HITLER'S
FORGOTTEN
FLOTILLAS

HITLER'S FORGOTTEN FLOTILLAS

Kriegsmarine Security Forces

LAWRENCE PATERSON

Seaforth
PUBLISHING

I would like to dedicate this book to Ian 'Lemmy' Kilmister. I hope he would have liked it. Long live rock and roll.

Frontispiece: *Räumboote* in action.

Copyright © Lawrence Paterson 2017

First published in Great Britain in 2017 by
Seaforth Publishing,
A division of Pen & Sword Books Ltd,
47 Church Street,
Barnsley S70 2AS

www.seaforthpublishing.com

British Library Cataloguing in Publication Data
A catalogue record for this book is available from the British Library

ISBN 978 1 4738 8239 3 (HARDBACK)
ISBN 978 1 4738 8241 6 (EPUB)
ISBN 978 1 4738 8240 9 (KINDLE)

Typeset and designed by M. A. T. S., Leigh-on-Sea, Essex
Printed and bound in Great Britain by CPI Group (UK) Ltd, Croydon, CR0 4YY

Contents

The Aegean Sea

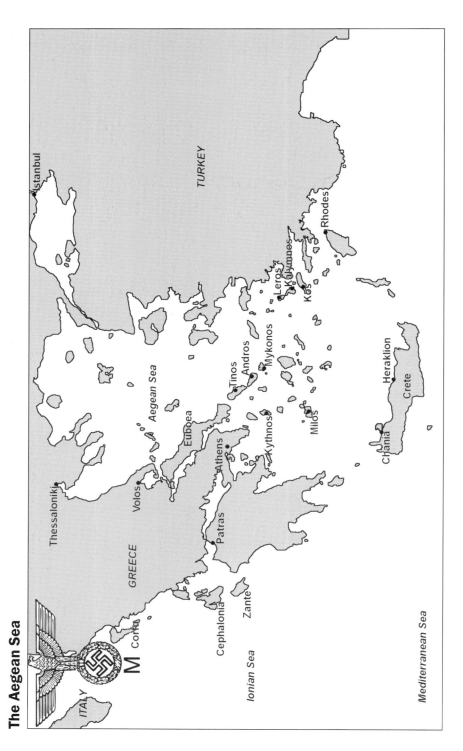

The Baltic

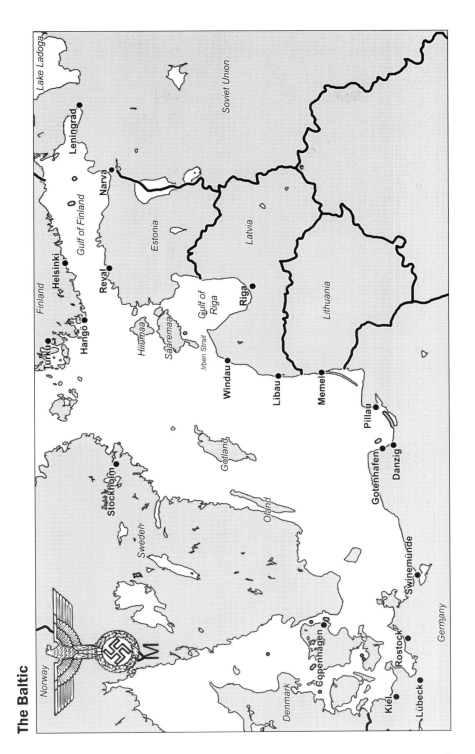

The Black Sea

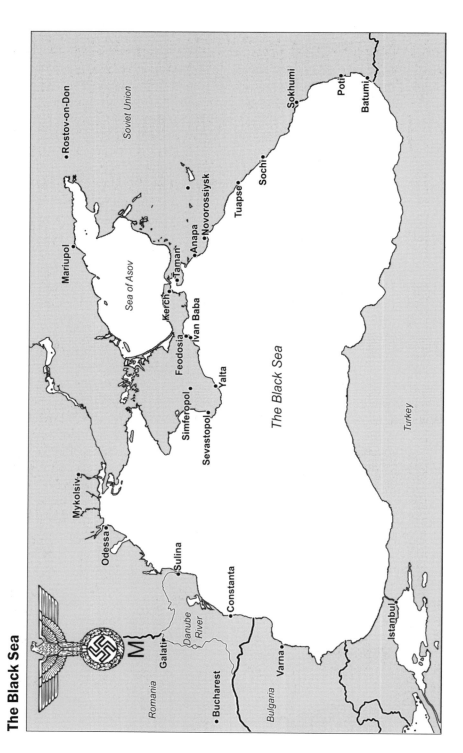

The English Channel

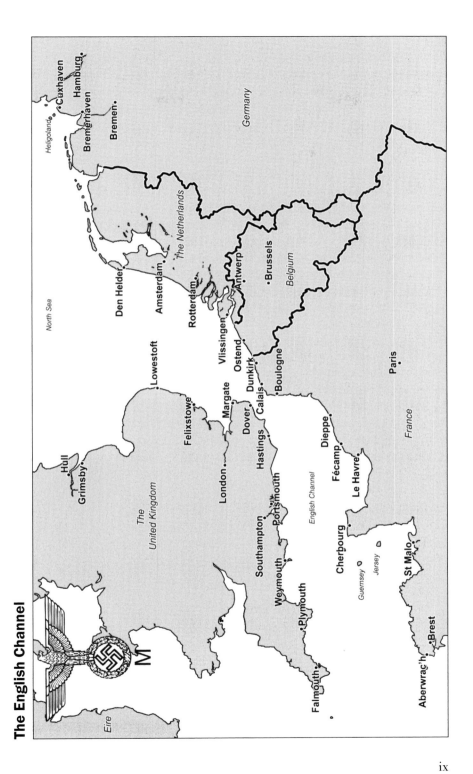

The Mediterranean

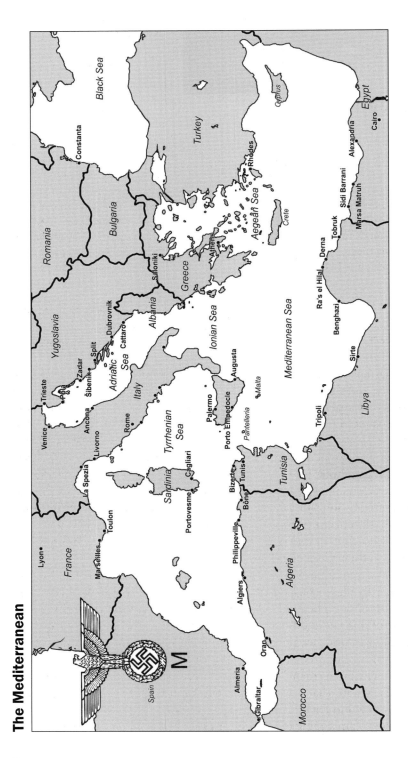

Introduction

At present the minesweeper is in the position of a person walking in the dark who can only feel for obstruction by stretching his arms behind him. Modern science has done much for the protection and improvement of the mine but at present cannot provide any means of giving warning to the sweeper of the danger which is before him.[1]

ALTHOUGH the above quote refers to the Royal Navy's minesweeping service, it is as relevant for all navies that fought during the Second World War, as well as those before and since. The Kriegsmarine was no different in this regard.

Much has been written about the large ships of the Kriegsmarine such as the *Bismarck* and the *Tirpitz* and as much about the U-boats that remained Germany's only real chance of success in the Atlantic war, but even then only a slender chance. There are some books, including one of my own, about the fast-moving *Schnellboote*, but very little about the other seagoing units, the backbone of any navy. Germany named them *Sicherungsstreitkräfte* – Security Forces – and most were grouped into flotillas and despatched to every theatre of war that German naval craft operated from with the exception of foreign ports inhabited by long-distance U-boats in the Far East. They were the most numerically significant portion of the Kriegsmarine and essential to enable the other branches of the navy to operate. For example, without mine-sweepers no other vessel could put to sea.

The role of the minesweeper, submarine hunter, escort vessel and patrol boat was hardly glamorous, which no doubt explains the dearth of books on them. A further complication is that the number of vessels involved was vast and a book of this size and type has nowhere near the space necessary to relate the fates of each unit, let alone each vessel within the units. However, I am hoping to give a comprehensive overview of the crucial role played by these small ships within Germany's naval war. There are books that carry ship lists available elsewhere that seek to name and number every craft, constantly updated as new information comes to light about the micro-entities of the Kriegsmarine. I am hoping that this book provides a window into the complex operations of the Security Forces; perhaps the briefest insight into their war that was fought in so many corners of occupied Europe.

My thanks to everybody who has helped me with this book, and I'd particulary like to mention Anna Paterson, James Paterson, Megan Paterson and Audrey 'Mumbles' Paterson (you can see a theme there I'm sure) who have always been supportive despite me waffling on and on at any given moment about events of over 70 years ago.

Glossary

Flotilla Types

AT-Flotilla – *Artillerieträgerflottille* (Artillery Carrier Flotilla); converted landing craft carrying heavy guns.

Donauflottille – 'Danube Flotilla'; river gunboats and assorted vessels for patrolling the Danube.

Hafenschutzflottille – Harbour Protection Flotilla.

G-Flotilla –*Geleitflottille* (Escort Flotilla); small destroyers or torpedo boats designed for fleet operations.

L-Flotilla –*Landungsflottille* (Landing Flotilla); comprised of purpose-built landing craft. (*Marinefährprahme*)

M-Flotilla –*Minensuchflottille* (Minesweeping Flotilla); conventional and auxiliary ships primarily intended for mine warfare.

R-Flotilla – *Räumbootsflottille* (Motor Minesweeper Flotilla); small shallow-water minesweepers.

Sp-Flotilla – *Sperrbrecherflottille* (Barrage Breaker Flotilla); converted vessels for the destruction of mine barrages.

UJ-Flotilla – *U–Bootsjagdflottille* (Submarine Hunter Flotilla); vessels whose primary duties were anti-submarine warfare.

Vp-Flotilla – *Vorpostenflottille* (Patrol Boat Flotilla); converted auxiliary coastal patrol boats.

General

ASW – Anti-submarine warfare.

BdA – *Befehlshaber der Aufklärungsstreitkräfte* (Commander of Reconnaissance Forces).

BSN – *Befehlshaber der Sicherung der Nordsee* (Commander-in-Chief Security North Sea).

BSO – *Befehlshaber der Sicherung der Ostsee* (Commander-in-Chief Security Baltic).

BSW – *Befehlshaber der Sicherung West* (Commander-in-Chief Security West).

FdM – *Führer der Minensucher* (Minesweeper Command).

FdV – *Führer der Vorpostenboote* (Patrol Boat Command).

GMSA – German Minesweeping Administration, set up after the war for the clearance of existing minefields.

Heer – German Army.

KFK – *Kriegsfischkutter* (Fishing boats for naval service).

KRG – *Korb Räum Gerät* (Basket Sweeping Gear).

Kriegsmarine – German Navy from 1935 to 1945.

KSV – *Küstensicherungsverbände* (Coastal Security Units).

KTB – *Kriegstagebuch* (War Diary)

LAT – *Leichte Artillerieträger* (Light Artillery Carrier).

Luftwaffe – German Air Force.

MAA – *Marine Artillerie Abteilung* (Naval Coastal Artillery Battalion).

MES – *Magnetischer-Eigenschutze Anlage*; Reducing a ship hull's magnetic field by use of electrical current, a process known to the Allies as 'degaussing'.

MFP – *Marinefährprähme* (German landing craft).

MGB – Motor Gun Boat, larger more heavily-armed development from ML (*qv*).

MGK – *Marinegruppenkommando* (Regional Naval Command, e.g., MGK West).

ML – Motor Launch, small British vessel designed for anti-submarine and harbour work.

MPG – *Motoren Pinass Gerät* (Motor Pinnace Gear).

MTB – Motor Torpedo Boat, similar to MGB but torpedo carriers with fewer guns. S-boat equivalent.

OKH – *Oberkommando des Heeres* (Supreme Army Command).

OKM – *Oberkommando der Marine* (Supreme Naval Command).

OKW – *Oberkommando der Wehrmacht* (Supreme Military Command – all three services).

RA – *Räumboote Ausland* (Foreign Minesweeper).

SAT – *Schwere Artillerieträger* (Heavy Artillery Carrier).

SDG – *Scheer Dracen Gerät* (Sheer Kite Gear).

S-Gerät – sonar carried for submarine detection.

Seeko — *Seekommandant* (Coastal Sector Command)

SKL – *Seekriegsleitung* (Naval War Staff),

SSG – *Schleppspulgerät*; towed looped cables used for detoinated magnetic ground mines.

Supermarina – Italian Naval Supreme Command.

VES – *Voraus-Eigenschutz Anlage*; Equipment for projecting a magnetic field in front of a ship to detonate magnetic mines).

VTE – Vertical Triple Expansion (engines)

Kriegsmarine Ranks

Seamen

Matrose	Ordinary Seaman
Matrosen-Gefreiter	Able Seaman
Matrosen-Obergefreiter	Leading Seaman
Matrosen-Hauptgefreiter	Leading Seaman (4½ years' service)
Matrosen-Stabsgefreiter	Senior Leading Seaman
Matrosen-Stabsobergefreiter	Senior Leading Seaman

(For engineering equivalencies above, replace 'Matrosen' with 'Maschinen')

Junior NCOs

–maat	Petty Officer
Ober-maat	Chief Petty Officer

Senior NCOs

Bootsmann	Boatswain
Stabsbootsmann	Senior Boatswain
Oberbootsmann	Chief Boatswain
Stabsoberbootsmann	Senior Chief Boatswain
Obersteuermann (ObStrm)	Quartermaster
Stabsobersteuermann (StObStrm)	Senior Quartermaster

Officers

Fähnrich zur See (FzS)	Midshipman
Oberfähnrich zur See	Sub Lieutenant
Leutnant zur See (LzS)	Lieutenant (Junior)
Oberleutnant zur See (ObltzS)	Lieutenant (Senior)
Kapitänleutnant (Kptlt)	Lieutenant-Commander
Korvettenkapitän (KK)	Commander
Fregattenkapitän (FK)	Captain (Junior)
Kapitän zur See (KzS)	Captain
Kommodore	Commodore
Konteradmiral (KA)	Rear Admiral
Vizeadmiral (VA)	Vice Admiral
Admiral	Admiral
Generaladmiral (GA)	No equivalent
Grossadmiral	Admiral of the Fleet
. . . dR	Naval Reserve

1

Development of Naval Mine Warfare and Auxiliary Ships in the Kaiser's Navy

THE Anglo-German naval arms race that preceded the First World War produced the Dreadnought battleship and advances in offensive weapons technology, particularly the submarine, and an equally important evolution of defensive weaponry – the naval mine. Indeed the first British warship sunk during that war was the cruiser HMS *Amphion* on 6 August 1914 after she struck a German mine off Britain's East Coast and went down with 150 crewmen killed.

Naval mines had existed in one form or another since the medieval Ming Dynasty employed prototype marine explosives to combat pirates in the South China Sea. Centuries later, the American David Bushell proved that gunpowder could be exploded underwater and subsequently attempted to sink British warships in 1777 during the American War of Independence by using floating 'kegs'. However, it was not until the Russo-Japanese War of 1904–5 that the true power of the weapon was demonstrated, with widespread destruction of both commercial and naval vessels. Both nations' mercantile trade was severely disrupted by either the sinking of freighters or denial of safe sailing routes. International observers from Great Britain were particularly alarmed; their island nation was reliant on maritime trade that flowed through its ports. The subsequent 1907 'Hague Convention VIII Relative to the Laying of Automatic Submarine Contact Mines' placed considerable restrictions on the use of such weapons, though by very virtue of its title it failed to restrict the variety of influence mines – acoustic and magnetic – under development. The convention consisted of thirteen separate articles, five of which governed the laying of contact mines:

Article 1. It is forbidden-
1. To lay unanchored automatic contact mines, except when they are so constructed as to become harmless one hour at most after the person who laid them ceases to control them;
2. To lay anchored automatic contact mines which do not become harmless as soon as they have broken loose from their moorings;
3. To use torpedoes which do not become harmless when they have missed their mark.

Article 2. It is forbidden to lay automatic contact mines off the coast and ports of the enemy, with the sole object of intercepting commercial shipping.

Article 3. When anchored automatic contact mines are employed, every possible precaution must be taken for the security of peaceful shipping.

The belligerents undertake to do their utmost to render these mines harmless within a limited time, and, should they cease to be under surveillance, to notify the danger zones as soon as military exigencies permit, by a notice addressed to ship owners, which must also be communicated to the Governments through the diplomatic channel.

Article 4. Neutral Powers which lay automatic contact mines off their coasts must observe the same rules and take the same precautions as are imposed on belligerents.

The Neutral Power must inform ship owners, by a notice issued in advance, where automatic contact mines have been laid. This notice must be communicated at once to the Governments through the diplomatic channel.

Article 5. At the close of the war, the Contracting Powers undertake to do their utmost to remove the mines which they have laid, each Power removing its own mines.

As regards anchored automatic contact mines laid by one of the belligerents off the coast of the other, their position must be notified to the other party by the Power which laid them, and each Power must proceed with the least possible delay to remove the mines in its own waters.

Events would later show that there was considerable latitude in the interpretation of these articles. The letter of the law may have generally been obeyed but the attempt to 'restrict and regulate' the use of naval mines was, in essence, an abject failure during both world wars.

Physical damage caused by naval mines can be divided into three categories. The first is that of a contact mine which simply blasts a hole in a ship's hull, causing injuries to crewmen by the blast itself and the ensuing fragmentation, and sinking the target vessel. The second results from an influence mine exploding a short distance from its target. The primary explosive pressure wave travels at the speed of sound in all directions and can reflect off the seafloor and strike the target almost simultaneously. An incandescent steam bubble also forms at the point of detonation which then quickly collapses from the bottom upward due to the water pressure differential, creating a column of water several dozen metres high if it reaches the surface. If this occurs beneath the centre of a ship, however, it will lift the ship upwards in the middle, weakening the keel; as the bubble then collapses the middle of the ship will fall into the void, breaking the keel and essentially splitting the ship in half. The 'bubble' can also attach to a ship's hull, like the result of a depth charge near-miss, which upon collapsing forms a high energy jet of water that can literally punch a hole straight through the hull, instantly killing any person in its path. The third can result from a mine exploding at some distance from a ship's hull. The resulting shock wave can cause the entire ship to resonate, shaking everything onboard to such an extent that machinery can be disabled and myriad leaks started. The effect on the crew can be particularly hideous, destroying leg joints and, in some cases, has been known to drive entire tibias upwards, splintering the victim's femur.

Mines were silent, effective and difficult to spot and to counteract with the improvised methods initially available. A dedicated ship was required that could quite literally 'sweep' a clear path through a mined area and following the end of the Russo-Japanese War, Russia ordered the construction of the world's first purpose-built minesweepers *Albatross* and *Baklan* for service in the Black Sea. Aware of the potential dangers of new and improved mines, Germany also began building the first of their own minesweepers during 1914. *M1* was launched from Geestemünde's Seebeck shipyard on 26 May 1915, and was completed and commissioned two months later. Previously, minesweeping had been the domain of fishing boats or obsolete gunboats trailing cables, but with the increasing use and sophistication of the naval mine, the Imperial German Navy finally had a vessel specifically designed for the task. By the end of the First World War, 176 M-class minesweepers had been ordered. An additional new design – the 'F-class coastal type' – had also been utilised; shallow-draught, flat-bottomed minesweepers intended for operations in rivers or shallow harbours. Following the end of hostilities in 1918, *F5*, *F6*, *F20–22*, *F25*, *F26* and *F36* remained in the German fleet, four were sold to Poland, two to

The value of *Vorpostenboot* and auxiliary minesweepers as U-boat escorts was established during the First World War.

Albania, one to Portugal and another to Iran. A second improved series was never completed, partially built hulks sold to Argentina, Colombia, Denmark and Portugal, where they were later finished.

Type 15/Type 16 Minesweepers

The Imperial German Navy was decimated by the end of the First World War, not simply by the conflict and ensuing revolution, but also by the draconian terms of the Versailles Treaty by which the victorious powers attempted to prevent future German militarisation. Nonetheless, a small minesweeping administration was allowed and indeed required by Article 193 of the Versailles Treaty (and Article 5 of the 1907 Hague Convention) and thirty-six Type 1915 and 1916 minesweepers were retained by the Reichsmarine in the 1920s.

The Reichsmarine's first new minesweeper unit was the formation of the 1st *Minensuch-halb-flottille* (Minesweeping Half Flotilla) in Kiel on 1 October 1924, the original complement of four later increased to six. Korvettenkapitän (KK) Hugo Schmundt originally commanded the Half-Flotilla, but by 1932 KK Friedrich Ruge was in command. Though later used as tenders and training ships when newer *M35*-class minesweepers began entering service, the original minesweepers that had been retained in 1918 would return to active service with the Kriegsmarine to bolster fleet numbers. In October 1940 a number '5' was added to the ship's original pennant number (if double digits) or replacing the original (if triple digits) in order to differentiate them from the modern 1935 boats; therefore *M28* became *M528* while *M102* became *M502*. The two Type 15s and thirty-five Type 16s underwent several design improvements providing different specifications for each stage, all those originally numbered *M121* onward completed after the war for peacetime minesweeping. The last of them, *M157* (redesignated *M557* and later sunk by a mine off Rügen on 27 December 1941), displaced 550 tons at full load, measured 59.6m overall length with a beam of 7.3m and a draught of 2.15m. Capable of 16 knots she was crewed by forty men.

Covert German naval development between the wars was generally sheltered behind dummy civilian corporate fronts. Kapitän zur See (KzS) Walter Lohmann, Chief of the Reichsmarine's Transportation Division and a man of experience in international business, was entrusted with administering an accumulated naval 'black fund' allowing armament development to progress under the noses of the Allied Armistice Control Commission. He was assisted by the man who would go on to head Germany's minesweeping service, Friedrich Ruge. Somewhat ironically, Lohmann was forced to resign in 1928 by pressure from within Germany after it became publically known that he had also poured money into various non-military ventures, both in an attempt to bolster the dwindling secret fund through profits as well as

Type 16 minesweepers sailing under the Reichsmarine ensign. These would form the early basis of Kriegsmarine minesweeper training flotillas and see action during the Second World War.

gradually accumulating a network of trustworthy agents in foreign firms. His ventures ranged from the Berliner Bacon Company (attempting to wrest the lucrative British bacon market from Danish firms) to a company attempting to raise sunken ships by encasing them in ice. His involvement with the Phoebus Film Company, which financially collapsed in August 1927, was exposed by the journalist Kurd Wenkel who was investigating the film company's hidden revenue source.[2]

Lohmann's resignation caused only a brief delay in the establishment of new 'fronts' behind which the military continued its secret work. In due course, three potential prototype *Schnellboote* were ordered from which the *Räumboote* (R-boats) evolved. While large minesweepers were ideal within the North Sea, a new class of vessel with a weak magnetic signature was desired for shallow coastal waters.

In 1926 three prototypes were developed. The Bremen firm of Abeking & Rasmussen, designers of minesweepers, torpedo boats and submarine chasers in the previous war, built the 'Experimental Boat K' with a stepped-planing hull, Travemünde's Caspar Werft built the 'Narwhal', with a large planning hull, and Lürssen built the 'Lür', a displacement-hulled boat. Attention primarily rested on the 'planing hull' concept that allowed a boat to effortlessly skim across the surface of the water in flat seas – 'planing' where the weight of the craft is supported by <u>hydrodynamic</u> lift rather than simple <u>hydrostatic</u> lift (displacement buoyancy). However, S-boats and R-boats were most likely to operate within the potentially turbulent North Sea and so it was Lürssen's displacement hull that was chosen by the Reichsmarine, a boat designed for a private customer, the *Oheka II*, boasting the features required and used as a design starting-point. The *Oheka II* carried the best features of a displacement hull – extreme seaworthiness even in heavy weather – and a planing hull towards the stern that would provide the requisite hydrodynamic lift when travelling at speed.

Räumboote

Alongside S-boat prototypes, Lürssen also built the prototype *Räumboot, R1*, commissioned in 1931. Of composite hull (double-skinned wood on light metal framing) the vessel measured 24.5m overall, with a beam of 4.38m and draught of 1.22m deep load. Armed with a single 20mm cannon (upgraded to two from *R17* onwards and then progressively up-gunned during the war) and crewed by between fifteen and eighteen men, *R1* could reach a maximum of 17 knots with her 700hp MWM diesels and deploy sweeping gear in a sea state up to 6 on the Beaufort Scale. The boats were reputed to be so lightly built that when the 20mm guns were fired they would shake the entire vessel noticeably.

With Lürssen's time devoted to S-boats, the firm of Abeking & Rasmussen took over the next phase of R-boat development, building *R2–R7* and *R9–R16* while the Schlichting-Werft at Travemünde built *R15* and *R16*. All these boats were commissioned between 1932 and 1934. Sea trials allowed the R-boat's specifications to be progressively altered, reflected in the vessels'

The first *Räumboote* commissioned into the Kriegsmarine, pictured here alongside a Type II U-boat in Neustadt harbour.

changing dimensions; *R16* measuring 27.8m long, the same beam as originally but a draught of 1.36m full load and a displacement of 52.5 tons. *Räumboote* were internally divided by five watertight bulkheads, the foremost of which was constructed as a collision bulkhead. A single scuttling charge was fitted in the diesel room, one in the W/T office, one in the men's quarters aft, and one in the petty officers' quarters forward. These were operated by a piston that once primed could not be rendered safe as the five-minute delay fuse burned down.

The second Lürssen R-boat design, *R8*, was of slightly wider beam and had also been fitted with the Voith Schneider propellers that delivered thrust in all directions and combined propulsion and steering into a single unit. Vessels so equipped did not require rudders, propeller blades protruding at right angles from a rotor casing and rotating around a vertical axis. The superb manoeuvrability that these propellers provided proved highly successful and they were installed from *R17* onwards on most boats. By 1943 when the R-boat fleet reached 177 craft, only 67 had traditional screws. However, with material shortages towards the end of the war, those constructed from 1944 onwards reverted to conventional twin-shaft screws.

As the war went on, R-boats became larger and carried more weaponry, requiring a concurrent crew expansion to an eventual maximum of forty-two aboard late-war boats. A typical R-boat complement would include an engine room crew of one Maat and three Matrosen to each watch, manning their stations below decks. The upper deck watches of an R-boat in action consisted of six men: one Maat for the forward 20mm gun; one Matrose for the stern 20mm gun if fitted (doubling as stern lookout to roughly 100° either side); one Matrose for bridge lookout, starboard (with an area from straight ahead to 100°); one Matrose for bridge lookout, port; one Matrose for helmsman and one Matrose for the telegraphs. The boat's captain – frequently either a junior officer rank or senior NCO – was continually on the bridge, there being no such thing as an officer of the watch. If sweeping gear was deployed, a man was detailed aft to supervise it.

Räumboote operated in pairs – a *Rotte* – generally being led by a command boat (*Rottenführer*) of the highest-ranking officer while the other (*Rottenboot*) was typically skippered by an Obersteuermann (ObStrm). Aside from sweeping, R-boats were also used for minelaying, with a carrying capacity of twelve mines that were mounted aft, six to each set of side rails, generally working in line-ahead formation, spaced approximately 100m from each other and each boat laying in succession from the back. When the laying boat was about to deploy its penultimate mine, a shaded blue light was used to signal to the next boat in succession. As the last mine was pushed overboard the blue light shone once more accompanied by a brief siren blast, the now-empty R-boat hauling out of line to run parallel to the main formation. Depth charges were sometimes carried, with stowage for eight, which were launched by simply being rolled overboard. Machine guns were sometimes mounted on the bridge for close combat and up to four MP38/MP40 sub machine-guns were also carried in the crew quarters. After combat experience, armour plating 10mm–12mm thick was fitted around the wheelhouse and bridge, which was situated abaft the wheelhouse on a raised platform with searchlights either side. Gun shields of the same thickness were fitted and plates extend 15cm on either side of the guns, which required a crew of four to operate.

Three main types of minesweeping gear were used in R-Boats. The first two – MPG or '*Motoren Pinass Gerät*' (Motor Pinnace Gear) and KRG or '*Korb Räum Gerät*' (Basket Sweeping Gear) – were known to the Allies as 'A' sweeps, consisting of a sweep wire strung between two or more ships, MPG requiring the R-boats to proceed 100m apart, KRG only 50m apart. MPG used kites, but KRG used a form of iron basket for depth-keeping; both were armed with explosive cutters (*Sprenggreifer*). The third method – SDG or '*Scheer Dracen Gerät*' (Sheer Kite Gear) – was a double sweep that could be towed by one vessel consisting of searching wires attached to paravanes, a single kite and floats.

M35 class Minesweepers

In May 1935 Adolf Hitler announced the rearmament of Germany and the abrogation of the Treaty of Versailles, the Reichsmarine being renamed the Kriegsmarine. Amongst an ambitious naval building programme, estimated

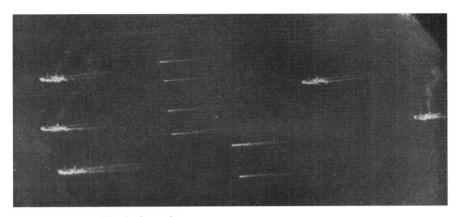

Minesweepers working in formation.

to reach compleation by 1944, was the construction of new minesweepers. The *M35* class minesweeper was developed along similar lines as proven First World War vessels. These ships had a full-load displacement of over 870 tons and carried a heavy armament for a minesweeper of two 105mm guns and one 37mm and two 20mm flak weapons, enabling them to tangle with enemy destroyers in the English Channel. A multi-purpose design, they could be fitted for minelaying and were able to carry thirty mines on hull rails as well as four depth-charge launchers for ASW work. The hull itself

The new generation of minesweepers; heavily armed and extremely effective, the *M35* class served throughout the war.

was of steel construction, divided into twelve watertight compartments while a double bottom covered most of the ships' waterline length. The first nine minesweepers of this class were ordered on 22 November 1935, and overall, sisty-nine units were commissioned between 1938 and 1943. *M1* was launched in Hamburg on 5 March 1937, and was completed by September 1938.

The *M35* class was constructed in three different series: Type 1935, ordered between 1935 and 1936; Type 1938 with increased hull dimensions providing better seakeeping qualities and allowing for the installation of additional generators for magnetic sweeps; and Type 1939(Mob) which had been ordered after the outbreak of war with emphasis on simplified construction. All of these Types were powered by Vertical Triple Expansion (VTE) engines and oil-burning boilers that required skilled maintenance and operation, capable of pushing the ships at speeds of up to 18 knots. The *M1* and *M2* had also been equipped with Voith Schneider propellers such as those fitted to *Räumboote*; originally it was planned to equip all *M35* series ships with these, though their complexity and issues of reliability rendered the idea void and the remainder of the series had two three-bladed propellers of 1.75m diameter. In October 1943, Fähnrich zur See (FzS) Gerhard Both saw firsthand the effect of the Voith Schneider propellers after he was taken aboard *M2* following the accidental grounding of his own ship, the destroyer *Z4*, in Norway in October 1943.

Voith Schneider propellers being manufactured.

Another attempt to refloat the destroyer was carried out by the minesweeper *M2* and an S-boat, both of which raced past our ship in order to achieve the desired lateral pitch, but this also failed to achieve anything.

Next the minesweeper came up on our starboard side in a right-angle approach and gingerly inched towards us, right against our hull. It attempted to shift our ship by pushing it carefully over on its side. Again, it was useless; on the contrary, this caused more damage, as in spite of the provision of fenders our hull was pushed in by as much as half a metre by the bow of the minesweeper . . .

Both and his fellow Fähnrich were then transferred to *M2* for transit to Bergen.

After we had eaten, we eight cadets closed ranks, went to the main deck and watched the manoeuvres of this vessel in a minor port en route. It was a manoeuvre of fantastic boldness such as we had never witnessed before. The captain directed his ship towards some old tub that had made fast alongside the little pier directly in line with our course; we were still steaming at cruising speed when only a ship's length away. Now, we had had more than enough of being shipwrecked, so we became very concerned and anxiously looked up toward the bridge of *M2*. 'Damn are they all fast asleep up there?' One of us dared to say it. We were only about ten metres away from that rusty old hulk when suddenly,

The Voith Schneider propeller in action aboard a test vessel. R-boats equipped with this system had an extremely high degree of manoeuvrability.

11

at last, vibrations in our vessel indicated that something was being done about the situation. Our boat swerved round and came to a dead stop in a perfect position alongside the other ship, without the precaution of fenders or anything else and, without the slightest bump. We were flabbergasted.[3]

Cuxhaven was designated as the North Sea base for Germany's minesweeper service on 22 October 1936. At the beginning of June the following year, Fregattenkapitän (FK) Friedrich Ruge took command as *Führer der Minensuchsboot* (FdM, Commander of Minesweepers); a post subordinate to *Befehlshaber der Aufklärungsstreitkräfte* (BdA, Commander of Reconnaissance Forces). Ruge held this office until on the outbreak of war the responsibilities of the minesweeper command were split geographically.

Friedrich Ruge, perhaps the most important figure in the development of the Kriegsmarine's minesweeping service.

Ruge had served in the previous war and, after detachment to study at the Berlin Institute of Technology for two years between October 1924 and 1926, was commander of *M136* of the 1st M-Half-Flotilla. His expertise led to posts as Advisor in the Inspection of Torpedo and Mine Affairs (2 October 1928–17 October 1928) and Advisor in the Mine Barrier Experiment and Instruction Command (18 October 1928–28 September 1932) before he had risen to command the 1st M-Half-Flotilla on 29 September 1932. Two years later he was transferred to the Baltic Sea staff office before his accession to FdM on 1 June 1937.

The commanders of the Kriegsmarine's first two minesweeper flotillas were from very different backgrounds. Korvettenkapitän Karl Weniger had served in the Imperial German Navy during the First World War aboard the battleships SMS *Nassau* and *Posen*. Following the end of hostilities he joined

Korvettenkapitän Karl Weniger (left).

the anti-communist Erhardt Brigade, the naval prototype of what would become the nationalist Freikorps. Later re-enlisting in the Reichsmarine, Weniger also helped organise the sailing events of the 1936 Olympic Games, his prowess in small sailing boats noted by fellow members of the Naval Yacht Club ('*Kaiserliche Yacht Club*'). Shortly thereafter he became actively involved in the development of '*Sperrwaffe*', weapons related to mine warfare and its countermeasures. Weniger, known as 'Minus' amongst his naval colleagues, was given command of the expanded 1st M-Flotilla during October 1938 while at the same time KK Kurt Thoma took command of the 2nd M-Flotilla.[4] Thoma, only two years Weniger's junior, had joined the Reichsmarine in April 1921 at the age of 19 and risen steadily through the ranks, being commissioned in 1925.

The 2nd M-Flotilla was established in 1936 with six Type 16 mine-sweepers, though new *M35*-class minesweepers were soon taken on, starting with *M1* on 3 September 1938.

> We made it a practice to select our minesweeper commanders and squadron chiefs from officers who had already had long service on minesweepers, thus making use of their practical experience as well as starting a 'minesweeper tradition'. With the revival of compulsory military service, reserve officers and short-term crews were also assigned for training, so that in case of war

Korvettenkapitän Kurt Thoma.

there would be an ample reserve of trained personnel to man the additional auxiliary minesweepers that would be taken into service – such as fishing trawlers and luggers.

Every year we staged a large minelaying and minesweeping exercise, conducted as much as possible under war conditions. I personally attended the one held in Helgoland Bay in June of 1939, and visited each boat in order

Preparing the sweep for use.

Pre-war portrait of a *Vorpostenboot* crewman.

to observe the exercise and to give the crews the feeling that the High Command considered their work important. For high morale is essential in an activity which ordinarily is tedious routine but which in time of war is absolutely necessary and, in fact, indispensible.[5]

Three other warship classes had been effectively used by the Imperial German Navy for defensive duties during the First World War, all of which would become a backbone of the Kriegsmarine's Security Forces: the *Vorpostenboote*, *Unterseebootsjäger* and *Sperrbrecher*.

Vorpostenboote

Vorpostenboote (patrol boats) were generally converted trawlers. Germany's trawler fleet underwent considerable technical development during the 1920s that enabled them to reach as far afield as Greenland. On average, 10 tons of coal and 5 tons of water were consumed daily by a trawler's steam engine to achieve a maximum speed of around 11.9 knots, the actual load capacity of fish being less than the capacity of coal and water. As the trawlers developed, so too did their tonnage, from an original 125–220 GRT to an average of 240–390 GRT in 1931. Several German shipbuilders also began constructing larger trawlers for export to the USSR, tending to be between 550 and 640 GRT. At the outbreak of war in 1914, the majority of ocean-going trawlers had been commandeered by the Imperial German Navy and converted into *Vorpostenboote*, successfully combining the tasks of coastal and harbour patrol, convoy escort and anti-submarine missions.

Vorpostenboote would become the backbone of the Kriegsmarine's Security Forces.

The end of the First World War and the later onset of the Great Depression caused a slump in German shipbuilding activity with large shipyards underutilised through a lack of overseas construction contracts or domestic repair work. In 1926, some influential Bremen merchants formed a co-operation of eight companies that became 'Deschimag' (*Deutsche Schiff- und Maschinenbau Aktiengesellschaft*) while the larger and more secure Blohm & Voss and Vulkan AG remained independent.[6]

Although Deschimag became Germany's greatest shipbuilding company, employing approximately 15,000 workers, by 1935 only Aktiengesellschaft 'Weser' (A.G. Weser) and Seebeckwerft remained active, experiencing a financial boom as a result of the Nazis' accession to power in Germany. The first two ships built by Seebeck after Hitler's inauguration were trawlers, both of which were named after prominent Nazis; the *Carl Röver*, named after the Gauleiter of Weser-Ems, and *R. Walter Darré*, the head of the Race and Settlement Office of the SS and Minister for Food and Agriculture. Both ships would later become *Vorpostenboote* and take part in the exercises *Festungskriegsübung Swine-münde* on 10 June 1937, later numbered *V209* and *V210* respectively during September 1939 and transferred to the 2nd Vp-Flotilla. At the turn of 1934/1935 AG Weser received its first defence contract, for the construction of the gunboat *Brummer*.

With a greater desire for self-sufficiency actively pursued by the Nazi regime, an expansion of Germany's deep-sea fishing fleet took place in the late

The *Unterseebootsjäger* was specifically equipped to combat enemy submarines. Most vessels of the Security Forces were equipped with ASW weapons, the depth charge in this photo providing a handy back-rest for potato-peeling duty.

1930s, trawlers of 400 GRT displacement becoming a standard design. During 1937 the Kriegsmarine tested the new German trawlers for potential suitability as *Vorpostenboote*, commissioning five of their own in March of that year so that future models would conform to a design that allowed military conversion with minimal work. Germany, one of the world's largest consumers of whale oil, also expanded its whaling fleet with ships built to reach Antarctic waters and these too would later be requisitioned by the Kriegsmarine.

The composition of a Vp–Flotilla varied depending upon the ships at hand and the armament available. The 15th Vp–Flotilla was an example of whalers being used, formed in September 1939 from nine whaling boats (*Walfang-boote*) that ranged between 348–381 tons each. Constructed by Deschimag, these steel-hulled vessels were extremely seaworthy and manoeuvrable, with a maximum speed of approximately 14 knots. The original crew complement of fifteen men was doubled with naval personnel, and the bow-mounted harpoon gun was replaced by a single 20mm C/30 cannon until its slow rate of fire led to substitution with the superior 20mm flak 38 from 1940. Racks for two to four depth charges were also fitted, though sonar gear was rare.

Trawlers, on the other hand, tended to carry heavier weapons. Typically they began the war with a single 75mm or 88mm First World War-vintage naval gun, rebored to fire newer ammunition, as well as a single 20mm C/30 with additional lighter machine-gun mountings and the same depth-charge complement.

U-Jäger

Specialised *Unterseebootsjäger* (submarine hunters) had been developed during the previous war; the small ships previously used called *U-Boots-Zerstörer* (submarine destroyers), originally small private yachts converted to naval use. With no detection equipment and limited armamens, they relied on the naked eye to find the enemy and a combination of luck and reinforcement to engage them. Their size limited them to coastal areas, being unable to weather heavy offshore seas. By 1939, *U-Jäger* were almost without exception requisitioned fishing or whaling boats, an initial plan for purpose-built naval vessels having been scrapped after *Oberkommando der Marine* (OKM) found little advantage in investing valuable resources to develop ships whose tasks could adequately be carried out by converted civilian craft. In appearance there was little to distinguish *Vorpostenboote* and *U-Jäger*, their spheres of responsibility overlapping in practice if not by design. Nonetheless, they remained separately-classed vessels albeit of similar purpose: the protection of German coastal interests. Generally, the *U-Jäger* conformed to the same broad specifications as *Vorpostenboote* and for all these vessels naval conversion included altering fish lockers to hold ammunition, expanded crew quarters and raising the wheelhouse to enable a clear view over any forward gun platform. *U-Jäger* could carry up to sixty depth charges with four side-mounted launchers and two stern chutes.

Many Security Force vessels, particularly *U-Boot Jäger*, carried 'S-Gerät' equipment, sonar comprised of an extendable hand-operated dome which, when fully lowered, protruded 90cm below the ship's keel. Sonar reflections were displayed on a cathode ray oscillograph and from its form, the general nature of the target determined; a submarine contact giving a sharp thin line, land bending the line slightly to one side while a wreck gave the line indistinct edges. Coupled with this was KDB hydrophone gear, consisting of six crystal units approximately 10cm in diameter, mounted in a single row on a retractable mounting 90cm in length. The extendable gear was trained to receive the maximum sound effect in earphones but was easily damaged and, at high speed, the rushing of water made reception very poor. The *S-Gerät* operator swept a defined sector reporting the range and bearing of any contact to the bridge where course was altered accordingly. At close range – 1000m or less – the ship's speed was reduced and KDB gear used for target confirmation, full speed then ordered and the attack begun.

Sperrbrecher

To counter the hazard posed by mines the Germans also invented the *Sperrbrecher*, literally 'barrage breaker'. The concept was first proposed in 1905 by naval reserve officers in Cuxhaven, and by 1914 it had been defined as a ship capable of deploying paravane minesweeping gear, anti–torpedo nets and conventional towed sweeps. On 3 August 1914, seven merchant steamers were put into naval dockyards for conversion to *Sperrbrecher*; the first, ss *Mecklenburg*, emerging two days later as *Sp1*. Altogether some thirty vessels served as *Sperrbrecher* between 1914 and 1918, another four as auxiliary *Sperrbrecher*, and eight of them were lost in action.

In 1937 the Kriegsmarine ordered fifteen ships (later modified to twelve) requisitioned and converted to Sperrbrecher for distribution between five Sperrbrechergruppen, three groups to be stationed in the North Sea and one in the Baltic. A shortlist of fifty-eight merchant ships was established that ranged from the 3164-ton MV Henry Horn of Hamburg's H. C. Horn Shipping Line to the 9626-ton freighter and passenger liner ss *Königstein* of Arnold Bernstein's shipping company, soon in jeopardy as its Jewish owner faced increasing exclusion in Nazi Germany. An estimated 120 man-hours were needed to complete the conversion, but by the outbreak of war only two unarmed auxiliary *Sperrbrecher* were available to FdM West for service within the Elbe – ss Bochum and Adalia – both of which were manned by their civilian crews with the addition of two naval signallers each.

In general a *Sperrbrecher* complement was approximately eighty-five men; a mixture of First World War veteran reservists, merchant seamen and young

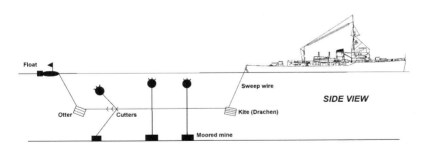

Ottergerät (Oropesa sweep)

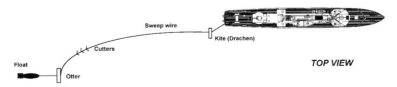

The Oropesa sweep was an extremely effective sweeping technique against moored mines.

Sperrbrecher came in a huge variety of shapes and sizes. This photo is *SpV 'Schwanheim'*, pictured later in the war after the addition of extra flak platforms fore and aft.

recruits. They carried a variety of sweeping gear including bow-mounted paravanes with towing-lines attached as far forward and low down as possible, raked outboard approximately 30m from the ship's centreline and held there by the paravanes to which they were attached. These swept a horizontal plane near keel level and any mine anchor-lines fouled were deflected into cutters that severed the cable from its base whereupon it would float to the surface. Supposedly – as specified in the Hague Convention – at that point the mine would be inert, though it was then dealt with by small-arms fire that was meant to hole the flotation chamber and sink the mine, though it sometimes also set off the explosive charge.

As the war progressed a *Geräuschboje-Turbine* was mounted on a spar attached to the bow and lowered by winch, the hydro–turbine turned by the ship's speed through the water causing an internal striker to hit the metal casing and create enough noise to detonate acoustically-triggered mines. This latter was a vast improvement on the unpopular *Knallkorpergerät* (KKG), an explosive sweep for acoustic mines which comprised a tube lowered into the sea through which hand grenades were pushed to detonate clear of the ship.

Immediately before the bridge were two extendible towing points on either side of the ship which could be run out and to which an Oropesa sweep (*Ottergerät*) was attached, two or more also fitted aft each capable of being run out to approximately 200m. The Oropesa Sweep was named after the

A *Sperrbrecher*'s holds filled with extra ballast intended to help keep the ship afloat if she was holed by a mine.

First World War trawler that had developed the method which consisted of a long thick wire cable fitted with wire cutters at periodic intervals. A steel 'kite' (*Drachen*) was attached to the wire a short distance from the point of tow which would keep the sweep positioned vertically, depth altered by the 'kite's' distance from the ship. Near the cable's end was an 'Otter', similar to the 'kite', but this time operating on the horizontal plane thereby determining the lateral drift of the sweep when under tow. Finally a float marked the end of the sweep cable, keeping the entire apparatus buoyant. As any mine's anchored chain became snagged it would rub along the sweep cable until encountering a cutter, which would then slice through the chain.

To neutralise magnetic mines, the Kriegsmarine used two systems: *Magnetischer Eigenschutz* (MES, known to the Allies as 'degaussing') and *Voraus Eigenschutz* (VES). The former was used on all major warships and entailed the reduction of a ship's magnetic signature by carrying electromagnetic coils that stretched the length of the ship and effectively wiped or reversed the hull's magnetic signature that triggered the mine. The VES system, on the other hand, was offensively orientated and used only on *Sperrbrecher* and some major surface units. This involved carrying thick electrically-charged cable loops wrapped around the outer hull of the ship's bow and encased in wood. Coloured alternately red and blue, each cable entered a central watertight junction box and generator powered by several

A *Flottenbegleiter*; purpose-designed escort vessels that failed to meet expectations.

ship or aircraft engines installed in the aft cargo compartment. This, often combined with iron ballast carried in the forward holds, would throw a strong magnetic signature far ahead of the bow and theoretically explode any magnetic mines lying in the ship's path. However, the weight of the iron ballast forward also necessitated the carrying of concrete or sand as ballast astern to even the ships' keel.

Both systems were trialled before the war, MES being installed aboard the test boat *Pelikan* (ex-*M28*) and the light cruiser *Nürnberg* which also had VES installed. Aboard the cruiser the VES comprised three vertical coils forward, amidships and aft magnetised with a 300kW electric charge. The test was a success, a magnetic mine being detonated 50m ahead of the moving ship at a depth of 28m. The decision was made to fit *Sperrbrecher* not yet under conversion with the VES system, which required major modification to the bow structure.

There was a final method of minesweeping for the deep-draught *Sperrbrecher*. To enable a brute-force approach, the holds were filled with buoyant material – a so-called *Scutzstauung* or 'protective cargo' – above a shock-absorbent layer of sand. For example, the holds of *SpVIII 'Neckar'* were filled with a lower ballast layer of 5600 tons of sand topped with 10,286 empty iron barrels and 32,286 empty wooden barrels. If all else failed, the *Sperrbrecher* would detonate mines by sailing into them and simply absorbing the punishment while hopefully remaining afloat.

Sperrbrecher were initially armed with a single 105mm C/96 gun mounted aft and two 20mm C/30 cannon either forward or near the bridge, though as the war progressed and Allied air power increased, so too did the weaponry carried. Eventually they were so heavily armed that the RAF referred to them as 'heavy flak ships'. The role of the *Sperrbrecher* was defined in instructions issued during April 1938: this included mine defence, merchant convoy escort, reporting of enemy aircraft and anti-submarine duties; all of which was controlled by the regional FdM.

Flottenbegleiter

The *Flottenbegleiter* (Fleet Escort) had also been developed for the Security Forces during the early 1930s, purpose-built fleet escorts whose principal role was to provide a fast inner escort screen for the 'pocket battleships' *Deutschland*, *Admiral Scheer* and *Admiral Graf Spee* while also being capable of minesweeping and ASW work. A design limit on this new class was a displacement not exceeding 600 tons, ships of that size unregulated by the London Treaty of 1930.[7] The concept was sound, as later evidenced by Allied frigate and destroyer-escort types; however, the German effort was a complete failure.

Planning was complete by 1934 and ten ships ordered, designated *Flottenbegleiter A* to *K*. Seventeen were originally envisioned but the exceedingly poor performance of the first ten led to all further construction being cancelled. The ships were top-heavy, sluggish in the water and too slow and cumbersome for their planned role. The design of the keel was found to significantly hamper seaworthiness, causing the ships to bury their nose in the water in all but calm seas. Correspondingly they were too unstable to provide an effective anti-aircraft platform or carry, let alone lay, mines. Their mine-sweeping capability was, at best, mediocre and they lacked the necessary detection equipment to become effective ASW vessels. Attempts were made to reduce the weight above the waterline but it did little to improve performance.

The *Flottenbegleiter* (whose pennant numbers were all prefixed with an 'F') were built by Germaniawerft (*F1*–*F6*), Blohm & Voss (*F7* and *F8*) and Kriegsmarinewerft (*F9* and *F10*), the first launched on 1 March 1935 and commissioned the following December. By the middle of August 1938, the final ship (*F10*) had been commissioned, the entire class had already been found to be not fit for purpose.

They carried two 105mm SK L/45 C/32 guns in shielded single mounts, four 37mm flak SK L/83 C/30 in twin mounts and four 20mm single flak weapons, and had capacity for up to sixty-two mines. The installation of stern mine rails caused the aft 105mm gun to be mounted a deck higher than originally planned. Plans to include torpedo tubes were scrapped as they would have pushed the design over its official 600-ton displacement, which it had already unofficially exceeded. The *Flotten-*

begleiter were 75.94m overall, capable of a top speed of 28 knots and manned by a crew of 121 men. They had no bilge keels, but a new type of Frahm anti-roll system which would prove a costly failure that was overly complex and decreased stability with the slightest handling error. The *Flotten-begleiter* were also used as test-beds for newly-designed high-pressure steam power plants, but they too had proven highly temperamental and prone to frequent breakdowns, so much so that sailors disparagingly referred to the unlucky units as the 'Horst Wessel flotilla' because they marched with the fleet 'only in spirit'.

The existing *Flottenbegleiter* were organised into two flotillas; 1st *Geleitflottille* (*F1, F2, F5, F6, F9* and *F10*) and 2nd *Geleitflottille* (*F3, F4, F7* and *F8*) with plans to limit their operational use to minesweeping. However, their continued poor performance and costly shipyard requirements led to their delegation to various non-combatant roles: *F1* was allocated as command ship to FdM Ost, *F2, F4* and *F7* were converted into torpedo recovery vessels for U-boats in training, *F3* and *F6* were scheduled for conversion to accommodation tenders with most weapons removed, and *F5, F8, F9* and *F10* were to be allocated to the ASW training school. However, the outbreak of war forced their commitment to active service to bolster an already under-equipped Kriegsmarine. Apart from *F3* and *F6* – both in shipyards undergoing conversion work to tenders *Hai* and *Königin Luise* – the *Flottenbegleiter* were grouped into a single *Geleitflottille*, serving within the North Sea under FK Friedrich-Wilhelm Pindter until his death on 14 December 1939. His successor was Kapitänleutnant (Kptlt) Hagen Küster who assumed command in January 1940. Though the ships had proven a complete failure, the idea of fleet escort ships remained alive and later several *Geleitflottille* were formed using captured destroyers and torpedo boats.

Command Structure

In June 1939 KzS Friedrich Ruge's office of *Führer der Minensuchboote* operated from his flagship, *F6 'Königin Luise'* in Cuxhaven, with the 1st and 2nd M-Flotilla, *Geleitflottille* and 1st, 2nd and 3rd R-Flotillas under his command.[8] The river minesweeping and patrol units of the *Donauflottille* (Danube Flotilla) commanded by KzS Hans Bütow remained independently also under BdA control near Linz, having been formed immediately after the *Anschluss* between Austria and Germany in 1938.

Separate geographical security commands already existed for the Baltic and North Sea, directly subordinate to OKM. In the Baltic, Konteradmiral (KA) Hermann Mootz was *Befehlshaber der Sicherung der Ostsee* (BSO, Commander-in-Chief Security Baltic), based at Kiel aboard his flagship, the aviso *Grille*. A school flotilla (*BSO Schulflottille*) in Kiel comprised his sole operational unit in June 1939. To the West, KA von Schrader was

Befehlshaber der Sicherung der Nordsee (BSN, North Sea), quartered aboard the survey ship *Meteor* alongside an equivalent school flotilla (*BSN Schulflottille*) in Wilhelmshaven. The regional *Befehlshaber der Sicherung* were in turn subordinate to the relevant geographical naval command, such as *Marinegruppenkommando West* or *Nord*.

With war imminent in August 1939, the office of FdM was removed from BdA jurisdiction and divided regionally between the two security commands. Ruge activated reserve flotillas and assumed the post of FdM Ost, a position created from existing staff from BSO. The office of FdM West was also created under the command of KA Hans Stohwasser, subordinate to BSN. The two officers would later switch positions once the invasion of Poland had begun, the majority of Ruge's staff having already been centred on the North Sea and familiar with that combat environment.

With mine warfare vessels catered for, patrol ships were in turn commanded by *Führer der Vorpostenboote* (FdV) *West* (KzS Otto Kahler) and *Ost* (KzS Helmut Leissner), the role of FdV *Nord* carried by FK Hans Fuchs as commander of 11th Vp-Flotilla but never fully established as an independent command. Those ships that didn't comfortably fit within the previous categories – the *U-Jäger* and minelayers – were directly subordinate to the office of *Führer der Sonderverbände*, who was again under the command of *Befehlshaber der Sicherung*.

2

Defending Germany's Coasts: Minesweepers, *Vorpostenboote* and *U-Jäger* of the Kriegsmarine, 1939–1940

NAVAL security of the Western Baltic, for which KA Mootz's BSO was responsible, was of crucial importance to Germany. It was through those waters that trade from Scandinavia flowed, in particular iron ore shipments from Sweden's Gällivare and Kiruna mines. The confined waters also provided perfect training areas for the resurgent Kriegsmarine and a nautical 'highway' for the transfer of military units headed to the East. Germany had delivered a successful ultimatum in March 1939 that the port city of Memel, ceded to the victors of the First World War and then forcibly occupied by Lithuania, be returned to Germany and the Reich had crept eastward. Hitler's next demand was for the return of the 'Polish Corridor' including Danzig but Poland remained unyielding and the stage was set for war.

Case White – the invasion of Poland

'Case White' – the plan for the subjugation of Poland – required decisive moves to be made by the Kriegsmarine and, therefore, the rapid creation of a substantial force able to carry out its tasks. Vessels allocated to mine-sweeping, escort, ASW and patrol duties in both the Baltic and North Seas were placed under the command of Ruge as FdM Ost. By the end of June 1939 the 1st and 2nd M-Flotillas were active along with 1st, 2nd and 3rd R-Flotillas and the eight escort ships of the *Geleitflottille* which had performed so disappointingly in sea trials. Within two months Germany teetered on the brink of war and while resources were poured into the completion of capital ships, destroyers and U-boats, both the 12th and 17th UJ-Flotillas were also commissioned, the former for use in the North Sea, the latter in the Baltic. Eight vessels were commandeered and earmarked for the 'Reserve Patrol Flotilla', the Kriegsmarine's first operational *Vorpostenboote*. This flotilla was assembled in just three days, orders for the charter of ten further trawlers, complete with civilian crews, being issued on the evening of 18 August. Towards the end of August the 5th R-Flotilla was complete while harbour defence flotillas in the Baltic and Kiel Canal were hurriedly formed.

Pre–war photo of a member of the 1st R–
Flotilla. Identifying cap bands were removed
during wartime for security purposes.

On 22 August 1939 the Kriegsmarine was fully mobilised. Harbour and coastal patrol stations were established along the German coast although conflict in the West was considered unlikely and naval units were concentrated in the East. The 11th R-Flotilla was also raised and stationed in the Baltic on 4 September 1939 though it was composed not of *Räumboote* but rather eight Finkenwärder fishing cutters and the tender *Weser*.

With full *Sperrbrecher* conversion incomplete, Ruge's two auxiliary *Sperrbrecher* were used, the 6121-ton SS *Bochum* making her first return journey between Cuxhaven to Heligoland on 1 September. The pair were soon joined by eight other auxiliaries for brief service on the Jade and Elbe rivers, though they would eventually be either returned to their owners or redesignated as transport ships by April 1940.

The obsolete *Deutschland* class battleship *Schleswig-Holstein* was to spearhead the attack against Danzig. The training ship used the cover of a visit planned six months previously for her presence in the Free City. On the night of 24 August *Schleswig-Holstein* took aboard 225 naval troops from Memel, the 3rd Naval Assault Company (*Marine-Stoßtrupp-Kompanie*) commanded by Oberleutnant Wilhelm Henningsen and formed in 1938 from a hand-picked cadre of artillerymen of Swinemünde's *Marine Artillerie Abteilung* (MAA) 123. Following advanced training in amphibious assaults the unit had first seen action during the Spanish Civil War when, under the command of Leutnant Walter Schug, they were landed on Ibiza by the 'pocket battleship' *Deutschland* to destroy a Republican radio station. They next took part in the reoccupation of Memel after disembarking from torpedo boats on 23 March 1939, though they faced no opposition from the Lithuanian garrison.

On the night of 24 August *M1* and *M3* of KK Karl Weniger's 1st M-Flotilla embarked Henningsen and his men in Memel and headed west to rendezvous

The obsolete battleship *Schleswig-Holstein* puts to sea. She would fire the opening salvoes of the Second World War.

with *Schleswig-Holstein* north of Stolpmünde to transfer the heavily-armed assault troops and seven motorcycles. Should the Polish defences be defeated, Henningsen's men were to protect the *Schleswig-Holstein*'s berth. The ship was to be moored in shallow waters so that, if damaged and holed, she could not sink completely and could continue to function as an artillery platform. The two minesweepers accompanied the battleship into Danzig to provide fire support if needed but, more importantly, security against enemy submarines. Indeed, at 0347hrs on the morning of 1st September, both minesweepers hunted what they at first took to be a Polish submarine, but turned out to be one of five German Type II U-boats operating in the Baltic.

Hitler's original planned invasion date was 26 August, the Kriegsmarine due to begin its part at 0430hrs. However, an 'Agreement of Mutual Assistance' signed between Great Britain and Poland at noon the previous day prompted a nervous Hitler to postpone until the morning of 1 September. The postponement allowed Hitler and Mussolini – his 'Pact of Steel' ally – to discuss the German plan to invade, Mussolini declaring Italy unprepared to wage war and formally a 'non-belligerent' nation.[9]

Amid this tension, on 30 August the Polish Navy ordered Operation Peking into effect, the withdrawal of their main surface force – the destroyers

Burza, Blyskawica and *Grom* – to the United Kingdom. The Kriegsmarine's numerical advantage, combined with complete aerial dominance, spelt certain destruction for the ships in the event of war. Sighted by U-boat and shadowed by aircraft and surface vessels that included *Vorpostenboot '7'*, the ships reached the North Sea at 0925hrs on 1 September, nearly five hours after *Schleswig-Holstein* had opened fire on the Polish enclave at Westerplatte.

Approximately 1500 local SS men joined Henningsen and his assault troops to attack the Westerplatte garrison but were repulsed with heavy casualties, Henningsen himself being badly wounded and dying in hospital the following day. The Westerplatte would prove a surprisingly difficult nut to crack and held out for seven days under intense infantry attack and naval and Stuka bombardment.

At sea the complexion of German dispositions had changed radically by that point. Two days after the attack on Poland, Great Britain and France declared war on Germany and additional units were placed under the command of *Marinegruppenkommando* (MGK) West including 4th and 6th M-Flotillas, 10th and 12th Vp-Flotillas and Harbour Defence Flotillas in Borkum, Wilhelmshaven and Cuxhaven. The auxiliary *Sperrbrecher* were also sent into the North Sea as minelaying by both sides intensified.

In the Baltic, the primary threat to Kriegsmarine forces was Poland's submarines. They had begun Operation Worek on the first day of hostilities, *Orzel, Wilk, Sęp, Żbik* and *Ryś* forming patrol lines after initial minelaying, the first two prowling the area of the Bay of Gdansk and the remaining boats off Hela to repulse any new German landing attempts. The submarines were attacked by minesweepers, U-boats and Luftwaffe aircraft. On 3 September *M3* and *M4* carried out a depth-charge attack on *Wilk* after the boat had laid twenty mines East of Hela, the Pole beingoptimistically claimed as destroyed. In fact one depth charge had exploded immediately above the boat, blasting it downward to the relatively shallow seabed, blowing the lights and causing a brief water leak through the diesel exhaust valve. However, the crew managed to stem the flow of water and, despite an oil leak developing, the boat slipped away under cover of darkness.

The following day *M4* was narrowly missed by two torpedoes fired by *Sęp* east of Hela and the submarine was depth-charged, suffering light damage before shaking the minesweeper off. By this time the minelayers *Hansestadt Danzig* and *Tannenberg* had begun laying extensive mine barrages around Danzig under escort by R-boats of the 5th R-Flotilla, and the training ship *Brummer* had also been pressed into service laying mines in Danzig Harbour itself, escorted by *M75, M84* and *M85*.

On 5 September *Wilk* was again depth-charged by ships of the 1st M-Flotilla, but again escaped serious damage. Despite Poland's valiant defence against the German invasion, there was little doubt as to the outcome of the battle, several ports already having been occupied by German forces and Gdynia under heavy fire. Less than two weeks after hostilities began, Polish submarines were ordered to retreat to England if possible, *Wilk* and *Orzel* the only pair to successfully escape the Baltic, the latter only narrowly managing to reach Rosyth in Scotland after having escaped internment in Estonia. The remainder were interned in Sweden after suffering severe battle damage and possessing insufficient fuel for the attempt, forced to seek shelter in neutral harbours. Despite German claims, none of the Polish submarines were destroyed.

Meanwhile on 13 September the *Schleswig Holstein* shelled Gdynia for the second time, the port expected to fall the following day. While R-boats swept a 400m-wide, 5m-deep sea lane off Hela for mines, Polish guns continued to fire at them while the larger ships of the 1st Minesweeper Flotilla supported the Army advance along the Hela peninsula with their own gunfire. It was a slow grinding battle against nearly 5000 strongly-entrenched Polish defenders, thick barbed-wire entanglements and defensive minefields. Heavy weapons were requested from other Army groups, as well as the naval railway gun *Gneisenau* temporarily under Army control. The harbour and its facilities were deemed of special interest to the German economy, particularly the export of coal from the industrial region of Upper Silesia. By way of contrast, even the occupation of Gdynia for naval use (to be renamed Gotenhafen after its conquest) was considered of secondary importance. Defending Polish artillery fire inflicted damage on *Schleswig-Holstein* and eleven minesweepers as the second obsolete battleship *Schliesen* arrived to add the weight of her guns to the attack on the Hela Peninsula. With no headway made by infantry units, the decision was made for the attackers to dig in and await the arrival of heavier weapons while the Kriegsmarine guns continued their attritional bombardments that sapped the defenders' strength and morale. Hitler had decided to starve the garrison into submission rather than lose more troops attacking overland.

Chief of Staff at MGK Ost, KA Hubert Schmundt, assumed direct control of the naval forces besieging Hela, while elsewhere in the Baltic minesweeping continued and lines of anti-submarine nets were laid, patrolled by R-boats and five trawlers of the 17th UJ-Flotilla which simultaneously carried out depth-charge exercises. Convoy routes linking Eastern Prussia with Germany were now considered secure and troops of the 23rd Infantry Division were transferred from Königsberg to Danzig via Stettin under minesweeper escort. On 14 September, Gdynia finally fell to German troops after a final failed Polish counter-attack, the defending troops' commander issuing the order to surrender before committing suicide in his headquarters.

Before the fall of Gydnia, the Kriegsmarine had considered using the riverine ships of the *Donauflottille* to reinforce the forces in Poland. In

Bow-mounted paravane sweeping gear being prepared for use. Note how exposed the forward gun crew would be; operational experience soon introduced gun shields on those ships that did not already have them.

conference with Hitler, Grossadmiral Erich Raeder raised the possibility of using the flotilla, which had been formed after the *Anschluss* with Austria, in both the Baltic and the North Sea. Comprised of the former Austrian gunboat *Birago*, six river motor minesweepers and six auxiliary river motor minesweepers, the Kriegsmarine exercised no operational control over the flotilla at that time as it was attached to XIV Army Corps and was only to be used in tactical co-ordination with the advance of ground forces. Divided into two groups, the first (comprising the heavier gunboat *Birago* and the auxiliary vessels) was tasked with guarding Bratislava harbour and bridges at both Bratislava and Engerau in occupied Czechoslovakia. The second group patrolled the river south of Marchek to safeguard the railway bridge.

However, as the tide of battle swung in Germany's favour, the *Donauflottille* was discounted for offensive action. With few duties, the formation was considered unsuitable for expansion beyond the completion of vessels already under construction. The commissioning of those ships was to be done singly and with only essential trials carried out that required little, if any, additional manpower. As winter approached and the Danube froze, the flotilla would be put into reserve, reducing personnel levels further. The *Donauflottille* would play no part in the conquest of Poland, though it would later be moved to the West as Germany prepared to attack the Netherlands, Belgium and France.

31

Schleswig-Holstein alongside an auxiliary of the Security Forces.

On 28 September the first three completed *Sperrbrecher* were commissioned into the Kriegsmarine in Hamburg; *SpX 'Vigo'*, *SpXI 'Petropolis'* and *SpXII 'Stolzenfels'* – the commander of the latter, Fregattenkapitän der Reserve (FKdR) Christian Schmidt-Prestin, an elderly landowner, distinguishing himself by reporting for duty in his Imperial German Navy uniform. Together they constituted *Sperrbrechergruppe 1*, departing Kiel on the first day of October for Baltic service. The group was attached to BSO and reached Pillau four days later, held in reserve for the three weeks that followed as the crew underwent final training.

The beginning of October saw increasing numbers of Polish troops deserting the Hela garrison as it continued to be battered by naval gunfire from *M4*, *M111*, *M132* and *Nettelbeck*. As distant Warsaw fell to German troops, the Commanding Admiral of the Polish Fleet despatched a message to Schmundt requesting a truce, the unconditional surrender of the Hela Peninsula subsequently being agreed to come into effect at 1100hrs on 2 October. Over 450 officers and 4000 men were taken prisoner, the Polish admiral being transported aboard the 1st R-Flotilla's depot ship, *Nettelbeck* (ex-*M138*), to a prisoner of war camp in Germany. By the time that the demoralised defenders were emerging, the Kriegsmarine Security Forces had suffered their first casualty to enemy action. One of twenty mines laid by the submarine *Żbik* during early September sank the minesweeper *M85* northeast of Heisternest.

In the forenoon of 1 October repeated submarine alarms off Neufahrwasser, later off Rixhoeft and Pillau. At 1440hrs minesweeper *M85* was lost about three miles east of Heisternest; the boat sank; 24 casualties. It has not yet been settled whether this was caused by a torpedo or a mine.

Minesweeper *M3* located a submarine near the point where the boat went down. It was not observed whether dropping of depth charges was successful. It is highly probable that this was the last remaining Polish submarine *Orzel*. Hela is issuing orders to her to surrender. However, it is not certain that the radio order has been received, as her radio apparatus is apparently out of order.[10]

Both *M3* and *M8* continued to bombard what was in actuality a phantom submarine, *Orzel* already being far to the north. The surviving forty-seven crew of *M85* were rescued by *M122* and R-boats and later used to crew two Polish *Jaskkóła*-class minesweepers – the *Zuraw* and *Czayka* – captured intact in Hela. These ships were recommissioned into the 7th M-Flotilla as *Oxhöft* and *Westernplatte* (later *TFA 11*) respectively.[11] Three other ships – *Komendant Pilsudski*, *Rybitwa* and *Mewa* – were raised from where they had been scuttled and repaired to become the Kriegsmarine vessels *Heisternest*, *Rixhöft* (later *TFA 8*) and *Putzig* (later *TFA 7*).[12]

On 6 October 1939, the last organised Polish resistance ceased when 17,000 men surrendered after the battle of Kock and Hitler announced the end of hostilities in a speech to the Reichstag. Upon the clearance of Polish minefields north and north-east of Hela, the Kriegsmarine was concerned with three primary tasks in the Baltic. Firstly, they were to patrol the Kattegat and prevent the ingress of British submarines into the Baltic or egress of any Polish submarines still trapped there. Secondly, they needed to control contraband shipped from Scandinavia and, thirdly, the sea lanes between East Prussia and Northern Germany required safeguarding. Security forces were also placed on high alert to sail from Danzig to the aid of some 70,000 German nationals in the Baltic States that looked increasingly likely to be occupied by Soviet forces. German and Soviet co-operation had resulted in a tangible anti-German mood sweeping through the region that felt threatened by Stalin's regime. German minesweepers were brought to operational readiness to sail as escorts for evacuation ships but Hitler restrained his naval chiefs, lest their preparation be misinterpreted by the Soviet Union as an aggressive move on the Baltic States themselves. Gradually tension relaxed sufficiently to stand the German ships down, though they remained in harbour until 9 October when the decision was taken to release them following Russia and Latvia agreeing diplomatic terms.

Expanding the Security Forces

By the end of the Polish campaign, the Kriegsmarine's Security Forces had expanded dramatically with the following new units:

Groups of eight fishing boats each were gathered to form the 2nd and 8th Vp-Flotillas, whalers comprising the 13th Vp-Flotillas during September and a group of coasters gathered to create the 10th Vp-Flotilla in Wesermünde;

22 September, 7th Vp-Flotilla in Kiel, consisting initially of seven ships with an eighth commissioned in October, and 11th and 17th M- Flotillas;

25 September, 4th Vp-Flotilla of eight trawlers in Bremerhaven;

26 September, requisitioned trawlers and whalers for the 12th and 15th Vp-Flotillas in Stettin, 18th M-Flotilla and single ships of the 15th M-Flotilla;

27 September, 11th UJ-Flotilla, 6th M-Flotilla in Cuxhaven (comprised of Type 16 ships) and nine trawlers of the 9th Vp-Flotilla;

28 September, the remainder of 15th M-Flotilla and 13th M-Flotilla was commissioned – though the latter was yet ready to proceed because conversion work on trawlers was incomplete – and eight loggers of the 14th M-flotilla;

30 September: *SpIV 'Oakland'* commissioned in Hamburg – the first *Sperrbrecher* equipped with VES gear;

1 October, 1st Vp-Flotilla (eight steamers that would later become *Sperrbrecher*) and 19th M-Flotilla were commissioned;

2 October, *SpI 'Bahia Camarones'*, *SpII 'Karl Leonhardt'* and *SpIII 'Robert Bornhofen'* commissioned in Hamburg, together comprising *Sperrbrechergruppe* 2;

3 October, *SpVII 'Sauerland'*, *SpVIII 'Neckar'* and *SpIX 'Lüneberg'* commissioned, comprising *Sperrbrechergruppe* 6;

4 October, eight trawlers each of the 3rd and 11th Vp-Flotillas and *SpV 'Schwanheim'*and *SpIV 'Magdeburg'* commissioned, together with *SpIV* comprising *Sperrbrechergruppe* 4;

5 October, 16th M-Flotilla was commissioned from nine modern trawlers (*M1601–M1609*).

On 12 October an additional six two-year old trawlers were taken into service as the 12th M-Flotilla while four *Sperrbrecher* were briefly gathered together as the 5th *Vorpostengruppe* during September, another four also forming the 6th *Vorpostengruppe*.

Kapitän zur See Friedrich Ruge returned to Cuxhaven on 17 October, released from the post of FdM Ost and returning as FdM West. With him were the ships of the *Geleitflotille*, the 1st, 2nd, 4th and 6th M-Flotillas, 2nd and 3rd R-Flotillas and reserve units of the 12th, 14th, 16th and 18th M-Flotillas all for operations within the North Sea. The elderly Type 16 minesweepers of the 7th M-Flotilla also transferred from the Baltic to Cuxhaven to begin operations in the German Bight, augmented by the ex-Polish vessels *Oxhöft* and *Westerplatte*.

Crew maintenance on one of the small
ships of the Security Forces.

While only a single ship from the Security Forces had been lost in the Baltic
during the Polish campaign, the primary threat remained that of mines,
ironically more often than not those from German fields. East of Copenhagen
the Danish Navy had laid a relatively small defensive minefield while the
Kriegsmarine had laid the thick mine barrages of Undine I, II and II,
stretching between Trelleborg in Sweden and Denmark's Faske Bay, as close
to the three-mile limit as was possible. While these three interlocking fields
had been laid efficiently and accurately by German minelayers, the
combination of strong currents, bad winter weather and occasional faulty
anchoring resulted in frequent 'drifters' which posed a potential hazard to all
shipping despite the fail-safe mechanism designed to render them inert if
separated from their mooring cables.

In the North Sea the Royal Navy laid a mine barrage the length of their
East Coast from Dover to the Orkneys between 20 and 50 miles wide,
leaving a narrow lane between the barrage and the coast for convoys. Over
6000 mines were also planted across the Dover Strait in an echo of the last
war's Dover Barrage. For their part, the Kriegsmarine laid contact mines
from the Netherlands' coastal waters off Terschelling, across the Heligoland
Bight to the entrance of the Skagerrak, at a distance of between 50 and
100km from the coast. Called 'Westwall', the most north-westerly point
was about half the distance between Skagerrak and Scotland. Naturally,

A typical converted trawler *Vorpostenboot*

each side also began offensive minelaying in any transit channels detected in the opposing fields.

Both the Axis and the Allies obeyed Hague Convention rules and declared mined areas as soon as hostilities had begun. Raeder also pointed out that Britain had assembled its merchant shipping in convoys protected by armed escorts and, therefore, strictly commercial trade routes to British ports no

The difficulties outfitting a wide array of auxiliaries frequently led to the use of whatever obsolete weapons were available, such as this machine gun aboard a *U-Jäger*.

Minelaying. Crewmen manhandle an EMC contact mine over the stern. With a 300kg explosive charge, they could be laid in water up to 500m deep.

longer existed. He reasoned that Article 2 of the Convention forbidding the use of mines 'with the sole object of intercepting commercial shipping' no longer applied. The mine war escalated and by August 1940 Germany announced a total blockade of the British coast and that the entire sea area surrounding Great Britain had been mined.

The Security Forces had begun to suffer a trickle of losses during the harshest winter weather for several years, including *V805 'Skolpenbank'* listed as missing on 18 October somewhere in the south–east corner of the declared mine area north of Schiermonnikoog. The last reported signals from the 397–ton steam trawler had been received eleven days previously and the area was checked for enemy minefields once the winter weather allowed, though none were found. It is possible that the ship struck a 'drifter', a mine broken loose from either a friendly or enemy field. It's furthermore possible that the harsh weather sank her, though the trawler had been typical of the requisitioned fishing vessels in naval use and was well suited to the North Sea. The mystery surrounding *V805*'s disappearance also prompted SKL to issue an edict that only the most necessary classified information be carried aboard the vessels lest they fall into enemy hands; even as a wreck it could be boarded and searched if in shallow water.

Three days later a *Vorpostenboot* was destroyed by a confirmed 'drifter' in the eastern Baltic. Flotilla leader *V701* '*Este*' struck a mine on 21 October while patrolling the mine barrage stretching across the Øresund. The 426-ton trawler had been built in Hamburg and launched only five years previously. Klaus Reichstein, a young member of the 7th Vp-Flotilla serving aboard a sister-ship, wrote about the loss of *V701* in a letter to Germany sent five days after the explosion.

I don't know if I already told you that I'm on a *Vorpostenboot*. You won't really get any reported exploits from us. Because, of course, we can't really actively attack with our paltry strength and puny speed. Our task is rather to determine the enemy's location, to report it but to defend ourselves against attacks, mainly from the air. Our attention is particularly on British submarines that almost certainly want to avenge the disaster of Scapa Flow somehow. Therefore we patrol our position in the vicinity of any mine barrier up and down, on alert day and night . . . Out there one experiences all kinds of things. We have had a lot of wind and correspondingly rough seas until now. The sea alone makes life aboard our small vessel quite uncomfortable. Add to that the dangerous proximity of the mines. Recently, in bad weather, we saw seven mine detonations within two hours. No one knows why they have exploded . . . But unfortunately, we received a bitter lesson a few days ago. The leading boat of our flotilla was blown into the air by mines. A few hours before the boat had been close to us. The accident happened within sight of us without our even being aware of it. Only four [*sic.* five] of the [75] crew were rescued by Danish fishermen.[13]

The skipper of the ill-fated *Vorpostenboot* was a veteran of the previous war, 43-year-old Kaptlt Dr Bruno Kindt, who had served as Watch Officer aboard the torpedo boats *S18* and *V1* during the conflict. During the interwar years he had received a PhD in chemical sciences before volunteering for naval service once more after the outbreak of war. Kindt was one of those lost, his body not washing ashore on the island of Amager until a month later.

The explosion was reported by Danish observers on the island of Møn and a Heinkel HE8 reconnaissance aircraft of the Danish Navy later found a raft with survivors in very poor weather conditions. Despite a dangerously high-running sea, the pilot landed his floatplane alongside the raft. Unable to take the men aboard the two-man aircraft, he secured them to his floats and flew them ashore. One other survivor made landfall in Denmark ten hours after the sinking, leaving the death toll at seventy men. During the following day seven bodies were recovered by Danish fishermen, another fifty later washing ashore. The bodies were buried in a communal grave in Denmark with a ceremony attended by the German ambassador Cécil von Renthe-Fink.

Another 'drifter' sank *V301* '*Weser*' on 25 November in the southern outlet

A grainy photo showing part of the Danish funeral ceremony for men of *V701* '*Este*' that was sunk by a drifting mine on 21 October 1939.

of the Great Belt with sixteen crewmen posted missing. At first, German authorities reported numerous Danish mines adrift in the area, which were very difficult to destroy with gunfire in the heavy seas. It was to one of these that they attributed the ship's loss, but Danish naval authorities firmly maintained that their mines were activated by electrical current from the mainland, being rendered completely harmless should they break free and therefore sever the electrical connection. Indeed, the harsh winter weather played a part in the sinking of these ships.

> Off Copenhagen shore: Gales have loosened several hundred mines in the German minefield . . . drifting mines exploded on the coast near the suburbs (of Copenhagen), breaking windows and frightening citizens with their terrific detonations. Naval crews have destroyed no fewer than forty-three mines from Koege Bay up to Amager Island, where 100,000 Copenhagen residents live in a district comparable to Brooklyn. Along the whole southern coast mine alarms often make it necessary to evacuate villages while experts empty or explode the mines. So many mines are floating around that it is impossible to destroy all of them in the bad weather.[14]

Danish and German pilot boats shuttled both military and commercial traffic through accepted channels within the mined areas, the Danish Navy patrolling north of the fields and informing all shipping of any sighted 'drifters'. Minesweeping continued and Danish authorities also requested the urgent removal of the wreck of *V301* which lay within their territorial waters, the Kriegsmarine undertaking work to clear the area for other ships. The Danes even agreed to German minesweepers entering their territorial waters to hunt for mines as well as a permanent German pilot service in both directions through the Great Belt.

Kriegsmarine operations against contraband shipments within the Kattegat and Eastern Baltic was continued by minelayers and vessels of the 11th U-J Flotilla and 9th Vp-Flotilla although results were deemed as moderate; dozens of vessels being stopped, many taken into one of the German Baltic harbours and searched though the majority were then released. Those vessels assigned to the interception of merchant shipping took up fixed positions during the day while patrolling Luftwaffe aircraft directed all foreign merchantmen towards them to be searched. During the hours of darkness, the German ships patrolled within assigned areas at low speed. Indeed by the end of October a survey of the merchantmen brought in to German harbours showed that from 103 vessels, sixty had been released, seven others were about to be released leaving thirty-six vessels suspected of having carried contraband. Among those thirty-six were seven against which Prize Law proceedings had been started, four vessels against which they were pending and twenty-three vessels which were considered 'doubtful'. The three large ships of *Sperrbrechergruppe* 1 were added to the picket lines, patrolling Swedish waters between Gotland and Öland at the beginning of December before returning to Hamburg for installation of VES equipment.

The Kriegsmarine also received reports of a brisk traffic of steamers from the Baltic States to Sweden carrying vital foodstuffs and pit-props ultimately bound for Britain. Frustrated by their inability to intervene, OKM extended contraband searches into the Gulf of Finland but Soviet authorities quickly requested them halted. They feared that the presence of German forces in the region could be construed as tacit Axis support for Finland during new Russo-Finnish negotiations over Soviet territorial demands. Mindful of the non-aggression pact between their two countries and agreement that Finland lay within the agreed Soviet sphere of interest, Raeder ordered operations restricted up to longitude 20° 30' East, thus concentrating on the Swedish area of the Eastern Baltic.

With winter closing in, levels of Baltic *Vorpostenboot* and minesweeper units decreased slightly. Ships of the 1st M-Flotilla equipped with *S-Gerät* had been hurriedly despatched to counter sighted Polish submarines, but

The officer leading a German prize crew climbs aboard an intercepted steamer attempting to reach Great Britain through the Baltic Sea.

they found nothing. Attention had moved west, Germany beginning to use its small destroyer forces for raiding into the North Sea and minelaying along the British East coast. These missions, coupled with U-boat transits from Brunsbüttel and Wilhelmshaven, required frequently-swept channels to be maintained. In November all minesweeping flotillas consisting of purpose-built ships were assigned to the North Sea. Frequently, multiple tasks were assigned during a single night's minesweeper operation and the converted trawlers of the auxiliary minesweeping flotillas lacked the required speed.

Controlling the Baltic Sea

As contraband continued slipping through the German net bound for Britain, much of it within Swedish territorial waters, German minelaying was extended to within three miles of the Swedish coast in disregard of Sweden's declared four-mile territorial limit. Subsequent frequent and dangerous clashes with Swedish units were reported, such as destroyers attempting to disturb German patrol boats engaged in stop-and-search operations with gunfire that they claimed were merely anti-aircraft gunnery exercises, while neutral steamers were warned by Swedish naval forces and lightships of the presence of German vessels warships. With a Swedish autogyro reported to be 'buzzing' and filming *Vorpostenboote* on 19 November, SKL authorised C/30 flak 'exercises' be initiated if warnings were ignored. Five days later, after diplomatic protests had been made, Raeder informed the Swedish Naval Attaché that any further interference would be met with 'force of arms'.

Meanwhile, the threat posed by British submarines had resulted in several depth-charge attacks by *U-Jäger* and *Vorpostenboote* reported near Heligoland, but with no clear results even after divers were sent to the scene of several claimed sinkings. However, the Royal Navy were indeed present in German territorial waters.

Lieutenant George D. A. Gregory had taken HMS *Sturgeon* from Rosyth for the boat's fourth war patrol on 11 November, patrolling the Heligoland Bight and Danish west coast. Fifty-six miles north-west of Heligoland, two *Vorpostenboote* were sighted and attacked.

> 1330 hours – Sighted a pair of armed trawlers bearing 070°, range 2.5 nautical miles. Position was 54°34'N, 06°28'E.
> 1400 hours – Started attack on these trawlers.
> 1555 hours – Fired two torpedoes at the first trawler.
> 1556 hours – Fired two torpedoes at the second trawler.
> 1558 hours – Heard a loud explosion. The result was not observed.[15]

Lookouts aboard both *V208* '*R. Walter Darré*' and *V209* '*Gauleiter Telchow*' were unaware of the impending danger and the 430-ton *V209* was hit in the stern and sunk, the first successful British submarine attack of the Second World War. Kapitänleutnant Dr Kurt Auerbach's ship went down quickly, taking the 40-year old captain, a veteran of the previous war, with it. The Germans remained ignorant of HMS *Sturgeon*'s presence and were uncertain whether the culprit had been a torpedo or a mine. An area of three miles circumference was scoured for possible enemy mines but declared safe.

The winter of 1939/40 was particularly severe in Northern Europe.

Trawlers converted to military use made perfect auxiliary warships, designed to withstand the conditions associated with high seas fishing.

Group West assumes that this loss is to be attributed to a Dutch drifting mine because of the faulty diaphragm safety devices found on a Dutch mine in the vicinity. There is no proof of this. From the nature of the detonation (sudden blowing into the air of the whole stern) the Naval Staff also considers it quite possible that it was torpedoed by a British submarine.[16]

Minesweeper *M132* was also sunk on 13 November in the Lister Channel between the German island of Sylt und Rømø, Denmark, after she was severely damaged by the accidental dropping of a depth charge from the *M61* travelling ahead of her. The minesweepers had been on an anti-submarine patrol when disaster struck though there were no casualties. The Kriegsmarine began salvage operations on the wreck, though they were soon abandoned in foul winter weather.

The threat posed by enemy aircraft had not yet fully developed. RAF Bomber Command had suffered disproportionate losses during its first few attempts at attacking German naval installations and they achieved little more on 3 December when twenty-four Wellington bombers attacked Heligoland by daylight, though they at least suffered no casualties. Bombs were dropped on the harbour with the exception of a single bomb that 'hung up' inside the bomb bay and was accidentally dropped on the island itself. This was the first British bomb to drop on German soil and provided grist to the German propaganda mill that the British would attack a densely populated area. The RAF claimed 'one cruiser' sunk but had in fact hit *M1407* '*Johann Schulte*' in the forecastle, penetrating straight through the hull and sinking the ship though the bomb failed to explode.

The following day, *UJ117 'Gustav Körner'* commanded by Kaptlt Dr Hans-Josef Klau struck a drifting mine and sank north–north–east of the wreck of *V301* in the Great Belt. Rescue attempts by her three flotilla-mates as well as the Danish torpedo boat *Dragen* and fishery defence vessel *Dugolf* were unsuccessful and only two men were saved, the 40-year old skipper not being among them. It soon transpired that Klau had made a navigational error that had led him directly into a German minefield.[17]

On 13 December, the cruisers *Leipzig* and *Nürnberg* were both torpedoed and damaged by HMS *Salmon* while covering five destroyers that had laid mines off Newcastle. The German cruisers had been reported by British reconnaissance aircraft as they lay waiting to rendezvous with the returning destroyers. Following the two torpedo hits Ruge despatched all available craft as escort, the cruisers capable of differing speeds and soon begame separated.

U-Jäger were frequently converted fishing boats and trawlers similar to *Vorpostenboote* and auxiliary minesweepers, with flak weapons added and an increased number of depth charges carried. Depth charges on their throwers can be clearly seen in this photograph.

The more seriously-damaged *Leipzig* which had taken a torpedo amidships was under escort by two destroyers as well as escort ships *F7* and *F9*, minesweepers *M9*, *M10*, *M12* and *M13* and R-boats *R33*, *R35*, *R36*, *R37*, *R38* and *R39* when they were sighted by HMS *Ursula* off the Elbe estuary the following day.

At 1115hrs, Lt.Cdr. G. C. Phillips detected what he took to be a cruiser and six destroyers by periscope, penetrating the protective screen and firing four torpedoes at a range of only 1,200 yards. Two tremendous explosions were heard, the second buffeting *Ursula* so badly that several lights blew. Believing his target cruiser to have been hit and sunk, Philips withdrew, skilfully avoiding the German ships hunting for him. His torpedoes had missed *Leipzig* and instead hit *F9*, which sank almost immediately with 120 men killed including *Geleitflottille* commander FK Friedrich-Wilhelm Pindter.[18] Only thirty-four survivors were rescued by *R36* and *R38*.

The loss of *F9* would be the sole casualty from the *Geleitflottille*, the ships being withdrawn from front-line service and the flotilla finally disbanded during May. The pennant numbers would be used again, but by other vessels more suitable for the tasks, notably captured French and Dutch ships. *F1* was decommissioned in December and would later return as fleet tender *Libelle* (later renamed *Jagd*), *F2*, *F4*, *F7*, *F8* and *F10* were rebuilt as torpedo retrieval ships while *F5* was moved to the *Sperrwaffen-Versuchskommando* (Mine Trials Command).

The escape of both British submarines from German countermeasures allowed the Kriegsmarine to determine that their ASW tactics were inadequate and ineffective, with not a single enemy submarine confirmed as destroyed following an organised hunt. Berlin ordered more efficient planning and execution of ASW operations by *U-Jäger* combined with the use of more depth charges and greater persistence in attack, like that shown by the Royal Navy. An increase in the use of ASW aircraft was also strongly advised, though interservice rivalry – the bane of all Hitler's military services – between the Luftwaffe and Kriegsmarine would always hamper this.

Deteriorating weather caused Kaptlt Helmuth Röhrig's *V704* 'Claus Wisch' to run aground on the Swedish coast east of Trelleborg at the end of December. The vessel had suffered severe icing during a south-westerly gale, rendering her uncontrollable. Two men were lost while the remainder were briefly interned by Swedish authorities, being released on 1 January and picked up by *V706* the following afternoon. Consideration was given to salvaging the stricken 256-ton trawler though the idea was abandoned after it was realised that, even in good weather, the task would take nearly two months with no guarantee of success at the end of it. The ship was already fifteen years old at the time of her grounding and permission was requested and granted to blow up the wreck after all useful material was salvaged.[19]

Though Röhrig had been released, tension with Sweden remained high during December. A Luftwaffe reconnaissance aircraft reported being hit and damaged by Swedish flak despite being within international waters, their location subsequently disputed by the Swedish torpedo boat that opened fire. At the end of November the Soviet Union attacked Finland after the latter refused to give in to Soviet demands. Subsequent Swedish coastal minelaying was read by the Germans as an offensive move against their anti-contraband patrols but justified by Sweden as defence against potential Soviet aggression. Indeed, on 10 December the Soviet submarine *SC322* sank the German freighter ss *Reinbek* in the Gulf of Finland while en-route from Leningrad to Oskarshamn. Two nights later Soviet submarine *S1* shelled and sank the German steamer *Bolheim* with fifteen rounds while the ship sailed from the Finnish port of Bjoerneborg, within the declared Soviet blockade zone. The steamer, which was fully illuminated with a large German flag picked out by spotlight, went down with the captain killed, twenty-seven crewmen reaching the Finnish shore in a lifeboat while the Soviets made no effort to rescue or assist the crew. Four other steamers were also fired on during the Russo-Finnish conflict, though without further loss.

The Kriegsmarine reckoned correctly that the so-called 'Falsterbo Channel' was being used within Swedish waters by neutral shipping in order to avoid German intervention. They further surmised that it might also be used by British submarines transiting into the Baltic and orders were issued for German patrol vessels to make the provocative move of running the channel as well, particularly by night. On 26 December minesweepers *M1106* and *M1103* were unhindered upon passing through the channel in broad daylight, though closely shadowed by a Swedish aircraft. The two German ships observed very heavy merchant traffic, at one point counting fifty-six ships travelling in both directions within two hours. Ratcheting the tension further, a Court of Maritime Inquiry and the Scandinavian press attributed the 12 December sinking by mine of the Swedish freighter ss *Torö* off Fasterbro to deliberate German mining of the Channel, rather than the result of striking a 'drifter'.

Perhaps surprisingly, these strained relations never reached breaking-point. During mid-December the Swedish Prime Minister Per Albin Hansson reshuffled his Cabinet to form a grand coalition and provide greater stability for the neutral nation. This new Cabinet was viewed by Germany as more favourably disposed toward the Reich and, although incidents would continue throughout the years that followed, the threat of conflict with Swedish forces receded. However, German military strategists continued to observe Swedish involvement – both tacit and overt – with Finland as they fought the Soviet invasion; 8000 Swedish volunteers were permitted to serve in Finland's ground war and joint Swedish-Finnish naval minelaying was undertaken in the Gulf of Bothnia. An entry in the SKL War Diary on 27 December 1939 now appears an ominous portent of things to come:

> Various reports confirm the assumption that the weakness of Russia's fighting strength, as clearly shown in Finland, coupled with the deficiencies in the Russian transport system and her industrial capacity, is having more and more effect on the Scandinavian, as well as the enemy powers. The standstill in the Russian operations in Finland seems to have strengthened Sweden and Norway in their will to resist aggression and to have lessened their fear of a Russian advance. A Russian setback will find the enemy powers more willing to help Finland; it will strengthen their fighting power and will to resist Germany. This lessening of Soviet pressure on the enemy's political and military position will bring increasing relief to him in the conduct of future warfare. Naval Staff is therefore of the opinion that the military and political weakness of Soviet-Russia, brought to light in Finland, should be taken into consideration in our attitude towards Russia. In making plans and decisions we should not overestimate the pressure which is imposed by the vastness of Soviet Russia and which is still perceptible despite the present pact of friendship. On the contrary we should let our military and political strength add weight in all negotiations with Russia more than perhaps it has done so far.

On 1 December 1939 *M14* was commissioned into naval service at Hamburg's Stülcken Werft. The *M35* series minesweepers, of which this was the latest, had proved extremely successful, being both versatile and exceptionally seaworthy. However, while the type would continue to be built – sixty-nine in total being constructed in eight different shipyards between 1937 and 1941 – they were expensive and their oil-fired boilers rendered them vulnerable to fuel shortages as the war progressed and the demand for oil increased exponentially.

A cheaper, simpler alternative to the *M35* was essential and thus the *M40* was born. Based on the Type 1916 minesweeper of the previous war, they were approximately 10 per cent smaller than the *M35*, displacing 775 tons as opposed to just over 870 tons for the previous design. The armament was reduced also, to one 105mm/L45, one 37mm/L83 and up to six 20mm flak cannon. Two Bauer-Wach exhaust-steam geared turbines powered by coal-burning Schultz boilers constructed by Germania Werft replaced the diesel powerplants of the *M35*. In total 131 were commissioned between 1942 and 1944, from *M401* onwards being built within captured Dutch shipyards. The first of the new type was launched on 5 May 1941 from the Schichau shipyard in Königsberg. As the war progressed and more new minesweepers became available, some flotillas of auxiliary converted trawlers were dissolved and the personnel moved to the newer heavy ships.

Combat in the North Sea

Despite the continued season of bad weather – the worst reported for 100 years in Northern Europe – German efforts at improved ASW tactics finally yielded success in the North Sea. On 7 January 1940 HMS *Undine* sighted what LtCdr. Alan Spencer Jackson, RN, took to be three trawlers 20 miles west of Heligoland. The boat was perhaps below operational par; the ASDIC had flooded due to a badly-fitted rubber seal and with poor hydrophone reception, Jackson was totally reliant on periscope observation to assess the situation. At 0940hrs, British time, submerged in a flat calm sea, Jackson fired a single torpedo at the leading trawler some 2000 yards away. The show passed closely astern as Jackson had underestimated his target's speed by two knots. He ordered the boat dived and attempted to sneak away in less than 30m of water, thinking it unwise for the periscope to break the calm surface once more. *Undine* had attacked Oberleutnant zur See (ObltzS) Peter Ottmar Grau's auxiliary minesweeper *M1204 'Anne Busse'* travelling in company with *M1203 'Bürgermesiter Smidt I'* on an anti-submarine patrol. The single torpedo track was sighted aboard the minesweepers which immediately commenced a depth-charge attack. A single distant explosion heard aboard *Undine* was explained by Jackson as his torpedo striking the sea floor, though a second confirmed that they were indeed under attack. As abruptly as they had begun, the first flurry of depth charges soon ended.

A short time later there occurred three more explosions, apparently nearer. The ASDIC being completely out of action and the hydrophones almost useless, I was unable to form any picture of what was happening on the surface. The depth of the water was 12–14 fathoms. Bearing in mind the experience of *Spearfish*, I proceeded at a depth of 40 to 50 feet as slowly as possible and turning to northward.

A period of complete quiet followed for about five minutes. Thinking there might be a possibility of attacking again or that the enemy had broken off the hunt, I returned to periscope depth and raised the Low Power Periscope, to look directly at a trawler on the starboard beam, so close that I could see only her port side from the bridge to the aft end of the engine room casing. I immediately ordered 'Down periscope, 60 feet!', but before the submarine had really started to go down there were three violent explosions, one aft, one forward and another. (I was informed recently by Leading Telegraph Monserrat that he heard a noise on the port side of the Control Room which sounded like a depth charge scraping the pressure hull, but I have no personal recollection of this.)

The submarine was blown upwards, some lights and glass broken, there was a steady leak in the engine room from near the hatch, a leak in the galley and I was later informed that the Fore End had flooded and had to be abandoned. Both sets of hydroplanes were reported out of action, (the fore hydroplanes hard–a–rise) but the after hydroplanes appeared to be working. I ordered 'Take her down, flood 0' but the submarine continued to rise until the periscope standards broke surface, giving many of the crew the impression that the drop keel had fallen off.

I therefore raised the Low Power Periscope and saw a trawler bows-on on the starboard beam at a range of approximately half a mile. Considering that it was impossible to get the submarine down again to a safe depth before being rammed, I ordered 'Surface, burn the C.B.s [Confidential Books], prepare the charge' and went to the bridge, followed by the Leading Signalman who acting on my orders, waved the Negative Flag, which was the best substitute for a white flag available.[20]

HMS *Undine* broke surface and came under concentrated gunfire before the surrender flag was observed and the twenty-nine crewmen began jumping into the freezing water. First Lieutenant Mike Harvey opened vents before he abandoned ship as, due to the flooding aboard the boat, the scuttling charges were inaccessible. However, the battered submarine continued to run at a speed of 6 knots, down by the stern and with rudder jammed hard to starboard. Jackson later surmised in his Admiralty report that the forward main vent had been damaged by an explosion and probably jammed shut, the submarine retaining enough buoyancy until completely flooded. The German flotilla commander, KK Fritz Petzel, aboard *M1201 'Harvestehude'*, had arrived as the submarine surfaced and managed to briefly board the boat and salvage some unburnt confidential papers. Grau and an Oberbootsmann also clambered aboard, trying to stop engines and close hatches in an attempt to capture the boat intact, but rising chlorine gas forced them to abandon the attempt despite *M1201* attached a towing hawser. An effort to return with gas masks by several German crewmen managed to finally kill the engines, but the boat sank faster beneath them and once more they were forced to depart. The minesweepers marked the spot with three buoys as *Undine* lay upright in only 37m of water.[21]

Efforts are being made to salvage her and the strictest secrecy is ordered . . . The sinking of this submarine has supplied the tangible success so long desired in our anti-submarine activities. It was all the more necessary since, on account of the complete lack of success so far . . . justifiable doubts were arising concerning the effectiveness of our anti-submarine defences. This success will provide the necessary impetus towards further vigorous prosecution of our anti-submarine activities.[22]

Later that same day ships of the 1st M-Flotilla sighted another submarine on the surface 20 miles west of Heligoland, which rapidly submerged as they gave chase. Eight to ten depth charges were dropped on the anticipated location, yielding no signs of success on the surface but resulting in breaking-up noises detected by hydrophone. A buoy was dropped to mark the site after further depth charges as heavy fog obscured the area. The minesweepers returned to Wilhelmshaven, leaving one of their number anchored on the spot overnight. Originally it was presumed that the attack had destroyed HMS *Seahorse*, though no wreckage has been found to confirm this. It also is possible that *Seahorse* was lost to mines north of Heligoland, while a third potential cause of the sinking was recorded by *Sperrbrecher IV 'Oakland'* which sighted a suspected periscope south-east of Heligoland on 29 December and, after altering course several times, rammed an obstruction just beneath the surface with her extended bowspar, the severe impact wrenching it loose. A heavy patch of oil was observed, though no wreckage was sighted.

Two days later HMS *Starfish* was detected by *M7* and attacked. Lieutenant Thomas Anthony Turner, RN, had taken his boat from Blyth on 5 January to patrol in the Heligoland Bight. At 0930hrs, British Time, he attacked at close range what he identified through his periscope as a German destroyer. Unfortunately, faulty communication between the captain and crew resulted in the four torpedoes remaining in their tubes. Returning to periscope depth for a second attempt, Turner was startled to find *M7* lying stopped less than 100 yards away. The S-*Gerät* operator above had been detected *Starfish* and ObltzS Heinrich Timm ordered an immediate depth-charge attack. Coincidentally, the full salvo of depth charges was not fired due to faulty communication aboard *M7* as well, only two stern charges being dropped for no visible result.

Timm continued to slowly stalk *Starfish* and six more charges followed nearly an hour after the first, a further pair within the hour that followed. In rising seas the S-*Gerät* was becoming unusable, but the damage had actually already been done. The first pair of explosions had damaged the power supply to the submarine's forward hydroplanes which remained locked in a 15° rise position. Both motors were immediately stopped and ballast tanks flooded to bring the boat gently on to the seabed only 30m below the surface while repairs were carried out.

Timm prowled the area above with guns manned and depth charges sporadically dropped, but failed to deliver the fatal blow. At approximately 1440hrs, sea conditions moderated and a more solid S-*Gerät* fix gave Timm the chance to drop twenty depth charges on the stationary boat, this time shearing rivets in the pressure hull and sending air bubbles to the surface. With the submarine's position now betrayed, Timm battered her further causing heavy flooding aboard *Starfish*. The submarine's engine crankcases and starboard main motor bearings were flooded, and torpedo trenches and bilges full of water with more pouring through the starboard engine clutch. With little chance that *M7* would abandon the hunt and no possibility of escape Turner ordered the boat's ballast keel dropped at 1932hrs and the *Starfish* surfaced rapidly at a 45° stern-first angle under the glare of *M7*'s searchlight and two light-buoys. The minesweeper immediately opened fire with machine guns before Turner showed a white surrender light and his crew began abandoning ship. As his flotilla-mate *M5* arrived on the scene, Timm brought *M7* alongside and secured a line briefly in an unsuccessful boarding attempt as HMS *Starfish* sank. Some of the British crew were taken aboard *M7* without even getting their feet wet, where they were well treated by their captors.[23]

> A most gratifying success, which is to be valued especially highly after the recent destruction of the submarine *Undine*. This will give our *U-Jäger* units more confidence and certainly, it is hoped, will convince the British submarine arm of the dangers of operating in the Heligoland Bight. The sinking will be kept secret in order to leave the enemy in doubt as to the type of German anti-submarine measures used.[24]

With severe ice in the Baltic, tugboats were necessary at all German bases except Warnemünde, Neustadt and Kiel. Operations against merchant shipping were being continued with the minelayer *Preussen* only, while the 17th UJ-Flotilla patrolled the Kattegat south of Anholt, regularly becoming stuck in thick ice as the temperatures plummeted.

By the beginning of February three ships of the 13th Vp-Flotilla were briefly active alongside *Preussen* though their operations were abandoned as thick ice obstructed passage in and out of port. Though the lack of Kriegsmarine interception allowed transit of potential contraband cargo to Great Britain, by the end of January the tally of vessels intercepted numbered 354. While 307 of these, all but one under neutral flags, had subsequently been released, the rest were retained. Through the Prize Court system the Reich had appropriated to that point ten ships totalling 21,004 BRT, their cargoes comprising: 1187 tons of provisions (in particular butter, bacon, eggs and condensed milk) plus 2280 tons of provisions which were not confiscated according to Prize Law procedure as they came under the German-Danish butter agreement, 28,766m³ of wood, sawn timber, plywood etc., 12,177 tons of cellulose, 678 tons of paper and 63 tons miscellaneous goods, particularly oil.

However, the winter had effectively curtailed further significant patrol action. *Befehlshaber der Sicherung West* (BSW, Commander-in-Chief Security West), requested an exchange with BSO of *Vorpostenboot* types: converted North Sea drifters swapped for trawlers still in the Baltic, the latter better suited to the heavy North Sea conditions and unable to operate in Baltic ice. However, the total number of trawlers available in two flotillas numbered only sixteen against two flotillas of twenty-four drifters, a severe numerical weakening of vessels available to cover the open spaces of the North Sea. A third ex-trawler flotilla was demanded by BSW which was flatly refused resulting in an exchange of only one flotilla of drifters (10th Vp-Flotilla) for one trawler unit. Requests from BSW for the formation of more flotillas were declined for logistical reasons; the Kriegsmarine simply did not possess the personnel or material.

Defensive and offensive minelaying continued between the two main antagonists and on 25 January the 7th M-Flotilla began sweeping mines from the first confirmed British minefield, west of Terschelling in a British-declared area. Three neutral steamers, the Swedes *Adolf Bratt* and *Vega* and the Finnish steamer *Indra*, had already been sunk within the region during October and December. Three British mines were again found and their anchors cut six miles north-west of Terschelling, one of which, a British submarine-laid mine, was towed as far as the lower Ems, where it was lost in the drift ice.

Luftwaffe reconnaissance flights south of Dogger Bank at the end of January sighted trawlers with no visible marking or flags which failed to communicate even after a warning burst of machine-gun fire. To their south, within visual range, a submarine was observed crash diving though it escaped before it could be effectively attacked. A periscope was later sighted on the Dogger Bank though no attack was made as anti-submarine hunts were forbidden in that area, air attacks at sea only being permitted within a strip 30 miles wide along the British coast. *U9* also reported twelve fishing smacks within the German declared area sailing along 'Route 1'. These were assumed to be Danish and orders were issued to two ships of the 16th and 18th Vp-Flotillas to find and intercept them. They were to be sunk if they could not be brought in as neutral vessels, though they escaped detection. In an attempt to separate neutral from Allied, the Danish Government was informed through diplomatic channels that fishing vessels were in jeopardy within the declared area and that they would be seized if discovered.

With fears over the possible presence of British trawlers within the Dogger Bank area, the Germans mounted Operation Wikinger, scheduled at first for the end of January but finally mounted on 19 February 1940. Six destroyers sailed at high speed through the swept channels of defensive minefields, though without the Luftwaffe fighter cover they had requested. A German He111 bomber of KG26, X *Fliegerkorps*, engaged on its own postponed anti-shipping strike sighted the ships and began shadowing, unsure of their nationality. Neither ships nor aircraft fired recognition signals and, believing the Heinkel to be British, the rearmost destroyers opened fire. Now convinced that they were enemy ships, the aircraft made two bombing runs and sank *Leberecht Maass* and *Max Schultz*, though the latter may have actually strayed into the flanking minefields during the chaos that ensued. In total, 578 men

Hans Bartels, captain of minesweeper *M1*.

were killed in the disaster.[25] *V803* was despatched to search for survivors while an exploratory sweep by the 1st M-Flotilla within Route 1 confirmed no presence of mines where *Leberecht Maass* went down.

The Security Forces' suspicion of unidentified trawlers was at an all-time high and it was perhaps this level of nervousness that resulted in the unnecessary destruction of four Danish fishing boats – *Ejjam* (E92), *Gerlis* (E456), *Mercator* (E348) and *Polaris* (E504) – during the night of 23/24 February. Kapitänleutnant Hans Bartels' *M1* sighted the first of the four small cutters from the major fishing port of Esbjerg in thick fog near the Dogger Bank in 'Weg I', a German path through defensive minefields. The small boat was illuminated by a handheld spotlight, *Ejjam* identified at a distance of only 150 metres. Bartels sailed past, his radio room reporting a flurry of 'very fast and blurred' Morse signals once they had passed from view. A second cutter was then seen four nautical miles away followed by a third. More Morse and coded radio chatter was reported and Bartels deduced them to be hostile, deciding to destroy the small vessels by ramming, lest gunfire warn other nearby boats and allow their escape in the thick fog. At 0135hrs *M1* rammed *Polaris* amidships, slicing the boat in two and both halves sinking in just over a minute. The second cutter, *Mercator*, went down in 40 seconds less than ten minutes later. At 0230hrs two more white lights were seen and four minutes later *M1* rammed *Gerlis*, the bow stubbornly floating for five minutes before slipping beneath the surface. Finally *Ejjam* was sighted again and rammed twice before she sank at 0255hrs.

The estimated crew numbers were four to five men. All boats were from Esbjerg.

The sinkings were made on the following grounds:

1. On 9 February I had already grown suspicious of some Danish fishermen. The reasons were laid down in the special report in the War Diary from 1 to 15 February.

2. From the middle of 'Weg I' to eight nautical miles East from its endpoint I have not seen Danish fishermen.

3. Coded radio transmission are not required by 'harmless' Danish fishermen.

4. The lead time from the first to the second boat with radio transmissions suggests that the fishermen had first adopted the German ship's course and speed and this information had been passed on to British submarines so that they could reach a favourable firing position in good time.

The assumption that they were in the service of the enemy was confirmed by the fact that:

a. After ramming of every launch and the vessels being cut in two, not even a single fish came to the surface.

b. Coded radio transmissions.

c. With two of the boats, the Danes were already sighted on their upper deck and made no signals with lamps while there was still time to ward off attack. They all sensed what was coming toward them and remained silent.

For military reasons, no survivors were taken.[26]

The Danish authorities were unaware of the fate of the four boats, although the following morning another Esbjerg-cutter *M. Harboring* sighted a mast projecting out of the water next to a channel buoy. The Danes pulled alongside to attempt salvage of the mast but instead found the bodies of two dead fishermen lashed firmly to it in what appears to have been an attempt to keep out of the freezing water. Nonetheless the two had died of exposure, father and son, Skipper Jørgen Jørgensen Bækby and Anders Jørgensen of the *Ejjam*.

Though the Danes remained ignorant of the exact details of what had actually happened, the cutters were assumed to have been sunk by German forces 'due to causes of war'. The Esbjerg fishing fleet walked a fine line; the Royal Navy would herd any of them encountered into British ports where they would remain, while German ships would do whatever they could to prevent this. However, reports were being received in Berlin that Danish public opinion was turning against Germany following these and other sinkings of Danish ships and consequent loss of life. As a result SKL issued a directive stating that armed force against merchant and fishing vessels encountered in these areas was only permissible in proven cases of the 'use of armed force, enemy escort, transmission of intelligence, forcible resist-

E348 'Mercator'; one of four Danish fishing boats rammed by M1 with all aboard killed.

ance, use of radio, enemy troop transports or sailing without lights.' Intense discussion followed within the Kriegsmarine command about Bartels' actions, though they ultimately endorsed his decision, given what the young captain knew or had surmised at that particular moment. However, they were compelled to stress within subsequent directives that the procedure he had followed would be exceptional, not standard. No further repercussions were expected, or received, from the Danish government.

German attention had now turned West, away from Denmark and Scandinavia, but while the difficult process of planning for an invasion of The Low Countries and North-Eastern France, fears of a British occupation of Norway were steadily increasing in Berlin. On 15 February 1940 the Royal Navy ignored Norwegian neutrality to rescue 299 captive British sailors from the German ship *Altmark* moored within Norwegian territorial waters. Hitler believed that this demonstrated ambivalence toward Norwegian neutrality that rivalled even his own. Where he had vacillated between concentrating his forces against Western Europe or countering the potential threat to Scandinavia and thence the Baltic, the Führer wavered no more: the invasion of Norway and Denmark would take priority over that of France and the Low Countries. On 1 March 1940, SKL recorded detailed instructions from Hitler on the method by which Norway was to be taken, the Kriegsmarine and Luftwaffe to 'bear the brunt of the first operation.' The invasion, code-named 'Weserübung' ('Weser Exercise') was confirmed, '*Wesertag*' set for 9 April 1940.

Raeder fully endorsed the invasion, convinced that Great Britain would attempt to cut off Scandinavian exports to Germany, bar access to the Atlantic and hinder operations in the North Sea. By British occupation of Norway, which was already demonstrating a marked anti-German posture not helped by Germany's ally the Soviet Union and its war with Finland, pressure could be brought to bear on Sweden with the aim of choking off the flow of all merchant traffic to Germany and possibly even forcing Sweden into the war on the side of the Allied powers.

Of an opposing point of view was Vizeadmiral (VA) Otto Schniewind, Chief of Staff at SKL. Schniewind believed it improbable that Great Britain was planning or even capable of such an operation, reasoning that British occupation of Norway would bring them into probable conflict with the Soviet Union and result in German countermeasures that could extend German operational bases to Denmark and Sweden. Correspondingly, he and his Chief of the Operations Division, VA Kurt Fricke, thought a German occupation of Norway to be extremely risky both strategically and economically. Following German seizure of Norway the country's neutral territorial waters would no longer be safe and with German naval strength still so low, the maintenance of iron-ore imports and the sea routes to *Basis Nord* (a secret U-boat enclave established in Soviet Arctic territory) could no longer be guaranteed. They pressed for the status quo to be maintained which allowed permitted Germany to use Norwegian territorial waters as a transit route in safety.

In this instance, Raeder was correct. Within the Allied corridors of power there were plans to neutralise Norway and thus German use of its sea lanes. While inexperienced and poorly-led Soviet troops finally managed to grind their way forward against Finnish defences following months of disastrous losses, the Allied Supreme War Council met in Paris on 5 February to consider sending an expeditionary force to aid Finland in their battle against Soviet aggression. Any Allied expeditionary force would only be able to reach Finland after disembarkation in Norway and transit through Sweden once those permissions had been secured. By landing in Narvik, the all-important Swedish Gällivore iron-ore mines were to be occupied as the troops moved East, under the guise of maintaining the Allied lines of communication. Despite misgivings about a confrontation with Russia, particularly from the French, plans were put into effect and while the British forces gathered in Scotland, French transport ships began to assemble in Brest and Cherbourg. It was a dubious arrangement that would more likely result in a 'quiet invasion' but, as Winston Churchill later wrote: 'The issue of what to do if Norway and Sweden refused, as seemed probable, was never faced.'[27]

As the news of the Allied application for transit rights to Finland, and Sweden's subsequent refusal on 12 March, became known internationally,

Scandinavian countries as a whole urged Finland to accept the armistice terms offerred by the Soviet Union. Despite Britain continuing to urge their resistance, Finland sued for peace with the Soviet Union on 13 March and the Allied plan was abandoned. Nonetheless, an alternative was sought and adopted. To frustrate the flow of trade to Germany through Norwegian territorial waters, British and French ships would lay mines along the Norwegian coast, forcing German shipping further out to sea and outside neutral waters where they could be attacked by the Royal Navy. This was in contravention of an agreement signed between Great Britain and Norway on 11 March 1940 by which exports to Germany, even of contraband, were permitted providing they did not exceed the levels of 1938 trade.

The mining operation was named Wilfred and set to be carried out on 5 April. A second prong to the idea was Operation R4; the landing of the 18,000 troops (those that had already been earmarked for Finland) in Narvik in response to what would undoubtedly be German reaction to the Allied infringement upon Norwegian neutrality. The Allied convoys were scheduled to begin sailing on 8 April.

Organisation of the Kriegsmarine Security Forces on 9 April 1940

Oberkommando der Marine Grossadmiral Erich Raeder

Marinegruppenkommando West Generaladmiral Saalwächter

Befehlshaber der Sicherung der Nordsee (**BSN**)
Vizeadmiral Eberhard Wolfram (Wilhelmshaven –Sengwarden)

Führer der Minensuchboote West (**FdM West**) KzS Friedrich Ruge	*Führer der Vorpostenboote West* (**FdV West**) KzS Heinz Schiller	*Führer der Sonderverbände Nordsee* KzS Kurt Böhmer
Führerboot 'F 6'	*Führerschiff 7 (Möwe)*	Minelayers:
Geleitflottille	2nd Vp-Flotilla	*Roland*
1st M-Flotilla	4th Vp-Flotilla	*Cobra*
2nd M-Flotilla	8th Vp-Flotilla	12th UJ-Flotilla
4th M-Flotilla	10th Vp-Flotilla	1st U-Jagdgruppe
6th M-Flotilla	12th Vp-Flotilla	2nd U-Jagdgruppe
7th M-Flotilla		3rd U-Jagdgruppe
12th M-Flotilla		4th U-Jagdgruppe
14th M-Flotilla		5th U-Jagdgruppe
16th M-Flotilla		5th V-Gruppe
18th M-Flotilla		6th V-Gruppe
2nd R-Flotilla		16th V-Ggruppe
3rd R-Flotilla		18th V-Gruppe
2nd Sp-Gruppe		
4th Sp-Gruppe		
6th Sp-Gruppe		
Minenräumschiff 12		

Marinegruppenkommando Ost Generaladmiral Carls

Befehlshaber der Sicherung der Ostsee (**BSO**)
Vizeadmiral Hermann Mootz (Swinemünde)

Führer der Minensuchboote Ost (**FdM Ost**) KA Hans Stohwasser	*Führer der Vorpostenboote Ost* (**FdV Ost**) KzS Helmut Leissner	*Führer der Sonderverbände Ost* KsZ Arnold Bentlage
Führerboot 'Jagd'	*Führerboot: Rugard*	Minelayers:
11th M-Flotilla	1st Vp-Flotilla	*Prussia*
13th M-Flotilla	3rd Vp-Flotilla	*Hansestadt Danzig*
15th M-Flotilla	7th Vp-Flotilla	*Emperor*
17th M-Flotilla	9th Vp-Flotilla	*Queen Louise*
19th M-Flotilla	10th Vp-Flotilla	*Tannenberg*
1st R-Flotilla	13th Vp-Flotilla	*Aviso Grille*
5th R-Flotilla	15th Vp-Flotilla	*Schiff 23*
11th R-Flotilla	*Schulflottille B.S.O.*	11th UJ-Flotilla
1st Sp-Gruppe		17th UJ-Flotilla

3

Expanding Horizons: German Pyrrhic Victory in Norway and the Fall of France, 1940

FOR those amongst the Kriegsmarine High Command who did not share Raeder's conviction of a British threat to Norway, the matter had passed beyond the purely military and had become a 'first class question of war economy and politics'. They reconciled the difficulties and hazards of the impending attack as a matter of accommodating the required military action, 'resolved to abandon all scruples and to sweep aside the difficulties that arise by using all its forces'.

Operation Weserübung – The Invasion of Denmark and Norway

It was to be a massive commitment; eleven groups of surface ships and nine of U-boats whose task was to provide a defensive screen for the landing forces. While *Gneisenau* and *Scharnhorst* would prowl offshore in support of the

Hitler visiting Norway in 1934 aboard the 'pocket battleship' *Deutschland*. The vital supplies of mineral resources that flowed from Scandinavia prompted the 1940 invasion at the same time that France and Great Britain were about to embark upon the same undertaking.

northern landings the following warship groups would mount the actual attacks on Norway (Weserübung *Nord*) between them carrying 8850 troops:

> Group 1 comprising ten destroyers (carrying 2000 troops from the 3rd *Gebirgs* Division, naval and Luftwaffe artillerymen and a naval signals group) and two freighters would strike at Narvik (the target code-named 'Nienburg');
> Group 2 led by the cruiser *Admiral Hipper*, accompanied by four destroyers (carrying 1700 troops of 3rd *Gebirgs* Division and more naval and Luftwaffe artillery and flak units) was to target Trondheim (code-named 'Detmold');
> Group 3 was to attack Bergen (code-named 'Bremen'), with the light cruisers *Köln* and *Königsberg* (carrying 1900 troops from the 69th Infantry Division, naval and Luftwaffe flak and artillery), the artillery training ship *Bremse*, two torpedo boats and the five boats of the 1st S-Boat Flotilla;
> Group 4 led by the light cruiser *Karlsruhe* (carrying 1100 troops from the 163rd Infantry Division, naval signals and artillery men) with two torpedo boats and the seven boats of the 2nd S-Flotilla were to land at Kristiansand (code-named 'Carlshafen') while the torpedo boat *Greif* would transport the ninety-strong 234th Bicycle Squadron of the 163rd Infantry Division and ten signals personnel to occupy Arendal and sever the telegraph communication between there and Britain;
> Group 5, assembled in Swinemünde, was charged with attacking Oslo and Oslofjord (code-named 'Oldenburg') centred on the heavy cruiser *Blücher* (flagship with Group commander KA Kummetz aboard), the 'pocket battleship' *Lützow* (originally planned for Trondheim but changed due to cracks discovered in the auxiliary engine casing ruling out a longer voyage) and the cruiser *Emden* (carrying 2000 troops from the 163rd Infantry Division) accompanied by torpedo boats and *R8* and *R19* of Kaptlt Gustav Forstmann's 1st R-Flotilla and *Rau 8*. Horten was to be attacked by two torpedo boats and the minesweepers *R17* and *R22* with *Rau 7*. The islands of Rauøy and Bolærne in Oslofjord were to be attacked by two pairs of *Räumboote*: *R20* with *R24* and *R22* with *R23* respectively.
> Group 6 was to sail from Cuxhaven to attack the telegraph station at Egersund (code-named 'Elsflet') with four minesweepers (carrying 150 men from the 69th Infantry Division): *M1*, *M2*, *M9* and *M13*. The group was commanded by KK Thoma, chief of the 2nd M-Flotilla, though *M1* was on temporary attachment from the 1st, suffering mechanical problems on the way out from Cuxhaven but able to rectify the problem with materials aboard ship before returning to port. Along with the possession of the harbour at Egersund, they were also to seize the undersea telegraph cable linking Norway to Peterhead in Scotland. By severing this link the Germans intended to eliminate its potential as a source of Allied intelligence also aiding the occupiers in gaining control of Norway's communications in order to pacify the population and discourage resistance.

The Kriegsmarine Security Forces were heavily committed to the invasion of Norway itself as well as keeping open convoy routes for resupply and reinforcement.

The remaining warship groups sailed for Danish targets (Weserübung *Süd*):

Group 7's objectives were the towns of Nyborg and Korsör that flanked the Great Belt. This attack was lead by the obsolete battleship *Schleswig-Holstein* with *Versuchsboote* (literally 'test-boats', generally obsolete vessels used as test beds for new equipment and machinery) *Claus von Bevern*, *Pelikan* and *Nautilus*, as well as six trawlers of FK Dr Dannenberg's *B.S.O. Schulflottille* and two cargo ships. The group put to sea from Kiel, KK Carl Bünte's *MRS12* proceeding ahead of the main group to clear a way through the Danish mine barrage;

Group 8 sailed from Travemünde bound for Copenhagen with the minelayer *Hansestadt Danzig*, ice-breaker *Stettin* supported by the 13th Vp-Flotilla;

Group 9 put out from Kiel and occupied the small Danish town of Middelfahrt and the bridge over the Little Belt with a combination of minelayers *Passat* and *Monsun*, minesweeper-test ships *M115 'Arkona'*, *M129* '*Otto Braun*' and *M157*, *Vorpostenboote V102 'Cressida'*, *V103 'Silvia'*, *Räumboote R6* and *R7* and the *U-Jäger UJ107*. The group was commanded by KzS Leissner, FdV Ost, from his 1,358-ton command ship *Rugard*.

The last two groups passed through the Kaiser Wilhelm Canal to Cuxhaven and from there landed at objectives on Denmark's North Sea coastline:

Group 10 sailed to Esbjerg and the island of Nordby with Group Commander (and FdM) KzS Ruge aboard the command/escort ship *F6 'Königin Luise'*, leading minesweepers of the 12th M-Flotilla, *M1201–1208*, and *M4*, *M20*, *M102* and *M84* and *R25*, *R26*, *R27*, *R28*, *R29*, *R30*, *R31* and *R32* of KK von Kamptz's 2nd R-Flotilla;

Group 11 comprising minesweepers *M134*, *M111*, *M136*, *M61*, *M110* and *M89* of KK Walter Berger's 4th M-Flotilla and *R33*, *R34*, *R35*, *R36*, *R37*, *R38*, *R39* and *R40* of Kaptlt Hagen Küster's 3rd R-Flotilla sailed for Thyborön, the Western entrance to Limfjorden. Küster was aboard the flotilla tender *Von Der Groeben* while Berger exercised command over the entire group as it sailed from Cuxhaven.

For the protection of the transport convoys and to safeguard the supply lines for the invasion troops, minelaying was undertaken by *Schliesen*, the minelayers *Roland*, *Cobra*, *Preussen* and *Königin Luise* and *M6*, *M10*, *M11* and *M12* which had been fitted with minelaying gear specifically for the operation. *Führer der Sondeverbände West*, KzS Böhmer, was tasked with co-ordinating the minelaying mission.

With limited carrying capacity for military equipment and fuel aboard the warships, separate transport groups (*Seetransportstaffel*) were planned, with seven steamers carrying heavy equipment and supplies for the troops of the initial assault and tankers laden with fuel. The steamers would adopt the guise of ordinary commercial traffic bound for Murmansk, docking in various Norwegian ports prior to the arrival of the invasion fleet. The transport ships and tankers began sailing on 3 April on the insistence of the Army. The Kriegsmarine was extremely concerned at the possibility of security breaches compromising the secrecy of the entire operation. Instructions were issued in the event of any German being captured by the enemy, they were to say nothing or, if forced to reveal information, claim that the troops were bound for Ireland. Indeed, on 4 April SKL protested loudly that the loading of army supplies onto transports in Stettin, which were flying the state service flag, was done in full view of 'interested spectators' while the 'Swedish consulate lies in the immediate vicinity'. With strong naval objections and the Army resolved on maintaining the supply schedule, OKW had compromised by permitting transport departures no earlier than 3 April; this later proved to be insufficient time for many of the vessels to reach their destinations on schedule.

Meanwhile the tasks of the Security Forces continued unabated. German minesweeping of the Kattegat and Great Belt reached a new level of urgency as it would be a major route for invasion traffic and supply convoys. The 13th *U-Bootsjagdgruppe* was tasked with operating at Denmark's northern tip and the Kattegat approaches to Norway, though ice and fog prevented the ships reaching their assigned area. Likewise the 15th and 19th M-Flotillas and 19th

R-Flotilla were unable to sweep within the Great Belt for periods at the end of March. *Sperrbrecher XI* cruised at the southern pilot station as escort for occasional supply shipping, the channels becoming increasingly obstructed by thick pack ice, requiring the temporary transfer of 13th *U-Bootsjagdgruppe* south of Anholt for the purpose of ice reconnaissance of the Belts and Sound. On the final day of March the *U-Jäger 'Gustav'* reported the destruction of an enemy submarine by depth-charge attack 15 miles north of Skagen, though it was never confirmed.

In the North Sea, vessels of the 11th Vp-Flotilla travelling along swept route 'Blau' were unsuccessfully attacked by six Wellington bombers on 1 April, while in the Skagerrak the 1st Vp-Flotilla took over the Little Belt's mine barrage patrol. The 17th UJ-Flotilla sailed for operations east of Skagen, going to the aid of the 4969-ton steamer *Curityba* of the 1st *Seetransportstaffel* bound for Bergen, which had run aground four miles north of Helsingborg. Alongside the *U-Boot Jäger*, the tugs *Preussen* and *Wotan* were despatched as the grounded steamer lay at the edge of Swedish territorial waters, its cargo of military supplies, horses and uniformed troops clearly visible. With belated hindsight, SKL recorded that the cargo 'should have been better camouflaged and that the soldiers and men in charge of the horses on board should have worn civilian clothes'.

Over the following days, as the Weserübung forces sailed, Allied reconnaissance reported German naval units moving along the Norwegian coast, speculating that they were attempting a breakout into the Atlantic. The advance echelon of eight disguised German tankers had quietly sailed to strategic positions along the Weserübung invasion routes, followed by the supply ships that would put into port objectives carrying heavy weapons.

On 8 April at 0600hrs the British government informed Norway that they were laying mines within Norwegian territorial waters, four destroyers having mined Vestfjord at 0500hrs. Troops of the joint Anglo-French 'Plan R4' were to be landed at Stavanger, Trondheim, Bergen and Narvik and had already embarked in preparation. In Berlin there was a certain degree of satisfaction with the Allied announcement: the Western Powers had now flagrantly violated Norwegian neutrality, providing a small measure of justification for the impending German invasion which could now be claimed as a response to the Allies' activities.

At sea, bad weather was enveloping the region and in rough seas and thick fog the opposing sides began to blunder into one another. The Polish submarine *Orzel* sank the 5261-ton German troopship SS *Rio de Janiero* of 1st *Seetransportstaffel* on 8 April (carrying 313 Luftwaffe personnel and anti-aircraft guns bound for Bergen) and noted uniformed soldiers amongst the wreckage. Norwegian fishing boats and a destroyer came to the surviving Germans' aid, also finding a startling number of troops and the Reuters News

Bad weather both hindered the Kriegsmarine invasion groups and helped to hide them from Allied reconnaissance.

Agency immediately reported the sinking of a 'German troopship' near Kristiansand. South of Oslo HMS *Trident* sighted a 'large laden tanker steaming westward outside territorial waters'. It was the naval tanker

Stedingen carrying Luftwaffe fuel for operations after the capture of
Stavanger airfield, scheduled for an airborne assault on the first day. The
tanker's Master, Kapitän Schäfer, turned to starboard and ran for Norwegian
waters when *Trident* surfaced to fire a warning shot. Two live rounds followed
and the German crew scuttled their ship and abandoned her, Schäfer being
taken prisoner as a single torpedo finished *Stedingen* off.[28] 'Weserübung has
left the stage of secrecy and camouflage according to the impression prevalent
in the evening. Our enemies have been warned. Since the element of surprise
is lost we must now expect engagements at all points.'[29]

However, the British Admiralty were momentarily distracted by the
sinking of the destroyer HMS *Glowworm* which had blundered into the
Admiral Hipper and managed to ram her before being sunk. At 0500hrs on 9
April the German Ambassador in Oslo 'requested' the Norwegian
government place their country under German 'military protection', as a
similar note was delivered to the Danish government. The latter acquiesced
under protest; the former refused.

Landings in Denmark proceeded as planned with no real resistance.
Troops successfully disembarked in Copenhagen from *Hansestadt Danzig*
before the ship departed for Warnemünde, and Group 'Rugard' putting
troops ashore near Middelfahrt to secure the bridge over the Little Belt.
Landings at Gjedser, Nyborg and Korsoer were carried to schedule while

German troops at Egersund after being landed by the minesweepers *M1* and *M9*.

Schleswig-Holstein ran aground near Vengeance Gruns, but was refloated in the afternoon and the Nyborg Group reached their objective soon afterward. At the German border there were brief skirmishes with troops of the ground forces, though they were eliminated after six hours with 200 German casualties.

The four minesweepers of Group Six destined for Egersund had departed Cuxhaven in the early hours of 8 April in heavy wind alternating with thick fog, only *M1* and *M9* managing to maintain contact in the vile conditions. The commander of the 2nd M-Flotilla, KK Kurt Thoma, led the group from *M9*, the four minesweepers carrying 150 bicycle troops of Reconnaissance Unit 169, under the command of Rittmeister Friedrich Eickhorn. Three of the minesweepers were part of Thoma's flotilla, with *M1* on attachment from the 1st M-Flotilla.

At approximately 0400hrs on 9 April 1940, *M1* and *M9* reached Egersund, the latter remaining offshore to secure the surrounding waters while Bartels' manoeuvrable *M1* carried Rittmeister Eickhorn and forty of his men into Egersund harbour, landing near the moored Norwegian torpedo boar *Skarv*. The 84-ton Norwegian ship had been ordered to a state of readiness as events unfolded elsewhere, though she was denied permission to patrol the harbour approaches. The destroyer *Gyller* was normally also stationed in Egersund

The moored Norwegian torpedo boar *Skarv* after its capture by German troops at Egersund.

but had been despatched on an escort mission, the single Norwegian sentry aboard *Skarv* mistaking the approaching *M1* for the returning destroyer. With the element of surprise, German infantrymen quickly boarded *Gyller* and seized control. Nonetheless, members of the Norwegian crew managed to destroy maps and important documents, as well as making a telephone call to their regional naval headquarters in Kristiansand before being locked in a shed under armed guard.

Though there was no garrison permanently stationed in Egersund, a 36-man light infantry platoon had arrived the previous day. As *M9* replaced *M1* inside the harbour to land further Wehrmacht troops, the Norwegian infantrymen were able to contact Stavanger and report a 'large invasion force' before being captured without resisting. Eickhorn left twelve men to guard the harbour while the remainder spread throughout the town to secure the telephone exchange, post office, police and railway stations. Within an hour *M2* and *M13* also arrived to land their troops and equipment. With Egersund secured, *Skarv* was formally surrendered to Eickhorn the following day and the minesweepers began their return to Kiel. In transit they were diverted towards Kristiansand to lend support to landings that had encountered heavy resistance. However, the port city was secured before the Thoma's group arrived during the afternoon.

Several of the German landings were hotly contested. With a number of supply ships and tankers sunk, troops in some areas soon found their situation desperate. This was particularly true in Narvik where, by 13 April, all ten destroyers involved in the landing had been sunk by the Royal Navy. Far to the south Oslo also proved a tough nut to crack, *Blücher* being sunk and *Lützow* badly damaged by shore batteries after failed attempts to bluff their way past the defences.

The warship group had made landfall at midnight, challenged by searchlights from the Norwegian patrol boat *Pol III* until the torpedo boat *Albatros* engaged the 214-ton converted whaler and sent her to the bottom. Her skipper Lief Welding Olsen was killed, the first Norwegian killed in the invasion, while fourteen crewmen were rescued and taken prisoner. The Oslo force then divided into smaller constituent groups targeting Horten and the islands of Rauøy and Bolærne. Near the latter, *R22* and *R23* encountered the obsolete Norwegian submarine *A2* and boarding parties captured her intact while *A3* and *A4* were scuttled in 10m of water before the Germans could seize them.

Both *R18* and *R19* had remained with *Blücher*, and they attacked and sank the 109-ton Norwegian cutter *Sørland* that had stumbled into them while on her way from Moss to Oslo with a cargo of paper. Mistaking the action for a military exercise, the *Sørland* took no evasive action until *R18* and *R19* opened fire, setting the small ship ablaze and killing two of the six crewmen.

The helmsman of a minesweeper.

Elsewhere in Oslofjord the attack on Horten was blunted by the minelayer HNoMS *Olav Tryggvason* and minesweeper HNoMS *Rauma*. The 1596-ton *Olav Tryggvason* was in Horten for minor engine repairs and so had only a skeleton crew aboard. Receiving warnings of foreign naval forces approaching, the skipper had moored his ship to a buoy within the inner harbour from where he could cover the entrance with his 105mm guns. Meanwhile, the minesweepers *Otra* and *Rauma* had been ordered north to sweep the declared British minefields laid for Wilfred. *Otra* received urgent instructions to contact and identify the inbound foreign warships and made contact at 0410hrs, establishing that the ships were German before being forced away from the fjord by heavy gunfire.

Approaching Horten, the torpedo boats *Albatros* and *Kondor* both had large numbers of troops aboard, the *Räumboote* placed in the vanguard carrying smaller assault groups for the initial attack. At 0435hrs they entered the harbour, the R-boats fully darkened and not identified by the Norwegians until only 60m away. The Norwegian skipper followed neutrality protection guidelines and first emitted a foghorn signal before firing a blank shot and two live warning shots. Only then did the Norwegians open fire in earnest.

The returned *Rauma* raced toward the R-boats and opened fire with her 76mm gun and two machine-guns, while *Olav Tryggvason* fired on *R17* and sank her, only fifteen of the forty-five embarked infantrymen reaching shore unscathed. Prepared depth charges aboard *R17* later exploded causing further

Norwegian minelayer HNoMS *Olav Tryggvason* alongside three *M35*-class minesweepers following the German subjugation of Horten.

casualties. Kapitänleutnant Siegfried Strelow's torpedo boat *Albatros* raced in and engaged the minelayer but was shelled and unable to return fire as the forward gun jammed after just eight shots. *Albatros* retired to open water with casualties and Strelow transferred the troops on board to *R21* to enable an assault on the nearby Bolaerne shore batteries that had caused such havoc among the capital ships.

In Horten *R27* reached the cover of a peninsula and landed her force of forty-five infantrymen while suffering several shell hits. Returning to the fight, the R-boat briefly ran aground, taking further punishment but also scoring hits on *Rauma* that caused severe damage and killed her commander, Lieutenant Ingolf Carl Winsnes. *R27* broke free and reached the open sea while the cruiser *Emden* began long-range – and ineffectual – supporting fire.

Finally, at 0735hrs, after threats of Stuka bombardment and overestimating the strength of the sixty-strong German landing party, the Norwegian land and naval forces at Horten surrendered. During the battle *Olav Tryggvason* had fired almost sixty 105mm shells, and suffered at least thirty-five hits from the R-boats' 20mm guns with two sailors wounded.[30]

After the costly Oslo landings were complete, the damaged *Lützow* returned to Kiel, travelling at high speed in order to avoid enemy submarines. However, HMS *Spearfish* torpedoed the ship, nearly blowing the stern off and wrecking the steering gear. While the crew prepared to abandon ship, five *Sperrbrecher* engaged on mine clearance in the Belt and the Kattegat arrived to assist. *Sperrbrecher V, VI, X, XI* and *XII* were all involved in the protection and towing-back to Kiel of the crippled ship, HMS *Spearfish* being unable to mount a second attack as the boat had fired its last torpedo.

The dangers posed by enemy submarines and mines could hardly be overstated. *Vorpostenboot V1507 'Rau VI'* was attacked and sunk by torpedoes from HMS *Triton* on 10 April in the Skaggerak. Lieutenant Commander E. F. Pizey, RN had already narrowly missed hitting *Blücher* inbound to Oslo, firing a full bow salvo of ten torpedoes at the heavy cruiser but all of them passed astern as *Blücher* increased speed. Pizey had better luck on 10 April when *Triton* sighted the eleven freighters of 2nd *Seetransportstaffel* under heavy *Vorpostenboot* and minesweeper escort.

> 1726 hours – Fired six torpedoes from 2500 yards (the last on board). Four hits were heard. *Triton* went to 85 feet upon firing and turned stern on to the convoy. Very shortly after the last torpedo explosion was heard, depth charging started. For the next hour at least 78 depth charges were dropped of which the ones dropped about 5 minutes after the last torpedo hit were the closest. These shook *Triton* considerably but no serious damage was done
>
> 2115 hours – Surfaced and set course for home as *Triton* was now out of torpedoes.

Three ships had been hit and sunk in the attack; two freighters, the 5219-ton *Friedenau* and the 3648-ton *Wigbert*, both carrying *Gebirgsjäger*, and the escorting *V1507*. The freighters had their passengers below decks and the loss of life was serious, a Swedish destroyer leaving neutral waters to render assistance, while the freighter *Hamm* later retrieved bodies and took them to Oslo. Other vessels, including *Räumboot R39*, joined the rescue and many survivors were pulled brought aboard in severe pain after time spent in icy water covered in a thick layer of diesel oil from the freighters' fuel tanks. Their eyes burned agonisingly while they were hosed down with fire-fighting gear before taken below deck and scrubbed with petrol and turpentine.

Minesweeper *M1101* became stranded on Hellene, south of Tjøme, after she struck a mine laid by HMS *Narwhal* on 14 April. The ship comprised part of the escort for the 3rd *Seetransportstaffel* of twelve ships carrying 8052 men of the 181st Infantry Division, 893 horses, 577 vehicles and 3450 tons of equipment from Hamburg to Oslo. *M1101* was the second of four ships lost from the convoy. One of the others, the 6148-ton SS *Florida*, was sunk by torpedo from HMS *Snapper* that same day.

Snapper had been ordered into the North Sea west of Denmark and on 12 April Lt. W. D. A. King, RN, shelled and sank the 322-ton German tanker

Moonsund off Larvik. Two days later he had missed *Schiff 35* 'Oldenburg' of the 6th *Vorpostengruppe* (serving as a Q-ship) with two torpedoes before sinking *Florida* later that day with one torpedo from a salvo of five. Despite depth-charging, King launched another attack early the next morning. At 0345hrs he sighted a single darkened ship, the remainder of the convoy slowly appearing from the mist as he watched. Fifteen minutes later King fired four torpedoes at a range of 1500 yards; hits were heard after which *Snapper* was hunted with depth charges for an hour before slipping away. King had hit two ships, the convoy escorts *M1701* 'H.M. Behrens' and *M1702* 'Carsten Janssen' which sank north-east of Skagen, Denmark, with forty men killed.

HMS *Tetrach* also claimed an escort ship on 23 April when Lt.Cdr. R. G. Mills, RN, torpedoed and sank *UJB* 'Treff V' in the Skagerrak. Mills had already unsuccessfully attacked the freighter *Ahrensburg* from a southbound supply convoy on passage from Larvik to Frederikshavn. The freighter had delivered troops and was escorted by *T153*, *T155*, *F5*, *F8* and R-boats *R33*, *R37* and *R40*. Two torpedoes missed and over two hours of depth-charging followed before a brief lull heralded the departure of the convoy and the arrival of a pair of *U-Jäger* of the 5th *U-Bootsjagdgruppe* to continue the hunt. Mills eased his boat to periscope depth and sighted *UJA* and *UJB* at a range of 1000 yards, approaching head on. Two torpedoes were fired to 'discourage their approach', one hitting *UJB* which made the fatal mistake of turning away and providing a broadside target rather than 'combing the tracks'. The sinking, however, went unnoticed aboard *Tetrach* which had dived immediately after firing. The submarine was hounded by the remaining *U-Jäger* throughout the night until the Germans abandoned their search, *Tetrach* finally surfacing at 2130hrs on 24 April 1940 and setting course for home.

Optimistically, during this period the torpedo boat *T153* and 17th UJ-Flotilla between them reported the probable destruction of three enemy submarines in all, two claimed as definite. In fact only HMS *Sterlet* had probably been sunk on 18 April in the Skaggerak south of Larvik by *M75* (the sinking originally being attributed to *UJ125*, *UJ126* and *UJ128*).

On the night of 13 April fifteen Hampdens of Bomber Command mounted the first RAF minelaying operation of the war in sea lanes off Denmark between German ports and Norway with a single bomber lost. Less than two weeks later, R-boats successfully recovered an aerial mine west of the Danish island of Samsø in the Kattegat. Uncertainty that had plagued the Kriegsmarine regarding the weapons' triggering system was eliminated. Fearing that they were triggered acoustically or by vibration, the fuse was confirmed to be magnetic and capable of being swept with existing gear. The efficacy of German VES gear was validated near Korsör when *Sperrbrecher IV* swept a ground mine that was 80m off the ship's port bow. In the Kattegat, *Räumboote* were soon able to determine the eastern edge of the British minefield off Frederikshavn while minesweepers secured transit routes in Mecklenburg and Kiel Bays with magnetic sweeps. All naval vessels and important merchant ships were ordered equipped with degaussing equipment to counter the mines' induction circuit triggers.

Further British aerial mines were recovered, one 2km west of Buelk lighthouse in a wheat field, another south of Oslo harbour on the island of Ulvoey and a third on land near Pelzerhaken. Countermeasures were requested by FdM West, that included the immediate requisitioning of numerous drifters and fishing smacks to be equipped with 20mm C/30 cannon and small searchlights in order to patrol river mouths and coastal waters while the number of *Sperrbrecher* available was increased.

Nonetheless, attritional losses continued in the Great Belt and the Sound: *V403* was damaged by a mine laid by HMS *Narwhal* and on 23 April *M1302* '*Schwaben*' was also lost to mines laid by the same submarine off Cape Skagen. *Sperrbrecher XI* '*Petropolis*' was damaged by an aerial mine while anchoring near the small Danish island of Sprogø within the Great Belt. Holed forward, the ship was forced to return to Hamburg for repairs that would last until August, the damage being so severe that *Petropolis* was decommissioned and returned to civilian service. The Allied mine offensive had truly begun to bite.

The Elbe is temporarily closed on account of the doubtful mine situation and the Weser and the Ems must also be closed to vessels with cargoes of ore until

Heavily-armed Kriegsmarine crewmen lower the colours of a Norwegian ship shortly to be recommissioned for German service.

German sailors aboard the Norwegian lifeboat *Biskop Hvoslef* of the *Redningsselskapet* (Norwegian Lifeboat Service). This is exactly the kind of craft requisitioned for use by the various *Hafenschutzflottillen* established in occupied harbours.

a check sweep has been carried out. Minelaying by enemy planes is beginning to make itself unpleasantly felt and causing serious interruptions on the traffic routes which are important to German war economy.

Numerous reports of submarine-chase in the Heligoland Bight have led Group West to make an urgent request for the return of the 12th UJ-Flotilla. Bearing in mind that the *Gneisenau* has struck a mine, the Group also requests the return of the 2nd M-Flotilla, as it has not enough vessels to keep the main channels clear.[31]

The Kriegsmarine established a widespread and comprehensive organisation for patrolling and reporting of mines that relied on numerous small vessels of the *Hafenschutzflottillen* (Harbour Protection Flotillas). By the middle of May 1940, fifty vessels were available within the Baltic, with sixty more scheduled for requisitioning. In the North Sea there were forty vessels available and a further thirty-eight due for transfer to the military. Escort and sweeping groups were formed with *Sperrbrecher* and minesweepers; though at that time only one *Sperrbrecher*, six ships of the 2nd M-Flotilla and a few belonging to the Minelaying Experimental Command were available. Twenty-five sets of cable remote clearance gear were in stock for fitting to requisitioned vessels, with an expected increase of fifteen per month up to

August 1940 and increased rate of production thereafter. The Germans were experiencing difficulties fitting *Sperrbrecher* with magnetic gear due to a shortage of raw materials: 10km of cable, 30 tons of copper, powerful electric motors and a great deal of iron were required for each ship during a conversion period of eight to ten weeks.

Despite the dangers of charted and declared mine barrages and the prliferation of 'drifters', the grave threat posed by enemy submarines remained. The lack of ASW equipment with which to take the fight to the enemy was lamented in Berlin.

> In Naval Staff's opinion the failure to date of anti-submarine defence and location is due to the lack of practice in look-out duties and servicing the location gear and to the apparently great liability of the sets to break down, according to reports to hand. From time to time so many sets are out of order that in individual flotillas only one or two hydrophone or sonar sets are available. In addition to this, it has so far only been possible to equip a limited number of defence vessels with sonar. The efficiency of the sets in the shallow water of the Kattegat must also be regarded as limited.
>
> It can be stated that German anti-submarine defence does not take into account the demands made on it and in the long run this gives rise to great anxiety for the future . . . It is the duty of all responsible offices to bring anti-submarine defence and training, which right from the beginning of the war has always been a special anxiety for Naval Staff, to the necessary zenith with the greatest speed and maximum effort, and to ensure that all submarine-chasers and defence vessels are quickly equipped with efficient location gear.[32]

UJ128 towing HMS *Seal* back to Germany.

Nevertheless, German forces remained capable of almost surprising success, no more so than the captured of British minelaying submarine HMS *Seal*. Lt.Cdr Rupert P. Lonsdale, RN, had taken HMS *Seal* into the Kattegat to lay minefield 'FD7' south of the Swedish island of Vinga. Lonsdale had shown considerable dash during his previous war patrol; creeping into Stavanger-fjord to attack German shipping but finding only neutrals and requesting – but not receiving – permission to attack a German seaplane base and land a shore party to sabotage railway lines.

HMS *Seal* had already suffered some damage while running shallow and being bombed by a Heinkel He115, but on 4 May Lonsdale laid his fifty mines successfully before sighting nine R-boats while in perilously shallow water and laying a zigzag course away from them. Straying into an uncharted minefield, *Seal* was severely damaged in the stern and took on enough water to pin her to the seabed. Unable to effect repairs, a last-ditch effort surfaced the submarine with no chance of submerging again. After unsuccessfully making for Sweden, *Seal* was attacked by a further He115 and two Arado Ar196 seaplanes. After briefly returning fire, the boat's Lewis gun jammed. With engines inoperative and unable to dive, Lonsdale ordered cipher material thrown overboard, the ASDIC equipment destroyed and the boat scuttled before the crew surrendered to *UJ128* that had arrived on the scene. Expecting their boat to sink, Lonsdale and his men were horrified to then see it towed to Frederikshavn where she would be examined, repaired and later commissioned into the Kriegsmarine.

Germany had begun the war with relatively meagre naval forces and an operation of the scale that it had undertaken in Norway tested it to its absolute limits. While the losses of destroyers and capital ships were extremely debilitating, there also remained a shortage of minesweepers and patrol vessels with which to fight what had become a coastal naval war that stretched far beyond the territorial waters of Germany. With fighting still taking place in Narvik, plans were now fully realised for the invasion of Western Europe. *Marinegruppenkommando West* suggested an attack by R-boats on Rottum and Delfzyl harbour in the Netherlands to precede the invasion, but the idea was vetoed due to insufficient craft being available. Indeed, Ruge observed that after FdM West had given up all new minesweeper, R-boat and *Sperrbrecher* flotillas to support the continuing battles in Norway, he could maintain only four flotillas at sea.

The supply routes from Germany to Oslo and beyond remained the Kriegsmarine's highest priority. In the far north Narvik was far from secure and within Oslofjord itself Generaladmiral (GA) Hermann Boehm (*Oberbefehlshaber Marineoberkommando Norwegen*, Commanding Admiral, Norway) reported that he could not defend the 50-mile stretch of fjord with only the vessels of the 1st R-Flotilla at his disposal. Newly-captured

Norwegian naval ships were being pressed into service, but they too were inadequate to the task and Boehm requested at least one UJ-Flotilla and a Vp-Flotilla of at least eight ships. His request was, however, impossible to entertain with the forces available. The tangled German naval hierarchy placed defence of the outer fjord beyond his sphere of control, those waters being the responsibility of the Baltic command that provided protection along the entire sea route to Oslo. All Norwegian trawlers and drifters commandeered by the Kriegsmarine were subsequently allocated to the Baltic, though procuring enough weapons to equip them also proved initially problematic.

As if to underline the urgent need for extra ships, French destroyers engaged on Operation Rake broke through German minefields and picket lines into the Skagerrak on the morning of 24 April. Vice Admiral Sir Max Horton had originally planned the operation with an Anglo–Polish force for the previous week, but potential Luftwaffe attack forced a cancellation. The French destroyers *Indomptable*, *Malin* and *Triomphante* of the 8th *Division de Contre-Torpilleurs* engaged *V702* 'Memel', *V709* 'Guido Möhring' and S-boats *S10* and *S12*, firing up to forty largely ineffectual salvoes before breaking off the engagement and heading away at high speed. During the brief battle *V702* received a 138mm shell hit directly on her navigation shack, demolishing it, while *V709* suffered only light splinter damage. The French ships unsuccessfully attacked *U26* during their return voyage and were themselves sighted by *U56* south of Skudesnes and later attacked by the Luftwaffe. *Triomphant* sustained damage to her port propeller shaft bracket, though all three destroyers reached Rosyth.

In those Norwegian harbours firmly in German hands the immediate shortage of minesweepers became apparent. On 11 April *Schiff 9* 'Koblenz' of the 16th *Vorpostengruppe* struck a mine that had been laid by HNoMS *Tyr* during the first frantic hours of the invasion. *Tyr*'s skipper, Captain F. Ulstrup, was notified of approaching German forces and raced from Bergen to mine the Lerøyosen roads. Seven mines were laid between Lerøy Island and Sotra and another sixteen near Vatlestraumen. However, time-delay mechanisms designed to safeguard the minelayer mean they were still inactive as the first wave of invasion shipping passed overhead and it was not until 4297-ton supply ship *Sao Paulo* arrived that the mines activated, one detonating and sinking the ship with heavy loss of life. With the position of the minefield betrayed, the need for a minesweeper was obvious though none were available. Instead *Schiff 9* 'Koblenz' of the 16th *Vorpostengruppe* and *V105* 'Cremon' of 1st Vp-Flotilla together with two motor launches belonging to the S-boat depot ship *Karl Peters* formed an improvised minesweeper unit and sailed into the area to begin clearance work. At 1925hrs on 11 April *Schiff 9* detonated a mine and went down in less than two minutes. As *V105* rescued survivors, she too struck a mine and exploded, one of the two motor launches being sunk by the blast. *Schiff 18 'Alteland'* recovered thirty-one men while sixteen others managed to swim ashore. Only five of the crew from *V105* survived.[33]

With the majority of Security Forces already committed, the interim naval commander at Trondheim requested immediate despatch of motor pinnace gear and minesweeping equipment with which to outfit commandeered Norwegian fishing smacks. Hydrophones and depth charges were also urgently requested, though there were none available. There were no harbour defence flotillas in operational readiness for deployment to conquered Norway and too few Security Forces available for the many tasks already running within the Baltic. Each flotilla tended to number a paltry eight vessels when at maximum strength and they were already engaged on vital tasks in home waters and the roads to Oslo. While Berlin made efforts to make sufficient harbour defence flotillas available as soon as possible, it would take time.

Not until 22 April did KA Otto Schenk consider that the situation along the southern Norwegian coast appeared stable. Schenk occupied the new post of *Admiral der norwegischen Südküste*, a position that would only exist for two months before he transferred to the Arctic and it was absorbed into Admiral Otto von Schrader's adjacent command to the north. With Norway's navy defeated and the Royal Navy heavily engaged around Narvik, Schenk maintained that only *Vorpostenboote* and minesweepers were required to safeguard the inner Oslo Fjord. With the 5th R-Flotilla, of eight boats, and

M1 during Operation Weserübung.

converted whalers '*Rau 7*' and '*Rau 8*' at his disposal he ordered speedy conversion of Norwegian whaling boats and captured torpedo boats to bolster his defences. Oslo and Kristiansand wee also soon equipped with ten converted drifters as emergency harbour defence boats, each carrying depth charges and minesweeping gear and armed with captured Norwegian guns. These '*Hafenschutzflottille*' would become a feature in all German occupied harbours.

To take control of the conquered Norwegian coastline between Vinjafjord and Kristiansund, which was geographically the closest to Great Britain, the post of *Admiral der norwegischen Westküste* was established in Bergen. The commanding admiral Otto von Schrader urgently demanded Security Forces transferred from the Baltic to his new command, but his demands were repeatedly denied; only two *Vorpostenboote* and *Sperrbrecher VII* considered for redeployment.

In Von Schrader's region *Schiff 18 'Alteland'* of the 16th *Vorpostengruppe* began operating in support of army units. South of Bergen, a small group of surviving Norwegian warships and auxiliaries which had gathered at Uskedal, were spotted by S-boats that had passed by during a reconnaissance sweep. Von Schrader ordered a direct attack on the port, spearheaded by the 1st S-Flotilla as well as *Bremse*, *Schiff 18* and *Schiff 221 'Veselgut'*, a 168-ton captured Norwegian trawler impressed into service by FdV for troop and supply transport. Both *Vorpostenboote* carried infantrymen into the attack as

Admiral Otto von Schrader (*Admiral der norwegischen Westküste*) addresses the crew of *M1*, Hans Bartels standing at left.

The cover of Hans Bartels' colourful and slightly inventive account of his service aboard *M1* during the Norwegian campaign, published in 1941.

five S-boats laid thick smoke screens to cover the landings. Norwegian artillery and guns aboard minelayer HNoMS *Tyr* opened fire and an S-boat was damaged before gunners on *Bremse* disabled the Norwegian ship, which was subsequently captured before she could be scuttled. The remaining defenders were quickly overwhelmed and the port fell to the Germans. Both *Vorpostenboote* returned to Bergen with prisoners aboard, LzS Klaus Feldt's *Schiff 18* towing the captured *Tyr*.[34]

Bartels' *M1* was also operating in close co-operation with the army, shuttling troops from Stavanger to Bergen. Von Schrader requested the minesweeper be left with him for 'special assignments (protection against mines, supplies for troops, bringing in merchantmen)' and *M1* remained the sole minesweeper allocated to him for quite some time. Bartels and Feldt both took part in amphibious operations against Norwegian units in Ulvik on 25 April. The minesweeper and S-boats landed troops at Granvin before the S-boats pressed on to scout the adjacent ford to the east, finding several apparently abandoned merchant ships at anchor.

Intending to capture them, the S-boats radioed Bartels for support. However, before *M1* arrived, men from *S21* and *S19* attempted to board the apparently deserted ships but were ambushed by Norwegian infantrymen

German minesweeper in action; once the sweep had cut a mine's anchor cable it would be sunk or detonated by small-arms fire.

firing machine guns from the village of Ulvik. *S19* was repeatedly hit as men attempted to find shelter, the boat reversing away from the fjord coastline under heavy fire. As *S25* raced in to pull escaping men from the water and return fire, *M1* arrived. Bartels, enraged to see Germans targeted while struggling in the water, ordered his gunners to immediately open fire. Ulvik was soon in blazing ruins, the Norwegian defenders retreating while two of the merchant ships slowly settled on the seabed, their seacocks having been opened before the Germans' arrival. The solitary prize, the steamer *Eidfjord*, was again boarded and sailed back to German-held territory. Von Schrader later visited Bartels and his crew for a tour of inspection in Bergen, coining the term 'Tiger of the Fjords' which was adopted by the crew of *M1* who painted an image of a tiger's head over crossed swords on their ship's bridge. A flag created from the same image would soon become famous in Norway.

Norwegian strategy had been to fight delaying actions against troops building up in Oslo and attempting to link up with other German beachheads to the north. British landings in Åndalsnes were made as part of a planned pincer movement to recapture Trondheim in conjunction with French troops at Namsos. However, further *Fallschirmjäger* drops and extremely effective air support from Luftwaffe dive bombers pushed the Allies back. Heavy air attacks on Trondheim harbour damaged the Norwegian torpedo boat *Trygg* and the Royal Navy ASW trawlers HMT *Bradman*, *Hammond* and *Larwood* of the 22nd Anti-Submarine Group, which were run aground to save their crews. Eventually the beachhead was abandoned and Norwegian strategy defeated as German forces from Oslo reached Trondheim. Organised Norwegian resistance in the area ended on 5 May after which the four damaged vessels in Åndalsnes were salvaged by the Kriegsmarine, later recommissioned as *Zick* (ex-*Trygg*), *V6112* '*Friese*' (HMT *Bradman*), *V6115* '*Salier*' (HMT *Hammond*) and *V6111* '*Franke*' (HMT *Larwood*).

However, in Narvik the struggle continued. German troops that included *Gebirgsjäger*, *Fallschirmjäger* and stranded German sailors were pushed out of Narvik on 28 May, French and Norwegian troops forcing the Germans east along the iron ore railway line towards Sweden. But this Allied success was in vain: three days previously the order for Operation Alphabet had been given in London beginning a general retreat from Norway. Hitler had unleashed his invasion on the Low Countries and France and so Norway was lost.

'Case Yellow' – the invasion of the Low Countries and France

While Weserübung had required the majority of German naval strength, in the West VA Eberhard Wolfram's diminished BSN command had continued to patrol German North Sea waters, in particular safeguarding the routes used by U-boats to and from their major bases. British bombers attacked *Vorpostenboote* off Wilhelmshaven on 15 April, losing one aircraft to defensive fire. *V811* '*Hugo Homann*' was sunk, but later salvaged and returned to active service albeit briefly – on 6 May she struck a mine dropped at the mouth of the River Ems and sank again. *V802* had narrowly missed an exploding mine in the same area eleven days previously. On 22 April the 151-ton Dutch trawler MV *Bep* (*Sch15*) was sunk by *V204* north of Terschelling with artillery fire following fears that the small vessel was reporting the location of German defensive minefields. The entire crew were rescued.

Bordering Germany, the Netherlands had mobilised its armed forces in 1939, a naval security service composed of converted steam tugs patrolling Dutch waters against incursions by any belligerent navy. During December 1939, the Luftwaffe had lost four Heinkel He59 floatplanes during a mining operation over England, three others being disabled and making emergency landings. One had put down at Schiermonnikoog and two *Vorpostenboote* entered Dutch territory with impunity to assist the stranded aircraft, towing it back to Germany. The incident convinced the Dutch that their picket ships were insufficient and the research vessel *Laman de Vries* was put into military service to monitor the Eastern part of the Wadden Sea.

As the German invasion of the West loomed, MGK West requested the transfer of *U-Jäger* formations from the Skaggerak to combat enemy submarines near Heligoland. However, troop convoys to Norway were sailing regularly, and were not expected to be completed before 11 May and required the strongest possible escort and minesweeping detachments. Indeed, even the threat of 'drifters' required a considerable commitment; the 5th R–Flotilla reported the destruction by gunfire of sixty-three drifting mines while on passage to Bergen. Correspondingly, forces available to FdM and FdV West at the beginning of May 1940 were severely limited. Only two *Sperrbrecher* were stationed in the North Sea and the majority of minesweepers available either old Type 16 boats or converted trawlers of the auxiliary units.

Of the *Sperrbrecher* in service, five were in shipyards undergoing repairs or being fitted with VES gear. As an emergency measure, auxiliaries (*Hilfs-sperrbrecher*) were commissioned, *HilfSp.A*, B and C being brought into active service on 17 May 1940 as a new *Sperrbrechergruppe* 1. The ships were pressed into action as mine clearance and icebreakers with only limited armament. Their curious 'half-military' status meant that they remained under the German national flag rather than the Kriegsmarine ensign, with half of the crew naval the other half civilian, including the masters who were designated Sonderführer which gave an equivalent military rank of Leutnant zur See. This unusual situation continued until 1 September 1940, when *HilfSp.A* was fully commissioned into the Kriegsmarine as *Sp24 'Waldtraut Horn'*, B commissioned as *Sp25 'Ingrid Horn'* and C retained her designation but was inducted into full naval service.

The invasion of the Netherlands, Luxembourg, Belgium and France was accomplished with a speed that surprised even the Germans. Luxembourg was subdued in a day and within four the Netherlands had surrendered, Belgium following suit two weeks later. Britain's troops and some of her allies' were evacuated from Dunkirk and its environs in Operation Dynamo, swiftly followed by Operation Aerial from the French Western Atlantic ports. It was a stunning defeat, won primarily on land and in the air with the Kriegsmarine playing at best a peripheral part, even during the Allied maritime evacuation. On 10 June Norway capitulated following the Allied withdrawal from Narvik, Italy plunging its tiny ineffectual dagger into France and declaring war on the Allied powers that same day. Border skirmishes followed in far away North Africa between British forces in Egypt and Italian troops in the Libyan province of Cyrenaica, an Italian colony since 1912.[35] Four days later Paris was surrendered to the Wehrmacht and on 22 June 1940 France signed an armistice that came into force three days later.

The sole remaining Breton thorn in the Germans' side after the capitula-tion of the coastal cities was the Ouessant Islands. Over 2500 French and British troops evacuated from Camaret and Le Conquet still remained on the desolate islands, gradually trickling away to England aboard any available vessels. Finally on 5 July 1940, three days after the surrender of the last French soldiers still manning the redundant Maginot Line and weeks after the official armistice, a single German Kapitän zur See supported by fifteen sailors arrived to take the surrender of Ouessant and its remaining 224-man garrison, these sixteen Germans ending the battle for France.

Though France was conquered, the war continued. *Sperrbrecher VII 'Sauerland'* suffered heavy damage after detonating a magnetic mine near Warnemünde, the ship being consigned to the shipyard for 15 months during which VES gear would be installed in an entirely rebuilt bow. A single *Vorpostenboot* was lost during the period of the invasion of France: *V801 'Bayern'* striking a mine north of Ameland on 9 June and going down with five crewmembers killed.

Ruge's minesweepers suffered losses on 19 June when elements of the 12th, 16th and 18th M-Flotillas were engaged in minesweeping operations in the Deutsche Bucht. At 0745hrs *M1802* hit a mine while leading the flotilla. Two men were killed outright and eight wounded before the 497-ton trawler sank. *M1803* and *M1805* were sent to assist, but only a minute later *M1601* also struck a mine, the damaged ship later being towed to Emden for repair. Although the battle for France had been won and British and Allied forces pushed back to the United Kingdom, nuisance raids were frequently mounted by small groups of RAF aircraft on the busy German minesweepers within the Channel. *Räumboote* of the 3rd R-Flotilla were strafed by one such attack in the North Sea as they routinely swept for mines, LzS Gerd-Dietrich Schneider's *R35* losing Matrosen-Gefreiter Alfred Habermann killed while Bootsmaat Helmut Schiller was badly wounded and died the following day in Leuwarden's naval hospital.

Conquered France was divided between German-occupied territory and that which remained under a new French government centred in Vichy, technically independent but politically dominated by Germany and economically dependent upon the Reich. The terms of the German-French armistice allowed an occupied area that included Northern France and the entire Atlantic coastline; the French Mediterranean remaining under Vichy control. German acquisition of the French Atlantic ports provided the perfect staging area for U-boats who were waging the convoy war. Whereas before the fall of France they had been forced to journey 450 miles through the North Sea and around the morth of the United Kingdom, they were now directly on the Atlantic fringe, giving them what amounted to an extra week in the combat area for Dönitz's convoy war.

The Kriegsmarine began the time-consuming task of clearing mines left by the retreating Allies from the captured harbours and from the Rhine, Moselle and Meuse rivers after Churchill had authorised their mining in Operation Royal Marine during May. Additionally, even while the fighting in France and Belgium had been raging, captured Dutch vessels were being examined for those that could be salvaged or converted for naval use.

Ex-lifeboat *HS114* of the *Hafenschutzflottille Kanalküste* tasked with patrolling the harbours of the English Channel. Lightly armed with two machine-guns, this is typical of the vessels requisitioned by the Kriegsmarine for such service.

Hafenschutzflottillen were almost immediately established in Harlingen, Holder, Ijmuiden, the Hook of Holland and Flushing, each comprised of six small armed fishing boats. Although thirty-one Dutch trawlers of the Ijmuiden fishing fleet had fled to England, it was estimated that at least 300 trawlers were still suitable for addition to the German Security Forces, five of them large steam trawlers to be converted to minesweepers. The Dutch harbours themselves were considered high priority for potential S-boat bases due to their proximity to the English coastline. Belgium also provided good harbours for S-boats and Zeebrugge, Nieuport and Ostend became focal points of Kriegsmarine occupation.

On 26 July minesweepers *M61*, *M89* and *M136* struck mines off the harbour entrance of the Hook of Holland and were lost but with only limited casualties. The commander of *M61*, ObltzS Georg Hindersin, was amongst those posted missing, though his body washed ashore later. Initial fears that the mines had been part of a cluster laid by Luftwaffe aircraft before the Dutch surrender were allayed after one was recovered intact and found to be part of a field laid by British destroyers during mid–May (Operation CBX3).[36]

In Dutch and Belgian waters a small group of coastal ships and river steamers were soon commissioned as *Sperrbrechergruppe Niederland*. The first of these, the 465-ton MV *Lies*, was converted in Werft Wilton, Schiedam, and commissioned as *NSI* (*Niederland-Seesperrbrecher 1*) on 29 July 1940. Eight more ships in total were complete by February 1941: *NSII 'Westerbroek'*, *NSIII 'Lola'*, *NSIV 'Beijerland'*, *NSV 'Import'*, *NSVI 'Havik'*, *NSVII 'Koert'*, *NSVIII 'Strijpe'* and *NSIX 'Goote'*.[37]

Somewhat confusingly, these former Dutch vessels were renamed once more. On 1 July 1940 FdM West redesignated all *Sperrbrechergruppe* as flotillas, reshuffling the strength of the service arm into newly-titled units; thus *Sperrbrechergruppe 1* became 1st *Sperrbrecherflottille* (1st Sp-Flotilla) and so on. *Sperrbrechergruppe Niederland* also became a flotilla after a delay of several weeks. On 25 September it was redesignated 4th *Sperrbrecherflottille* although the individual vessels would not have their numerical titles changed until 1 August 1941.

The 1st Sp-Flotilla was moved to Cuxhaven for operations in the Deutsche Bight. Fregattenkapitän Lothar Köhler's 2nd Sp-Flotilla travelled to Biscay and would eventually be based in Royan. The first of the flotilla's ships to head West, *Sp5 'Schwanheim'*, cleared mines before Dunkirk, Calais and Boulogne whilst en-route at least 263 magnetic mines that had been laid by the Luftwaffe before the conquest of France was complete.

French harbours were prioritised for development as naval bases and stocks of captured weapons, fuel, supplies and ships were examined by German officers despatched immediately to hasten the ports' levels of readiness. Minesweepers, R-boats and *Sperrbrecher* swept clear channels through minefields that had been laid by the Allies and the Luftwaffe, marking the safe passage routes with buoys. Anti-aircraft units were swiftly installed at critical points and construction of coastal artillery positions began along the Channel coast. Fishing restrictions were imposed on the conquered countries; for example within the Netherlands only Ijmuiden and Scheveningen were left as fishing ports to a sea area within a three-mile coastal limit between Zandvoort and Kijkdnin, and night fishing only permitted from Ijmuiden.

The Channel Islands were geographically closer to occupied Normandy than England and were duly occupied. Once aerodromes on the islands were no longer required for the evacuation of Allied troops the British government had designated the islands as demilitarized, though they failed to inform the Germans. The newly established *Marinebefehlshaber Nordfrankreich* (Naval Headquarters Northern France), VA Eugen Lindau, had already planned the occupation of the islands by naval assault as Operation Green Arrow (*Grüne Pfeile*) but a chance Luftwaffe landing discovered the islands to be un-defended and rendered the operation unnecessary. By the first week of July, mixed Kriegsmarine and Army troops had landed on Guernsey, Jersey, Alderney and Sark. Somewhat piqued, SKL recorded regret that the 'Kriegsmarine is not thus the first to carry out the landing on the British Channel Islands and the first therefore to gain a footing on British territory'.

While France collapsed, pressure had perceptibly eased in freshly conquered Norway. The routine business of minesweeping and securing maritime transport routes had begun in earnest and made considerable headway. *Marinegruppenkommando West* planned to leave 1st and 18th M-Flotillas, 5th R-Flotilla, 12th UJ-Flotilla and *Sperrbrecher VII, 18* and *47* permanently in Norway at the expense of defences within the North Sea and Heligoland Bight while the 11th Vp-Flotilla and 2nd M-Flotilla were scheduled to be withdrawn upon completion of the major troop transports from Germany.

However, although the threat level in Norwegian waters had diminished, it had not disappeared. On the penultimate day of May, the 291-ton *V1109* '*Antares*' sank off Bud after hitting a mine laid by the British submarine HMS *Narwhal* nearly three weeks previously. Eighteen men were rescued but seventeen were posted missing, including a Norwegian pilot.[38] Less than three weeks later, on 18 June, the minesweeper *M5* and 1828-ton Swedish SS *Sonja* were both sunk by mines laid by the submarine HMS *Porpoise* as part of minefield FD18 south-east of Fiskolmnes Light four days previously.

On 25 June HMS *Snapper* sighted a convoy comprising the German merchant ships *Robert Sauber, Makki Faulbaum* and the Norwegian *Bygdøy* and *P.G. Halvorsen*, escorted by *V1107* '*Portland*' and her flotilla-mate *V1108*. *Snapper* fired three torpedoes. Though two hits were heard, a second salvo of two torpedoes missed entirely. The submarine skipper had overestimated the freighters' sizes and claimed a 5000-ton merchant sunk south-west of Feistein. He had actually destroyed the 286-ton *V1107* and hit the 2515-ton SS *Robert Sauber* with a dud torpedo that caused minor impact damage. *Snapper* was able to retreat unscathed, the Germans believing that *V1107* had struck a mine and that *Robert Sauber* had been damaged in the explosion.

On 18 July HMS *H31* was four days into the boat's third war patrol, sent to relieve HMS *Sturgeon* on station. Lieutenant Malcolm David Wanklyn sighted what he took to be a screened convoy outside of firing range. He had found a minelaying force of the 12th UJ-Flotilla and after closing Wanklyn fired torpedoes that hit the 422-ton converted trawler *UJ126* '*Steiermark*', commanded by flotilla leader Korvettenkapitän der Reserve (KKdR) Heinz Peters, at 0855hrs, sinking her with nine crewmen killed.

Occupying Europe – preparations for Operation Seelöwe
In France, FdM Friedrich Ruge had travelled aboard *R27* to bays flanking Brest to oversee the selection of French vessels suitable for requisitioning as minesweepers. He needed ships to create the flotillas necessary for the control of hundreds of miles of newly-occupied coastline. For traditional trawler forms, the conversion work itself was relatively standardised and very similar to that of the *Vorpostenboote*. Generally a trawler's deckhouse was converted

for use as a radio-room, complete with hydrophone receiver if available, while a fixed, enclosed wheelhouse was added above. This allowed unobstructed vision over the forward gun platform that carried the boat's main armament. The wheelhouse would in turn be crowned with a signal mast. The stern was structurally altered for use of minesweeping equipment, while *Schlepps-pulgerät* (SSG) towed magnetic loop gear was housed in the deckhouse. Like larger minesweepers, the trawlers were equipped with MES degaussing gear.

Such *Hilfsminensuchboote* generally had light armament; a 37mm cannon mounted on the forecastle, a 20mm cannon abaft of this, and a further 20mm behind the wheelhouse. This, however, varied dependent on what was locally available. Some were issued heavier 88mm or 105mm guns, often captured models as there were frequent shortages of weapons. Two depth-charge throwers with three charged each were aft to port and starboard, while the holds were converted for ammunition storage and accommodation for about twenty-five men.

The requisitioning of large numbers of civilian vessels placed certain strains upon both the local economy and that of the Third Reich. Military vessels could be seized as legitimate spoils of war but vessels requisitioned from private individuals or companies required financial compensation. For example, the Dutch tugboat *Cycloop* belonging to the salvage firm Doeksen & Zoon was requisitioned by the Kriegsmarine on 4 September 1940 and numbered *R46S* to tow gunnery targets. The cost of the requisition was Hfl 28.05 per day and this payment was maintained until the end of the war. Coupled with this financial burden was the effect on local food supplies and trade as merchant and fishing vessels were taken for naval service.

Nonetheless, Ruge's primary concern was the immediate establishment of Security Forces for permanent stationing in the French ports. An officer and 100 men were ordered to Brest from the minesweeping personnel reserve in Cuxhaven, while the 3rd R-Flotilla was immediately moved from Denmark to France. The newly-established 4th R-Flotilla began operations in the Channel and the 2nd R-Flotilla, already having swept the entrance to major harbours from Le Havre to Lorient, was then engaged on escort duties for occupation troops and prisoners to and from Ouessant before being posted to Boulogne and Saint-Nazaire. Alongside the *Vorpostenboote*, *U-Jäger* and auxiliary minesweepers, numerous craft were taken for service in the various *Hafenschutzflottillen*. The fishing cutters of the makeshift 11th R-Flotilla that had served in Dutch waters during the fighting in May were disbanded on 16 October, the vessels being released to form *Hafenschutzflottillen* while the crews were transferred to larger R-boats that would become the 7th R-Flotilla, destined again for Dutch and Belgian waters

Returning to Cuxhaven, Ruge began a drive to recruit enough men to man six new R-Flotillas for stationing between the Netherlands and Biscay. The prospect of hostilities in the Mediterranean now that Italy had entered the war was not yet something that could be addressed; many Kriegsmarine officers clung to the forlorn hope that Germany could remain outside this theatre of operations, but they did not fully believe it. To compound Ruge's problems, during July verbal instructions from OKW were issued in preparation of an amphibious invasion of England: Operation Seelöwe (Sealion).

The original plan called for the embarkation of six infantry divisions and four Panzer battalions in a first wave that would hit beaches along the south coast of England between Ramsgate and the Isle of Wight, the Army calculating that it would be possible to launch two waves within the first 24 hours of the attack, using the same vessels that had transported the initial assault. Raeder and his staff were aghast. The Army clearly had little concept of what such an invasion entailed, going so far as to term it a 'river crossing on a broad front'. Even without the interference of the RAF and Royal Navy, it would be impossible to transport such numbers of troops even if the Kriegsmarine managed to requisition every barge and fishing boat in occupied Europe. Coupled with this, the expected bad weather within the English Channel would begin shortly after the landings and resupply by ships would become increasingly difficult. Furthermore, the Luftwaffe had suffered surprisingly heavy losses during the invasion of the Netherlands, including 276 transport aircraft with many crews, thus making both large-scale parachute drops and aerial resupply of the invasion force virtually impossible at that time. Nonetheless, considerable energy was spent on developing a basic plan for the attack at the request of the Führer. German Security Forces would be fully committed to the invasion; five ships of the 15th Vp-Flotilla (*V1505*, *V1507*, *V1508*, *V1510* and *V1512*) were even fitted with *Sturmboote* (assault boat) launching gear and transferred to FdV West during September 1940.

At sea, the war continued. *Vorpostenboot V1501 'Wiking VII'* was sunk by mine off Frederikshavn on 1 August, though she was later salvaged and repaired, and in the Channel a month later *UJ121 'Jochen'* struck a mine while approaching Ostend harbour and sank with thirteen crewmen killed and several severely wounded. The stricken hulk temporarily blocked the harbour whch was used by S-boats. Three days later *V201 'Gebrüder Kähler'* was also sunk by a mine in the Dunkirk Roads and *V403 'Deutschland'* sunk by another in the Westerschelde. The perils of war were not the sole cause of losses: *V304 'Breslau'* was wrecked in a severe storm near Ijmuiden.

Preparations for Seelöwe reached their peak in September. Minelaying ships earmarked for the operation – *Schiff 23 'Stier'*, *F6 'Königin Luise'*, *Schwerin*, *Preussen*, *Hansestadt Danzig*, *Grille*, *Tannenberg*, *Cobra*, *Kaiser*, *Roland* and *Togo* – escorted by six torpedo boats were moved to the Netherlands and Belgium, though four ships in Ostend were damaged in an

RAF raid. Those designated as the *Westgruppe* (*Schiff 23*, *Tannenberg*, *Cobra*, *Togo* and *Schwerin*) moved on to Cherbourg under heavy destroyer escort, reaching port on 11 September.

By the middle of the month a huge invasion force of transports, barges, lighters, tugboats and motorboats of various types and sizes had been gathered together between Rotterdam and Le Havre. Troops had been rehearsing disembarkation from crudely-adapted landing craft and the invasion scare had reached fever pitch in England; air attacks mounted by the Luftwaffe on 7 September were so intense that the code-word signifying invasion imminent – 'Cromwell' – had been given in South-East England, church bells rung and the Home Guard mobilised. Bomber Command had begun raids that sank nearly 200 barges by mid-September while the Royal Navy also mounted spoiling attacks with motor gunboats and destroyers, sinking German trawlers near the Channel ports and bombarding harbours such as Cherbourg and Le Havre.

Raeder then presented Hitler with a stark warning that the levels of commitment to Seelöwe could be maintained only until mid-October without jeopardising other theatres of action and finally a conference on 14 September resulted in its indefinite postponement (though Hitler was unwilling to cancel it formally lest the enemy's morale receive an unwelcome boost), and the massed invasion shipping was ordered to be dispersed. Finally, on 12 October, the Führer decided that until Spring 'preparations for Seelöwe shall be continued solely for the purpose of maintaining political and military pressure on England'. The so-called Battle of Britain was over and the Luftwaffe had failed to gain the requisite air supremacy over Great Britain to permit any invasion and it was ultimately abandoned. In reality Hitler's attention had already turned to the East.

Protecting French and Norwegian ports

Germany's greatest hope of defeating Great Britain now lay with Dönitz's U-boats. Their French Atlantic ports now required constant defence and minesweeping. With this increased territorial responsibility came the establishment of new posts in the naval hierarchy. On 27 October 1940 *Befehlshaber der Sicherung West* (BSW), was established by transferring the existing staff of BSO from the Baltic to Trouville in France. Vizeadmiral Hermann Mootz was appointed BSW, co-ordinating control of units stretching the length of the Dutch, Belgian and French Atlantic coast. Operationally subordinate to *Marinegruppenkommando West* and dependent on *Kommandierender Admiral Frankreich* for logistics, Mootz's new office in turn controlled *Führer der Minensuchboote West* (FdM West) and *Führer der Vorpostenboote West* (FdV West) as well troop services for *Führer der Minenschiffe* (FdMinsch).

As Mootz and his staff relocated to their new office, VA Hans Stohwasser replaced him as BSO Ost in Aalborg, vacating his post of FdM Nord that he had held for the previous two months. Stohwasser created a new staff from the experienced personnel that had previously served as KzS Leissner's FdV Ost personnel, the latter position being abolished and Leissner becoming Stohwasser's chief of staff. Stohwasser had served as FdM Ost since October 1939 until the post's dissolution in August 1940, controlling the forces at his disposal from his command ship *F3 'Hai'*. FdM Ost's responsibilities were transferred to FdM Nord, Stohwasser handling the transition of duties for two months from Aarhus in Denmark, before passing the reins to KzS Böhmer who would hold the post until March 1942 when another complicated change occurred and his position was abolished, being replaced by a new *Fuhrer der Minensuchverbände Ost*, operating from the fleet tender *Rugard*. It was a time of expansion and reorganisation as the Kriegsmarine consolidated its hold on a coastline that now stretched from the Norwegian border with Finland in the Arctic Circle to the Franco-Spanish border on the Bay of Biscay.

The busy convoy routes between Germany and Norway remained perilous: the 449-ton auxiliary minesweeper *M1306 'Hermann Krohne'* sank after striking a mine north of Hanstolm within the Western approaches to the Skagerrak the same day that the 510-ton converted motor vessel *UJ173 'Heinrich Wesselhöft'* became stranded on rocks north-west of Stavanger and had to be abandoned. The stricken motor ship remained there until October when efforts to salvage her ended in the vessel sinking in 30m of water. The continued expansion of the Security Forces remained crucial as British submarines also began prowling the waters of the Bay of Biscay, laying mines and attempting to intercept the newly-arriving U-boats, though their presence appeared unexpected to some in MGK West.

On 22 September, the Norwegian freighter *Tirranna* was approaching Bordeaux at the end of a lengthy journey. The 7230-ton ship had been captured by the German raider *Atlantis* south-east of Mauritius, her cargo of flour, wheat, wool, mail and 178 military vehicles destined for Suez. A small German prize crew of sixteen men was put aboard as well as a considerable number of prisoners from the raider's other victims, including British women and children. The captured ship then set course for Saint-Nazaire, traversing the Indian Ocean and rounding South Africa into the Atlantic without encountering the feared British blockade.

Tirranna's prize crew were informed by wireless that Saint-Nazaire was still heavily mined and, unable to contact MGK West by radio, LzS Louis Mundt had gone ashore alone to telephone for instructions on heading onward to Bordeaux.

He had a devil of a job getting through on the telephone to Naval HQ. Whoever-it-was he spoke to seemed almost irritated at being interrupted in whatever-it-was he was doing and Mundt began to feel somehow apologetic for bothering him. The he spoke to Someone Else, someone who seemed to treat the arrival of this laden prize from halfway across the world with about as much enthusiasm as a lock-keeper disturbed from his Sunday dinner to arrange passage of a dinghy.

Tirranna was to wait where she was. Owing to enemy minelaying she wouldn't possibly enter the Gironde without a sweeper escort. She would be met the following morning . . .

'But what about enemy submarines?' Mundt protested.

The Voice laughed. 'Don't worry, Lieutenant. There are no submarines in this area.'[39]

Minesweepers waiting for the order to sail from Bordeaux and meet the incoming prize never received their instructions in time. Instead the submarine HMS *Tuna* sighted a dark grey unmarked and unescorted ship and put three torpedoes into her. The ship exploded and *Tuna* headed back out to sea as two armed trawlers were sighted making what appeared to be a half-hearted ASW sweep with scattered depth charges. Eighty-seven of the men aboard *Tirranna* were killed, three of them from the ship's original crew.

Two days later *Tuna* made a second successful attack, torpedoing the 1281-ton German aircraft catapult ship *Ostmark* as she travelled escorted by minesweepers *M6* and *M12* thirty miles off l'île de Noirmoutier. *Ostmark*

The stern section of *Sp2 'Athen'* beached near Boulogne after being snapped in half by a mine explosion.

was one of four Lufthansa catapult ships designed to assist large Dornier Do18 flying boats in their Atlantic crossings to South America. They had been recalled to France by the Luftwaffe during September and *Tuna* fired six torpedoes from the range of nearly four nautical miles, hitting the ship and sending her down to the seabed 65m below. A single minesweeper attempted to locate the submarine by combing the tracks of the sighted torpedoes, but the hunt was swiftly abandoned while twenty-three survivors were pulled from the water, only a single man lost in the sinking.

Despite these successful torpedo attacks, mines remained the primary threat both in the Channel and Biscay both those laid by the RAF and Royal Navy, HMS *Porpoise* laying a barrage of forty-eight near Isle d´Yeu and HMS *Cachalot* another fifty in a line before Lorient. *Cachalot*'s field (FD27) appears to have been responsible for the destruction of *M1604 'Österreich'* which detonated two of them off Penmarc'h and sank.

The first *Sperrbrecher* had begun operating in the West by this stage, *Sp5 'Schwanheim'* working the waters off Dunkirk, Calais and Boulogne and the recently-commissioned *Sp2 'Athen'* soon arriving in the Channel. *Athen* had joined the 2nd Sp-Flotilla on 8 September, replacing the elderly *SpII 'Karl Leonhardt'* which had been returned to merchant service at the beginning of February. On 22 September *Sp2 'Athen'* struck an aerial mine near Boulogne that snapped the ship's keel in two, the forepart sinking while the aft section of the ship was grounded on the sandy beach nearby. In October the stern was towed to the Wilton shipyard in Schiedam where a new forward half was built and attached, the ship eventually re-entering merchant service during November 1942.

The number of *Sperrbrecher* had increased three-fold during 1940 and never again during the entire course of the war would so many new *Sperrbrecher* be commissioned; thirty-one new ships being made operational. However, raw materials for the new ships remained problematic.

> At present there are 25 sets of VES remote clearance gear; there will be an increase of 15 per month up to August; rate of production will be increased later. Great difficulties are being encountered in fitting up the *Sperrbrecher* with magnet gear (raw material situation), 10km of cable, 30 tons of copper, powerful electric motors, a great deal of iron required. Conversion period required to date (8–10 weeks) must be reduced at all costs.[40]

A total strength of fifty-six active *Sperrbrecher* was desired with a further twenty-eight in reserve, though this number had already been established before the fall of France. The acquisition of foreign merchant ships from occupied territories at least increased the potential *Sperrbrecher* fleet and by the end of 1940 the 3rd and 4th Sp-Flotillas were in service. Of course, attritional losses continued from such dangerous work. As well as *Sp2* having been blown in half, *Sp11 'Zeus'* suffered severe damage after detonating a mine off Korsør in the Great Belt. The engine room was flooded and the ship was towed to Kiel, later being transferred to Copenhagen for repairs that would take until April 1943 and the ship's return to service with the 3rd Sp-Flotilla. *Sperrbrecher 38 'Porjus'* of the 1st Sp-Flotilla was sunk on 1 December 1940 after being rammed while lying at anchor by the German steamer *Tilsit*.

While the Battle of Britain had raged, mines had continued to exact a toll from the Security Forces; *UJ175 'Perseus'* was destroyed off Ameland Island, *M3407* was sunk off the Hook of Holland, *M507* was sunk off Boulogne though later salvaged, repaired and returned to service, and the 259-ton *Schiff 13 Düsseldorf* was sunk in shallow water off Dieppe on 23 August but also salvaged and returned to service as *V607*.

Räumboot R21 was damaged by a mine explosion near in the German Bight on 14 August and four days later the First World War-vintage escort ship belonging to the 4th R-Flotilla, *Von der Groeben*, hit a mine north of Dunkirk and was severely damaged. She was beached by her captain near Boulogne but later salvaged and returned to service as *M507*. Ten days later a second R-boat tender, *Raule* (ex-*M133*), was also damaged by a mine in the Westerschelde.

While the Germans suffered a steady stream of casualties and damage, they were not alone. The submarine HMS *Sealion* was rammed by *U-Jäger UJ123* on 6 August while running at periscope depth after an attack on a German convoy near Norway's South coast, damaging the periscope shears. Although *Sealion* managed to slip away without further harm, the repairs that followed in port kept her out of action until late October. HMS *H49* had already attacked a German convoy off Terschelling Island and sunk 2,186-ton cargo steamer *Heimdal* before running afoul of the 5th UJ-Flotilla. Korvettenkapitän der Reserve Wolfgang Kaden was leading *UJ111*, *UJ116* and *UJ118* in an ASW sweep when they sighted *H49* approximately 3km away. Caught in shallow waters, Lieutenant Richard Evelyn Coltart, RN, immediately dived his submarine to 60ft and attempted to creep away, enduring over two hours of depth-charging before the boat finally broke up, twenty-six men being killed and only a single survivor, George William Oliver, rescued by the Germans. In the boat's final moments Kaden had continued depth-charging to ensure that his target was destroyed, despite a growing oil patch on the surface. Oliver was blown out of the wreck through the engine room hatch by a pressure wave from ruptured compressed air bottles. The shocked Leading Stoker was sighted afloat on the long swell after being in the water for twenty minutes. He was pulled aboard a *U-Jäger* and rubbed down with schnapps to remove the thick diesel oil from his skin before being transported ashore to captivity.

Grossadmiral Raeder inspects *Zwerg 7*, one of the smallest purpose-built minesweepers of the Kriegsmarine.

Regular German supply convoys were now running along both the Norwegian and French coasts as well as to the Channel Islands. In Biscay, the U-boats bases at Brest, Lorient, Saint-Nazaire, La Pallice and Bordeaux had all become operational for the Atlantic U-boats and Italian BETASOM[41] boats in Bordeaux. While Allied bombing of the ports almost inexplicably lagged behind offensive action by submarines in the Bay of Biscay, German escort vessels were in high demand to shepherd U-boats to and from harbour and sweep the transit routes clear of mines. *Sperrbrecher* soon became indispensable, preceding the U-boats through the dangerous approach channels both inbound and outbound.

By December 1940 the Kriegsmarine's Security Forces had increased dramatically in size and location,; divided between theatre commands MGK West, MGK Nord and *Komandierenden Admiral Norwegen*. Under the latter office was established the *Küstensicherungsverbände* (KSV, Coastal Security Units). Hans Bartels, former commander of *M1*, was responsible for creating the first such formation, *KSV norwegische Westküste* during May 1940. Bartels based his small unit of only four fishing boats and two *Vorpostenboote* in

Bergen, commanding from the the headquarters ship *Tan*. Bartels' unit was responsible for local minesweeping, patrolling and ASW work, later also adopting the roles of gunboats and minelayers.

Kapitänleutnant Bartels would soon run afoul of naval bureaucracy while attempting to add improvised but effective elements to his meagre command. He had already managed to accumulate a sizeable force of forty-five vessels which were divided between 51st, 53rd and 55th Vp-Flotillas and 52nd M-Flotilla. These were to become his '*Tigerverbänd*', flying the pennant that had been adopted by *M1*, Bartels going so far as to issue his own commemorative pin with accompanying certificate to flotilla men who had excelled themselves.

On 13 October three of Bartels' minesweepers – *M5207 'Gnom'*, *Kobold 1* and *Kobold 3* – were lost to mines laid by HMS *Narwhal*. Bartels recognised the urgent need for small vessels which could operate in shallow water without risk of grounding and to that end commissioned the construction of twelve diminutive vessels based on Norwegian fishing boat designs and christened '*Zwerge*' ('dwarves'). They became the smallest purpose-built minesweepers in German service, weighing only 3.5 tons. *Zwerg 7* was taken to Berlin where Raeder inspected her, receiving the four-man crew at OKM headquarters. However, Bartels' independent spirit would be temporarily curbed when he was transferred as IWO to the destroyer *Z24* to, as Raeder put it, 'relearn naval discipline'.[42]

During October 1940, Kaptlt Dr Heinrich Behlen was put in charge of KSV *Polarküste*, based originally in Tromsø with headquarters ship *Nordwind*, before relocating to Kirkenes. Like Bartels' unit, Behlen's flotillas were made up of requisitioned Norwegian trawlers and whaling boats during 1941 and responsible primarily for convoy protection. During February 1941, the third region, KSV *norwegischen Nordküste*, was established in Trondheim under the command of FK Alexander Magnus.

The *Küstensicherungsverbände* were distinct from the *Hafenschutzflottillen* established in all major occupied ports. The latter utilised whatever local craft they could obtain – from pinnaces, barges and tugs to passenger paddle steamers armed with flak weapons or, at best, a 75mm gun – to conduct local surveillance and security. They were generally subordinate to the location's naval commander (*Seekommandant*) but frequently worked in concert with the Security Forces. In areas with fewer operational units, such as the Adriatic and Aegean, there was a constant amalgamation of harbour defence craft and security vessels used to overcome logistical difficulties in order to achieve the common goal of local naval defence.

Modernising the Fleet: *M40* minesweepers

During 1940 a redesign of the Kriegsmarine minesweeper was finished. The new *M40* class reverted to economical coal-fired boilers, no longer dependant on oil fuel supplies which would become increasingly problematic. Having more design traits in common with the Type 16s of the last war, the *M40s* were smaller than the *M35s*. Able to make 17.2 knots, they displaced 775 tons full load, measuring 62.3m from stem to stern with a waterline length of 57.6m, draught of 2.82m and a beam of 8.9m that allowed more room for newly-developed influence sweeps than was available aboards *M35s*. More powerful auxiliary engines were also installed in order to produce the current necessary for magnetic minesweeping. Crewed by between fifty-four to seventy-five men, typical armament would comprise a single 105mm gun, one 37mm and up to six 20mm cannon. For ASW work thirty-six depth charges could be thrown by four launchers while minelaying capacity remained twelve mines on stern rails. At least 10 per cent smaller than the *M35*, they were considerably cheaper to produce, required less exacting specifications and used less shipyard manpower. Of the 131 that were built between 1940 and 1942, the majority were constructed outside of Germany, most in Dutch shipyards.

The *Räumboote* had also been modernised during 1940, the first 'Type *R41*' coming off the slipway at Travemünde's Schlichting Werft in April 1940. Only the first three of the series, *R41* to *R43*, were built in Travemünde, the remaining eighty-six all built by Abeking & Rasmussen, Lemwerder. The boats' displacement under full load had increased by 10 tons to 135 tons, the length and beam also fractionally increased while they remained shallow draught with only 1.51m clearance required under deep load. *R41* to *R48* were propellled by MWM diesels while *R49* to *R129* carried MAN diesels, the maximum speed capable a respectable 20 knots, though maximum endurance of 900 nautical miles was only possible with an average speed of 15 knots. The crew of twenty could handle a payload of ten mines if required, two 20mm cannon or a mixed armament of 20mm and 37mm as well as depth charges. During 1940 the Burmester yards in Burglesum and Swinemünde also began launching R-boats, the series numbered *R151* to *R217* of similar dimensions, the entire series powered by MWM diesels. Highly manoeuvrable, fast and robust, the *Räumboote* remained at the cutting edge of Germany's coastal minesweepers.

Kriegsmarine Security Forces in the West – December 1940

Oberkommando der Marine
Grossadmiral Erich Raeder

Marinegruppenkommando West
GA Saalwächter

Befehlshaber der Sicherung der West (BSW)
VA Mootz

Führer der Minensuchboote West
KzS Ruge
2. FdM Niederland – FK Bramesfeld
2. FdM Nordfrankreich –FK Weniger
2. FdM Westfrankreich – FKdR
Lautenschlager
1st M–Flotilla
2nd M–Flotilla
12th M–Flotilla
14th M–Flotilla
15th M–Flotilla
16th M–Flotilla
32nd M–Flotilla
34th M–Flotilla
36th M–Flotilla
38th M–Flotilla
40th M–Flotilla
42nd M–Flotilla
44th M–Flotilla
1st R–Flotilla
2nd R–Flotilla
3rd R–Flotilla
4th R–Flotilla
7th R–Flotilla
2nd Sp–Flotilla
4th Sp–Flotilla
Minenräumschiff 11
Minenräumschiff 12

Führer der Vorpostenboote West
(FdV West)
KzS Schiller

2nd Vp-Flotilla
3rd Vp-Flotilla
4th Vp-Flotilla
7th Vp-Flotilla
13th Vp-Flotilla
15th Vp-Flotilla
16th Vp-Flotilla
18th Vp-Flotilla
20th Vp-Flotilla
12th UJ-Flotilla

Kriegsmarine Security Forces in the Baltic and Norway – December 1940

Oberkommando der Marine Grossadmiral Erich Raeder

Marinegruppenkommando Nord GA Carls

Kommandierender Admiral Norwegen
Admiral Boehm

11th M-Flotilla
17th UJ-Flotilla

Admiral norwegen Westküste
VA von Schrader

4th M-Flotilla

Admiral norwegen Polarküste
KA Schenk

KSV norwegen Westküste
Kaptlt Hans Bartels

51st Vp-Flotilla
53rd Vp-Flotilla
55th Vp-Flotilla
52nd M-Flotilla
54th M-Flotilla

KSV norwegen Polarküste
Kaptlt Dr Behlen

59th Vp-Flotilla
61st Vp-Flotilla

Befehlshaber der Sicherung der Nord (BSN)
KA Wolfram

Befehlshaber der Sicherung der Ostsee (BSO)
KA Stohwasser

FdM Nord
KzS Böhmer

3rd M-Flotilla
6th M-Flotilla
13th M-Flotilla
17th M-Flotilla
18th M-Flotilla
31st M-Flotilla
5th R-Flotilla
1st Sp-Flotilla

FdV Nord
FKdR Fuchs

8th Vp-Flotilla
11th Vp-Flotilla
12th Vp-Flotilla
11th UJ-Flotilla
2nd *Flakjägergruppe*

Bewachungsverband Ostseezugänge (BEWA Ost)
KzS Karstens

10th Vp-Flotilla
19th Vp-Flotilla
Netzsperrverband 1

FdV Ost

9th Vp-Flotilla
17th Vp-Flotilla
BSO *Schulflottille*
3rd Sp-Flotilla

Temp attachments:
3rd M-Flotilla
19th M-Flotilla
8th Vp-Flotilla
Sperrbrecher 12
Sperrbrecher 13
Sperrbrecher C1

4

Establishing the Security Divisions, 1941

O N 9 January 1941 VA Hermann Mootz vacated his post as BSW to oversee the testing of newly-constructed warships, his place briefly being taken by VA Hermann von Fischel who occupied the post for a month in which the Kriegsmarine command structure in the West was drastically altered. The existing BSW staff was dissolved and replaced by men who had previously staffed the offices of FdM West and FdV West. Installed in Paris, under the command of the newly-promoted VA Friedrich Ruge, the border between BSW and BSN was moved west so that the Netherlands was removed from Ruge's sphere of operations.

The FdV and FdM commands were also fused and Security Divisions (*Sicherungsdivisionen*) established in their stead on 17 February 1941. Each Division was responsible for a sector of coastline and the incumbent work such as the protection of naval bases, requisitioning new vessels, the formation of new flotillas and general convoy protection, minesweeping, minelaying and ASW operations.

Admiral Hermann von Fischel (*Befehlshaber der Sicherung West*) inspects a minesweeper crew.

U30 arrives in Lorient on 7 July 1940 under escort from the 2nd R-Flotilla (identified by the 'Trident' flotilla marking on the port bow). Fritz-Julius Lemp's *U30* was the first U-boat to refuel in a French port.

Four *Sicherungsdivisionen* were initially created. The 1st *Sicherungsdivision* was responsible for the Netherlands and Germany's North Sea coast with its headquarters in The Hague under the command of FK Heinrich Bramesfeld who built his staff around the existing core of FdM *Niederlande*. Kapitän zur See Karl Weniger, previously FdM *Nordfrankreich*, based his new 2nd *Sicherungsdivision* in the Château du Souverain-Moulin near Boulogne. His responsibility stretched over an area covering Belgian and Northern French coastal waters to Cherbourg, his units based in Bruges, Ostend, Dunkirk, Boulogne-Wimereux, Dieppe, Le Havre, Ouistreham, and Cherbourg as well as the Channel Islands. Kapitän zur See Heinz Schiller based the 3rd *Sicherungsdivision* initially at Brest before moving to Trez Hir near Plougen-velin. His zone stretched from the Western portion of the English Channel to the Loire estuary, the main ports used by his forces being St Malo, Brest, Concarneau, Benodet and Lorient. The final French Atlantic unit, 4th *Sicherungsdivision*, was based at Larmor-Plage near Lorient, KzS Anselm Lautenschlager being responsible for the region between the River Loire and the Spanish frontier, using the ports of Nantes/Coueron, Paimboeuf, Saint-Nazaire, Les Sables-d'Olonne, La Pallice, Royan, Pauillac, Bordeaux, Bayonne and Saint-Jean-de-Luz.

Defending the Capital Ships

Between December and February 1941 Brest played host to the heavy cruiser *Admiral Hipper* which made a successful raiding sortie into the Atlantic, sinking seven ships and seriously damaging two more from the slow convoy SLS64 bound for England from Freetown. Engine trouble forced her back to

A fairly typical early-war *Vorpostenboot* off the French coast in the Bay of Biscay. The main armament of single-barrelled flak weapons is plainly visible.

Brest where she was the target of the heaviest British air raids to date against the harbour. Raeder was convinced of the need to bring *Admiral Hipper* back to Kiel, a thirteen-day journey that ended on 15 March.

One week after *Admiral Hipper*'s departure, Brest hosted two more capital ships. Escorted by three *Sperrbrecher* and two torpedo boats, the battleships *Scharnhorst* and *Gneisenau* arrived at the end of a successful raiding mission in the North Atlantic during which they had sunk twenty-two enemy merchant ships. *Gneisenau* was the first to arrive, rounding Pointe de Petit Minou at 0700hrs on 22 March, and manoeuvred into Basin Number 8 at Lanninon for routine maintenance. Later that afternoon her sister-ship steamed into the Rade de Brest.

The British Admiralty discovered their presence within five days with the aid of a coded message from French Resistance member Jean Philippon, code-named 'Hilaron'. Philippon had previously been Second Officer aboard the French submarine *Ouessant*, scuttled in the Penfeld before the French surrender. He continued to work in the naval arsenal under the provisions of the German-French armistice, the intelligence he provided bringing RAF bombers on a series of heavy air raids against the two ships, scoring no direct hits but leaving an unexploded bomb lying beneath the docked *Gneisenau*. The ship was temporarily moored in the harbour without the benefit of extensive torpedo net protection. It was a target too tempting for the British to pass up.

On 6 April 1941, Coastal Command's 22 Squadron, based at St Eval in Cornwall, ordered six aircraft to attack her with a mixture of torpedoes and mines. However, pouring rain had softened the grass airfield and only four of the bombers were able to get aloft, three of which then lost their way in pouring rain. Only Beaufort number OA-X/22, flown by Flying Officer Kenneth Campbell, reached Brest. Approaching at low altitude between the cliffs of the Crozon Peninsula and the northern fringe of the Goulet de Brest, Campbell launched his torpedo moments before the thick curtain of anti-aircraft fire that came from land batteries, *Gneisenau* and ships of the 7th Vp-Flotilla sent his Beaufort plunging into the harbour. Though there were no survivors, Campbell's torpedo struck the *Gneisenau* in the stern, breaching the hull and flooding generator and turbine housings. German divers recovered the Beaufort crew's bodies and they were buried with full military honours, Campbell being posthumously awarded the Victoria Cross.[43]

Gneisenau was once more moved into dry-dock, triggering further air raids, and on 11 April a combined force of Blenheim, Wellington and Manchester bombers from eight different squadrons hit the ship, killing seventy-eight crewmen and causing further damage. As aircraft battered Brest, the remaining Atlantic ports also came under air attack while Allied submarines were routinely despatched to patrol the port approaches and attempt to intercept U-boats in transit to and from them.

HMS *Snapper* departed the River Clyde on 29 January 1941 on one such mission. The usual skipper, Lt King, had been hospitalised with influenza and his place had been taken by Lt Geoffrey Vernon Prowes. Prowes proceeded into Biscay submerged by day and surfaced by night and it is estimated that she arrived at her patrol area during the early hours of 2 February. Final communication with the boat was made on 7 February when *Snapper* was instructed to begin her return after dark on 10 February and rendezvous with the submarine tender *Cutty Sark* near Trevose Head. *Snapper* failed to arrive and repeated contact requests remained unanswered.

Although the exact details of *Snapper*'s loss are unconfirmed, during the night of 10 February, *M2*, *M13* and *M25* of Benodet's 2nd M-Flotilla were conducting a routine sweep for mines near Ouessant Island when tracks of three torpedoes were sighted. Taking evasive action, a British submarine was observed breaking the surface nearby, possibly a momentary error in depth-keeping while torpedoes were fired resulting in the submarine 'porpoising'. Immediately attacking, the minesweepers attempted to ram the submarine which submerged with only seconds to spare, one of the minesweepers losing its sweeping gear after it became entangled in the submarine's conning tower. The German ships then made a prolonged series of depth-charge attacks lasting several hours and totalling fifty-six separate charges. Despite no wreckage being recovered, the strong sonar fix that had been obtained on the

The addition of captured minesweepers, such as this Dutch *Jan van Amstel*-class vessel, helped bolster the strength of the Kriegsmarine. The outbreak of war caught Raeder's navy unprepared, understrength and undermanned.

submarine suddenly ceased, the target claimed at the very least to have been badly damaged.

In the meantime the Security Forces continued to suffer a steady flow of casualties. Three days into the New Year, *M3410 'Kasia'* of the 34th M-Flotilla was wrecked on the Dutch coast, the crew rescued by lifeboat. The flotilla had been formed from requisitioned small Dutch vessels in June 1940 and the 113-ton *M3410* was the first boat to be lost. The winter weather also sank the 45-ton fishing boat *HS76 'Julius Ruh'* of the *Kanalküste Hafenschutz-flottille*, wrecked in stormy weather near Dunkirk on 3 February and *HS68 'Albinus'* wrecked in thick fog entering Calais harbour. During January three ships were lost to enemy mines: *V303 'Tannenberg'* and *V306 'Fritz Hincke'* both sunk near Ijmuiden and *UJ175 'Mob FD-31'* of the 17th UJ-Flotilla sunk two days later off Feiestein. The 'Mob FD' patrol ships had been designed in 1940 as a special project on which to base *Vorpostenboot/U-Jäger* construction, twenty-one of them being launched by November 1941. The

A message for England. Probably taken in the war's early months, these chalked cartoons appear to depict Neville Chamberlain and Winston Churchill.

inspiration lay in the specifications of the Norderwerft trawler *Uhlenhorst*, including enhanced compartmentalisation, a strengthened stem and stern and a double bottom for about half of the length. Cuxhaven's 4th *Hafenschutzflottille* lost the 200-ton converted herring drifter *H415 'Schaumburg Lippe'* in the Elbe near light vessel Number 4 after colliding with the minelayer *Cobra*. Her sister-ship *H401 'Hannover'* pushed the damaged vessel aground where salvage attempts subsequently failed and the vessel written off as a total loss. The same flotilla would also lose *H453 'Gretchen'* in the Elbe after she collided with Marker Buoy 7 during April.

The British begin raiding Norway

A more serious loss for the Germans was to follow during March. With Norway conquered, Hitler's fears rose of a potential British offensive to recapture the country and its valuable resources. On 4 March 1941, troops from the newly-established British No. 3 and 4 Commando as well as Royal Engineers and fifty-two men of the Royal Norwegian Navy mounted Operation Claymore, an attack against factories on the Lofoten Islands that produced fish oil for use in the manufacturing of glycerine for the German armaments industry. Claymore was just the first of twelve Allied raids on Norwegian soil – four of them in 1941 alone – and not only did it serve to heighten Adolf Hitler's paranoia about an attempted invasion, but its also yielded a major breakthrough in deciphering the Kriegsmarine's Enigma code.

The operation involved the Royal Navy's 6th Destroyer Flotilla led by HMS *Somali*. The day before the actual landing, a Luftwaffe weather flight spotted the approaching ships and the alert status along the northern Norwegian coast was raised to 'increased watchfulness'. As the Claymore ships approached the Lofoten Islands, lookouts aboard *Somali* sighted the 376-ton armed trawler *NN04 'Krebs'* of Narvik's *Hafenschutzflottille*. Sailing near one of the commandos' landing zones on Svolvaer, *Krebs* was fired on at a range of just under two miles, returning fire despite being massively outgunned. She failed to hit her attacker though one shell ripped through *Somali*'s flags. The trawler's wheelhouse then took a direct hit which killed the captain, LzS Hans Kapfinger, and several crewmen, more shells hitting the boiler room and magazine. *Krebs* lost power and steerage and slowly began steaming in a lazy circle before stranding on a low rocky islet named Flesa while most survivors abandoned ship.

With troop landings to support, *Somali* left the stricken trawler, only passing the wreck hours later as she drifted in the centre of a small fjord on Scråven Island after refloating on a rising sea. Lieutenant Sir Marshall Warmington, signals officer aboard HMS *Somali*, led a boarding party to search for any valuable intelligence material. A wounded German stoker had managed to burn some secret papers before jumping ashore on Flesa, but Warmington retrieved a naval grid map and some personal papers and documents before discovering two Enigma rotors in a cupboard after shooting the lock off with his pistol. Five wounded German were rescued, two of whom were severely injured, one with a head wound and the other bleeding profusely after having most of the muscle of his arm shot away. After evacuating the trawler *Somali* sank the stubborn ship with depth charges and shellfire, eighteen of the twenty-five crew going down with her. It was only later that the significance of some of the documents was revealed: Warmington had taken the Enigma key tables for February and the inner and outer plugboard settings. It was a vital break for the cryptanalysts of Bletchley Park.

Increasing Anti-Aircraft Capabilities against RAF Coastal Command

During February 1941 RAF Coastal Command was placed in large part under the operational control of the Admiralty. The RAF had not begun the war with any defined anti-shipping doctrine but rather had concentrated upon the presumed task of strategic bombing while the Royal Navy blockaded Germany. Coastal Command had been created in 1936 as a defence against U-boats that had been so successful against British mercantile traffic during the previous war. Once hostilities began it become rapidly apparent that the Royal Navy was stretched to its limits in all theatres and Coastal Command's remit extended to attacking Germany's convoy routes.

Vorpostenboot flak gunners.

Through 1940 their results had been dismal despite their best efforts: 161 aircraft lost for the sinking of only six ships and another fourteen damaged. Outdated equipment, lacklustre intelligence, poor serviceability of aircraft, low morale and a lack of cohesive tactical doctrine had combined to thwart Coastal Command's efforts. They had focussed on the valuable mineral shipments from Norway to Germany, with *Vorpostenboote* and *Sperrbrecher* escorts providing effective protection. With the Admiralty's assumption of control, Coastal Command started receiving more suitable aircraft such as Beauforts and Beaufighters, though these were soon transferred to the Mediterranean to attack Rommel's maritime supply lines.

Nonetheless, their fortunes improved during 1941. The cipher used by German and German-occupied dockyards (*Werftschlüssel*, also used by small patrol craft that did not carry Enigma) was broken in February 1941, providing intelligence from signals traffic alerting dockyards to convoy departure and arrival times. Luftwaffe Enigma codes had also already been broken, particularly important convoy traffic being escorted by fighters and thus betraying its value. These sources of intelligence were aided by the expansion of the RAF's Photographic Reconnaissance Unit from twelve aircraft to seventy-two. Finally, from August 1941, Kriegsmarine Enigma was regularly broken which provided information about pending convoys and the results of previous attacks. One of the first such signals was transmitted by *V2012* reporting a successful strike against the SS *Viborg* that had damaged the freighter. While the Germans remained ignorant of their codes' penetration, the increased efficacy of Coastal Command resulted in *Vorpostenboote* and *Sperrbrecher* in the English Channel and North Sea having their anti-aircraft armament increased incrementally over the years that followed. The threat posed by these 'flak ships' was never underestimated by Allied aircrews.

> Much has also been said of the activity of the flak-ships. The Germans are using them in ever increasing numbers to protect shipping, of which the value, always great, grows daily. Sometimes as many as five have been observed escorting a single vessel. Their crews are not unnaturally light on the trigger. 'Just as we were right over the ship it spotted us,' reported the pilot of a Hudson who met one such vessel off Norway. 'The Germans opened up first with machine-gun fire; then the heavier guns started firing. It seemed to me, at that moment that they were throwing up everything except the ship herself.' It was bombed and left burning.[44]

The escorts themselves became targets. On 5 May, BSN, KA Wolfram, ordered an experimental sailing of *Sp10 'Vigo'* equipped with a barrage balloon to assess its value at sea. During the test mission the *Sperrbrecher* was attacked by an RAF bomber which caught the balloon's cable with its right wing, was put into a spin and hit by heavy flak before two Bf110 fighters finished it off. The trial was therefore deemed a success and many *Sperrbrecher* were subsequently equipped with a 77m³ balloon towed by a thick cable up to 250m in length.

Minesweepers at sea, one towing a barrage balloon designed to ward off low-flying enemy aircraft.

Onboard anti-aircraft flamethrower, seen here being fired aboard *Sperrbrecher 16 'Tulane'*. An inaccurate and unpopular weapon, it was carried to ward off low-level aircraft attacks but was rarely used in combat.

Experiments with an on–board flamethrower designed to combat low-flying aircraft soon followed. Tested aboard the *Geleitschiff Möwe* and deemed satisfactory, flamethrowers were installed aboard several *Sperrbrecher* and minelayers. A firing tube was attached to the head of the aft mast, capable of projecting a burst of flaming oil up to 50m in length and enough fuel was carried for up to fifty three-second bursts. However, this imprecise weapon was unpopular with *Sperrbrecher* crews. Frequently, after firing, burning oil would run down the exterior of the pipe and pose an extra fire hazard for both ship and crew. Correspondingly, and contrary to standing orders, the flamethrower was rarely used in combat.

Later during 1943 a third anti-aircraft device was widely installed aboard *Sperrbrecher*. This was the *Raketenabwurfgerät* (Rocket Launcher) capable of firing either an explosive projectile carrying a 3.7kg time-fused warhead designed to explode anywhere between 400m and 800m from the ship, or trailing an anti-aircraft cable 100m long which was then suspended by parachute. Cheap to produce and easy to install, they became widely carried and although no known casualties were caused to attacking aircraft, they functioned as a healthy deterrent.

Wie werde ich Offizier der Kriegsmarine?
(Kriegsausgabe)

Kriegsmarine recruiting booklet. Manpower concerns within both the Kriegsmarine itself and the shipyards that supplied new vessels or repaired existing ones hampered the growth of the Security Forces.

It was, of course, not only direct attack that caused casualties amongst the Security Forces, but also the perils of their day-to-day tasks. During April the 289-ton *V709* '*Guido Möhring*' was sunk while attempting to assist French fishermen to extricate a spent British torpedo caught in their nets. After arriving alongside the stationary French vessel, a diver equipped with cutters struggled to free the torpedo which exploded unexpectedly. The blast killed several Germans instantly, severely damaging *V709*'s hull below the waterline. While rescue craft were summoned from Lorient, the *Vorpostenboot* settled deep into the water while the crew vainly tried to shore up the damage with wood. In deteriorating weather, *V709* was abandoned before she heeled over to port and sank.

Manpower Shortages

With steady losses, the Kriegsmarine needed to boost its recruitment levels. OKW had always regulated the distribution of new recruits between the three services, the Army and Luftwaffe receiving priority over the Kriegsmarine. During September 1939 Raeder's service had been assigned only 9 per cent of the available manpower pool, both volunteers and those drafted for service.

By October 1941 this had risen to 10.2 per cent and by November 1942 the annual naval quota was fixed at 30,000 men though, of these, priority was of course given to U-boat crews. On 15 June 1943 Dönitz reported his ongoing manpower concerns in a conference with Hitler.

> If the Kriegsmarine does not receive the requested personnel, then, from January 1944 on, no newly commissioned *Vorpostenboote*, minesweepers, S-boats etc could be manned. By 1 January, 1944, the last available soldiers would be transferred to U-boat training. The remaining training schools of the Kriegsmarine would run out of men in the winter of 1943–1944. The Führer declares that a cessation of the U-boat war is out of the question; that he would have to allocate personnel as they become available, and orders a list of the required personnel with the date when they will be needed drawn up and submitted to him. He will see to it that appropriate action is taken.[45]

The supply of skilled dockyard workers was also a constant problem, somewhat assuaged by the labour pool found in newly-conquered territories. Engineers, technicians and dockyard workers of the occupied countries worked within shipyards and ports which both maintained naval vessels and converted new ones. In France, some 2000 men worked for the Kriegsmarine in this capacity, authorised by the Vichy government at the beginning of August 1940 although workers in Brest and Lorient had already started on the conversion of trawlers to *Vorpostenboote*. It was not until March 1944 that Frenchmen and other European volunteers could enlist for service in the ranks of the Kriegsmarine itself. Complicated negotiations between Dönitz and Heinrich Himmler, the head of the SS, had taken place, the SS having prior claim on foreign volunteers as a way of circumventing recruitment limitations imposed by OKW. Himmler eventually relented and foreigners deemed to have a working knowledge of maritime affairs were transferred to 28th *Schiffsstammabteilung* (Training Detachment), also used by the Waffen-SS for the basic training of recruits from Belgium, the Netherlands, Latvia, Ukraine, Spain, France and Denmark. Once naval instruction was completed they were generally assigned as replacements for ships of the Security Flotillas in the Baltic. In January 1943, some 200 Frenchmen were also formed into the *Kriegsmarinewerftpolizei* which handled shipyard security at some French ports. However, following the 20 July plot against Adolf Hitler, Himmler reversed his decision and many of the erstwhile foreign members of the Kriegsmarine were transferred *en masse* to the Waffen-SS.

Additional infrastructure required for the Security Forces in conquered territories was relatively minimal beyond facilities already available for the Kriegsmarine. In each port where a Security Flotilla was based, the administrative staff would be billeted ashore, while in general the crews were accommodated aboard ship. As air raids began in earnest, the decision was taken to construct reinforced concrete shelters to protect the Kriegsmarine's most valuable assets. In the Atlantic ports and Norway these were the U-boats, whereas along the Channel coast shelters were built for use by both S-boats and R-boats, replacing vulnerable depot ships and providing protection while the boats were in harbour or undergoing maintenance. While not as large as the U-boat bunkers, they were still monolithic constructions built by the workers of the Organisation Todt. Bunkers were built in Ijmuiden, Ostend, Dunkirk, Boulogne, Le Havre and Cherbourg, Boulogne and Ostend being the first to be made operational during the middle of 1941.

Despite British coastal forces growing in size and ability along their southern coast, the Germans successfully sailed convoys through the English Channel. While accidents, mines and enemy attack continued to exact a toll on the Security Forces, growth outpaced losses throughout 1941. By the end of the year the four Security Divisions based in Western Europe had increased in size.

1st *Sicherungsdivision* (operational area from Hanstholm, Denmark, to the Scheldte, Belgium):
>13th Vp-Flotilla; transferred from the Baltic to Rotterdam.
>20th Vp-Flotilla; established in July 1940 from German trawlers and based in The Netherlands.
>22nd M-Flotilla; formed on 1 September 1941 from Type 40 minesweepers.
>32nd M-Flotilla; formed on 16 June 1940 from requisitioned Dutch fishing boats.
>34th M-Flotilla; formed as *Küstenminensuchflottille* in The Netherlands on 13 June 1940 and redesignated minesweeping flotilla in July 1940.
>*Flußsperrbrecher 201, 202, 203, 204* and *Sperrbrecher 145, 147, 148, 149*; designated *Sperrbrechergruppe Niederland* in June 1940, then 4th Sp-Flotilla from 25 September 1940. Briefly reorganised as the short-lived 5th Sperrbrecherflottille between November and December 1941.
>*Minenräumschiff 12 'Nürnberg'*

2nd *Sicherungsdivision* (operational area in the English Channel from Dover to the Scheldte):
>36th M-Flotilla; formed from captured Belgian fishing boats on 26 July 1940 and based at Ostende.
>38th M-Flotilla; formed on 4 July 1940 using captured trawlers and based at Le Havre.
>2nd R-Flotilla; transferred to Dutch and French waters, based principally in Dunkirk.
>4th R-Flotilla; formed on 1 April 1940 and later transferred from the North Sea to Boulogne.
>15th Vp-Flotilla; transferred from the Baltic to Le Havre during autumn 1940.
>18th Vp-Flotilla; created from the 18th *Vorpostengruppe* in October 1940 and moved to Brügge.

Korvettenkapitän Burkhard Heye pictured in convoy with vessels of his 4th Vp-Flotilla near Bordeaux.

3rd *Sicherungsdivision* (operational area along the French north-west coast and Brittany).

2nd M-Flotilla; transferred first to Dutch then Channel waters before being stationed in Bordeaux and Royan.

40th M-Flotilla; formed in Brest on 1 July 1940 from requisitioned French fishing boats.

46th M-Flotilla; formed at St Malo on 8 December 1941 from requisitioned French trawlers.

14th UJ-Flotilla; formed in May 1941 at Lorient from requisitioned and newly built trawlers – emerging from the reorganised 13th U-Bootjagdgruppe that was disbanded in Stavanger, transferring to France, based in Lorient and Auray.

2nd Vp-Flotilla; transferred from Wilhelmshaven to St Malo in May 1940.

7th Vp-Flotilla; moved from Kiel to Brest in May 1940.

6th Sp-Flotilla; formed on 1 July 1941 in Nantes, transferring to Concarneau on 6 July.

4th *Sicherungsdivision* (operational area the southern French Biscay coastline).

8th M-Flotilla; formed in Kiel on 14 March 1941 from Type 35 minesweepers and transferred to Royan.

42nd M-Flotilla; formed in La Rochelle on 8 July 1940 from requisitioned French fishing boats and transferred to Les Sables d'Olonne.

Kapitän zur See Heinrich Bramesfeld, the second commander of the 2nd *Sicherungsdivision* responsible for the English Channel zone of operations following the death of Korvettenkapitän Karl Weniger.

44th M-Flotilla; formed in November 1940 at La Rochelle from requisitioned French fishing boats.

4th Vp-Flotilla; transferred from the North Sea to Bordeaux.

2nd Sp-Flotilla; formed in Wesermünde on 1 July 1940 and transferred incrementally to Royan by 9 August 1941.

Operation Cerberus: The 'Channel Dash'

During the spring of 1941 a third heavy ship appeared in Brest. *Prinz Eugen*, commanded by KzS See Helmuth Brinkmann, had departed Germany in company with *Bismarck* for action against North Atlantic convoys. However, the raiders met with disaster. After a promising start – the famous sinking of HMS *Hood* – the two formidable ships were harried by considerable British forces, *Prinz Eugen* dashing for Brest while the *Bismarck* was sunk on 27 May.

The presence of three large warships in Brest during June 1941 provoked a surge in British bombing and *Prinz Eugen* was hit next, a bomb penetrating her port side, killing fifty men and temporarily immobilising her. With *Gneisenau* already damaged, only *Scharnhorst* was able to leave Brest during July for exercises near La Rochelle though she too would not remain unscathed and returned to Brest suffering a 7° list to starboard after being hit by a British bomb.

Their continued presence in France was in line with Raeder's belief of a 'fleet in being' that posed a significant potential threat to the enemy and

Sperrbrecher 19 'Rostock' leads *Scharnhorst*. The passage of three heavy German ships through the English Channel in broad daylight was a stunning victory for the Germans, though ultimately a strategic defeat.

required them to dedicate resources to counter it. However, Hitler had become increasingly obsessed with the possibility of an Allied invasion of occupied Norway and demanded the ships return to Germany. Planning for the operation was exhaustive and it wasn't until early 1942 that the Kriegsmarine finally attempted to bring their ships home.

The British Admiralty anticipated just such an plan, aware of the precarious position of the ships in Brest. However, expecting the three ships to make their attempt under cover of darkness the Royal Navy was caught off-guard by the daring German decision to send them dashing up the English Channel with strong Luftwaffe and Kriegsmarine escort in broad daylight. Raeder's staff planners had decided that it was more important to conceal the ships' departure from Brest in darkness than actually pass through the Channel during those hours. Boats of the 13th M-Flotilla, 20th Vp-Flotilla and *Sperrbrecher 145* in company with *M1407* began covert minesweeping missions of the route to be taken by the three ships in what was code-named Operation Cerberus. The minesweeping was continued by assorted other units under a bewildering array of code names including Mandarine, Torero, Ganges, Korsika and Labyrinth.

The planned transit of the large ships would take 14 hours to complete and *Scharnhorst*, *Gneisenau* and *Prinz Eugen*, escorted by six destroyers, cleared the Brest net barrage at 2245hrs on 11 February 1942, slipping past the submarine HMS *Sealion* that had been despatched to watch for just such an event. Their departure was also missed by patrolling radar-equipped aircraft due to faulty equipment. Admiral Otto Ciliax, C–in–C of German battleships and previously captain of the *Scharnhorst*, commanded Cerberus. The Luftwaffe's *Luftflotte* 3 provided dense fighter protection (Operation Donnerkeil) with a continuous strength of sixteen fighters to be maintained

Depot ship for the 3rd R–Flotilla *Von der Groeben*, formerly the minesweeper *M507*, photographed here in Saint–Malo.

Laying mines from a Kriegsmarine ship.

by relay over the ships during the hours of daylight and a larger reserve force on immediate standby. This support was controlled by Oberst Adolf Galland, with a Luftwaffe liaison officer, Oberst Max Ibel, aboard the *Scharnhorst*.

The naval escort was formidable; one destroyer flotilla, three torpedo boat flotillas and three S-boats flotillas were accompanied by eleven flotillas under VA Ruge's control. Altogether the overlapping Security Forces running the length of the Channel comprised 1st, 2nd, 4th, 5th and 12th M-Flotillas, 2nd, 3rd and 4th R-Flotillas and 13th, 15th and 18th Vp-Flotillas. The converted trawlers of the auxiliary flotillas stood no chance of keeping pace with the fast-moving main body, but they would provide outpost support and additional flak cover for the expected British interception.

[Orders] provide that on D-day the route which the Brest group is to follow for its Channel breakthrough be swept in sections by the 2nd 12th and 1st Minesweeper Flotillas, and the 2nd and 4th R-Flotillas. In case of bad weather the 4th Mine Sweeper Flotilla will supplant the 4th R-Flotilla. Otherwise, the 4th Mine Sweeper Flotilla is to remain on alert in Boulogne. The 3rd R-Flotilla will be on alert in Calais. Furthermore, an attempt will be made to have two steam trawler-type vessels each in readiness in Cherbourg, Le Havre, Fecamp, Dieppe, Boulogne, Calais, and Ostende.[46]

It was not until 1042hrs that patrolling Spitfires sighted the German ships, the aircraft obeying orders to maintain radio silence and therefore unable to report the Cerberus forces until they landed 27 minutes later. The British responded with air and naval attacks that were hampered by poor co-ordination and bad weather, although pressed home with great courage and dash. Ultimately they were unsuccessful. Damage was inflicted on *Scharnhorst* and *Gneisenau* by mines, though all three capital ships reached Germany. The sole loss to the Germans was a small *Vorpostenboot*, the 292-ton *V1302* 'John Mahn'. At 1550hrs, Coastal Command Hudson bombers attacked the Cerberus squadron, two bombs hitting *V1302* on the port side and ripping the hull open. The ship sank in 35 minutes, all twelve crewmen going with her to the bottom. Cerberus had succeeded and British prestige had suffered another humiliating blow at a time when the war was swinging against them in North Africa. However, though deemed a German triumph, the removal of the potential threat posed by the battleships and heavy cruiser to shipping in the Atlantic was actually a strategic victory for the Allies. Despite the British press not fully realising it at the time, and lambasting the military command, the balance of power in the Atlantic Ocean had tipped irrevocably in their favour.

Italy forces German Commitment to the Mediterranean

By the time that the large ships had returned to Germany, two new theatres of operations had opened that would alter the course of the war. During September 1940 an ill-conceived Italian invasion of British-occupied Egypt had been launched from the Libyan province of Cyrenaica. The Italian advance was soon checked and then beaten back by British forces during December, throwing the Italians westwards in disarray. In the meantime, Mussolini, somewhat irked by German troops being moved into Axis Romania without his knowledge or consent, had begun what would swiftly become a second unsuccessful venture in October 1940 when Italian troops attacked Greece. Believing the country to be something of a soft target, Italian troops were woefully unprepared for the ferocity of the Greek defence and counter-attack. Turkey had immediately declared itself neutral in the Graeco-Italian war and by early November Italian troops were retreating back past their start-lines in Albania, comprehensively beaten by Greek forces. To compound Italian woes, the Royal Navy launched a devastating air raid on their fleet anchorage at Taranto on the night of 11 December 1940, the loss of several capital ships swinging the Mediterranean naval balance of power firmly in favour of the British.

Though irritated by his troublesome ally's military folly, Hitler dedicated German forces to both theatres of action. Raeder had long pushed for naval operations in the Mediterranean, despite his previous conference with Admiral Domenico Cavignari in June 1939 in which the Mediterranean had been designated an Italian sphere of responsibility. After the signing of the Anti-Comintern Pact between Germany and Italy in 1937, Italian military chiefs had urged talks between military chiefs of staff and despite prolonged German hesitation, Raeder and Cavignari had met in Fredrickshaven on 20 June 1939. By the end of their conference agreement was reached on the exchange of technical information and the respective nation's worldwide areas of operations. Germany remained responsible for the North, Baltic and Arctic Seas as well as the Atlantic Ocean, while Italy was made responsible for the Mediterranean, Black and Red Seas. The Indian and Pacific Oceans became an area of shared responsibility, though a separation of forces committed to those areas was also foreseen. This agreement – like that reached between the German and Italian army chiefs – paved the way for parallel wars rather than a true alliance of nations with one common goal; Italy's catastrophic attempted invasion of Greece the result.

With Italy now humiliated and her status as junior partner in the 'Pact of Steel' confirmed, Raeder pressed for a German commitment to the Mediterranean. He reasoned that if British strength both there and in the Near East could be nullified then Italian forces would be able to complete an invasion of East Africa and the Indian Ocean would then be under Axis domination. His plans involved the conquering of Gibraltar with Spanish assistance (Operation Felix), the invasion of Malta (Operation Herkules) and the seizure of the Suez Canal followed by a push through Palestine and Syria to the Turkish border, placing Axis forces in a good position to assist a future invasion of the Soviet Union and its Caucasian oilfields. If the agreement of Vichy France could also be secured, airbases in Vichy-controlled North Africa could even assist in the Battle of the Atlantic. Of course, the requisite agreements from either Pétain or Spain's General Franco were never secured and Raeder's grand plan failed whereupon Hitler, disappointed by Vichy and Spanish obduracy, looked to the East once again.

Yet the arrival of British troops in Greece to bolster the Hellenic forces placed an Allied presence on Germany's future southern flank of the planned invasion of the Soviet Union. After Mussolini's appeals to bolster exhausted Italian troops in Cyrenaica, Hitler despatched the first units of what would become the Afrika Korps and opened German operations in North Africa. On Wednesday 12 February 1941, General Erwin Rommel arrived in Tripoli at the head of the 5th Light Division. Ten days later he attacked El Agheila.

While Rommel swung into action, Hitler concurrently ordered planning for the invasion of Greece and Yugoslavia, the latter having suffered an anti–German coup d'état after the government that had signed the Tripartite Pact on 25 March was deposed. This invasion began on 6 April and by the end of that month mainland Greece was occupied by the Wehrmacht, the last Allied bastion of Crete falling to a German airborne attack in May. The conquered territory was then divided between three Axis powers: Germany, Italy and Bulgaria. The bulk of Greece would be under Italian control with German forces holding the strategically important regions of Athens, Thessaloniki, Central Macedonia, Florina and several Aegean islands, including most of Crete. While Bulgaria occupied most of Thrace, the Italians took control of the Ionian and Aegean islands, the Peloponnese, Thessaly and the majority of Attica. With this expansion of occupied territories, the Kriegsmarine would be required to furnish further Security Forces for the region as OKM noted that protection of the various German-occupied areas could 'only be guaranteed if coastal forces and occupation of the hinterland is in the hands of German forces'.[47]

5

Sun and Steel: The Security Forces move into North Africa and the Soviet Union, 1941–1942

DURING February 1941, MGK West had ordered the establishment of *'Dienststelle Admiral Z'* for the control of potential forces in the Southern European region. The post became *Admiral Südost* (Admiral South-East) during April and finally *Marinegruppenkommando Süd* in July 1941. The original commander, KA Lothar von Arnauld de la Perière, a U-boat ace of the previous war, was killed in an aircraft crash at Le Bourget in February as he travelled to take up his new post, and he was replaced by Admiral Karl-Georg Schuster. With headquarters in Sofia, Bulgaria, this new command was responsible for the impending German commitment to the Balkans and the Black Sea. However, apart from the craft of the *Donauflottille* and transport units, no vessels were as yet directly under Schuster's control. Instead they were grouped into regional sub-commands: *Kommandierender Admiral Schwarzes Meer*, established in Bucharest and *Kommandierender Admiral Ägäis* in Philippopel, Bulgaria, which moved to Athens and then Thessaloniki following the Greek surrender (the latter post had begun life as *Dienststelle Marinebefehlshaber 'A'*, then becoming *Marinebefehlshaber Griechenland* in April 1941 and finally *Admiral Ägäis* in July). Konteradmiral Hans-Hubertus von Stosch held the post until September 1941, his remit involving coastal defence and the organisation and protection of supply convoys to North Africa. With only a light naval commitment at this point of the war, his command comprised combined German and Italian elements.

In April 1941 the Kriegsmarine commissioned the first of four *Küstenschutzflottillen* for service in the Aegean. The *10. Küstenschutzflottille* was based in Thessaloniki under the command of KKdR DrIng. Heinz Peters, the former commander of *UJ126* and the 12th UJ-Flotilla. His unit was comprised of three types of vessels; minesweepers, of which he had fourteen requisitioned and converted Greek vessels (numbered '*10M1*' – '*10M4*' and '*10M7*' – '*10M14*', '*10M17*' and '*10M19*'); five *U-Jäger* which were again requisitioned locally ('*10V1*' – '*10V5*'); and, in 1942, an additional force of four *Marinefährprähme* (*F308*, *F327*, *F330* and *F370*).

Marinefährprahme

The *Marinefährprähme* (MFP, naval ferry barges) had been developed as a direct result of the aborted Operation Sealion. Preparations for the invasion of Great Britain had starkly highlighted the lack of suitable landing craft, forcing a reliance on hastily-converted civilian barges. All branches of the Wehrmacht were invited to submit proposals for landing craft designs, the Luftwaffe developing the *Siebel Fähre* (Siebel ferry, named after its creator, aircraft designer Luftwaffe Oberst Fritz Siebel) constructed of two bridge-building pontoons connected by a platform with BMW aircraft engines mounted astern for propulsion. The remainder of the platform carried the payload; vehicles were able to embark and disembark via a bow ramp. Constructed in moderate quantities, variants were built that carried artillery, headquarters facilities and field hospitals.

Meanwhile, Kriegsmarine experimentation had resulted in a list of requirements for a vessel capable of being used either a landing craft or supply vessel. It needed to be cheap to construct, have a retractable bow ramp, a large carrying capacity and the ability to operate in sea state 5 (wave height of 3m). The resultant 155-ton design incorporated all of these features, constructed of riveted steel with a raised stern and bow complete with ramp. The aft portion of the cargo area was enclosed by a steel roof giving a maximum clearance of 2.74m, the forward section featuring removable corrugated iron shutters. Three six-cylinder Deutz diesel truck engines were

A Siebel ferry puts out from harbour. Designed by the aircraft designer Luftwaffe Oberst Fritz Siebel, these were one solution to the lack of efficient landing craft highlighted during preparations for Operation Sealion.

MFP *F387* puts to sea in Dutch waters. This particular MFP would soon be transferred to the Mediterranean. (Bundesarchiv)

placed in a stern engine room above which the wheelhouse was mounted, both protected by 20mm–25mm armour plating. The craft could make 10.5 knots but were found to be only able to manage sea state 2 at full load. *Marinefährprähme* were equipped with MES mine defence which interfered with magnetic compass navigation, requiring pilot boats to guide them in operation. At first they were equipped with two 20mm flak but, like most Kriegsmarine security vessels, they would be considerably up-gunned as the war progressed. The original crew complement was two officers and ten men.

Highly successful, MFPs were built in over a dozen different shipyards in both Germany and occupied territories, resulting in a wide range of modifications to the general design. The initial model became known as 'Type A', three variants following:

Type B, where the load floor was lowered to provide a cargo area clearance of 3.19m;
Type C, with an additional 10cm added to the height odf the cargo area;
Type D, with the fully-riveted construction changed to partially welded. The hull was lengthened and widened and the carrying capacity increased to 140 tons, capable of accommodating a Tiger I heavy tank. The wheelhouse and engine room were moved slightly forward with reinforced armour and weaponry added, particularly for defence against aircraft. By this stage, the crew had also increased to a standard twenty-five men.

Additionally, like its Luftwaffe counterpart, different requirements resulted in specific variants as the war progressed and their employment frequently became more akin to that of the *Vorpostenboote*. Three MFPs were converted into hospital vessels, four into tankers, four into repair ships, forty into dedicated minesweepers or *Sperrbrecher* and one into a *U-Jäger*; *UJ118*. The dedicated *Minenfährprähm* were used primarily in the Adriatic and the Black Sea, carrying anywhere between thirty-six and fifty-four mines depending

An *Artilleriefährprähme* at sea. The existing *Marinefährprähme* hull proved highly adaptable for conversion to accommodate specific requirements, amongst them a relatively stable gun platform for naval fire support.

on the variant; the mines were loaded via the front ramp on installed rails and dropped over the stern. Alternatively, if the situation required retasking, the rails could carry sixteen *Sturmboot* for infantry amphibious landings.

Additionally, 141 were permanently converted into gunboats (*Artilleriefährprähme*). This was achieved by fitting armament consisting of two 88mm and one 75mm gun and two 20mm *Vierling*. The cargo hold was converted into a magazine protected by armour 100mm thick, bolstered by 10cm of concrete filling the adjacent bulwarks. The overall increase in weight reduced the *Artilleriefährprähme*'s maximum speed to 8 knots. The crew quarters were also enlarged to accommodate the extra gunners. Of shallow draught, they became extremely effective in inshore waters, operating in Northern Europe, the Black Sea (all such vessels had their pennant numbers prefixed 'AF'), within the Mediterranean ('KF') and on the Danube ('AT').

In December 1941, it had become apparent that many MFPs would be required for transport and supply operations in the Black Sea and the Aegean; the Allied submarine menace was guaranteed to increase rather than decrease while there would be little opportunity to bolster German ASW defences. For this reason, barges were considered the safest and most suitable means of transport, requiring no escort and the risk of loss of materiel and personnel in each case being relatively small. Schuster proposed that Von Stotsch at once order the construction of fifty MFPs, the best building facility beingfound in Palermo. As SKL recorded, it was likely that 'the Seelöwe will be asleep for quite a while' and the barges were not needed in France.

By the end of 1941 three more *Küstenschutzflottillen* had been established in the Aegean; the 11th at Mudros, the 12th at Piraeus and the 13th at Suda in Crete. All three flotillas comprised the same basic sub-division of vessel types as Peters' flotilla in Thessaloniki. Apart from these auxiliary units, the first unit of the Kriegsmarine Security Forces to serve in the Mediterranean was the 21st UJ-Flotilla, patrolling the waters between the Dardanelles and Crete. Based in Piraeus, the flotilla was commanded by FK Günther von Selchow who had successfully led the 11th UJ-Flotilla since the outbreak of war. Coupled with the, requisitioned *U-Jäger*, von Selchow would also control the minelayers *Bulgaria*, *Drache* and *Zeus* as well as the auxiliary minelayers *Otranto*, *Alula* and *Gallipoli*.

Operation Barbarossa: the invasion of the Soviet Union

While the Southern Front was being established in the Mediterranean, on 22 June 1941 German forces launched Operation Barbarossa and attacked the Soviet Union, opening the Eastern Front. Raeder had consistently lobbied for German forces to concentrate all of their power on the defeat of Great Britain before any diversion of strength elsewhere, but Hitler believed that a swift victory over the Soviet Union would eliminate the last existing threat on mainland Europe and allow Germany to then deal with the troublesome island nation. On 18 December 1940 Adolf Hitler had put his signature to a decree distributed to the military services, designated 'Directive 21'. In it he outlined the plan to 'crush Soviet Russia in a lightning campaign, even before the termination of hostilities with Great Britain'. Somewhat counter-intuitively – but coinciding with Raeder's desire to keep naval striking power in the Atlantic – the role of the Kriegsmarine during this huge offensive was to be primarily defensive in nature:

> In addition to defending the German coast, the Kriegsmarine will have the mission of preventing enemy naval forces from forcing their way out of the Baltic Sea. Once the Leningrad area has been seized, the Russian Baltic Fleet will have been deprived of all its bases. Since its situation will then be altogether hopeless, major naval engagements prior to that time must be avoided. After the Russian fleet has been eliminated, it will be important to establish full-scale maritime traffic in the Baltic, including the logistical support of ground forces in the Northern part of the Russian theatre (mine sweeping!).

Correspondingly, the Kriegsmarine's commitment to Barbarossa in the Baltic was relatively small compared to the strength of the Soviet Red Banner Fleet. Operating in tandem with the offensive formations of twenty-eight S-boats and five U-boats, the Security Forces' primary task was establishing minefields. Ten minelayers were allocated for service in the Baltic, the full strength available in June 1941: *Brummer* (ex-*Olav Tryggvason*), *Tannenberg*, *Hansestadt Danzig*, *Königin Luise*, *Cobra*, *Kaiser*, *Preussen*, *Roland*, *Skagerrak*, and *Versailles*, all controlled by *Führer der Minenschiff* KaptzS Arnold Bentlage. A large minesweeper contingent was also committed – the 5th,

15th, 17th, 18th and 31st Flotillas – as well as *Sperrbrecher 11 'Belgrano'*, *Sp169 'Ceres'*, *Sp6 'Magdeburg'* and *Sp138 'Friedrich Karl* from the 1st and 6th Sp-Flotillas and *Räumboote* of the 1st and 5th R-Flotillas. *Vorpostenboote* from 3rd VP-Flotilla and trawlers of the 11th UJ-Flotilla were also assigned to minelaying, ASW work and escort duties.

There were also two *Minenräumschiffe*, *Minenräumschiffe 11 'Osnabruck'* and *MRS 12 'Nürnberg'*, allocated to Barbarossa. These were large converted merchant vessels that carried a number of small pinnaces equipped for minesweeping in extremely shallow or estuarine waters;

On 26 February 1941, Admiral Otto Schniewind, SKL Chief of Staff, and Generaloberst Franz Halder, the Army's chief planner for Barbarossa, had met to discuss the issue of naval support for Army Group North which was tasked with occupying the Baltic States. Schniewind had informed Halder that no major warships would be available to support the advancing land forces. However, supply convoys of freighters and barges could travel through the Baltic dependent on the developing naval situation and the ability of the Germans to lay the extensive defensive minefields planned.

On 29 May the naval Barbarossa forces, commanded for the duration of the immediate invasion by Generaladmiral Carls as MGK Nord, began moving to their jumping-off points in the Baltic, including ports in Finland. *Minenschiffgruppe Nord* was stationed in Turku, comprising *Tannenberg*, *Brummer*, *Hansestadt Danzig* and half of the 5th R-Flotilla with a covering force of S-boats from 2nd S-Flotilla. Further east, in Porkkala, *Minenschiffgruppe Cobra*, comprising *Cobra*, *Königin Luise* and *Kaiser* with the remainder of the 5th R-Flotilla and S-boats of the 1st S-Flotilla, was ready to begin the laying of the first major minefields.

Finland had become a willing ally in Germany's Eastern ambitions after months of Soviet demands for resources and military access following their defeat in 1940. However, their role was at first covert, simply allowing German forces the use of their ports and coastal waters. It would be three days after Germany launched its attack that Finland would move into open action, the start of their so-called Continuation War. Opposite Finland, the Baltic States of Lithuania, Latvia and Estonia were also highly sympathetic to a Soviet defeat. They had been plundered by a Soviet occupation that had begun on 14 June 1940 while the world's attention was focussed on the German war in France. With their elected governments forced to step down and replaced by Soviet puppet regimes, mass deportations had followed. thousands being shipped to almost certain death in Siberia. In August 1940, the Soviet Union formally annexed all three states, making them a part of the USSR.

Beginning on the night of 19 June, Kriegsmarine minelayers began sowing three huge barrages ('Wartburg I–III') stretching from the northernmost East Prussian port Memel to the Swedish island of Öland, to protect German home waters. Initially, the fields contained 1500 mines and 1800 explosive buoys to prevent minesweeping. These thick barrages required accurate piloting and escorts for ships traversing them, provided by the 11th UJ-Flotilla based in Memel and Stolpmünde. The Russian light cruiser *Kirov* observed the minelayers west of Libau (known as Liepāja in Latvian), but did not intervene; Soviet standing orders forbade any offensive action. *Minenschiffgruppe Nord*, with six R-boats escorted by four S-boats, began sowing the 'Apolda' minefield between Örö and Takhona, blocking the entrance to the western Baltic north of Dago Island. A Soviet destroyer and three patrol boats were visible but again did nothing to intervene. However, at 0221hrs in the light summer night, two Soviet fighters strafed the ships with machine-gun fire, but were chased away by German flak without casualties.

Minenschiffgruppe Cobra, with five R-boats and escorted by S-boats, laid the 'Corbetha' field between Kallbadagrund and Pakerort, effectively blocking the central Baltic north of Estonia, once again observed by silent Soviet warships as they dropped 400 EMC contact mines and 700 floating mines. Elsewhere S-boats and minesweepers added their own small mine payloads to the growing defensive fields. Early the following morning, Operation Barbarossa began and the Wehrmacht marched eastwards.

The initial Soviet naval response was also to begin laying defensive minefields across the entrance to the Gulf of Finland. Providing cover for the minelayers, the heavy cruiser *Maxim Gorky* and three destroyers left the Gulf of Riga and ran into German mines, the cruiser losing her forecastle and the destroyer *Gnevnyj* sinking. *Maxim Gorky* was towed to Reval (Tallinn), made seaworthy and moved to Kronstadt a few days later.

Operation Barbarossa achieved stunning success on land, despite large pockets of dogged Soviet resistance. The Wehrmacht rapidly advanced through the Baltic States and on 29 June Libau, which had been abandoned by the Soviet Navy, was occupied by elements of the 291st Infantry Division though heavy street fighting raged for several days. Windau had also been abandoned while Daugavgriva and Riga were on the verge of evacuation before the German onslaught. The loss of Libau was particularly serious for the Soviets as they had significantly reinforced the port as the principal base of the Soviet Baltic Fleet. Minesweepers of all flotillas committed to Barbarossa continued minelaying along the existing 'Apolda' field as well as the 'Juminda' barrage east of Tallinn, which wouldlaid primarily by *Cobra*, *Kaiser* and *Königin Luise*. This would become probably the most successful single German minefield of the war: 2828 mines and 1487 explosive buoys accounting for twelve warships and thirty-five merchant ships sunk, with another three warships and eleven merchant ships severely damaged.

On the morning of 4 July, S-boats and their tender *Adolf Lüderitz* sailed

The minelayer *Roland* in port. Extensive mine barrages would become a central feature of the Security Forces' Baltic war against the Soviet Union.

from Memel to Libau to continue covering minelaying operations, the final field being sown by *Brummer* that night under S-boat escort. The German stock of mines had now been exhausted. Two nights later the S-boats covered minesweeping in the approaches to Riga by *MRS11 Osnabrück* and *M31*, clashing with Soviet destroyers in a battle in which no serious damage was suffered by either side.

The German 'Wartburg' minefields connected at their northern end with Swedish defensive fields laid on 28 June following German requests. However, notification of the Swedish barrage, though passed to OKM, never reached German ships and, somewhat ironically, the most significant losses suffered by the Kriegsmarine in the Baltic during July 1941 were to these 'neutral' mines. On 9 July, as the three minelayers *Hansestadt Danzig*, *Preussen* and *Tannenberg* headed west escorted by the 5th R-Flotilla, they blundered

127

into the mines and were sunk. Nine men were killed aboard *Hansestadt Danzig*. *Tannenberg* slowly sank, and *Preussen*'s forward bulkhead ruptured after the mine blasted the auxiliary engine room, the crippled ship being scuttled with explosives. A fourth minelayer, *Königin Luise*, would also be lost to a Soviet submarine mine on 25 September while returning to Helsinki.

Other German ships were destroyed in the morass of minefields throughout the Baltic during July. Between 22 and 26 June, the Soviet minesweeper *T204* laid several defensive minefields totalling about 207 mines near Libau that would sink the minesweeper *M3134* on 1 July and *UJ113 'Nordmark'* nine days later. The mines laid by *T204* stayed active for weeks, eventually also sinking *V309 'Martin Donandt'*, *M1708 'Aldebaran'* and *M1706 'Gertrud Kämpf'*. The minesweepers *M201* and *M3131 'Nordmark'* were sunk in the Irben Strait by Soviet mines of a different field and *R53* and *R63* damaged. *Minenräumschiffe 11 'Osnabruck'* was travelling under the escort of the minesweeper *M23* from Riga to Pernau via the Irben Strait when *M23* was heavily damaged by a mine and beached, later being successfully salvaged.

On 5 July MGK Ost ordered *MRS11 Ösnabruck* to deploy her twelve small motor pinnaces to sweep for mines in the shallow waters of Riga harbour. Escorted by *M23* and *M31* of the 5th M-Flotilla, the three ships avoided Soviet bombing before encountering a Soviet force consisting of the destroyers *Serdityi* and *Silnyi* and two minesweepers engaged in minelaying off the Sworbe Peninsula. The Soviets opened fire at long range, straddling *Ösnabruck* which returned fire when her lighter guns were in range. *M31* attempted to lay smoke but the machinery malfunctioned. However, as she turned to begin the attempt the attacking Soviets misidentified her as a destroyer preparing to fire torpedoes and abruptly broke off the action. The gunners aboard *M31* hit *Silnyi* which laid smoke and retreated, further long-range gunfire achieving little more than churning up the sea as the battle petered out.

Soviet surface forces also launched more determined attacks on German convoys in the Gulf of Riga, four MTBs attacking a convoy of ten supply ships and transports under the combined escort of minesweepers, *Vorpostenboote* and S-boats on 13 July. Soviet aircraft added their weight to the assault, as did the cruiser *Kirov* and supporting destroyers. Once battle was joined, further MTBs engaged the S-boats in running battles while the larger Soviet ships attempted to attack the convoy itself. Ultimately, only the landing ship *Deutschland* was sunk with minimal loss of life, though minor damage was suffered by other ships as the Germans withdrew behind smoke screens and under Luftwaffe Stuka cover. The new Soviet naval attacks, while only causing minimal damage, at least served to delay German attempts to force the Irbe Strait and transport troops by sea for an assault on Estonia.

Nonetheless, despite steady casualties, the Germans prevailed. Over following weeks German troops battered their way eastward through the

The sinking of the minelayers *Hansestadt Danzig*, *Preussen* and *Tannenberg* (pictured) by Swedish mines on 28 June 1941. As a second ship burns in the distance. *Räumboote* of the 5th R-Flotilla rescue the crew.

Baltic States; Lithuania was occupied by 24 June, Latvia by 10 July and Estonia's capital Tallinn (Reval) falling on 28 August. The Security Flotillas continued their dual roles of minesweepers and minelayers, as well as escorting supply convoys and hunting enemy submarines. The Soviet Red Banner Fleet had been successfully bottled up to the east in Leningrad, where it became the object of Luftwaffe attention that strived, unsuccessfully, to destroy both it and the city's defences.

With the Estonian mainland conquered there only remained the islands of Ösel (Saaremaa) and Dago (Hiiumaa) which controlled the sea lanes to and from the Gulf of Riga. The low-lying islands had been heavily fortified by their Soviet garrison that numbered over 20,000 men, including naval troops, engineers and regular infantry.

To conquer the islands, two distinct plans had been formulated by Army Group North; Beowulf I, to be launched from Latvia, and Beowulf II from the western coast of Estonia. While the battle for Tallinn raged, it was Beowulf II that was put into effect using elements of three infantry divisions and supporting Brandenburger commando troops. The plan required three diversionary attacks: Südwind, against Koiguste Bay, Sutu Bay and Kuressaare on Ösel; Westwind against Vormsi and Ösel's offshore islands; and Nordwind directed against Dagö Island. Beowulf II was launched on 8 September.

The diversionary attack Westwind utilised the *Erprobungsverband Ostsee* (Test Detachment Baltic), under the command of KzS Johannes Rieve for the first time. This unit had begun studying amphibious assault methods and incorporated five *Schwere Artillerieträger* (SAT), three *Leichte Artillerieträger* (LAT), twelve steam tugs, twelve MFPs (type AF46), twelve lighters, thirty motor boats, three motor yachts, thirteen coasters (six fitted with *Sturmboot* launching ramps), twenty-six Siebel ferries, five freighters and the hospital ship *Pitea*. By 10 September 1941, elements of *Erprobungsverband Ostsee* were based in the port-cities of Liepaja, Riga, Roja and Ventspils in Latvia. This was to be the first operational use of the MFP and its variants and began with an attack against the small Estonian island of Vormsi, capturing 200 Soviet prisoners. Then began assaults on the remaining Estonian islands.

The Westwind assault on Ösel opened on 13 September, the commander of 11th UJ-Flotilla, FK Günther von Selchow, exercising tactical command

Landing craft of Operation Beowulf.

while the main Beowulf II attack developed elsewhere. For Westwind the commander of 5th M-Flotilla, FK Rudolf Lell, controlled two LATs (*Getchen II* and *Orion*) as well as four minesweepers, four R-boats and seven tugs which landed troops on the small fortified island of Abruka South of Kuressaare. At daybreak KKdR Hellmut Stimming, commander of 17th M-Flotilla, launched an attack against Kuressaare itself with the SAT '*Robert Müller*', the LAT '*Germania*', seven minesweepers and four tugs from Riga. Four more minesweepers and seventeen large transport vessels attacked to the East in Koiguste Bay. The sole German ship lost was the 467-ton *M1707* '*Lüneburg*', disabled by a Soviet mine and then hit by a 130mm shell that blew a hole in her stern, the crew abandoning ship and losing one man, Matrose Heinz Bahr, in the sinking.

By 21 October 1941 all of the Estonian islands were firmly in German hands and the Soviets had lost approximately 19,000 men captured and 4700 killed while German casualties amounted to 2850 men. The *Erprobungs-verband Ostsee* had proved highly successful and the unit was disbanded in December 1941 with elements used to create the 13th and 17th *Landungsflottillen*.

War in the Arctic

Alongside the Baltic, the invasion of the Soviet Union opened two other theatres of operations for the Kriegsmarine. In the Arctic, Soviet naval forces had been slow to take the offensive although the German land assault on Murmansk had rapidly degenerated into static trench warfare after early gains and the front line subsequently barely moved for years. Soviet troops successfully landed on the Rybachiy Peninsula in July 1941 ensuring that a significant portion of the available German troops were pinned down containing the bridgehead which they never managed to eliminate.

With German troops firmly entrenched, in August 1941 the Royal Navy despatched the light cruisers HMS *Aurora* and *Nigeria* and the destroyers HMS *Icarus*, *Antelope* and *Anthony* as escorting force for the passenger liner SS *Empress of Canada*. Their mission was the demolition of the coal mines on Spitzbergen and the evacuation of Soviet and Norwegian citizens. The island's weather, radio and power installations were also to be destroyed in order to deny them to the Germans. By 3 September these tasks were completed although not without difficulty as the Soviet miners had plundered their settlement's vodka stocks and required some 'manhandling' by the British in order to get them aboard the evacuation ships. After delivering the Russians to Archangelsk and returning for the Norwegian miners, the cruisers were advised of a nearby German troop convoy and, leaving the destroyers to shepherd the liner back to Britain, turned to intercept. At 0126hrs on 7 September they made contact with the German convoy consisting of the transports *Barcelona* and *Trautenfels* carrying 1500 *Gebirgsjäger*, escorted by the gunnery training ship *Bremse*, *V6103* '*Nordlicht*', *UJ1701* and *R162*. The first shells from HMS *Nigeria* were fired at 0129hrs, *Bremse* mounting a gallant rearguard action as the rest increased speed for the safety of the Norwegian fjords. Outgunned, *Bremse* closed the distance and laid smoke while opening fire with all guns while taking heavy punishment herself. Over the course of little more than quarter of an hour *Bremse* was reduced to a smoking wreck and sank. As the damaged British withdrew, *Vorpostenboote* mounted a rescue operation but only recovered thirty-seven men, the captain, KK Hermann von Brosy-Steinberg and 159 others going down with their ship. As a consequence, German troop movements by sea in the polar region was temporarily suspended, the extra time and difficulties encountered by marching overland hindering Wehrmacht efforts to launch a offensive that could break the stalemate.

Initial attempts at using S-boats within the Arctic had failed dismally, the waters being far more suited to the converted trawlers of the Security Forces which were soon in action against the Soviets, controlled by KSV *Polarküste* headquartered in Tromsø. Their primary job was convoy protection between Hammerfest and Kirkenes once sailings had resumed. Supply and troop convoys were desperately needed by the land forces in the northern theatre, a region otherwise accessible by only a single difficult road. It was not until 7 July that Soviet submarine activity was first detected off Vardø, the surfaced *Shch401* attacking *UJ177* and *UJ178* with torpedoes after mistaking them for cargo steamers. The *U-Jäger* located *Shch201* and fired several shells, forcing her under where they hammered her with eight depth charges, disabling the stern hydroplanes and blowing several fuses and electrical circuits aboard the submarine. Though damaged, *Shch401* successfully escaped.

Soviet appeals for British assistance brought two Royal Navy 'T'-class submarines to Polyarnyy, arriving in early August and beginning attacks on German shipping in Kola Bay. Eight Soviet submarines were also transferred from the Baltic Sea via the Stalin River/Canal system although results were poor in the first months of the war against Germany. A change in tactics that lessened the grip of shorebound headquarterson operations was subsequently introduced as minelaying by four 'K'-class submarines also began; the minesweeper *M22* was severely damaged by one of their minesat the entrance of Bok Fjord in early November.

On 3 December the Soviet submarine *K3* attacked the escorted steamer *Altkirchen* near Hammerfest. The boat's first Arctic patrol had involved minelaying outside of Mose Fjord, which would later sink the Norwegian coaster *Inge* on 30 January 1942. Having completed this. the Soviet skipper took his large submarine on patrol, firing four torpedoes at *Altkirchen*, which were sighted and evaded at the moment that *K3*'s conning tower broke surface

The opening of the war against the Soviet Union extended the duties of the Security Forces into the Arctic Ocean.

due to bad depth-keeping after the torpedoes had left the tubes. The steamer's three *U-Jäger* escorts sighted *K3* and opened fire, driving her under where they subjected her to accurate depth-charging that cracked one of her fuel bunkers. Trailing oil, there was little chance of escaping submerged and so the Soviet submarine surfaced and opened fire with its guns, hoping to take advantage of the boat's surface speed. The Soviet gunfire was devastating, the fifth salvo from the boat's 100mm and two 45mm guns hitting the stern of *UJ1708* and probably detonating the depth charges as the ship immediately exploded and sank. A second escort, *UJ1416*, was also severely damaged and forced to break off the pursuit while *UJ1403* failed to significantly damage the escaping sub. During the action *K3* had fired thirty-nine 100mm rounds and fifty-seven 45mm shells, the boat returning to base for repairs on 5 December.

Both Royal Navy submarines experienced greater success than the majority of their Soviet counterparts. HMS *Tigris* sank 2397 tons of merchant shipping while HMS *Trident* sank three freighters totalling 12,984 tons and damaged a fourth. Both submarines also tangled with German escorts. At 0040hrs on 27 September, Cdr. G. M. Sladen's HMS *Trident* fired a full bow salvo of six torpedoes at what he thought were merchant ships sailing unescorted, hitting the lead vessel which slewed sideways out of formation. Sladen identified her as a trawler while bringing *Trident* closer to finish her off with gunfire. The target was *UJ1201* which had suffered severe damage and twenty men killed in the blast, but nonetheless turned to engage *Trident*. A second escort, *UJ1211*, also increased speed toward *Trident* which crash-dived. Structurally weakened, *UJ1201*'s bow broke off, the stern section later being towed to Hammerfest, while *UJ1211* dropped six depth charges on HMS *Trident* below, causing minor damage and disabling the submarine's gyro and magnetic compasses. After the attacks subsided and everything had remained quiet for an hour, Sladen surfaced and could plainly see *UJ1201* astern, lying dead in the water and apparently sinking with a lifeboat full of survivors visible nearby.

HMS *Trident* also accounted for a second *U-Jäger* during her next patrol. In the course of two attacks on a widely-dispersed convoy of three escorted merchant ships, Sladen hit *UJ1213 'Rau IV'* with one of two torpedoes that sank her by the stern while other escorts dropped ineffectual depth charges at random. Allied submarine commanders had already noted a tangible sense of disorganisation in German ASW tactics and a sense of their unwillingness to engage upon an extended hunt, something that would definitely hamper the efficacy of Germany's *U-Jäger* throughout the war. The root cause may have been the general level of inexperience to be found among the auxiliary vessels of the Kriegsmarine as limited personnel numbers frequently led to the transfer of more experienced men to the U-boat service, still considered the cutting edge of Germany's blunted naval sword. A British Admiralty interrogation report from 1942 of the captured crew of *UJ1404* provides some insight into this:

> A large proportion of her peacetime crew was transferred to the naval service, and remained on board when she was taken over and converted by the Navy in 1939, but they were gradually drafted elsewhere. At the time of her sinking, only one man of her pre-war crew remained. He did not survive . . . The Captain, Leutnant zur See Max Berner, a reserve officer, was killed in action. The crew did not seem to have a very high opinion either of his capabilities or his personality. They described him as unusually stupid in service matters and needlessly callous towards his men . . . Only a sprinkling of the survivors were experienced men. One, for instance, had served since 1935 in the Navy, while another had been a deep-sea fisherman for years before the war. The large majority, however, were very young and inexperienced, mostly aged about 21.

By the end of 1941 the German Security Forces were exhausted. The vessels of the 15th M-Flotilla were in desperate need of repairs after strenuous operations in the East. However, they were called upon to provide relief for ships of the 3rd M-Flotilla whose engines had become completely run down by missions in Norwegian waters. At that point there was only one seaworthy vessel in the 7th R-Flotilla and the 12th UJ-Flotilla was operating far below its effective strength. Urgent appeals were made by GA Boehm, who directly quoted an SKL directive of 31 October 1941, which stated that '*U-Jäger*, minesweeper and R-boat flotillas are either to be brought up to strength or

Christmas aboard a German auxiliary warship of the Security Forces.

to be replaced by new flotillas'. He emphasised his need for escorts with reports from Army units in the polar region suffering such shortages of food that their very survival depended upon the success of maritime supply.

Conversely, to attempt to interfere with British convoys that had begun to supply the Soviet Union via the Arctic, minelaying by the 3100-ton *Ulm* was undertaken after the ship was transferred from the English Channel. Departing Narvik at 0400hrs on 24 August, *Ulm* was under destroyer escort with a distant screen of two U-boats, though once the U-boats considered the region clear of enemy forces *Ulm* then proceeded alone. Under British aerial surveillance and intercepted by HMS *Onslaught*, *Martin* and *Marne* after one day at sea, *Ulm* was sunk after a ferocious bombardment that caused the minelayer to break up and go down in less than three minutes.

On 5 January 1942 GA Rolf Carls of MGK Nord gave a complete inventory of all minesweepers, R-boats and *Vorpostenboote* under his command that demonstrated the critical point his forces had reached. It was no longer possible to transfer further units to other theatres of operations without completely jeopardising Norwegian naval security. However, raw materials, building yards and manpower were insufficient in Germany to begin the necessary expansion of its Security Forces, not least of all due to the unforeseen extension of Kriegsmarine responsibilities into new theatres.

135

UJ1029 of the 12th UJ-Flotilla, stationed in Norway.

The German Naval Staff was compelled to prioritise allocation of whatever forces were available in order to meet the most urgent need at any particular moment. This exhaustive decision-making required a fully-accurate picture of where they would be best employed and remained a problem that plagued the Wehrmacht and Waffen-SS as the scope of Hitler's war expanded beyond expectations and Germany's actual capabilities.

War in the Black Sea

While the offensive against the Soviet Union in the Arctic Circle had stalled, thousands of kilometres away Army Group South was advancing into the Ukraine and towards the Black Sea. Undoubtedly weakened by the diversion of forces that had been used for invading Yugoslavia and Greece in April 1941 and who were still refitting, the southern Wehrmacht forces faced a stiffer Soviet defence than they had anticipated. The port city of Odessa held out under siege for two months before the defenders successfully evacuated to the Crimean Peninsula which became the scene of some of the fiercest fighting on the Eastern Front during 1941. The prize, Sevastopol, was put under siege on 30 October 1941 but stubbornly refused to crack. The key to the Soviet ability to hold both cities was their own Black Sea Fleet, comprising one battleship, five cruisers, three destroyer leaders, eleven modern destroyers, four old destroyers, forty-four submarines, two gunboats, eighteen minesweepers and eighty-four MTBs. Opposing them was the well-trained yet tiny Royal Romanian Navy comprising four destroyers, six fleet torpedo boats, one submarine, five midget submarines, two minelayers and seven

MTBs. During the second half of 1941 the Soviet fleet mounted daring, well-planned and well-executed raids on German Army positions that ranged in size from small commando operations to major amphibious attacks on the eastern Crimea that forced the diversion of German troops from Sevastopol, extending the siege by months and therefore denying the use elsewhere of the heavy weapons deployed against the city.

Elements of the Croatian Naval Legion were also present in the Black Sea during 1941, the Legionnaires wearing German uniforms and initially numbering 350 men but later increasing to approximately 1000. The Croatian Black Sea contingent arrived in Varna on 17 July, training on Romanian minesweepers and submarines and was commissioned as the 23rd M-Flotilla after relocating to Genichesk on the Ukrainian coast of the Sea of Azov. The unit was not initially equipped with ships but subsequently secured forty-seven damaged or abandoned fishing vessels, many of them pinnaces, repairing and crewing the vessels bolstered by local volunteers. The flotilla did not put to sea until April 1942, having served as coastal infantry to that point. The Germans for their part could field only the riverine vessels of the *Donauflottille*.

After the outbreak of war and with no perceived threats in Austria, the *Donauflottille* had been downsized and eventually transferred to the Netherlands during the Spring of 1940 for river patrols. In April 1941 the unit was transferred back to the Danube and placed under the command of the *Admiral Südost/Chef der Marinemission in Rumänien* (Head of the Naval Mission to Romania). Once Barbarossa had begun, the flotilla moved to the Black Sea port of Constanța and became an important original component of Axis naval forces in the region. Korvettenkapitän Fritz Petzel assumed command in July 1941 as the flotilla went to war against the Soviet Union.

The strength and composition of the *Donauflottille* fluctuated greatly during the course of the war, with auxiliary units added as required and if available. The river monitors *Bechelaren* and *Birago* were joined by the former Czech minelayers *FM1* and *FM2*, the captured 180-ton Yugoslavian minelayers *Alexandra*, *Sisak* and *Alzey*, the 222-ton *Wallner Theresia* (which would be destroyed by a mine in Ochakov on 25 October 1941), the former Czech mine barges *MZ1* and *MZ2*, the 635-ton *Sperrbrecher 191 'Motor I'* (commissioned into the flotilla on 7 August 1941 in Brăila, Romania), the auxiliary minesweeper *Alberich*, the converted naval tug/auxiliary minesweeper *Drossel* (taken onto strength on 12 August 1939, transferred to Romania in March 1941 and sunk by a Soviet mine on 24 October in Ochakov), the Hungarian patrol ship *Zagon*, the former Dutch patrol vessel *Zeeland*, Austrian 'Krems' type patrol boats and a depot ship of the 'Kriemhild' type, built in Linz and used as accommodation, transport, supply carrier and floating workshop. There were also twelve purpose-built

Flussräumboote (river minesweepers) constructed by the Lürssen shipyard in Vegesack, Germany between 1938 and 1939, numbered *FR1 to FR12*. The latter's design was undertaken by naval engineers not connected to Lürssen, based on existing Austrian plans that had been drawn up before the Anschluss. The *Flussräumboote* were 15.42m overall length with a 3.3m beam and draught of 88cm. They were capable of a top speed of 12.4 knots, were armoured and carried one small-calibre turreted machine-gun, later replaced by a 20mm MG151 cannon or a MG131 machine-gun. All twelve were ordered from Lürssen in June 1938, *FR1* being launched in September. Each had twin three-bladed screws, turned by Kämper diesel engines and carried some hull armour. The bow was reinforced for icebreaking on the Danube. To accommodate restrictions on weight and draught, the boats were built of a composite of armoured steel for the engine room and helm, shipbuilding steel for below the waterline and the engine mounts and an aluminium, copper and magnesium alloy for the remainder of the hull.

FR1 was commissioned on 9 September 1938, the next five following in rapid succession. These first six boats were stationed in Linz where they underwent intensive trials under the watchful eye oftheir designers, *FR1* actually capsizing during testing which led to the hulls of *FR7* to *FR12* being extended by 2m at the stern making them less sensitive to shallow water and reducing the power needed to propel the boats. The twelve 'FR' boats were soon transferred to the Black Sea to augment Axis minesweeping capability. However, three were sunk by mines during 1941: *FR5* and *FR6* (sunk by Soviet magnetic mines on 6 September in the mouth of the Danube), and *FR12* (sunk on 11 October by a Bulgarian mine), although *FR5* was salvaged and later returned to service. Interestingly, during June 1942, it seemed possible that the *Donauflottille* would be taken over by the SS:

> The SS, which is responsible for policing rivers in occupied territories, is interested in setting up the organization required for this task. The *Donauflottille* is being mentioned in this connection. The Chief, Naval Staff is of the opinion that the navy does not object at all but that it cannot permit the SS to extend its activity to maritime police duties.[48]

The ex-motor vessel *Motor I* had been converted into an experimental *Sperrbrecher*, equipped with VES and designated *Sp191* on 7 August 1941. She would not be the only *Donauflottille* boat thus converted; the 383-ton motor ship *Keppler* commissioned as *Sp192* on 10 April 1943 and the 383-ton *Albrecht Dürer* as *Sp193* on 26 June that same year.

Before the end of 1941 there were also two German minelayers operational in the Black Sea. The first was the 170-ton ex-minsweeper *FM36*, re-christened *Xanten* after being purchased from Romania by the Kriegsmarine and commissioned in October 1941, later redesignated *UJ116* during 1942. The second was the 222-ton *Theresia Wallner*, a river minelayer capable of carrying thirty mines. She was diverted for use in the Black Sea, but she was sunk along with the auxiliary minesweeper *Brusterort* on 25 October 1941 by mines laid by Soviet minesweepers.

On 26 December 1941, Soviet troops made successful seaborne landings on the northern coast of the Kerch Peninsula, establishing five bridgeheads, each holding up to a battalion of infantrymen. While the Wehrmacht was still heavily engaged in attempting to batter Sevastopol into submission, the Soviet ability to land troops in force with naval gunnery support threw the Germans momentarily off balance and caused great concern in Berlin. The besieged Sevastopol garrison was supplied by ships, supported and protected by the Black Sea Fleet who took the opportunity to provide fire support against the besieging Axis troops. When surface ships were judged vulnerable to Luftwaffe attack, submarines were used with equal effectiveness supplying

A river minesweeper (*Flussräumboot*), like those supplied to the *Donauflottille* that saw action in the Black Sea.

2300 tons of ammunition, 1100 tons of food and 574 tons of fuel while evacuating 1400 wounded over the course of seventy-seven missions to the port city. In Berlin, OKW recognised the clear dominance of the Soviet Navy in the Black Sea and immediate plans to transfer U-boats, S-boats and *Räumboote* there were drawn up.

The first four *Räumboote* to be despatched were captured Dutch vessels, former *Mijnenveegeboten MvI, MvII, MvIV* and *MvXII*. Designated *Räumboote Ausland* (Foreign) they were numbered *RA51, RA52, RA54* and *RA56* respectively. Small, shallow-draught vessels, they had been captured at an advanced stage of construction in Amsterdam's De Vries-Lentsch shipyard. Displacing only 51 tons they had a waterline length of 22m, beam of 4.5m and a draught of only 1.3m full load. Two Kromhout diesels gave the boats a top speed of 11 knots, 6 tons of fuel being carried in the bunkers. Lightly armed, they carried one 37mm C/30 flak and up to a maximum of three 20mm C/38 cannon alongside the standard Oropesa sweeping gear. Two other Dutch boats had also been commissioned – *RA53* (ex-*MvIII*) and *RA55* (ex-*Mv11*) – and together the six had comprised part of 36th M-Flotilla, alongside captured Belgian vessels, during the minesweeping operations in the Baltic in October and November 1941. Somewhat confusingly, their appellation had been different at that time, numbered *R201 – R206* before the change was made to adopt the '*Räumboote Ausland*' titles at the end of 1941. By then two of the boats had been lost in the Irben Strait; *RA55* (*R205*) destroyed by a mine on 1 October 1941 and *RA53* (*R203*) by another on 19 November, the stern destroyed and the bow section towed to Windau but judged to be beyond repair.

By the beginning of March 1942, the plans were complete. Six S-boats, eight large *Räumboote*, four small *Räumboote* (the RA boats) and fourteen fishing smacks were to be transported to the Black Sea, S-boats leading the way, and once they had reached Dresden, the R-boats would leave Northern Germany. Transporting the craft from Germany to Romania was an impressive logistical feat. Each vessel had her superstructure and all weapons removed, the stripped hull being towed along the Elbe from Hamburg to the Dresden suburb of Übigau where they were lifted by slipway from the water and craned across to eight-axle trailers for a 450km overland transfer via autobahn to Ingolstadt in southern Germany. Pulled by heavy Kuhlemeyer trucks the trailers (each with solid rubber tires) travelled at a maximum of 8km/hr with rotating shifts of drivers for nearly 60 hours. The manpower required included shipbuilders, drivers, traffic police, security troops and engineers assigned to remove any potential obstacles along the route and to check the structural integrity of any bridges that had to be crossed. Workshop vehicles, communications vehicles and fuel-tanker trucks accompanied each R-boat transport to supply and replenish the heavy Kuhlemeyer trucks. Once in Ingolstadt the boats were returned to the pontoons which had been moved by rail from Dresden and then towed along the Danube River by tugboat to Galaţi in Romania. There the boats were reassembled and would complete the journey to Sulina under their own power.

On 16 April, the four RA-boats were in Hamburg replenishing their supplies before continuing the journey via Dresden and Übigau the following day. Still nominally on the strength of the 36th M-Flotilla, the four boats finally arrived in Constanţa from Sulina at 1900hrs on 8 June 1942. Vizeadmiral Hans-Heinrich Wurmbach (*Kommandierender Admiral Schwarzes Meer*), who had recently moved his headquarters from Bucharest to Eforia near Constanţa, was on hand to greet the new arrivals.

Commander, *Donauflottille* (KK Friedrich-Karl Birnbaum) put into Constanţa from Sulina with four motor minesweepers (RA). These were brought to Sulina from Germany by the Danube route. I welcomed the motor minesweepers upon their arrival and inspected the leading boat. Unfortunately, the length and shape of the bow is not entirely suitable for the rapidly-rising short seas we have here. On passage from Sulina to Constanţa with sea state 4 on their starboard bows, the group showed a loss of speed of one and a half knots. However, on the whole the group will be a valuable addition to our minesweeper strength urgently needed for work in Crimean waters.[49]

They became operational on 10 June, Wurmbach's intention being to transfer them to the small port at Ak Mechet on the western edge of the Crimean Peninsula in order for them to sweep the approach channels used by the recently-arrived *Schnellboote*. He had intended the FR boats of the *Donauflottille* to use Ak Mechet as far back as December 1941, but the winter weather and the general naval situation did not allow it. During their passage to the Crimea, the RA-boats were instructed to sweep the routes from Ochakov to Skadovsk and onwards to Ak Mechet with Oropesa gear. The four were now under the command of the *Donauflottille*, Birnbaum having been designated *Räumchef* Crimea.

Marinefähreprahme also began service in the Black Sea as both transports and auxiliary escort craft. The relatively cheap vessels were being built in both Axis and occupied countries at a tremendous rate and in Varna, Bulgaria, they were in production in three different shipyards. On 26 February 1942 the 1st L-Flotilla was established in Varna, under the command of Kaptlt Max Giele. Originally designated the 1st *Landungs-Lehr-Flottille*, the unit reached operational status and was immediately involved in mining operations to close Perekop Bay to Soviet forces. The flotilla's first casualty was damage from a floating mine to *F130* on 29 April 1942 as she travelled in company with *F132* and *F139* from Constanţa to Skadovsk. The MFPs were carrying 50 UMA mines, 200 explosive floats and fuel, sweeping gear, small arms and food to Skadovsk for use by 'Group Lex', a separate formation of MFPs engaged in minelaying. The mine exploded against *F130*'s starboard bow, the skipper immediately running her ashore where she was beached on a strongly inclined shoreline, the stern barely clearing the surface in 2m of water and with a strong starboard list. The entire crew were taken off after both stern anchors had been drooped to keep her in place, Romanian troops beginning the arduous task of unloading her cargo. Soon, *F130* was flooded as far as the waterline although her radio gear and engine had been undamaged by the blast. Salvage attempts were mounted by other MFPs and river minesweepers of the *Donauflottille* and by 3 May most of the stored small arms, mines, sweeping gear and depth charges had been removed despite the heavy swell. Two dockyard engineers were despatched from Odessa who surveyed the vessel and found the hull breach, the craft eventually being raised and taken for repair in Varna.

The flotilla lost its first vessel totally destroyed on 3 June when *F145*, skippered by StrmMt Maiss, was sunk by a Soviet mine while en route to Ochakov after delivering fuel and equipment for S-boats, one nautical mile south of Karabatsch. Nine men were killed and eight wounded. The stretch of water in which *F145* sank had just been declared mine-free by Odessa's 16th *Hafenschutzflottille*, who came out once again to sweep for mines but again found nothing.

Two of the flotilla's MFPs were assigned as convoy escorts on 10 June. *F133* and *F134* had been launched on 18 April 1941 and commissioned during November. With minesweepers *FR2*, *FR4*, *FR7*, *FR8* and *FR10* they were to escort the freighters *Ardeal*, *Bar Ferdinand* and *Oituz* from Ochakov headed South. At 1414hrs the following day Wurmbach received a radiogram from the naval communications centre in Odessa: 'Heavy explosion aboard the second steamer of the southbound convoy, very thick smoke.'

The 5695-ton Romanian ss *Ardeal* had been hit by the first of three torpedoes from the Soviet submarine *A5*. The American-built 'Holland' class submarine was commanded by Captain (Third Class) Gregory Aronovich Kukui and had recently arrived in Sevastopol from Poti. It was the boat's eighth war patrol and Kukui cruised near Odessa, creeping submerged in the port approaches during daylight hours and then withdrawing to the east to recharge the batteries on the surface at night. During the morning of 11 June, he sighted the German convoy and after positioning his boat, hit *Ardeal* with his first torpedo, the Romanian ship being beached nearby in order to save both herself and the Luftwaffe stores she carried. The escort located *A5* and both MFPs depth-charged her with fiften charges over a 20-minute period before temporarily losing contact. One hour later, as Kukui risked a look through his periscope, he was sighted and depth-charged once again, three charges landing close enough to wreck the boat's gyrocompass, twist the conning tower hatch and damage several other instruments. The German hunters sighted a large oil patch, both remaining on the scene until dark whereupon they put in to Odessa. However, although damaged, *A5* moved away and managed to make enough onboard repairs to remain on station for another week before heading to Tuapse. While the two MFPs were ordered to return at dawn to resume the hunt – soon curtailed due to fog – naval inspectors examined the beached *Ardeal* and found that despite a large hole in the port side on the waterline, the bulkheads were holding and the ship was later salvaged.

This latest submarine attack prompted Wurmbach to cancel further supply convoys through Odessa Bay due to lack of ASW vessels. Thicker minefields flanking the convoy route appeared his sole alternative, coupled with intensive sweeping for enemy mines revealed by the interrogation of captured Soviet sailors. Odessa's 16th *Hafenschutzflottille* carried out a preliminary sweep but with no results, and they and the FR and RA minesweepers from the *Donauflottille* were then placed by Wurmbach directly under the control of a 'Naval Special Duties Detachment'.

The shortage of minesweepers resulted in a defensive posture beingtaken by the Kriegsmarine in the Black Sea while land operations also bogged down against stiff Soviet resistance. Eight large R–boats under construction in French shipyards had originally been earmarked for transfer to the Black Sea.

The award of the Iron Cross Second Class to this Matrosen-Obergefreiter gunner.

The funeral of KzS Karl 'Minus' Weniger; commander of the 2nd *Sicherungsdivision* killed by British aircraft while aboard boats of the 3rd R-Flotilla on 1 October 1940. The *Räumboote* were consigned to the shipyards and later transferred to the Black Sea.

However, due to 'technical reasons' and the pressing time element, the decision was cancelled and the boats retained upon commissioning by MGK West. Instead SKL ordered eight boats from the 3rd R-Flotilla to replace them, which were transferred with officers and crews by the same route used by the *Schnellboote* of the 1st S-Flotilla. Most of the R-boats were already in the shipyards undergoing repair after a serious air attack while minesweeping in the English Channel on 1 October 1940.

Never one to avoid service at sea, the popular commander of the 2nd *Sicherungsdivision*, 42-year-old KzS Karl Weniger, had accompanied the boats of the 3rd R-Flotilla sweeping off Dieppe. In the early evening they were attacked by eight Hurricane IIbs of Manston's RAF 615 Squadron engaged on their routine fighter sweeps of Northern France. 'The almost daily "beat up" this time was an attack on eight "E boats" [*sic*] off Dieppe which were successfully shot up. Several of them were stationary, and flames and smoke were seen coming from one of the boats as the Squadron left the scene.'[50] In mere minutes the R-boats had suffered heavy casualties; Weniger, the flotilla commander Kaptlt Richard Rossow, two officers and eight seamen were killed while twenty men were seriously wounded and another sixteen lightly injured. The damaged R-boats limped back to base whereupon KK Arnulf Hölzerkopf, former commander of the 42nd M-Flotilla, took command. Eight of those damaged boats were chosen for service in the Black Sea: *R33, R35, R36, R37, R163, R164, R165* and *R166*. Three of the remaining four – *R34, R38* and *R40* – were released for service with the

A Kriegsmarine flak gunner. The threat posed by enemy aircraft increased dramatically on all fronts as the war progressed and the Luftwaffe's strength ebbed away.

newly-formed 12th R-Flotilla in Bruges, which would eventually transfer to the Mediterranean in 1943.

Following a brief minesweeping operation near Calais, the flotilla arrived in Cuxhaven by the end of March, moving on to Hamburg to begin the journey to Romania. Ochakov was to be the flotilla's home port and *R35* and *R166* were the first pair to become operational in the Black Sea on 30 June 1942. The first combat mission followed a few days later as they escorted a small convoy of towed barges from Sulina to the Bug estuary. The addition of minesweepers came none too soon for Wurmbach as he lost the only *Sperrbrecher* available at that time in the Black Sea. On 1 July *Sp191* '*Motor I*' struck a mine eight miles west of Ochakov and sank while escorted by four small boats of the *Donauflottille* .

The Southern Front: with Rommel in North Africa

Concurrent with Black Sea deployments, German naval strength in the Mediterranean had also increased. Following the establishment of the 21st UJ-Flotilla in the Aegean in December 1941, the commitment of further

Security Forces was scheduled to the Mediterranean basin. A strong U-boat presence had become established since *U371* passed through the Straits of Gibraltar on 21 September. Vizeadmiral Karl Dönitz had protested strongly about the commitment, considering the Mediterranean unsuitable for U-boat operations and an irritating diversion of strength from the Atlantic where the convoy war would be decided. Raeder too had opposed the deployment, reckoning that safeguarding of Axis supply lines to North Africa was a task wholly unsuited to U-boats and better handled by more effective Italian ASW units. Hitler overruled them both, however, throwing what he considered to be visible support for the embryonic Afrika Korps who, with Italy's already poor showing, remained the sole hope for Axis domination of North Africa. Therefore, by the end of 1941 twenty-seven U-boats had entered the Mediterranean but, despite some stunning initial successes against the Royal Navy, five of them had already been sunk. None would ever return to the Atlantic.

Rommel had requested German R-boats and S-boats for protection of vulnerable supply convoys straggling across the Mediterranean as early as March 1941. However, the decision was taken at OKM to refuse him due to the anticipated operational demands of Barbarossa which was in the advanced stages of preparation. The provision of such forces to the Mediterranean was only examined in July 1941, initially dependent on the successful 'end of the Eastern campaign'.

Unsurprisingly, Rommel's supply situation deteriorated rapidly. The Afrika Korps had made an initial lightning advance between February and May 1941, bypassing the besieged Allied garrison in Tobruk and reaching the Egyptian border, before a critical lack of supplies had brought them to a halt. For nine months the defenders of Tobruk denied the port to Axis forces while also tying up valuable units needed in the push towards the Suez Canal. Rommel's supply lines across the Mediterranean were threatened by British naval and air forces and in North Africa itself stretched all the way back to Tripoli. A British counter-attack mounted during November, Operation Crusader, pushed the Afrika Korps back to El Agheila where Rommel waited to resupply. The Allies destroyed significant quantities of material bound for Tripoli, aided enormously by having broken Germany's Enigma codes. Raeder reported the dire state of affairs to Hitler in a conference at the Wolfsschanze during the afternoon of 13 November:

> As feared by Naval Staff since July, the situation regarding transports to North Africa has grown progressively worse and has now reached the critical stage. It is pointed out that the Naval Staff has always fully recognised the dangerous situation caused by British naval superiority in the Mediterranean and constantly emphasised the need for speedy introduction of the proper German measures (This point was raised in personal conversation). Today

the enemy has complete naval and air supremacy in the area of the German transport routes . . . The Italians are not able to bring about any major improvements in the situation, due to the oil situation and to their own operational and tactical impotence . . .

Recently the transport situation in the Aegean Sea has also greatly deteriorated. Enemy submarines definitely have the upper hand.[51]

As a result both the Luftwaffe and Kriegsmarine began slowly increasing their commitment to the Mediterranean. To supplement locally-constructed *Marinefähreprahme*, the first *Räumboote* were despatched from Germany in December 1941. The 6th R-Flotilla had been established in Cuxhaven on 28 July, formed around a core of the smaller 46-ton R-boats of the 5th R-Flotilla – *R9, R10, R11, R12* and *R13* – which were, in turn, replaced by larger updated 125-ton *R41*-class boats fresh out of the Abeking & Rasmussen shipyard. Two boats from the Schlichting shipyard – *R15* and *R16* – were added to the flotilla which was initially commanded by Kaptlt Richard Rossow before Kaptlt Peter Reischauer replaced him during August 1941.[52]

The small boats could be transferred to the Mediterranean through the river and canal system of Western Europe. Permission was granted to transit through Vichy France and the first three boats left Cuxhaven on 19 November 1941. They proceeded first to Rotterdam where they were modified in closed bunkers to allow passage through narrow locks and under low bridges while disguised as civilian air traffic control vessels. All deck weapons were dismounted, the wheelhouse lowered and the boats repainted. With the crewmen in civilian clothes they entered the Rhine River, travelling South in planned daily stages until Strasbourg where their route led into the Rhine-Rhône canal. Passing through 167 narrow locks they proceeded to the Belfort Gap in the Vosges Mountains, then west along the Doubs to the Saône and the border with Vichy France. From there they joined the River Rhône at Lyon and followed the waterway south until Port-Saint-Louis in the Rhône estuary west of Marseilles. Once all the boats had arrived, the flotilla was remilitarised and divided into two groups which sailed to La Spezia for overhaul in the shipyard there. Finally, on 18 March 1942, Reischauer's flotilla left La Spezia to headsSouth in stages to Trapani where, on 3 April, the first four R-boats escorted the freighter *Una* to Tripoli, arriving four days later with the remainder of the flotilla arriving later that same day escorting the supply ship *Atlas* (later sunk by HMS *Thrasher*).

The 6th R-Flotilla was ready to operate in support of the Afrika Korps, whose military fortunes had markedly improved. On 21 January 1942, with supplies stockpiled, Rommel had launched a surprise counter-offensive at El Agheila (Operation Theseus) that carried his troops to within sight of the Egyptian border. An intensified Italian air campaign began in early February

Räumboote were an essential addition to the Axis war effort in North Africa.

against the island of Malta to remove the threat posed to Axis supply convoys by Royal Navy forces stationed in Valetta.

Alongside the R-boat presence in North Africa was Kaptlt Fritz Scheck's 2nd L-Flotilla which had been formed in Palermo during October 1941 from fifteen MFPs built in the Italian Cantieri Navali Riuniti shipyard. Used both as transport and escort craft, the MFPs were based in Tripoli. On 19 April 1942, *F154* and *F156* were carrying supplies from Benghazi to Derna when they were engaged by gun from submarine HMS *Thrasher*. Hit twice, *F154* returned fire with both 20mm and her single 75mm gun, forcing *Thrasher* to dive to safety. Two depth charges were dropped, purely in an attempt to frighten the British crew as their location had been lost, and both *F154* and *F156* reached their destination without casualties.[53] At that stage the 2nd L-Flotilla was technically part of German Transport Command, under the overall control of the *Deutsches Marinekommando Tunisien*. Later the unit would be subordinated to 7th *Sicherungsdivision* following the latter's creation in Trapani during March 1943.

By 26 May, the 6th R-Flotilla and 2nd L-Flotilla were both situated in Derna, Cyrenaica, as the front line moved east. To date 42,849 tons of supplies for Rommel's troops had been unloaded at Derna since 7 March and control and protection of supply traffic from Benghazi was subsequently handed over from Italian to German control. Two of Reischauer's R-boats had been subordinated to Benghazi's Italian Naval Command for the escort of local coastal convoy traffic in response to increased British submarine activity.

Rommel's advance had once again bypassed and laid siege to the Allied garrison in Tobruk. This time, however, there was no guaranteed resupply possible by the Royal Navy. On the afternoon of 28 May the first German assault on Tobruk was planned with naval forces leading the way. Operation Hecker was an amphibious landing of *Kampfgruppe* Hecker (led by Oberst Hermann-Hans Hecker, *Pionier Führer Afrika*) comprising men of the 13th Brandenburger Company, 33rd and 39th *Panzerjäger* Battalion, 778th Pioneer Landing Company and the Italian 3rd San Marco Marine Battalion. Their plan was to cut the main British supply route by landing 30km east of Tobruk while Rommel's main forces attacked the Gazala Line. The assault troops were embarked on Scheck's *Marinefährprähme* accompanied by Reischauer's R-boats and an S-boat escort. However, after only a few hours at sea the operation was cancelled by radio and the amphibious force returned to Derna, *F149* being attacked that night by *MTB309* and *MTB312* but two torpedoes passing under the shallow-draught vessel. An attempted attack with depth charges was driven off as *F149* returned fire and the opposing sides lost contact in the confusion that followed with no loss to either side.

By mid-June optimism was high that Tobruk and Bir Hakheim would soon fall, allowing the proposed invasion of Malta (Operation Herkules) to begin. Egypt and the Suez Canal were within the grasp of the Afrika Korps, Rommel himself describing the naval supply operations as 'first rate'. Finally, on 20 June, Tobruk fell to the Axis advance.

The town and harbour of Tobruk was taken by German panzer forces at 1842hrs.

The Admiral, German Naval Command, Italy thereupon immediately ordered the 3rd S-Flotilla and the 6th R-Flotilla to leave Derna. The task of the *Schnellboote* will be to intercept any enemy ships that may have been left in Tobruk and that now may attempt to flee. Subsequently the flotilla will form a patrol line North of Has Azzaz in order to protect the 6th R-Flotilla. The task of the latter will be to sweep a lane into Tobruk.

The significance of this brilliant victory of the forces in North Africa is tremendous. Quite apart from its political importance and the prestige gained . . . together with its potential effect on the enemy and on all neutrals, the fact that we now hold this coastal fortress and excellent harbour has definite tactical and strategic implications requiring very quick military and naval decisions. The fall of Tobruk leaves the route to Egypt open and Operation Aida [the invasion of Egypt and capture of the Suez Canal] has suddenly moved into the realm of possibility. It is obvious that the primary task for the time being is to exploit fully the defeat of the enemy 8th Army. This will create the basis for later carrying out the operations with the Nile Delta as their ultimate goal. This victory will also extend the task of the Naval Staff, since [we] now will have to assume responsibility for transporting and con-voying increased troop and supply shipments, together with the Luftwaffe. It will no longer be possible to delay carrying out operation 'Herkules' now, if the victory at Tobruk is not to remain a mere episode but is to be the beginning of a large operation which may decide the outcome of the war. Recognizing his critical situation, the enemy will put all of his available forces into action, particularly his air and naval forces. He will desperately attempt to prevent our conquest of the Delta by trying to smash our troop and materiel supply. The battle for air and sea supremacy in the Mediterranean has entered its decisive phase. The faster we are able to deal the first blows, the more effective they will be. Every delay gives the enemy the time he needs for bringing up reinforcements.[54]

This appreciation of the situation was accurate; the crucial phase of the war in the Mediterranean had been reached, through the use of relatively meagre forces. The decisions on how to immediately follow the fall of Tobruk would go a large way to determining the course of the entire war on the Southern Front.

6

War in the North and West: The Security Flotillas in Western Europe, the Baltic and Norway, 1942–1943

AS soon as France fell to the Wehrmacht, the British began minelaying off major harbours. The RAF predominantly used Hampden aircraft during 1940 to lay small fields of 1500lb parachute mines during missions code-named 'Gardening', that forced frequent port closures. British aircrews followed specific minelaying guidelines that included a flight path initially following aircraft engaged on a conventional bombing raid elsewhere. Assisted by Pathfinder aircraft dropping coloured markers on a nearby land waypoint, the 'Gardening' bomber would then alter speed and release its mines – the 'Vegetable' of which generally only two were carried – at intervals of three to five seconds, continuing along a straight course in order to mislead any observers as to the mine's location. The weapons themselves were evolving into models of greater sophistication that included acoustic and delayed triggers. Coastal Command Beaufort squadrons joined the 'Gardening' forces and during 1942, forty-eight such missions were undertaken against Saint-Nazaire alone. However, thanks to their diligence and determination, German minesweepers maintained high levels of success.

Räumboote sail into action from a French Channel port.

By the utmost exertion the German mine defence was, generally speaking, able to master the situation in a very short time so that our losses were kept within reasonable bounds. Only in the case of surprisingly extensive use of new fuses or other devices (e.g. first appearance of the acoustic mine) did sweeping take a few days longer with a temporary increase of losses. The mine offensive resulted in the reorganization to the smallest detail of routing and in the increase of protective equipment on naval and merchant ship. These countermeasures proved their worth. Not until the winter of 1944–45 did the mine offensive begin to cause us really serious difficulties.[55]

The threat lay not only from mines and Coastal Command but also from increasingly aggressive British MTB and MGBs. Working together, the gunboats would strive to draw escort forces away while torpedo attacks were made on the merchant ships. By the end of 1941 the Royal Navy possessed seven mixed flotillas of MTBs and MGBs active in home waters.

At the beginning of March MTBs torpedoed the tanker *Memelland* which managed to struggle into Dunkirk's outer harbour under tow before being beached and her 7000 tons of fuel oil unloaded. Two nights later the 4th MTB Flotilla attacked another German convoy north of Cap Griz Nez and torpedoed the 3493-ton steamer *Abbeville*. The cargo ship was travelling in ballast to the North Sea and future troop transport duties but broke apart and sank. Escorting *Räumboote* of the 2nd R-Flotilla engaged the attackers while *Abbeville* burned; damaging one of the attackers who had been reinforced by MGBs. Peter Scott was aboard *MGB322*:

Harpy Lloyd had taken John Weeden and Robert Varvil after a small convoy, and it appeared that one of the boats was in trouble. John Hodder and 'Flatters' Sidebottom were just off this very minute to the rescue, and if I would like to go with them I would have to run.

Ten minutes later, and not twenty minutes since my train had pulled into Dover station, I was steaming out of the harbour entrance on the bridge of a 'C' Class MGB (322), under the command of Lt. J. H. Hodder, R.N.V.R., while close astern followed *MGB330* (Lt. D. C. Sidebottom, R.N.V.R.).

MTB31, commanded by John Weeden, had made a signal to say that she was near the North-East Varne buoy and required immediate assistance. In bright moonlight we set course for the North-East Varne, and soon after we sighted a dim flicker of light and turned towards it. In a haze of smoke we came upon the burning wreck of the MTB. Some of the crew were still on board and shouted to us as we drew alongside. 'There's a raft with the wounded on it about a quarter of a mile away to the eastward' they said, and Sidebottom went off to find it, while we made fast alongside the burning boat.

The First Lieutenant was on board organising a fire party, and they were ready to take the hoses which had been laid out in readiness on our decks. Apparently they had successfully torpedoed a ship, but had been pursued by

R-boats and badly shot up. John Weeden had been seriously wounded and so had the Coxswain [H. Unsworth] and one or two others, and the Seaman Torpedoman [Able-Seaman Frederick Jackson] had been killed. The boat had run clear before the engines packed up and the fire took hold.

Macdonald, the First Lieutenant, an imperturbable New Zealander, had placed the wounded, including the Commanding Officer, in the Carley Raft, while he and the able-bodied members of the crew had abandoned ship by holding on to the splinter mattresses, which had been cut adrift to act as additional rafts. For some time they had lain off, but then the boat did not blow up and the fire seemed, if anything, to be abating. So Macdonald, who was a great swimmer, swam back and climbed aboard, and finally got some more of the crew back, and began to tackle the fire. It was at this stage that we had put in our most welcome appearance.

It seemed that *MTB31* was not past salvage. The fire, though not yet extinguished, was no longer spreading. The engine-room and tiller-flat were slowly flooding, but it was only a short distance to Dover . . . [56]

The survivors successfully reached England while a few nights later the 3rd R-Flotilla was again in action defending a large convoy from MGBs off Griz Nez. However, this time German light coastal flak batteries also opened fire, hitting *R164* and *R165* though without causing any casualties.

Despite aggressive Royal Navy coastal forces, the English Channel remained a primary route for German surface ships to the Bay of Biscay. In fact, between April and June 1941, twenty-nine major ships and eleven destroyers had passed through the English Channel unscathed. Disguised merchant raiders were also successfully routed that way, *Ship 28 'Michel'* making the voyage during March 1942. After departing Flushing on 13 March, *Michel* rendezvoused with a strong escort that included five torpedo boats, nine R-boats of the 2nd R-Flotilla and eight minesweepers of the 1st and 2nd M-Flotillas. The raider was bound for the South Atlantic, the minesweepers clearing a path as the convoy headed west hugging the coastline, while torpedo boats shielded them to seaward. The British were aware of the ships' movements and planned an interception, but careless radio chatter gave their approach away and attacks by MTBs and MGBs were repulsed with ferocious gunfire, the attackers illuminated by star shells from German coastal batteries. Two attacks failed and a third involving five Royal Navy destroyers was also beaten off, *Michel* suffering no more than splinter damage and some small-calibre hits. *Michel* reached Le Havre that afternoon under strong Luftwaffe escort and later continued to the Bay of Biscay unmolested. Her minesweeper escorts were attacked by Spitfires, but suffered no serious damage or casualties after mounting strong flak defence.

Mines remained the primary threat, *Sperrbrecher 162 'Delia'* of the 6th Sp-Flotilla sweeping eleven closely-grouped magnetic mines from the route code-named 'Rosa' though she and an ore steamer under escort were damaged by one exploding. Traffic between Ostend and Boulogne was immediately rerouted as 'Rosa' was deemed 'no longer under control'. The wooden-hulled minesweeper *M3615* was sunk off Dunkirk as the result of a mine explosion in water only 10m deep, illustrating that wooden ships were not safe against non-contact mines in shallow water. It was also clear that timer fuses were being introduced, allowing the first vessel to activate a chain of processes delaying the explosion. This was designed to either destroy the minesweeper herself as she passed overhead or the vessel that followed. Magnetic and acoustic firing triggers were also adjustable, allowing activation by a particular strength of magnetic field or a specific frequency of noise.

Bad weather severely hampered Channel operations during January 1942, though the six vessels and escort ship *Von Der Groeben* of the 3rd R-Flotilla departed the Hook of Holland on 23 January, due to begin their transit to the Black Sea. In the North Sea six ships of the 1st M-Flotilla sailed from Cuxhaven on 20 January to begin Operation Weichsel, the laying of three dense barrages in the Hoofden area which would also require the participation of the 4th and 5th M-Flotillas and 5th R-Flotilla to complete. Though the operation went to plan, every ship of the 1st M-Flotilla reported ice damage to their propellers, requiring shipyard time in Rotterdam. Sweeping was curtailed on 1 February as thick drifting ice continued to pose a hazard to all shipping, though R-boats were active again in the Channel a day later.

The German garrisons of the Channel Islands lacked any dedicated Security Forces and on 3 February a British and a Polish destroyer mounted Operation H to intercept convoy traffic between Alderney and Cherbourg. Alerted to German ship movements by the Quesnard Light illuminated on the north-eastern end of Alderney and the harbour lights shining, the destroyers waited under a full moon in a cloudless sky. Two small vessels were sighted in the early hours of the next morning, the 114-ton schooner *Hermann* and the 174-ton coaster *Schleswig-Holstein*, and both were rapidly destroyed by gunfire followed by depth charges as the vessels sank. Aboard were forty-two infantrymen, forty-three flak gunners and forty-three German, Flemish and French Organisation Todt workers heading for leave on the French mainland, bodies washing ashore for several days afterwards.

On Jersey the *Seekommandant Kanalinseln* was established in July 1942, the islands falling under the jurisdiction of the Kriegsmarine's 2nd *Sicherungsdivision*. However, it was not until the Allied invasion of Normandy in 1944 that a Vp-Flotilla and two minesweeper flotillas were stationed in the islands. Until that time, coastal defence was handled by the *Hafen-schutzflottille Kanalinseln*, split between the islands and St Malo.

While S-boats and destroyers attacked British East Coast convoys with minelaying and torpedoes, the Security Forces thickened defensive German

Bootsmann aboard a small vessel of the *Hafenschutzflottille Kanalinseln*, based between the Channel Islands and St Malo.

mine barrages in the German Bight. On 12 March the 5th *Sicherungsdivision* was formed under the direction of FKdR Max Klein, ex-commander of the 13th M-Flotilla. Klein's division was created from the flotillas already operational in German North Sea waters and was headquartered in Cuxhaven, directly subordinate to BSN, VA Eberhard Wolfram. The initial strength of his forces included seven minesweepers, one R-boat, one *Sperrbrecher*, four *Vorpostenboot*, one *U-Jäger* and one *Flakjäger* flotillas.[57]

The 2nd *Flakjäger* Flotilla had been established during July 1940 specifically for air defence, originally being designated 2nd *Flakjägergruppe* (*Nordsee*). A plan to establish the 1st *Flakjägergruppe* (*Ostsee*) was cancelled due to the low level of aerial threat in the Baltic. Originally subordinate to FdV Nord, the unit was redesignated on 1 November while under the command of KK Dr Felix Fischer. The 2nd *Flakjäger* Flotilla was equipped with converted whalers and Customs boats armed with twin 20mm and 37mm guns: *Flakjäger 21* (ex-whaler)'*Wiking 8*', *Flakjäger 22* (ex-whaler) '*Wiking 10*', *Flakjäger 23* (ex-whaler) '*Wiking 9*', *Flakjäger 24* (ex-whaler) '*Wiking 6*', *Flakjäger 25* (ex-Customs vessel) '*Yorck*', and *Flakjäger 26* (ex-Customs vessel) '*Nettelbeck*'.

Coastal Command came under harsh criticism for their failure to stop the paasge of *Scharnhorst*, *Gneisenau* and *Prinz Eugen* through the English

Channel. But, while acutely embarrassed, lessons were taken and learned. The severe casualties amongst attacking torpedo bombers indicated that they required escorts to suppress or neutralise enemy flak and the RAF were keen to have a standardised type of aircraft that could handle both roles. Coastal Command began re-equipping with Beaufighters during the summer of 1942 and the development of formidable and effective 'Strike Wing' tactics would see formations of up to thirty-five Beaufighters armed with 20mm cannon employed as flak suppressors, covering a main strike force of torpedo-armed Beaufighters ('Torbeaus').

Operation Chariot: the British Commando raid on Saint-Nazaire

Simultaneously, other branches of the British armed services evolved throughout 1942, including the Combined Operations Headquarters, and in March it mounted a daring raid to neutralise the threat posed by the *Bismarck*'s sister-ship *Tirpitz* in the Atlantic. *Tirpitz* had been declared operational in January and the fear that she could reach the Atlantic on a convoy raiding mission resulted in a plan to destroy the only dry-dock capable of handling a vessel of that size, the Normandie dock at Saint-Nazaire, the largest dry-dock in the world upon its completion in 1932. Destruction of the dock gate would render it unusable, but it was constructed of reinforced concrete on a solid rock base with thick welded gates impervious to bombing. The daring plan involved crashing an obsolete ex-American destroyer, HMS *Campbeltown*, into the dock gate laden with explosives while Commandos raided the harbour to destroy equipment, installations and whatever ships or U-boats could be found. *Campbeltown* was structurally altered to resemble a Kriegsmarine torpedo boat and would be accompanied by *MGB314* (the headquarters ship), *MTB74* and sixteen motor launches. Additionally there was a covering force of destroyers, HMS *Atherstone* and *Tynedale*, and the submarine HMS *Sturgeon* supplying a navigational beacon to guide the attackers into the Loire estuary.

The mission was set for 28 March, though as the attacking force sailed through the Bay of Biscay on the previous day they chanced upon *U593*. The U-boat was also headed for Saint-Nazaire and was chased below the surface at high speed with gunfire, then depth-charged by HMS *Tynedale* and *Atherstone*. The U-boat was blown temporarily back to the surface where she was again fired upon, visibly heeling over and submerging. *Kapitänleutnant* Gerd Kelbling's boat survived and escaped, but only reported British ships headed 'West' five hours after the initial sighting.[58]

Five German torpedo boats sailed from Saint-Nazaire to investigate but failed to make contact. This left the harbour occupied by twelve vessels of the *Hafenschutzflottille* and eight auxiliary minesweepers, which had been engaged in clearing fields laid by the Royal Air Force's 'Gardening' missions. *M1601*, *M1602*, *M1605* and *M1607* were all at the quayside in the Vieux Basin du Port, while both *M1606* and *M1608* were at the quayside in the Basin de Penhoët in which *M4221* and *M4225* were also moored. Two *Sperrbrecher* were also present; *Sp137* '*Bottilla Russ*' anchored near the East Jetty and *Sp3* '*Belgrad*' in the Basin de Penhoët. A trio of armed tankers, *Passat*, *Schlettstadt* and *Uckermark*, as well as five tugboats were in harbour while *V414* and *V415* patrolled offshore between Noirmoutier and Saint-Nazaire on picket duty.

At 0100hrs the following morning *HS1* of the *Hafenschutzflottille* detected unidentified darkened ships in the Chenal des Charpentiers, but was unable to report the sighting as she was not equipped with a radio. Luck and daring allowed the British force to reach within 2500m of the port entrance before a searchlight belonging to naval flak *Abteilung* 703 crackled into life and was trained on the ships at 0122hrs. The incoming craft flew Kriegsmarine ensigns and the nearby *Sperrbrecher Sp137* issued the first challenge. Neither the commander, ObltzSdR Carl von Appen, nor the First Officer was aboard and the *Sperrbrecher*'s two helmsmen took charge. A large percentage of the crew were also ashore and so it was largely technical crew members who manned the guns. A rapid signal flashed in reply: 'Two damaged ships. Request permission to enter port without delay.' Valuable minutes were lost while the German hesitated until flak weapons aboard the *Sperrbrecher* began shooting at *MGB314*, which immediately replied, pumping shells into the *Sperrbrecher* and seriously wounding both helmsmen and silencing the guns. The *Sperrbrecher*'s Chief Engineer took command while German guns ashore opened fire.

HMS *Campbeltown* successfully rammed the lock gates and landed eighty Commandos into an inferno of gunfire. Other Commandos were being put ashore although most of the British Motor Launches were destroyed by the storm of German gunfire, while crewmen ashore were quickly formed into small combat groups to defend the port. After hours of ferocious combat, the British survivors withdrew. Ultimately, the raid was a success but a costly one. Of the 622 men of the Royal Navy and Royal Marine Commandos who took part in the raid, only 228 returned to England. Five Commandos later evaded capture and escaped back to England via neutral Spain and Gibraltar, while 169 men were killed and another 215 captured. The Germans lost 42 men killed and 127 wounded during the battle itself and a further 96 men killed and 116 badly and 130 lightly wounded when the timed explosives aboard *Campbeltown* finally exploded. Heinz Hunke was aboard *M1601* '*Oldenwald*' when the attack started.

Our ship was stationed in the old basin of the Saint-Nazaire port, tied up to the quay facing the entrance to the U-boat pens. We placed the ship there to protect the individual berths of the U-boat base and could fire seaward against the British launches. After the fighting that night and during the morning that followed we walked along the port and on the wreck of the *Campbeltown* where men from our ship found a case containing secret documents related to the raid. Five minutes before the explosion I was back aboard my ship. When it exploded around midday it destroyed the lock gate and our crew suffered two dead and two wounded.[59]

A second delayed explosion – that of a timer-fused torpedo fired by *MTB74* into the basin entrance – occurred at 1630hrs on 30 March as Organisation Todt workers attempted to clear away the wreckage. Panicking, many of the Todt men fled, their khaki overalls being mistaken for British uniforms by the jittery Kriegmarine sentries nearby and some being shot dead.

The naval coastal batteries and naval anti-aircraft batteries, as well as *Sperrbrecher* 137 . . . minesweeper flotillas, and harbour patrol boats, succeeded in destroying all but a few (one to four) of the enemy vessels before they reached the shore. The crew of the destroyer put the pump of the lock out of commission, and entered the nearest streets and houses, where they were annihilated or captured by naval detachments and an Army detachment which had been alerted in the meantime. Three vessels of the 16th Minesweeper Flotilla took part in the land fighting, and protected the open side of the submarine pens . . . Unfortunately, the explosives on the destroyer exploded at 1145hrs when German personnel were already aboard to secure documents and equipment, and there were numerous curious bystanders, mostly French shipyard workers, in the vicinity, so that the number of casualties on our side increased considerably. Fortunately the secret documents and the enemy's latest mine chart had been removed from the destroyer previously.

Four vessels of the 5th Torpedo Boat Flotilla, which were engaged during the night in sweeping the routes because of mine danger, received the first report of the attack at 0315hrs and returned at top speed to St. Nazaire. One British motor gunboat [*ML306*] was captured by the *Jaguar* after a short engagement, and was later brought in by *Vorpostenboote* [*V414* and *V415*].[60]

Though casualties had been heavy, it was an important success for the Allies at a time when their military fortunes had ebbed on all fronts. The threat of the *Tirpitz* had also dramatically diminished, the Normandie lock remaining out of action for the remainder of the war.

A second major amphibious raid was planned by the British against the coast of Aquitane for the beginning of April. Convoys transporting minerals crucial to Germany's armaments manufacturers, particularly iron ore and

Heavily-armed Kriegsmarine sailors during the mopping-up after the battle in Saint-Nazaire following the landings by British Commandos in Operation Chariot.

wolfram, sailed regularly from Bilbao in Spain, to the Gironde or Bayonne and a Commando raid was planned to cause maximum disruption. A strong naval contingent was to escort men of No 1 and No 6 Commandos into the mouth of l'Adour, the troops disembarking from landing craft and attacking coastal defences and enemy shipping in harbour. However, the landing was thwarted by high seas and aborted after German artillery from MAA 286 opened fire on 'a suspicious vessel'. A single landing barge ran aground on rocks off the North Pier in l'Adour and had to wait until just before dawn before the tide refloated them and they withdrew under covering fire from a destroyer outside of searchlight-range. At 1400hrs the next day the minesweeper *M4206* sighted an abandoned British landing craft ten miles north of St. Jean de Luz that had been damaged by gunfired and was three-quarters waterlogged, but it sank during an attempt to tow it ashore.

English Channel battleground; the destruction of *R184*

Convinced of the need for increased coastal fortifications, the Germans expended massive resources on the creation of the Atlantic Wall, particularly the construction of concrete fortifications around the main ports and docks. The Kriegsmarine had already begun an intensive minelaying scheme to create a west-east barrier between Boulogne and Cherbourg that would provide protection for convoys travelling along the Normandy coast, an area considered unlikely as a potential Allied landing ground by OKW. All available minelaying craft were used to lay the dense field of deep mines, including dedicated minelayers, destroyers, torpedo boats, minesweepers and

Räumboote. This frequently brought them into contact with British forces either attempting to disrupt the minelaying or in the process of laying their own barrages. In one instance, on the night of 9 July near Boulogne, boats of the 12th R-Flotilla fought a sharp engagement with two destroyers, four MTBs and two MGBs, *R178* claiming an MGB sunk after 'ramming and by shelling her with incendiary ammunition at a range of 20 metres'. Both *R176* and *R178* were heavily damaged and disabled after the battle.

During August 1942 the Allies obtained their first proper glimpse into the operations of the Kriegsmarine's *Räumboote* following the capture of twenty-five of the 28-man crew of *R184* from KK Herbert Nau's 10th R-Flotilla. The flotilla had been formed in Cuxhaven during March from new boats constructed in Bremen. *R184* had been launched on 11 April, commissioned one week later and underwent engine trials in the Weser River. After flotilla manoeuvres were complete, the boat was fitted with gun shields and bridge armour plating at the Howaldtwerke yard and after degaussing travelled to Cuxhaven for final formation exercises in the North Sea. On 8 July *R183*, *R184*, *R185* and *R186* left for Rotterdam, arriving two days later (*R187* delayed by engine trouble) and then sailing onward first to Ostend then Dunkirk and finally Boulogne. At 2055hrs on 25 July, the flotilla escorted a small convoy of three unarmed tugs bound for Dieppe, from where they moved onward to Ouistreham. After further days of exercises the R-boats travelled to Calais to embark mines at the Quai du Rhône.

On 16 August *R184* sailed with boats of the 10th and 12th R-flotillas, each carrying twelve mines. The crew were lacking one man, Matrosengefreiter Peter, who was serving a six-day prison sentence for drunkenness, but did carry an extra petty officer, ObStrm Eberhard Reiners, who was in training to take command of his own boat. *R184*'s skipper was ObStrm Helmut Welzer, a veteran of auxiliary cruiser operations. At 2000hrs they departed Calais and divided into two groups, each detailed to lay a minefield in a south-easterly direction from Dover running parallel to the coast. Nau led the flotilla aboard *R179* as they sailed north-west for 30 minutes, changing course frequently before reaching the position to begin minelaying.

Unfortunately they had been detected by British radar while travelling at half speed nine miles from South Foreland. Two MGBs from Ramsgate and three from Dover raced to intercept, the Ramsgate boats *MGB6* and *MGB10* making contact at about 2125hrs, five minutes after *R184*'s group had dropped its final mine, and opened fire, taking the Germans completely by surprise. British coastal artillery also began shelling the Germans. Welzer was severely wounded in the stomach by gunfire that penetrated the bridge, Funkgefreiter Hans Ochs signalling for urgent help from the flotilla's medical officer. The second round that hit *R184* went straight through her engine

Wartime postcard with a 1941 painting by Adolf Bock depicting British aircraft being shot down by *Vorpostenboote*. Bock was also the designer of the Kriegsmarine's *Flottenkriegsabzeichen* (High Seas Fleet War Badge)

room and put both engines and the steering gear out of action. Fuel oil ignited and soon the boat was ablaze, as the German gun crews continued to return fire until all ready-use ammunition had been expended. The boat's smoke screen apparatus was hit, acid pouring out and severely burning several men. Preparing to scuttle the boat, Ochs set fire to the captain's cabin and smashed the wireless transmitter with a hammer while three hand grenades were thrown into vulnerable parts of the boat.

R184 lay motionless and both MGBs attempted to board and take her in tow. However, the flames were completely out of control and shortly after everybody had abandoned ship, *R184* went down, three of the crew having been killed in the attack. Fifteen survivors were taken prisoner, while another ten were picked up from a life raft the following day by *MTB204* while on patrol. 'Survivors were considerably disappointed at the lack of team spirit shown by the other R-Boats, who dispersed for home the moment they realised they were being attacked, instead of coming to *R184*'s assistance.'[61] Three other boats of the 10th and two of the 12th R-Flotillas had been damaged during the action but managed to get back to base, the survivors maintaining that they had lost track of *R184*'s location.

Operation Jubilee: the British and Canadians attack Dieppe

Three days after this battle a second major Allied raid was mounted on French soil. This time the objective was to take and temporarily hold the port of Dieppe. Once again, the operation was planned by Combined Operations Headquarters, originally as a division-sized attack but later downsized to a brigade; initial plans to secure its flanks with airborne troops were altered to use seaborne Commandos instead. Originally known as Operation Rutter, the Allied code name was changed after several delays to Operation Jubilee.

The plan called for Commandos to silence the coastal batteries atop imposing promontories flanking either side of the Dieppe landing area while elements of 2nd Canadian Division supported by Churchill tanks put ashore at Pourville, Puys and the Dieppe seafront. Support would be provided by British and Polish naval forces and the Royal Air Force.

Unlike Operation Chariot, Jubilee was a disaster. A chance encounter with one of the regular German convoys that sailed along the French Channel coast presaged the bloodbath to follow. At 2000hrs on 18 August, Convoy 2437 consisting of the small coasters *Iris*, *Spes*, *Ostflandern*, *Hydra* and *Franz* escorted by *UJ1411* '*Treff III*' (skippered by flotilla commander Kaptlt Reinhard Wurmbach), *UJ1404* '*Franken*' and the minesweeper *M4015*, departed Boulogne bound for Dieppe. Travelling at approximately 6 knots, the escorts were warned by shore radar of the presence of enemy high-speed craft astern of their position. Some twenty minutes later, the hydrophone gear aboard *UJ1404* detected enemy vessels approximately seven miles astern and to port, whereupon the convoy altered course very slightly. Leutnant zur See Max Berner reasonably assumed that it was likely to be a force of MTBs or

Battered but still battle-ready; a *Vorpostenboot* in the English Channel.

MGBs on a raiding mission, though within 15 minutes *UJ1411* unexpectedly encountered Naval Group 5, part of Operation Flodden, the section of Jubilee tasked with taking and holding the Berneval coastal artillery battery.

Naval Group 5 was commanded by Commander D. B. Wyburd and carried 325 men of 3 Commando, 40 US Army Rangers, five Free Frenchmen and an officer and three men from 'Phantom', the special signals unit tasked with establishing communications with the raid's operational headquarters in Uxbridge. The majority of the troops were carried aboard Eureka boats, small spoonbill-bowed plywood vessels that could carry up to twenty-five troops and a crew of three or four. An armoured bulkhead provided the only protection while a Royal Navy gunner manned a single Lewis gun. Of limited range, the boats that night each carried sixteen two-gallon cans of petrol strapped to any available upright. Escorting the small infantry boats were *LCF(L)1* (Landing Craft, Flak, Large) – armed with twin 4in dual-purpose guns and three 20mm Oerlikons – and *ML346* which carried a 3-pounder gun and a 20mm cannon. In the van sailed *SGB8* (Steam Gun Boat 8, renamed HMS *Grey Owl* in 1943) which boasted more formidable armament, being in the heaviest class of vessel operated by British coastal forces. She was armed with a 3in gun aft, three single 2-pounders, two 20mm Oerlikons, two twin Browning machine-guns and a single 21in torpedo tube abreast of the funnel on either side. The steam gunboat was considered quieter at high speeds than either an MGB or MTB, though frequent bursts of sparks from the funnel gave cause for concern amongst the small force, for whom stealth was crucial.

Despite the German convoy having been detected by British radar, no attempt was made to divert escorting destroyers to intercept and both sides blundered into one another, a German star shell from *UJ1411* beginning the sharp engagement that followed. Aboard a Eureka boat nearest *SGB8* was Sub Lieutenant D.J. Lewis, RCNVR.

At 3.30 a.m. [actually, at 0347 hours], a starshell went up on the starboard hand and lit the whole fleet in a horrible quivering semi-daylight. Our boat was leading the starboard column. It was immediately enveloped in the hottest tracer fire I have ever seen. The air was filled with the whine of ricochets and the bangs of exploding shells, while after every burst of the streaking balls of fire came the clatter of Oerlikons. The SGB's thin armour was riddled and the shells exploding inside filled her boiler room with [superheated] steam. One of the burst[ing shells] struck LCP (L) 42. Sub Lieutenant C. D. Wallace [RCNVR] of Montreal . . . was killed instantly . . . In my boat men threw off their blankets, fumbled for tin hats and weapons. The flak was flying but a few feet ahead and a few astern. Some was right above us . . . Our boat put on full speed and went under the stern of the disabled SGB . . . At full speed we tore away from the lashing streams of flak . . . Astern we could see star shells, flak converging, and a big flash which died down and then blew up and lit the sky. I never found out what this was.[62]

The Allied group attempted to battle their way through the German convoy, calculating that any violent manouevres would scatter the small craft. *SGB8* battered her way forward, her radio antennae destroyed by German gunfire and within minutes all her guns were silenced with 40 per cent of the crew badly burned by escaping steam or wounded in the action. The boiler was repeatedly hit by German fire and soon *SGB8* lost power and lay dead in the water. Meanwhile the LFC skippered by Australian Lieutenant T. M. Foggitt, opened fire with all available weapons, concentrating on *UJ1404* which was soon ablaze. The fierce gunfire had killed LzS Berner, ObStrm Franz Schwenn taking command as the *U-Jäger* took multiple hits in her engine room. The trawler's steering gear was damaged and she began to circle, most guns out of action and the bridge, forecastle and W/T office all hit repeatedly and in a shambles. With the ship in danger of breaking apart, survivors attempted to lower the aft whaler but this too was found to be practically destroyed by gunfire. Those men that were left then abandoned ship by jumping overboard as *UJ1404* began to founder.

During the confused action, *ML346* closed what they took to be the damaged *SGB5* but was in fact the remaining German escorts, who drove them away with heavy fire. The commander of *UJ1411* reported exchanging fire with 'numerous gun boats and MTBs', sinking at least two and ramming a large landing craft. However, no Allied vessels were lost and although *UJ1411* attempted to ram one of the Eureka boats, the small damaged landing craft reversed out of the *U-Jäger*'s path at the last moment.

Almost inexplicably, the nearby destroyers ORP *Slazak* and HMS *Brocklesby* did not intervene in the battle despite seeing and hearing the gunfire. It wasn't until 0530hrs that HMS *Brocklesby* came across the drifting wreck of *UJ1404* and sank her with gunfire, rescuing twenty-five of the crew from the water. who had already abandoned ship. Both the German convoy and the Allied assault group had been scattered by the brief battle, some of the latter returning the England with engine damage, others towing *SGB8* while several carried on to their objective.

Though many at MGK West believed that the engagement was most likely the result of an MTB attack on a German convoy, on the coast the battle had served to bring defences to some level of alert. Despite all surviving convoy escorts having had their radios disabled during the mêlée, the battle had been observed from the shore. At 0510hrs the Kriegsmarine Communications Officer at Le Havre reported: 'Three miles off Dieppe surface forces attacking convoy.' Though MGK West had then advised Army Group D and

Luftflotte 3 headquarters by telephone that it was most likely nothing out of the ordinary, at 0535hrs the three ships of *Hafenschutzflottille* Dieppe patrolling off the harbour were also attacked and a visual signal fired that alerted the entire coastal region and brought Wehrmacht troops into action. The *Hafenschutzflottille* vessels were later able to make port without loss.

> The convoy was dispersed in the course of the engagement; *U-Jäger UJ1404* was driven off and was in flames when last sighted 10 miles North of Dieppe at 0603hrs. Other reports stated that she blew up. Sub chaser *UJ1411* and minesweeper *M4015* fought separate engagements during which *UJ1411* fired on and rammed a large assault boat carrying 20 to 30 men, destroying it. Hits were scored on several motor gunboats and a flotilla leader. One large gunboat was sighted burning, and one motor gunboat was seen drifting bottom up. During the engagement numerous enemy planes strafed our vessels. Two bombers and one fighter were definitely shot down, and one fighter was probably shot down. The convoy was brought into the roadstead of Le Treport where it can be protected from the shore.
>
> This engagement alerted the coast sector from Boulogne up to Cherbourg against the enemy landing which started on the coast near Dieppe at 0600 . . . The first news concerning the details of the operation did not start coming in at the Naval Staff until noon, and all reports came from other branches of the Armed Forces. Only after 2000hrs in the evening did Group West transmit details of vital interest for the Kriegsmarine. Thus the real importance of the engagement between our convoy and the enemy landing force as the initial phase and a warning signal very unfortunately failed to receive full recognition on that day. For the same reason, no mention of the importance of this engagement is to be found in the special communiqué from the Führer Headquarters announcing the success of the German coast defence and the crushing defeat of the attacker with explicit reference to the political pressure by Stalin which had forced the British to commit this act of desperation.[63]

The landing was indeed a disaster; of 6106 men who had left England, 1027 were dead by the end of the day and 2240 captured. The order for withdrawal had been given at 0950hrs following pitched battles against well-motivated Wehrmacht troops and under intense pressure from the Luftwaffe which fielded its new Fw190 fighters, outclassing the covering RAF, which lost 106 aircraft to the Germans' 48.

The rest of Convoy 2437 was taken to Le Treport, though the 159-ton armed tanker *Franz* had attempted to add the firepower of her 88mm gun by sailing towards Dieppe's beach and firing upon the waiting landing craft and Canadian troops. She was hit and driven ashore in flames by gunfire from *ML346*, British sailors removing Franz's ensign as a trophy before retreating. During the battle LzSdR Hermann Bögel's *M4040 'Odenwald'* was credited with shooting down four enemy aircraft, the skipper later being awarded the Knight's Cross on 15 October as a result of the action.

Though Operation Jubilee could hardly be described as successful, it had two important results. Firstly, in conjunction with Chariot, it helped convince OKW to fortify ports they believed (incorrectly) would be a focal point of any Allied invasion of the Continent for their supply capacity. Secondly, it showed to the Allies the folly of just such an attack, leading to the design and construction of the floating 'Mulberry' harbours that could be employed along any suitable stretch of coastline, such as that that of Normandy.

In the meantime, Allied submarine patrols in Southern Biscay to disrupt mineral convoys from Spain yielded some results on 12 June when *M4212* struck a mine laid by the Free-French *Rubis* at the southern tip of the convoy route, the minesweeper sinking with eleven crewmen killed. Mines from *Rubis* would later claim the 288-ton Vichy tugboat *Quand Même*, *M4401* and *V406 'Hans Loh'* all sunk and *M4448* seriously damaged on 20 September and beached nearby.

Minefields in the English Channel had also taken a steady toll of the Security Forces, demonstrated by the combined loss of several vessels in early October 1942. The raider *Komet* was travelling through the English Channel in stages towards the Atlantic for her second mission escorted by boats of the 2nd R-Flotilla. Her departure from Le Havre was delayed by bad weather and once underway, in spite of minesweeping of the route, *R77*, *R78*, *R82* and *R86* were all sunk by mines before they had reached Dunkirk. *Komet* ploughed on,

The disaster of Operation Jubilee. German troops inspect a Daimler Dingo scout car abandoned after the withdrawal of the surviving Canadian troops.

The foreship of the small 499-ton *Sperrbrecher 142 'Westerbroek'* showing the swastika recognition symbol for the benefit of German aircraft. *Westerbroek* was sunk on 15 September 1942 by a mine.

losing the escorting 498-ton *Sperrbrecher Sp143 'Lola'* on 9 October to another undetected mine. It was a severe blow to the minesweeping strength in the area: between June and December 1942 ten *Sperrbrecher* were lost to mines in the sea lanes between Norderney and Dunkirk.[64]

Two other *Sperrbrecher* were lost in December 1942, both to destroyers. The newly-commissioned 1236-ton *Sp178 'Gauss'* and the smaller 387-ton *Sp144 'Beijerland'* of the 4th Sp-Flotilla were preceding a convoy from Boulogne to Le Havre under *Vorpostenboote* and minesweeper escort on the night of 12 December. It was a clear but moonless night with a slight wind ruffling the sea as they made passage at an average speed of 7.5 knots along the darkened coast. At 1040hrs north-east of Dieppe they were intercepted by six destroyers on Channel patrol. For two hours the battle raged, all six attacking destroyers receiving damage: HMS *Whitshed* holed on the waterline by gunfire, HNoMS *Eskdale*'s wheelhouse damaged forcing her to withdraw from the battle, HMS *Vesper* hit eight times and her commanding officer wounded and HMS *Worcester*, *Albrighton* and *Brocklesby* damaged by near-misses. While the smaller escorts herded the German merchants into Dieppe, both *Sperrbrecher* fought desperately but *Sp178* was hit amidships by a torpedo from HMS *Whitshed* that sent her under in ten minutes with only three of her crew of 102 surviving. As the destroyers concentrated fire on the remaining *Sperrbrecher*, *Sp144* was torpedoed by the Norwegian *Eskdale* and went down with no survivors.

A further extraordinary British Commando raid in December 1942 cost the Germans another *Sperrbrecher* in the port of Bordeaux. Tasked with sinking merchant shipping that had been bringing crucial supplies of raw materials from the Far East, ten Royal Marine Commandos were dropped off the coast south-west of Point de Grave by HMS *Tuna* in small camouflaged two-man collapsible canoes named 'Cockles'. Slipping through the various German naval patrols they managed to plant limpet mines that disabled six ships, including the *Sperrbrecher Sp5 'Schwanheim'*. Halfway through planting two limpet mines on the *Sperrbrecher* the pair of commandos heard an audible clang from above and looked up to see the outline of a German sentry looking directly down at them only five metres distant. As they drifted

Sperrbrecher 11 'Belgrano' sinking after hitting a mine on 23 October 1942 near Ameland. The wreck was later towed to Hamburg and repaired in time for service with the post-war German Minesweeping Administration.

with the slight current the sentry followed them, evidently unsure of what he was seeing, until the canoe drifted below the bow and out of the sentry's field of vision. They could still hear his footsteps as they gently drifted away from the ship.

Though the raid was successful, all the ships were later repaired. Eight of the ten Commandos never returned, two dying of hypothermia and six being captured and executed according to Hitler's infamous 'Commando Order', while the two survivors managed to escape to Britain through neutral Spain. Though Raeder later expressed disquiet about uniformed soldiers being executed, this was not the only time that the Kriegsmarine obeyed Hitler's orders and handing captured uniformed men over to the SD for interrogation and execution. Six Norwegian and one British man that made up the crew of *MTB345* were intercepted and taken prisoner by R-boats on 28 July 1943 before they could scuttle their boat. The crew of *RA202* had boarded the boat which lay at anchor under camouflage netting, attempting to refuel from hidden depots along the Norwegian coast before hunting for targets. After a brief gun battle in which three Norwegians were wounded, the boat was captured, later recommissioned into the Kriegsmarine. Admiral von Schrader had co-ordinated the German attack and, perhaps because of their previous mission that dropped an agent ashore, labelled the crew as 'pirates not soldiers' and they were subsequently interrogated by the Kriegsmarine, handed over to the SD, tortured and shot.

The Baltic

In the Baltic, the Security Forces continued reinforcing the mine barrages established at the beginning of Operation Barbarossa. They also continued fouling the Skagerrak to prevent British submarines from entering the Baltic. On 6 January 1942 the newly-commissioned minelayer *Ulm* began her first minelaying mission in company with *Roland*. They laid an experimental field of the new EMF contact mines, most of which exploded after being laid and the ships returned to Fredrikshaven to be replenished by lighters from shore. The second minelaying proved more successful, although a crewman named Giese was killed when his braces became entangled in a mine's horns and he was dragged overboard with its heavy sinker. Minelaying in the Skagerrak extending towards the southern coast of Norway' continued with several different minelayers, generally under Luftwaffe escort and sometimes the R-boats of Kaptlt Werner Dobberstein's 5th R-Flotilla.

The winter of 1941/42 was once again severe and ice did not fully clear from the Gulf of Finland until May 1942. During that month German and Finnish reconnaissance aircraft detected at least twenty-five Soviet submarines conducting trials between Kronstadt and Lavansaari, fitted with wooden fenders and cutters to counter contact mines. The German and

Finnish naval authorities discussed methods to completely close the Gulf of Finland to any potential breakout of Soviet submarines, extending the existing minefields while reinforcing surface patrols. The Finns, for their part, also demanded the allocation of anti-submarine nets, though they were in insufficient supply.

Finnish forces had broken through the Irben Strait and conquered the Baltic islands of Suursaari and Suur-Tytärsaari supported by the 1st M-Flotilla, so that by the summer of 1942 only Lavansaari and Seiskarisaari remained in Soviet hands. During early June the minesweepers laid three minefields – 'Tiger I', 'II' and 'III' – each of fifty-four EMC mines near the two islands to interfere with supply traffic between them and also to block the approaches to Kronstadt. These were swiftly followed by three more lines of mines, code-named 'Brummbär I', 'II' and 'III'.

During the winter naval forces in the Eastern Baltic had operated under the control of *Marineverbindungsstab Finnland*, co-ordinated by the Naval Attaché in Helsinki. However, on 8 May FdM Ost, KzS Böhmer, and his staff arrived in Helsinki to assume direct control of Kriegsmarine surface forces. By 25 April in the Gulf of Finland he had at his disposal 1st R-Flotilla, 18th, 31st and 34th M-Flotillas, 12th UJ-Flotilla, 3rd and 17th Vp-Flotillas, 27th L-Flotilla, the minelayers *Kaiser* and *Roland* as well as FK Johannes Schur's *Küstenschutzflottille Ostland* (subordinate to *Marinebefehlshaber 'D' / Marine-befehlshaber Ostland* in Reval) and the 17th M-Flotilla, which was soon to be transferred from the North Sea.[65]

Böhmer's initial responsibility was the establishment of the anti-submarine mine barrages 'Nashorn', extending from Nargen on the Estonian side of the Gulf of Finland to the area of Porkkala on the Finnish side, and 'Seeigel' that stretched between the islands of Aspoe via Vigrund to Cape Kurgalski. This latter barrier numbered 4569 mines when combined with the complementary Finnish 'Rukajarvi' barrage. The Germans planted 100 moored mines, magnetic ground mines and a combination of horned and anti-submarine mines that were covered by both coastal artillery and Böhmer's flotillas to prevent sweeping by the Soviet Navy. By the end of the year several different barrages had been completed or were in the process of being laid, some 12,000 mines being planted within the Gulf of Finland.

However, despite this formidable defence, some Soviet submarines managed to reach the open Baltic. Twelve Soviet submarines were sunk, eight while attempting to break out and four within the Western Baltic. Those that managed to pass the barriers inflicted some casualties on Axis forces, sinking at least twenty ships and damaging eight others. While this figure remains relatively minor compared to the 1900 ships that carried 5.6 million tons of cargo and more than 400,000 troops through the Baltic in 1942, the fact that any Soviet submarines had managed to pass through the barriers disturbed

Kriegsmarine officers. It demonstrated the tenacity, resolution and skill of Soviet submariners who, in the face of daunting prospects, continued to attempt penetration of the Axis minefields. Several skirmishes were also fought with Soviet MTBs; *UJ1216 'Star XXI'* was torpedoed and sunk by *TK152* on 26 August with one officer and seventeen men rescued by other *U-Jäger*.

By late October most naval operations in the Baltic had ceased as once again the winter ice took hold. At the end of 1942 the Böhmer wrote in his War Diary:

> In contrast to the summer of 1941 the enemy demonstrated activity at sea which had not been observed among the Russians up to that time. They made ready and committed a large number of patrol boats and motor mine-sweepers, many minesweepers as well as MTBs and a few gunboats. They have two to three submarines in constant operation in the Baltic. The Russian MTBs were likewise very active and frequently sought out suitable targets among our anti-submarine patrol forces near Hogland [Suursaari], and they even scored one success in torpedoing *U-Jäger UJ1216* . . . Several times in this year the Russians attacked trawlers and minesweepers in the U-boat hunting area with aerial torpedoes. The attacks were poorly executed and remained unsuccessful.[66]

The year showed the crisis that was enveloping the security flotillas. In May 1942, SKL had concluded that the German convoy situation was 'very difficult' because of the strain put upon existing crews and their vessels which were overstretched in every way. The successful importation of 43 per cent of Germany's ore requirements was dependant on safe mercantile passage through the Baltic, Norwegian waters and the Bay of Biscay. A critical lack of escort vessels endangered this life blood of Germany's war economy. Indeed, on 30 April 1942, of 201 escort vessels stationed in the area controlled by MGK West, 115 were unserviceable through damage or essential main-tenance. A crisis in manpower and equipment was crippling Germany's ability to safeguard its supply convoys, the Kriegsmarine only mustering approximately a quarter the strength that SKL had demanded during the summer of 1940 if it was to effectively control the occupied coastline stretching from the Arctic to the Spanish border. A lack of manufacturing steel, dockyard space and dockyard workers conspired to prevent the construction or conversion of anywhere near enough vessels for the Security Forces. The Third Reich had passed its high-water mark and now there was only the slow ebb to follow.

A lookout keeps watch aboard a pristine-looking naval auxiliary.

Artillerieträger

Development of the purpose-built *Artillerieträger* was at least a partial answer to this problem. Plans for a large 175-ton *Räumboot* capable of a top speed of 25 knots had been put forward and construction begun before being halted in April 1942 due to a shortage of copper. The new boats had been intended as convoy escorts – quick to build and robust – though their dependence on scarce materials defeated the object. Only twelve were eventually completed between 1943 and 1944 after the acute copper shortage had been resolved. However, the requirement for a cheap, effective escort remained.

Ruge was the first to propose the conversion of existing MFPs into dedicated *Artillerieträger*, reckoning their rectangular hull shape would require minimal conversion to carry heavy weapons while provide ample space for crew and ammunition. Their shallow draught, even with the extra weight, would also render them safer from torpedo attacks than a conventional hull. By June 1942 SKL had given the go-ahead to begin construction of the first version. Longitudinal strength was improved by filling bulkhead gaps with concrete, increasing the weight-bearing ability and also providing extra splinter protection for the gun crews. Additional armour and a soundproofed radio room were also installed. The main armament was two 88m flak guns with additional 20mm cannon fore and aft. However, initial tests in the English Channel demonstrated that the *Artilleriefährprähme* Type AC (AF-AC1) was only capable of operating in a maximum sea state of 3 and was not a very stable gun platform.

Improvements soon followed, including a remodelling of the bow (later returned to its original form but with the loading ramp welded shut),

An *Artillerieträger* of the 6th AT-Flotilla in dock for maintenance.

improved armour and weaponry plus the ability to construct various versions in sections and transport them by road and rail. While the myriad design improvements yielded different variants, the general effectiveness of the *Artilleriefährprähme* was unquestionable and they served in all European theatres of war as coastal escort and bombardment vessels.

Befehlshaber der Sicherung West, VA Ruge, reported that during February forces under his command had escorted 112 U-boats to and from harbour as well as 282 coastal freighters totalling 185,000GRT. Seven enemy air attacks, one MTB attack and one submarine attack were made on the convoys with only *V408 'Haltenbank'* sunk. Twenty-seven ground mines and fifteen moored mines had been cleared and three enemy planes claimed shot down. However, Ruge also noted a noticeable revival of enemy surface force activity along the French Channel coast that exploited gaps in mine barrages and a renewal of attacks by enemy submarines on the ore traffic from Bilbao.

In fact the sinking of *V408* heralded the arrival of a new enemy to the Bay of Biscay; USS *Blackfish* had sailed from the United States and taken part in Operation Torch before being based in Scotland for Biscay operations. Lt.Cdr. John Frederick Davidson encountered the *Vorpostenboot* on 19 February:

> At 1740 sighted two small vessels . . . No Spanish colors on bow; so went to General Quarters and made approach to attack. Vessels were in approximate column and were running about one half mile outside of 3-mile limit . . . At 1749 recognised German colors. At 1950 fired two torpedoes from bow tubes at leading ship [*V404*] and at 1752 fired two torpedoes at second ship [*V408*]. Ships had been identified as converted trawler type AS vessels with guns mounted fore and aft. Forward gun appeared to be about a 4-inch. One vessel appeared to have radar. One torpedo hit was made on second target and we were immediately counter-attacked with depth charges and something which

Three vessels of the 6th AT-Flotilla in harbour; the flotilla's 'crossed shells' insignia can be seen painted on the stern.

Another view of a vessel from the 6th AT-Flotilla.

sounded like bombs which did not produce much shock. Five bombs and four depth charges were dropped while we were going deep, the third depth charge being very close and jarring the ship considerably. Fortunately the fourth charge was quite far away as it was later discovered that the conning tower door frame had been cracked and main induction partially flooded, and it is my considered opinion that another charge as close as number three would have flooded the conning tower.[67]

The American submarine bottomed out in 368ft of water, later surfacing under cover of darkness and beginning the voyage to Plymouth for repairs.

The English Channel

The Royal Navy had also steadily strengthened its coastal forces in the English Channel and North Sea during the later months of 1942. The famous 'Dog Boats' were now operational, 'Fairmile D' MTB and MGBs, bigger and more heavily armed than their predecessors and designed to combat S-boats. Slower than their opponents, their 30-knot maximum speed made them faster than R-boats, though not as manoeuvrable. As well as convoy defence, the Dog Boats were frequently sent on offensive sweeps along the Belgian and Dutch coast.

During March 1943, for example, several such missions resulted in losses to both sides that demonstrated the difficult and dangerous work of attacking and defending small coastal convoys. On the night of 9 March, Royal Navy MTBs attacked a convoy off Terschelling escorted by minesweepers and *Vorpostenboote*. In the confused melee, *MTB622* was hit by several large-calibre shells and caught fire, eventually exploding with only ten survivors, including several wounded, rescued by *V1300*. The following night the Free French MTBs *96* and *94* sank minesweeper *M4620* off Morlaix after attacking a convoy of steamers under auxiliary minesweeper escort. Twenty-eight of the German crew survived with twenty-nine posted missing. Further east a convoy of the 18th Vp-Flotilla and two steamers came under fire from a British long-range coastal battery while travelling from Boulogne to Dunkirk. As German shore batteries returned fire, *V1802* sustained damage and casualties from shell splinters. Shadowed by an enemy aircraft until 0525hrs, the convoy was then attacked by *MTB24*, *MTB35* and *MTB38* off Gravelines, and the 3176-ton steamer SS *Dalila* was sunk by torpedo with twenty-six crewmen killed. On the night of 13 March two steamers – the 1495-ton Swedish SS *Hermod* and the 4398-ton SS *Liège* – were sunk by torpedoes from *MTB617*, *MTB628* and *MTB624* in an attack that went completely unseen; the sole German response being a starshell fired in the wrong direction by the escorting *Vorpostenboote*. Two nights later Danish steamers, SS *Maria Toft* and SS *Agnete*, carrying cargo from Rotterdam to Copenhagen were sunk by *MTB88* and *MTB93* despite the escort of *Vorpostenboote* from the 13th Vp-Flotilla.

With four steamers sunk by MTBs, convoys were ordered to use the route between the Elbe and the Hook of Holland only in daylight between 0400hrs and 2200hrs, putting into Den Helder or Borkum if necessary. Delays to scheduled traffic resulted, but the risk posed by MTB attack under the cover of darkness was deemed too great. *Marinegruppenkommando West* expected a resultant increase in enemy minelaying and strongly resisted the scheduled return of minesweeping units transferred from the iced Baltic Sea during the winter lull.

As if to underline this point, at 1910hrs on 17 March *R40* and *R177* both struck Mark XXV snagline mines four miles south-west of Boulogne, the former's bow being completely blown off although there were few casualties. The British Mark XXV was intended for use against S-boats and R-boats, triggered by any of four switch horns which had fishing lines and bottle corks attached that floated at propeller level.

Towards the end of April, the destroyers HMS *Albrighton* and *Goathland* plus supporting MTBs intercepted the fully-laden 4983-ton Italian tanker SS *Butterfly* travelling under the escort of *UJ1402*, *UJ1403*, *V424* and *V722*. Sailing in three columns, German lookouts sighted silhouettes to starboard at 0245hrs, although intelligence reports had indicated the possible presence of ships of the 24th M-Flotilla in the area and for eight crucial minutes the German convoy commander hesitated to change course. The decision was taken for him when shells began falling nearby.

V722 was hit almost straight away on the stern, the rudder and engine both failing as more concentrated fire rained upon the *Vorpostenboot*. Gunners at the 88mm continued to fire, registering a direct hit on HMS *Albrighton*'s bridge, killing eight men and wounding twenty-five others. The destroyer was less than 200m away and both sides blazed away with all available weapons. The auxiliary's 37mm cannon engaged an approaching British MTB to starboard, before a direct hit killed the gun crew. *V722*'s skipper,

An account from *Die Kriegsmarine* magazine of the battle involving *V722* and the tanker *Butterfly* that resulted in the awarding of the Knight's Cross to Steuermannsmaat Karl-Heinz Fischer (pictured top left).

30-year-old LzS Jonni Johannsen, ordered his crippled ship abandoned but as lifeboats were lowered to starboard, a prolonged burst of machine-gun fire swept across the deck, killing Johannsen and several of his men instantly, stored depth charges being hit but failing to explode. The IIWO counter-manded the order and survivors attempted to save their ship. By 0340hrs the German minesweepers *M422*, *M475* and *M483* (with flotilla commander KK Fritz Breithaupt aboard) were approaching along with *V210* from St Malo. Losing the upper hand, the British attempted to disengage although the battle was still raging at dawn.

With daylight came twenty-four Spitfires of 310 (Czech) and 313 (Czech) Squadrons along with four 263 Squadron Whirlwinds that began strafing the German ships, which in turn were engaged by two Luftwaffe Bf109 fighters, a 310 Squadron Spitfire V, piloted by Flying Officer Otto Pavlů, soon being shot down. Squadron-mate Otto Hrubý, flying next to Pavlů's plane, and Sergeant Vavřínek from 313 Squadron both witnessed a shell explode in Pavlů's cockpit, the stricken Spitfire turning upside down and crashing into the sea. *V722* came under direct attack from the Whirlwinds, the engine ventilators between bridge and smokestack being smashed by the impact of a bomb that failed to explode.

German losses were heavy. *UJ1402* had been hit and holed beneath the waterline. While the crew attempted to shore up the damage from inside, her depth charges detonated and she disintegrated in a searing flash. *Butterfly*, hit repeatedly by shellfire and burning out of control, eventually broke up and sank at 0600hrs.

Aboard *V722*, eighteen of the forty-one crew lay dead and another nineteen wounded. Steuermannsmaat Karl-Heinz Fischer took command after the IIWO was added to the casualty list. Despite blood streaming down his face from a head wound, he disengaged the ship as the battle petered out, sailing her towards Brest which the battered *Vorpostenboot* reached later that day. *V722* was found to have suffered 148 shell hits and over 600 holes from machine-gun fire. Fischer, already the bearer of the Iron Cross 1st and 2nd Class, received the Knight's Cross from Dönitz on 6 May 1943.[68]

Norway

The rugged Norwegian coastline was difficult for the Security Forces to patrol as they attempted to counter covert agent and Commando landings. On 31 March 1943 a *Räumboot* intercepted the Norwegian cutter *Brattholm* near Rebbenes in Karlsøy carrying a twelve-man sabotage troop. The small Norwegian craft had escaped to Iceland in November 1940, and was later requisitioned by the Norwegian authorities for service with the 'Shetland Bus', a clandestine ferry organisation formed by SOE for shuttling spies and equipment to Norwegian resistance groups. Attempting to escape, the cutter was hit by gunfire which killed Per Blindheim and injured two others who later died in hospital. Scuttling their small craft, eight of the Norwegians were taken prisoner and later interrogated, tortured and shot by the Gestapo, only Jan Baalsrud successfully escaping to Sweden.

Germany remained reliant on the safe passage of Norwegian coastal convoys for both the support of Army units within the Arctic Circle and import of raw materials. During the first six months of 1942, 872 freighters carrying 2,608,057 tons of supplies had shuttled between Kirkenes and Narvik, keeping the Wehrmacht war machine moving. Naval interdiction, primarily by submarine attack, was infrequent but the Norwegian coast would soon become a regular hunting ground for Coastal Command.

Their first raid that used the new Strike Wing tactics had taken place on 20 November 1942 in Dutch coastal waters. Twenty-four Beaufighters with Spitfire escort had launched the attack; three Beaufighters were shot down and two others crashing upon landing at their home airfield for the sinking of a 449-ton Dutch steam tug requisitioned by the Kriegsmarine as a salvage vessel. Future raids were suspended and did not resume until April 1943, once tactical mistakes had been analysed and rectified. On 18 April a second convoy was attacked off Den Helder and the 4006-ton Norwegian MV *Høegh Carrier* was sunk carrying a cargo of coal with two stokers killed and no loss to Coastal Command.

Emboldened, the RAF increased the tempo of shipping strikes while the Kriegsmarine could do little to improve defences beyond adding more guns, the Security Forces being overworked and spread increasingly thinly with new theatres of war opened. During May the new BSN, KA Ernst Lucht who had replaced Wolfram during April, maintained that only increased Luftwaffe protection could successfully defend coastal approaches. While others pressed for convoys to revert to night sailing, Lucht felt there was little to be gained at that time of the year due to the short hours of darkness. The Luftwaffe was, however, already stretched beyond its own limits.

In the Baltic, BSO VA Hans Stohwasser ordered two *Sperrbrecher* attached to each convoy rather than one due to the discovery of new British ground mines incorporating a combined magnetic-acoustic trigger combination. However, following heavy *Sperrbrecher* losses and a lack of replacement ships, the majority of escorting would be carried out by auxiliaries fitted with a towed cylinder gear, reducing convoy speed from an average of 9 knots to 5 or 6 knots; the number of convoys also decreased due to the doubled commitment of escorts.

When the Baltic winter ice cleared, German and Finnish ships immediately began to refresh the mine barrages at Porkkala ('Nashorn') and Hogland ('Seeigel'), the Germans laying 1965 mines in one seven-day period during May 1943. A net barrier was at last stretched parallel to 'Nashorn', extending

An RAF Coastal Command Beaufort bomber attacks a German freighter and *Vorpostenboot* (left).

60m into the depths and patrolled by *U-Jäger*. Soviet submarines attempted to pass through the formidable lines of defences but without success despite Red Air Force support. Nonetheless, the increase of air attacks on ships patrolling the barrier and German-held ports caused great disruption. A direct bomb hit on *M15* killed four men including commander of the 3rd M-Flotilla, KK Kurt-Joachim Schwarte, and his adjutant on 31 July. *M459* was hit during the course of a separate attack, severely wounding several men including the minesweeper's skipper although three of the attacking aircraft were shot down. Heavy damage was inflicted for the first time on German naval installations in Tallinn, the engineers' supply dump being destroyed with all equipment and material, while two small craft of the Ostmark River Police were damaged during the same raid. The culmination of this concerted Soviet effort saw 465 separate aircraft attacks within a single week between 18 and 25 August 1943, sinking several small auxiliary minesweepers. Both *M17* and *M30* were also damaged while patrolling 'Seeigel', four men being killed and two wounded on board the latter. The Luftwaffe was powerless to intervene as was the Finnish Air Force, despite assurances having been given. Half of the Security Forces' vessels were eventually disabled with severe losses of personnel.

> Our own forces were further weakened by the withdrawal of the 25th Minesweeper Flotilla and by the [ships'] insufficient anti-aircraft-gun armament and lack of protective shields. Commanding Admiral, Baltic, reports that it will be impossible to hold position Seeigel any longer if sufficient fighter protection is not given at once by the Luftwaffe. The situation is similar West of Seeigel and off Nashorn. Therefore an urgent strengthening of the fighter forces is requested for the whole Gulf of Finland.[69]

The Security Forces and convoy traffic were subsequently forced to withdraw during daylight. Despite this, the barriers remained effective and during 1943 not a single Soviet submarine reached the open sea. All Security ships were ordered equipped with extra 20mm cannon and four *Artilleriefährprähme* of the 24th L-Flotilla and extra boats of the 3rd Vp-Flotilla were assigned as anti-aircraft escorts to particularly valuable freighters and tankers sailing between Germany and the Baltic states.

In Denmark – long considered a 'model occupation' – civil unrest had begun during August. German authorities had exerted relatively little pressure upon the country following its capitulation in 1940, especially in comparison to other occupied states. The Danish military had continued to exist, albeit in somewhat reduced form, larger naval vessels remaining in harbour while minesweeping and patrol craft operated under their own national flag.

During the summer of 1943, demonstrations against Denmark's collaborationist policies resulted in increased levels of sabotage and nationwide strikes, Esbjerg workers leading the way on 10 August. German troops clashed with mobs of civilians and the Wehrmacht prepared plans for Operation Safari, the seizure of army and navy assets.

Vizeadmiral Hans-Heinrich Wurmbach, *Kommandierender Admiral Dänemark* (Commanding Admiral Denmark) since March 1943, attributed the increase in cases of sabotage to the import of British explosives and the landing of agents in Denmark via the Danish fishing fleet that still plied the waters of the Skagerrak and North Sea. Incoming fishing boats were subject to more intense searches by German coastal patrols and suspicious craft were fired on more than once. Minesweepers of the 29th M-Flotilla observed unidentified fishing vessels within a prohibited area on the evening of 24 August and fired several warning shots, driving them hurriedly away. Five more vessels under the Swedish flag were then encountered that evening after the Germans had discovered that only one of seven light buoys laid during the previous night was still alight, the switches of the remainder having been unscrewed and removed. Ignoring orders to stop, the Swedish boats sailed north-east across a German minefield as the minesweepers opened fire and sank two while the remainder faded into the darkness. The Swedish News Agency later reported that twelve people had been killed by German 'destroyers', maintaining that the vessels had been clearly identified as neutral.

Regional tensions increased with dockyard strikes affecting five *Vorpostenboote*, a *Sperrbrecher* and two steam tugs awaiting repair in Danish yards. Finally, Safari was ordered for 29 August after demands for Denmark's government to institute a range of emergency measures to crack down on the population were refused. At 0400hrs the operation began. The Danish naval authorities, having anticipated the move, ordered the wholesale scuttling of their fleet. German torpedo boats and Security Forces entered Danish harbours while elements of the 25th Panzer Division disarmed the army, serious resistance only being encountered during the occupation of Copenhagen's Naval Arsenal.

While a small number of ships escaped to Sweden and Great Britain, the Danes scuttled thirty-two of their larger vessels. The Kriegsmarine seized fourteen large ships and fifty small patrol boats, an additional fifteen of the scuttled ships later being raised and refitted. Initial German plans to accept Danish volunteers to man the vessels, either as civilian crews with German officers or as foreign Wehrmacht volunteers, were thwarted by Hitler's declaration that Reichsführer-SS Heinrich Himmler had been granted permission to recruit 4000 volunteers from the Danish armed forces for Waffen-SS service; any naval recruitment being ubsidiary to this. Correspondingly the 255-man minimum requirement to create a Danish *Küstenschutzflottille* was to be drawn from existing German units already experiencing a manpower shortage.

The Kriegsmarine was not only short of men but also ships. One solution was the creation of the *Kriegsfischkutter* (KFK). Before the war, German authorities had authorised design of the *Reichsfischkutter*, a trawler primarily constructed of wood over a steel frame by privately-owned shipyards to a standardised design that was suitable for deep-sea fishing but would, in the event of hostilities, be immediately returned to state control and converted to military use. During 1942 the Kriegsmarine called for renewed construction of these vessels, resulting in Germany's largest single shipbuilding programme. In total, 1072 of these trawlers were ordered from forty-two different yards in seven countries, including seventeen in neutral Sweden, unaware that they were building a military vessel, the contract being made with the Reich's Ministry of Food and Agriculture.

The first – *KFK1* – was launched by the Hamburg shipbuilder Eckmann during March 1943, though the majority built in Germany were manufactured at Swinemünde's Burmester shipyard. The remainder were constructed by twelve Dutch, six Belgian, two Bulgarian, two Greek and one Ukrainian yards and by the end of the war 612 had been completed. Each KFK was about 110 tons displacement, crewed by a complement of between fifteen to eighteen men. Powered by a single-shaft diesel engine, they could make 9 knots. The basic armament comprised one 37mm SK C/30 cannon mounted in the bow and a single 20mm C/38 astern but there was considerable latitude in what actual armament was carried, including the fitting of the fearsome *Vierling* four-barrelled 20mm flak atop the vessel's superstructure. With dimensions of 24m length, 6.4m beam and a draught of 2.75m, with little modification these extremely seaworthy craft could carry Oropesa and influence minesweeping gear, or *S-Gerät* and depth charges for use as *U-Jäger*. Small and lightly armed they may have been, but they were a welcome addition to the Security Forces, being both versatile and sturdy in service.

Larger vessels required more substantial commitment from Germany's industrial complex. In January 1943 Raeder had resigned as Kriegsmarine C-in-C, being replaced by Grossadmiral Karl Dönitz. U-boat production had increased dramatically once Dönitz had established his rapport with Armaments Minister Albert Speer. Dealing directly with Speer, Dönitz was

A seemingly successful *M43*-class minesweeper with three confirmed aircraft kills and one probable. Of prefabricated construction, 160 ships were ordered but only seventeen had been commissioned by the end of the war.

able to largely sidestep the internecine wrangles that bedevilled competing branches of Hitler's Wehrmacht. Alongside the increase in U-boat manufacturing, Speer was also able to boost production of S-boats and minesweepers. The results would be impressive; during 1944, eighty-seven new minesweepers were built as opposed to fifty-two during the previous year. Concurrently, during 1943 a new minesweeper type was designed with the aim of utilising prefabrication methods similar to those which would be used to construct the new generation of Type XXI U-boats.[70]

M43 Class Minesweeper

The *M43* class minesweeper was essentially a simplified version of the *M40*, originally intended to be made in block sections three to five tons each by AG Neptun, Rostock, with final assembly distributed between eleven shipyards. However, this block system was abandoned as logistically difficult in favour of prefabrication created by Dr Woldemar Rodin of F. Schichau GmbH, Königsberg. Nine further months of design work were completed before the seven prefabricated sections were perfected. These comprised the aftership, crew accommodation, engine room, boiler room, foreship, deck and bridge, upper deck and superstructure. The minesweepers could also be used as torpedo training ships equipped with two midships-mounted torpedo tubes, while others were supposed to fulfil an ASW role with extra depth charges.

The anticipated production time was three to four weeks per section, one week for assembly and launch, two weeks for final fitting-out and another week for sea trials. However, by the time the new type was ready for manufacture, Germany's infrastructure was being gradually destroyed by bombing and delays of up to six months became commonplace. In total, 160 ships were ordered with the building of sections begun for forty-nine of them. The first keels would be laid in 1944 and *M601* was launched in Rostock on 31 August. By the end of the war only seventeen had been commissioned.

Despite increased production of minesweepers, U-boats remained the priority. May 1943 had seen Dönitz concede defeat in the Atlantic as losses became untenable against dwindling success. Improved Allied tactics and technology had beaten his outdated boats and while this superiority dealt the German U-boats a body blow, code-breaking had finished them off. The Enigma machine, on which the Wehrmacht depended so heavily, had now been penetrated by the Allies at all levels in all services. The Germans no longer held any secrets.

7

War in Southern Russia: The Security Forces in the Black Sea, July 1942–1944

THE Black Sea *Räumboote* continued to escort supply convoys during July 1942 for Wehrmacht forces poised to finally batter Sevastopol into submission. Already, between 20 April and 3 July 90,000 tons of supplies had been delivered to the Crimean front by sea and 5000 tons of material transferred back to Romania. The Soviet Navy had disrupted these convoys for eighteen days in June with mines and torpedoes but the large ships of the Soviet Black Sea Fleet had not interfered. On 7 July, *R165*'s arrival in Sulina raised the 3rd R-Flotilla's operational strength to four boats. By then Sevastopol had finally fallen, organised resistance collapsing three days previously although scattered fighting continued for days afterwards.

Temporarily assigned to 'Naval Special Duties Detachment', the R-boats were scheduled to begin minesweeping duty off Crimea's west coast once additional flotilla boats had arrived and routine engine overhauls had been completed. Until then they remained constantly in action under the control of FK Birnbaum, the *Donauflottille* commander. Birnbaum was tasked with clearing a route along the Crimean coast from Eupatoria to Feodosiya with branches into active harbours. He had been named *Räumchef Krim* (Barrage Commander, Crimea) and co-ordinated the activities of the 'Naval Special Duties Detachment'. He planned and executed a landing of 'agents, prisoners of war and shock troops' between Cape Fiolyent and Khersones, south-west

Constanţa harbour photographed in 1942.

of Sevastopol, on 13 July using R-boats and MFPs to land troops. Mopping up lingering pockets of resistance, '111 prisoners, among them a Commissar, Staff Officers and women' were brought in while twenty-nine 'Russians who resisted' were shot. This operation was probably not connected to the orgy of violence unleashed against Sevastopol's captured Soviet Jews who were shot on the outskirts of the city, but there can be little doubt as to the fate of the Commissar who was subject to Hitler's *Kommissarbefehl* that called for their summary execution as purveyors of 'Judeo-Bolshevik ideology'.

The Wehrmacht prepared for a push east across the Kerch Strait on to the Taman Peninsula. German and Romanian troops were advancing into the Caucasus as part of Operation Edelweiss, their objective the oilfields at Baku.

German and Romanian troops in the Constanţa shipyards. German-Romanian co-operation was perhaps at its most efficient between their naval forces.

By the beginning of August they had passed Rostov and were headed south towards the coastal port of Novorossiysk, trapping Soviet forces on the Taman Peninsula. While the Soviet Black Sea Fleet began evacuating troops from the Sea of Azov, the Germans planned an amphibious assault across the Kerch Strait, code-named Operation Blücher. Intended for five entire divisions, four specially equipped tank-landing MFPs were requested. They were transferred from the Palermo shipyard, first to Piraeus and from camouflaged as merchant vessels and travelling onward to Thessaloniki in preparation for transfer into the Black Sea. The *Marinefährprähme* A1s were capable of carrying captured 52-ton KV1 tanks, not the newly-developed Tiger Is being rushed into service as the latter was too wide for the cargo bay. The hull was strengthened as was the loading ramp so as to bear the weight of the Soviet vehicles and the cargo bay roof removed. It was not until the development of the Type C2 that Tiger Is could be carried aboard MFPs.

Although bad weather hampered operations during late July, *R33* and *R164* finally arrived at Sulina, the last of the 3rd R-Flotilla's eight vessels now being fully operational in the Black Sea. They moved eastward to the advanced harbour at Ivan Baba, while MFPs prepared for transfer into the Sea of Azov for supply missions near Rostov.

Generalfeldmarschall Wilhelm List's Army Group A was tasked with conquering the entire eastern Black Sea shore, eliminating the Soviet Black Sea Fleet and its harbours. Kriegsmarine forces were to directly facilitate and defend the Army's crossing of the Kerch Strait. *Marinefährprähme* were shuttling supplies across the Sea of Azov to the Don River which led northeast to troops attacking Stalingrad. Road and rail transport was proving problematic in the occupied Soviet Union and the Kriegsmarine was frequently asked to operate as far east as possible. Army Siebel ferries were already sailing from Mariupol, one sunk by a Soviet mine on 28 July with heavy casualties after the retreating Soviets sowed the Sea of Azov with magnetic and acoustic mines.

The passage of the MFPs through the Kerch Strait would be covered by the Luftwaffe, whose task was to intercept enemy reconnaissance aircraft and also mask the sound of their engines by operations over the Taman Peninsula. The column of vessels was nearly 2000m long and vulnerable to Soviet artillery fire, so Army gunners planning to lay a thick smoke screen along the strait's northern shore. Vizeadmiral Wurmbach moved his headquarters temporarily to Kerch to directly oversee the operation himself, while sweeping of the southern strait was already underway by R-boats.

During the early afternoon of 1 August, MFPs of the 1st Landing Flotilla arrived at Sevastopol and Balaklava. They were to break through the Kerch Strait during the night of 2 August in Operation Regatta under close escort by the 3rd R-Flotilla. At 2300hrs they passed Cape Takil, hugging the coastline and screened to seaward by S-boats and Italian MAS boats. While the Luftwaffe mounted its covering missions and smoke was fired across the strait, four MFPs and half of the 3rd R-Flotilla successfully passed into the Sea of Azov. Two MFPs had already dropped out with engine failure before reaching the strait, two others and *R163* turning back at Yenikale and headed for Kerch after one of the barges was damaged by a Soviet mine. Leaving the disabled MFP behind, *R163* and the remaining barge made a second attempt to pass through the strait and successfully reached the Sea of Azov later that morning. The MFPs moved onwards together to Mariupol, which was under heavy Soviet air attack and in flames when they arrived. Over the course of two nights – 7 August and 9 August – fifteen more MFPs and R-boats successfully passed through the Kerch Strait without enemy interference in Operations Regatta II and Regatta III.

The R-boats immediately began minesweeping operations, accompanied by several of the MFPs that had been equipped for the task, the remainder already being engaged on supply missions and preparation for the upcoming Blücher offensive. Additionally, the Luftwaffe had despatched two Ju52/MS

Sperrbrecher 192 'Kepler' of the *Donauflottille* showing not only the heavy allocation of flak weaponry but also the cruciform iron bars of the CAM magnetic-minesweeping system on the ship's narrow deck.

'Mausi' aircraft to assist in mine clearance. They were equipped with a suspended magnetised ring capable of detonating magnetic mines.

Wurmbach ordered Birnbaum to oversee minesweeping operations within the Sea of Azov, the Kerch Strait and off the Caucasus coast from his headquarters at Ivan Baba. The recently-captured harbour of Akhtarsk in Krasnodar had been badly damaged but would potentially provide an advanced supply base for the Wehrmacht if free from mines. Elements of the *Donauflottille* were to also enter the Sea of Azov and work had already begun to convert two of the flotilla's motor vessels into *Sperrbrecher*, the 383-ton MS *Kepler* and her sister-ship *Albrecht Dürer*. The two riverine vessels were small and rather than the VES system installed aboard larger *Sperrbrecher* they utilised the CAM (Canona Antimagnetica) system. Of Italian design, this consisted of two large cruciform iron bars mounted on the vessel's upper deck. Both bars were alternately polarised with electrical current flowing through them, generating a magnetic field that could detonate mines 40m away. It required no elaborate wrapping of the hull with copper wire (which was in short supply) and as it was mounted on deck, maintenance was simplified. Purchased from the Italians and designated '*Kreuzpolgerät*' the system was installed aboard both *Sperrbrecher*, although shipyard congestion and weather-related delays caused by frost and snow meant that they would not be in service before 1943. A fourth *Sperrbrecher* was planned for the Black Sea. The 836-ton *Potemkin* had served as a Soviet troop transport before the fall of Sevastopol. Sunk by Luftwaffe aircraft on 4 May in Kerch harbour, she was later raised and repaired but was unfinished before events on the Eastern Front overtook the Kriegsmarine.

On the night of 19 August *R36*, *R37* and *R166* encountered a small convoy of Soviet steamers off Temryuk and attacked, sinking two of the escorts and driving the remaining ships back into harbour. Four nights later the besieged Soviet port was taken by Romanian troops of the 6th Cavalry Division, pushing two Soviet marine brigades into the Taman pocket and providing another front-line port for the unloading of Axis supplies. The harbour entrance was temporarily blocked by a scuttled lighter until Army engineers partially demolished the wreck. With speed and supplies essential, MFPs began unloading supplies seaward of the wreck despite periods of bad weather. *Räumboote* combed the area for mines while engaging Soviet shore batteries in an inconclusive duel. Within hours the first dock space had become available in the harbour itself. On 27 August the R-boats landed sixty men of '*Einsatzkommando Neumann*' to fully inspect the devastated port of Temryuk, *R36* leading the group under the guidance of a Russian pilot. The *Einsatzkommando* secured important documents and Soviet military maps, while establishing that the port itself had been virtually destroyed by retreating Soviet forces and Luftwaffe bombing.

Kriegsberichter Horst Grund (left), a photographer of the Propaganda Kompanie who saw action aboard vessels of the Security Forces in the Black Sea.

During September the number of MFPs allocated to the Black Sea MFP was fifty-six. Of these twenty-five were in service, nineteen either 'working up', in transit on the Danube or awaiting transfer from Germany, eight were unserviceable awaiting repair and four had been lost to enemy action. On 12 September KK Hölzerkopf was informed that his 3rd R-Flotilla would receive the new *R151*-class boats *R196*, *R197*, *R208* and *R209* which were to be accepted from the building yards at Swinemünde and Burglesum (Bremen) on 16 September and 8 October respectively. Their transfer to Korneuburg on the Danube near Vienna had been hastened, where their final assembly would be completed before continuing on to the Black Sea.

Taking the Taman Peninsula

At 0200hrs on 2 September, the long-awaited Operation Blücher, the attack across the Kertch Strait, began with three assault detachments of the 46th Infantry Division landed by MFPs, Siebel ferries and *Sturmboote* covered by the 3rd R-Flotilla with S-boats and Italian MAS guarding the flank to the south. With strong Luftwaffe support, German troops quickly took several villages south and south-west of the bridgehead while MFPs provided supporting fire. By 1500hrs the northern part of the Taman Peninsula was in German hands, followed by landings on the promontory south-west of Tamanskiy that encountering little resistance. Romanian cavalry advanced from Temryuk and it appeared that the battle for the Taman bridgehead would be over in days, possibly leading to the wholesale collapse of the Soviet forces in Krasnodar. Swept approach channels to the new bridgeheads were marked by R-boats as they cleared the area, although bad weather caused delays in resupply and reinforcement, while to the south German forces battled into the outskirts of Novorossiysk.

However, the Kriegsmarine's Black Sea strength was almost exhausted. By the middle of September only three S-boats and three Italian MAS were operational. The MFPs that had taken part in Blücher had added valuable fire support but received considerable damage from Soviet fire and the elements, requiring urgent repairs. They had ferried 21,144 men, 9229 horses and 3802 vehicles as part of Blücher, but OKW vetoed their withdrawal as the operation relied completely upon naval support. The R-boats were also

A boat of the 3rd R–Flotilla at sea; the flotilla insignia of a moose head silhouette visible on the bow amongst the dazzle camouflage.

showing the strain of constant deployment, engine overhauls frequently having to be delayed due to 'military necessity' while the crews grew increasingly fatigued. Even Wurmbach himself was relieved by his deputy VA Hellmuth Heye so that he could begin what would become five months of sick leave before reassignment to Denmark. Soviet submarines and aircraft soon began to make their presence felt as Kriegsmarine offensive pressure slackened, *R163* being briefly put out of commission with bomb splinter damage in Ivan Baba at the beginning of August and freighters bound for Kerch were torpedoed. Nevertheless, by the night of 9 September, all of Novorossiysk harbour was finally under German control, tiny Soviet enclaves on Mount Myskhako being the sole remaining enemy presence nearby. While storage facilities in Novorossiysk harbour had been completely destroyed, the main pier, coal yards and railway sidings were intact and promptly requisitioned for naval use.

Elements of the 3rd R-Flotilla moved to a forward base at Anapa, while at the end of September the 31st G-Flotilla was formed in Sevastopol specifically for convoy escort, the unit's commander KK Helmut Dreschler appointed *Geleitchef Krim-Kaukasus* (Escort Commander Crimea). Dreschler's new flotilla comprised fifteen steamers (numbered *G3101* to *G3115*) and fourteen converted trawlers that operated as auxiliary R-boats and minesweepers (numbered *G3161* to *G3170* and *G3181* to *G3184*).

On 14 October Heye summoned Kaptlt Giele to his headquarters to discuss the difficulties facing the 1st L-Flotilla and the siphoning-off of some of his existing overworked MFPs to form the 3rd L-Flotilla for 'special operations'. The new unit would be placed under the direct control of KA Ernst Scheurlen, who had arrived in the Crimea during July as *Führer des Marineeinsatzstabs Krim*, his command establishing supply bases in Kerch, Taman and Temryuk.

The following general picture emerged, which I have reported to Group South in the interests of the expected detailed orders on the co-ordination and operations of these vessels:

1. Nine barges in a state of growing disrepair on ferry duties on the Kerch route, two more whose repair will soon be completed, total 11 MFPs available.

2. During the next few days 17 MFPs are to be withdrawn from the Azov traffic, escort duties and Training Squadron Giele, in addition to two still under repair or conversion. Once these 19 MFPs have been withdrawn there will be none available during the next two weeks for the actual task, of supplying S-boats, German and Italian U-boats.

We may perhaps at the beginning of November have seven barges, provided trained crews are obtainable and the boats require no running in.

4. The next ferry barges do not arrive till mid-November.

5. In order to save time it is proposed to assemble the 19 MFPs belonging to

Siebel ferries were also used extensively in both the Black Sea and the Sea of Azov for fire support and transport missions, operated predominantly, but not exclusively, by the Luftwaffe as shown here.

Operations Staff, Scheurlen (Crimea) in an Eastern port, preferably Berdyans'k, and to carry out their exercises there. Constanţa not only involves a longer assembly period but also a later and longer advance to the East, at the expense of the time devoted to training and exercises.

6. Expert opinion regards repairs and additions as imperative if the boats are to be used at sea, particularly in view of the deterioration in the weather.

7. I have informed the relevant commands of the coming withdrawal of the MFPs and that, until November, there will be none available for escort duties and supplies.[71]

It was a bleak assessment and during October the 3rd L–Flotilla was formed in Berdyans'k on the Sea of Azov, its assembly organised by ObltzS Carlheinz Vorsteher before immediately being handed over to KK Gustav Strempel. The unit was designated a 'tactical flotilla' for use in minelaying and ASW work, as opposed to the transport duties of the 1st L–Flotilla's 'Blücher boats'. The flotilla was to be composed of three sub–units of seven MFPs each (though MGK Süd limited the initial strength to two groups lest the Blücher transport boats be unable to draw replacement craft). Experienced crews were transported from Germany and France in order to speed up the flotilla's combat readiness and exercises began at Constanţa using MFPs temporarily withdrawn from Blucher for repairs. The flotilla's own craft gradually arrived from Varna's Karolovag shipyard and from Germany via the Danube, though the latter were delayed due to the river's low summer level. Scheurlen's staff moved to Berdyans'k with radio vans, trucks, cars, signals equipment, fuel and accommodation ready for action.

Predictably, local requirements meant that some of the new flotilla boats were committed to transport duties before their 'special operations', pressed into service in the Kuban Strait as the Crimean-Caucasus supply system had experienced unwelcome disruption with the withdrawal of even the minimum number of craft for repairs. During October alone 20,100 troops, 7185 horses, and 954 vehicles were transported from Kerch to the Taman Peninsula, the barges returning with 3149 troops, 160 horses, 545 vehicles and 414 cattle. The use of Siebel ferries had been severely restricted due to their reliance on aviation fuel, and the MFPs that had been in action since the beginning of Blücher were showing severe structural and mechanical wear and tear.

However, even if MFPs had been available in greater numbers they were not equal to the task of keeping the Soviet Black Sea Fleet in check. *Schnellboote* and the six small U-boats of the 30th U-Flotilla would have been hard-pressed to combat an enemy superior in both size and numbers. Heye recognised the Wehrmacht's weak position on the eastern seaboard and he feared an inability to combat a determined Soviet amphibious counter-attack if supported by strong naval forces.

Winter weather brought extra difficulties, including a reduced radius of action for S-boats and R-boats as they required a greater fuel reserve should bad weather force an unexpected return to the lee of the coastline. *R33* was laid up with severe bearing and shaft damage on 18 October and towed to Mykolaiv on the Bug River for repair. *R36* was also soon out of action with damage to the boat's starboard engine. None of the front-line harbours had effective repair facilities and long voyages to the west were required for vessels needing shipyard time, MFPs requiring transfer to Varna as it was the only shipyard that could handle them.

Minefields were laid at the end of October to protect the convoy routes running from Constanţa to Kerch, though the task was too large to be carried out effectively. The initial section covered the sea area south of the island of Fidonisi although even Heye himself professed no confidence in the idea of flanking minefields as an effective method of convoy protection. But he had no alternative; his ASW capability was minimal, not helped by the diversion of the 3rd L-Flotilla to transport Luftwaffe ground troops across the Kuban Strait.

By the end of the first week of November ice had begun to form in the Sea of Azov and the 3rd L-Flotilla's transport duties became a matter of urgency, both to release the 1st L-Flotilla boats, now in an extreme state of disrepair, for shipyard time and also to complete the passage of troops across the Kuban Strait and enable the flotilla to withdraw west to ice-free waters.

> The withdrawal of Operations Staff, Scheurlen's ferry barges simply for a transport operation is regrettable in view of the training necessary for the special duties planned, more particularly since the time available is extremely limited owing to the ice that normally sets in mid-December in the Sea of Azov. It should also be remembered that the barges are not built for such permanent traffic and that their engines will soon break down, thus disabling them for the military operations shortly planned to take place.[72]

Ice in the Gulf of Taganrog forced the flotilla from Berdyans'k to the ice-free harbour of Sevastopol where the dry-dock, slipway and engineering sheds were undergoing repair to make them operational so that the long transit to Bulgaria was unnecessary. The coastal minesweepers of the *Donauflottille* and their repair ship *Uta* were also ordered to lay up at Linz over the winter months, the craft being unsuitable to the harsh winter sea conditions and allowing their crews to be used aboard more seaworthy vessels due for commissioning.

With the redirection of the 3rd L-Flotilla to purely transport operations, Scheurlen's *Führer des Marineeinsatzstabs Krim* was dissolved during November 1942, he himself being ordered to return to Germany as quickly as possible. The redundant operations staff were returned to their former commands but remained ready to reassemble at short notice if required. A number were employed as staff for the 1st L-Flotilla in which discipline, administration, welfare and medical inspection had been neglected due to a lack of available staff officers. With the cancellation of 'special operations', the 3rd L-Flotilla was at least well placed to transport supplies across the Kuban Strait – including urgently-required winter clothing – allowing the 1st L-Flotilla boats to finally transfer to Varna for a complete overhaul and a return to operations in Spring 1943, twelve also being scheduled for transfer to the Mediterranean (*F314*, *F315*, *F316*, *F322*, *F363*, *F367*, *F369* and *F372*) and the Aegean (*F308*, *F327*, *F330* and *F270*) where Kriegsmarine strength had also dwindled considerably. Meanwhile, VA Witthoeft-Emden arrived on 19 November to relieve Heye as *Admiral Schwartz Meer*; a day that would prove decisive for the Wehrmacht in the Soviet Union.

To the north-east the Soviets launched Operation Uranus as the German Sixth Army lay partially paralysed by the onset of winter and battle exhaustion in Stalingrad. The offensive broke through the Romanian forces north of the city, while the following day a second major offensive smashed the Romanian lines to the south. By 23 November the two prongs of the Red Army's advance had met at Kalach and Sixth Army was completely surrounded in Stalingrad. Axis forces throughout the entire Caucasus were thrown onto the defensive, an attack being expected against the Taman Peninsula. On 16 December Soviet forces launched Operation Little Saturn that hammered Axis forces within the Ukraine, pushing them away from Stalingrad and sealing the fate of the Sixth Army while the German 1st *Panzerarmee* was pushed back to Rostov and 17th Army towards the Taman Peninsula.

Transport missions across the Kuban Strait continued into December. At 0640hrs on 19 December, *F336* detonated a mine under her stern while two minutes later *F538* was blown 15m into the air and split in two by a second mine, the stern sinking first while the bow remained afloat for several minutes before also going down. Only one man was rescued unharmed from *F538*, a second being pulled from the water with serious injuries and the remaining thirteen either killed or missing. The damaged *F336* suffered no casualties and remained afloat, being towed into Kerch harbour. Both MFPs had strayed outside of the swept channels due to a navigational error.

The Soviets began deploying increasing numbers of destroyers on convoy harassment missions, though they were remarkably ineffective despite the dearth of Luftwaffe aircraft to counter them and lack of comparable defensive forces. U-boats of the 30th U-Flotilla were unequal to the task of convoy defence and both S-boats and R-boats were frequently defeated by bad weather. Maritime supply of the Army suffered during the winter due to the combined hazards of enemy action and bad weather. The movement of men and equipment increasingly relied on an already-overworked railway network and supplies of depth charges bound for the Black Sea also suffered as the available transport was prioritised for Army needs. Only half the normal depth-charge load per vessel could be carried from February 1943.

The December Soviet offensive had battered its way through to the shores of the Sea of Azov and, quite uncharacteristically, Hitler authorised a withdrawal into the Taman Peninsula not only to protect the eastern approaches to the Crimea but also to provide a potential launching point for renewed offensive operations against the Caucasus in 1943. Luftwaffe reconnaissance noted a steady build-up of Soviet forces in ports along the Black Sea and the expected storm finally broke on 4 February 1943 when elements of three Soviet infantry brigades landed at Cape Myskhako near Novorossiysk and were soon firmly established ashore.

The Kerch Strait received increased Soviet minelaying and both *F126* and *F472* were equipped with towed-loop minesweeping gear and assigned to the area to hunt for mines, while the 3rd R-Flotilla was split between escorting convoys from Constanţa and two craft, *R163* and *R165*, maintaining the swept channels around the Kuban Strait. The reactivated *Donauflottille* took command of the two MFPs while their coastal minesweepers began periodic operations whenever the weather permitted. Flotilla minelaying was also aided by the addition of ten MFPs. Should Novorossiysk Bay fall to Soviet troops, traffic crossing the Kuban Strait would be particularly vulnerable to Soviet coastal forces based in such proximity. Even complete destruction of the port by the retreating Wehrmacht would not prevent Soviet use of the bay for at least MTB and gunboats. Therefore defensive minelaying was undertaken between Cape Takil' and Cape Panagiya, effectively covering the Strait's southern approach. The first field of 153 UMA mines were placed 27m apart with 116 explosive buoys sown amongst them to prevent minesweeping, though the second phase of minelaying was disrupted by heavy swell resulting in the mines being laid closer together than planned and therefore insufficient for the task. The last ten to be laid also turned out to be duds and came to the surface where they were detonated by gunfire. On 24 February a final section was to be added to the barrage but the mission was disrupted by a freshening north-westerly wind and strong tides. As the MFP returned to Kerch *F143*, carrying thirty-four inactive UMA mines, struck a Soviet mine on the coastal route near Eltingen and sank with the entire crew of twelve men. Only 103 mines aboard three MFPs remained available to finish the ragged minefield which was completed the following day.

Transport missions in the Kerch Strait increased in number, those MFPs not used for minelaying, minesweeping and ice-breaking reverting to

The addition of four-barrelled '*Vierling*' flak guns to *Artillerieträger* helped combat the increased Soviet air superiority in the Black Sea as the Wehrmacht began its steady retreat west.

transport tasks under the command of KA Scheurlen who had been reassigned as *Führer des Marineeinsatzstabs Kerch* in February. *Marine-gruppenkommando Süd* had informed Witthoeft-Emden that the Crimea and Caucasus would rely solely on maritime supply with all Ukrainian railways being choked with traffic for other destinations. On 2 February Sixth Army had surrendered at Stalingrad and the front lines everywhere were in a perilous position. The Crimea was to be held at all costs. Naval reinforcements were urgently required for the Black Sea and Witthoeft-Emden ordered the formation of the 5th L-Flotilla. The flotilla commander, FK Karl Mehler, first gathered his staff in Antwerp before transferring to Kerch by the beginning of March. The flotilla itself was not fully operational until the following month. One more L-Flotilla, the 7th, was also created, based in Varna with a single group in Kerch and becoming operational in July 1943 under the command of KK Bernhard Stelter.

In February the 3rd AT-Flotilla was formed in Constanţa under the command of Kaptlt Curt Richter. Originally the unit was designated 3rd *Marineartillerieleichterflottille* and would also be temporarily known as *Artillerieträgerflottille Asowsches Meer* while serving within the Sea of Azov. The flotilla numbered eight MAL-type small fire-support landing ships (*MAL1–MAL4* and *MAL8–MAL11*). These 140-ton vessels measured 34.2m long and 7.72m wide with a draught of just 87cm full load. Two 260hp Deutz diesels gave a top speed of 8.5 knots and a range of 790 nautical miles. Each vessel's armament of two Army 88mm and two 20mm cannon and one anti-aircraft rocket launcher was manned by a maximum of twenty-nine men. Built by Krupp in Rheinhausen they comprised an open hold with gun positions and the unarmed variant was able to carry 200 troops or 80 tons of cargo. Disassembled in sections they were transported by truck and rail from Germany to the Black Sea and reassembled there. The first three were operational in Constanţa on 26 April, travelling to Sevastopol under escort by *R37* from where they were scheduled to be transferred to the Sea of Azov following an inspection by *Admiral Schwarz Meer*.

Thick glutinous mud obstructing the approaches to the eastern landing stage hindered troop trasnport across the Kuban Strait until timber was delivered by barge to build new landing ramps. Hitler himself impressed upon the Kriegsmarine that the transport of troops to and from the Taman Peninsula was the 'most vital naval task since the Norwegian operation'. Constant Soviet air attacks posed the most immediate threat; on 26 February alone *F176* received a direct bomb hit on her stern which detonated the ammunition, wrecking the boat with eight men injured and leaving *F372* lightly damaged with one man killed and two wounded.

Nevertheless, during March 1943 the Kriegsmarine safely transported 22,026 men, 1655 prisoners, 1551 civilians, 19,835 horses, 5534 horse-drawn

Lookout duty on patrol in the Black Sea; another atmospheric photograph taken by Kriegsberichter Horst Grund.

vehicles, 930 transport vehicles and 1650 tons of supplies across the Kuban Strait. At that point the advance harbours at Anapa and Novorossiysk were still in German hands though rigged for demolition. Risky convoys of MFPs acting as both transports and escort were run from Kerch to Anapa were vulnerable to Soviet artillery fire from their strongly-held Cape Myskhako beachhead. The vessels also attracted the attention of Soviet airborne forces: paratroopers landed north of Anapa on 20 March to sabotage any MFPs in harbour with delayed demolition charges. Five of the raiders were captured and the remainder driven off.

To stabilise the Taman Peninsula, the Soviet Myskhako beachhead had to be eliminated. The German Seventeenth Army planned Operation Neptune to overrun it, the 3rd R–Flotilla being tasked with intercepting inbound Soviet supply traffic. On 13 April *R35*, *R36* and *R165* completed the first of these night operations, greatly hindered by bad weather and finding no supply traffic or patrol activity. Taking the opportunity to mount a reconnaissance mission, Kaptlt Helmut Klassmann discovered a battery of searchlights between Cape Doob and Cape Myskhako that swept the entrance to the bay every ten minutes. The following evening the three R–boats repeated their mission, lurking in attack positions less than a mile off the coast. Though they had a clear view of the Soviet landing points they still observed no enemy vessels, taking the opportunity to calculate navigational aids for the upcoming Neptune attack which would be difficult due to the proximity of German defensive minefields covering Novorossiysk.

Originally scheduled for 6 April, Neptune was repeatedly postponed as bad weather prevented Luftwaffe support. Vizeadmiral Gustav Kieseritzky (who had replaced Witthoeft-Emden as *Admiral Schwartz Meer* in February) had been ordered to support the Army landings; to prevent enemy reinforcement and supply by sea and tie down opposing light naval forces. Anapa was the planned jumping-off point, but Kieseritzky could only muster four boats of the 1st S-Flotilla, eight Italian MAS boats and *U24*. He therefore decided to use *R35*, *R36* and *R165* of the 3rd R-Flotilla, reasoning that their 37mm main armament and armoured bridges made them more suitable than both the Italian MAS and S-boats whose torpedoes were useless against small vessels and which mounted only 20mm cannon. Kapitän-leutnant Klassmann had replaced Hölzerkopf as commander of the 3rd R-Flotilla during March and he opted to lead the three R-boats personally. Extra berths were provided at Anapa by laying mooring buoys north of the mole, with shore billets hastily arranged and six days' worth of provisions for the crews shipped ashore. The buoys were highly vulnerable to enemy attack as they lay unprotected offshore, strong northerly winds also violently pitching the moored vessels, so much so that crewmen were ordered to sleep ashore so that they could rest between night missions. Sufficient fuel for four separate sorties was provided. The R-boats were operationally directly off the enemy beachhead, while the S-boats would be concentrating on the area between Suchuk and Cape Doob and the Italians between G'helonjik and Cape Idokopas. *U24* would operate offshore between Idokopas and Tuapse. Klassmann and KK Georg Christiansen, commander of the 1st S-Flotilla, conferred about operational conditions near Myskhako, including minefields and a large wreck off the cape that posed a navigational hazard.

The R-boats sailed at 0545hrs on 16 April and were in position from 2000hrs though the sky was clear and they had a bright moon behind them, rendering them highly visible from the Soviet-held coastline. At 2350hrs they sighted and engaged a single gunboat and MTB headed on a south-easterly course. The action lasted 35 minutes before the Soviets retreated, the R-boats then moving on to bombard the enemy landing stages at Myskhako. Coming underaccurate artillery fire from the shore, they retreated to Cape Doob where no traffic was sighted and the returned to Anapa.

Operation Neptune began at 0600hrs on 17 April when the infantry began their ground assault. Klassmann put to sea again, standing off Myskhako from 1940hrs. As soon as they arrived on station the three boats came under heavy artillery fire from batteries in Kabardinka Bay and were soon embroiled in an action taking place between S-boats and Soviet MTBs. Repeatedly machine-gunned and bombed by aircraft, one man aboard *R35* was wounded and a 20mm gun put out of action. After midnight they had three further clashes with Soviet light forces and shelled the Myskhako landing stages again while coming under fire from guns ashore. During the early hours of the morning the enemy gunfire abated and the R-boats returned to Anapa.

The following evening they sailed at 1900hrs and again shelled the Soviet beachhead four times, destroying an ammunition carrier, the resultant fire engulfing a landing stage which subsequently exploded. Three skirmishes with Soviet MTBs were inconclusive and the R-boats had returned by 0445hrs the following morning.

Ashore, German troops had become rapidly bogged down against stiff Soviet resistance and it soon became apparent that the original timetable of four days would be completely insufficient; the R-boats, S-boats and MAS boats would henceforth be rotated in their operations so as to allow rest and recovery time between missions. Meanwhile the remainder of Klassmann's flotilla was still engaged on minesweeping and escort duties. On 20 April at 0123hrs the 6875-ton Romanian steamer SS *Suceava* was torpedoed and sunk while travelling from Sevastopol to Constanţa under escort. The ship, representing about one-quarter of the available Axis freight capacity in the Black Sea, was hit by three torpedoes and sank within four minutes with twenty-six men lost including KzS Boy Federsen, commander of all maritime transport in the Black Sea. The attack took place in bright moonlight in calm weather with no visible torpedo tracks. *R164* stopped her engines and detected the sound of a submerged submarine by hydrophone, but *S33* escaped unscathed.

Kieseritzky repeated the demands for *U-Jäger* that he had made since his assumption of the Black Sea command. His ASW force was completely insufficient and plans to equip twelve converted trawlers with the necessary gear were the subject of frustratingly repeated delays. It was not until June 1943 that the 1st UJ-Flotilla was formed in Sevastopol under the command of ObltzS Hans-Herbert Böttger. Before then there had been little success against Soviet submarines, although on 17 December 1942 the converted minelayer *UJ116 'Xanten'*, attached to the ASW contingent of the *Donau-flottille*, sank the Soviet *M31*. The submarine had attempted to attack a small convoy in the Bay of Zhebriyany, escorted by *UJ116* and other flotilla craft. The submarine was detected and forced momentarily to the surface before diving again whereupon *UJ116* made sonar contact and dropped thirty-six depth charges that brought debris and oil to the surface, no trace being found of the twenty-one crewmen.

Missions in support of Neptune continued, S-boats torpedoing the landing stages and all vessels engaging Soviet coastal forces and land-based artillery. It became apparent that Soviet forces were being strengthened and the German boats were continually put at a disadvantage by bright moonlight silhouetting them against the horizon. The three R-boats spent one night in Ivan Baba to rest and recuperate fully as Soviet aircraft bombed and strafed Anap, their main targets being the airfield and harbour mole. The urban area adjacent the harbour was almost completely destroyed, naval personnel being in bunkers that at least afforded some protection against direct hits by light bombs. By 23 April it was clear that Neptune had failed. The Luftwaffe was no longer able to mount attacks of any scale and while Soviet counter-attacks on land were being repulsed, it was clear that the German beachhead at Novorossiysk was close to collapse. Kieseritzky urgently enquired about the status of the operation and was informed by Army Group A that requests to discontinue the attack had been made but not yet granted. So the boats sailed once again that night, while MFPs were used to evacuate wounded from Anapa.

Klassmann's boats were heavily bombed by aircraft on their outward passage and once off Myskhako were engaged six times by MTBs and patrol vessels that were protecting small supply ships running to the landing stages. One MTB (possibly *CKA041*) and a transport vessel estimated at 100 tons were set ablaze, the former sinking while the burning transport dropped out of the convoy and headed south-east. A second MTB was hit and observed breaking away behind a thick smoke screen. In total the R-boats fired 1091 37mm and 1150 20mm rounds before retiring to Anapa, the guns of *R36* no longer operable after the fierce action.

On 24 April Army Group A finally suspended Neptune in the face of mounting casualties and little headway, and *R165* sailed for Sevastopol to resume minesweeping operations. With Soviet forces launching concerted attacks against German positions on the Taman Peninsula, *R35* and *R163* were moved into the Sea of Azov to patrol north of Temryuk to prevent any attempted landings. Reinforcements were urgently requested for the region and Kieseritzky inspected the three new *Artillerieleichter*. His impression was less than favourable.

1100hrs: I went to Sevastopol to inspect the naval gunnery lighters which arrived there this morning. The inspection showed that in their present condition they are not operational either in their equipment or personnel.
1) Some of the pontoons are not watertight because their flange-joints leak; as a result the ammunition and supplies carried were partially swamped. The joint strengtheners already delivered will have to be added in Sevastopol.
2) The vessels have not full anti-magnetic protection; degaussing equipment not yet built in as it is still at testing stage.
3) Crews for the most part have no naval training, gun crews have no training, and there is no one trained to take charge of fire control. As, in my opinion, the strength of the naval gunnery lighters lies in well-directed fire from the

88mm gun, these deficiencies are of decisive importance.

For these reasons I have given the following orders:

a) The joints are to be reinforced immediately by Naval Fitting-Out Depot Sevastopol.

b) Degaussing equipment will be put in later in Sevastopol as soon as we have the results of the trials with naval gunnery lighter No. 4 in Constanţa.

c) The flotilla will carry out a short ten-day training period with a final inspection in Sevastopol before the boats are transferred to the Sea of Azov.[73]

Klassmann's flotilla divided operations between Myskhako and the Sea of Azov, basing itself midway at Kerch between patrols. At 0950hrs on 29 April the 1756-ton German steamer *Arkadia*, on passage to Constanţa under R-boat escort, ran into a German minefield by mistake and sank in seven minutes with no casualties. Assuming a navigational error, *R36* was despatched to investigate the sinking by finding the wreck and calculating its exact position. However, *R36* also struck a mine, the boat's bow being blown off back to the bridge though miraculously nobody was injured and the engine undamaged. The shattered boat was towed to Constanţa. Investigations into both sinkings concluded that the steamer was probably sunk by an error in navigation resulting from a stronger southward current caused by the spring thaw in the Danube. The lack of such environmental details, only picked up through practical experience in the area, had not been passed on to the inexperienced young officers in command of convoy ships due to the frequent rotation of naval officers in Romania's Kriegs-marine command.

On 5 May, Soviet troops captured Krymsk, north-east of Novorossiysk, three weeks later beginning an offensive against German units sandwiched between the Sea of Azov and the Black Sea, but were repulsed after desperate defensive fighting. Soviet submarines continued to attack coastal convoys, MFPs *F329* and *F307* being attacked by gunfire by *L4* south of Sudak on the Crimean coast on 23 May. Unable to achieve a torpedo firing position, the submarine surfaced and fired eight 102mm shells, the first time that a Soviet submarine had attempted a surface attack so close to the Crimean coast, a sign of increased confidence. *L4* surfaced on the convoy's starboard quarter at a range of about 3000m and opened fire, *F307* immediately turning towards the submarine and returning fire with her 75mm gun while *F329* turned to port to use the boat's 20mm guns followed by the main gun. The Germans claimed to have scored at least three hits before *L4* submerged amidst 'thick smoke'. *F329* had been hit on the port side level with the wheelhouse, all three engines and the rudder being disabled and four men killed and two wounded. *F307* came alongside to render assistance, abandoning the pursuit of the retreating submarine. This decision was later criticized by Kieseritzky.

Depth charges dropped at once at the place of submerging might have been successful under the particularly favourable conditions, as there were oil traces from the damaged submarine. The decision of *F307*'s commander to assist the badly damaged *F329* instead of attacking the limping submarine can be attributed to his lack of experience. Most boats have only a leading seaman in charge. I cite this incident to direct all naval forces once more that their main task is to destroy the enemy regardless of their own situation.[74]

The gunboats of 3rd AT-Flotilla were finally committed to action and during early morning on 5 June *MAL1* joined a patrol line that included MFP *F401*, two *Hafenschutzflottille Mariupol* boats and two boats of the *Küstenschutz-flottille* along with five combined operations vessels. They encountered the Soviet *SKA Nr-011*, *BKA Nr-112* and *BKA Nr-114* attempting to land troops, which opened fire with 45mm guns upon their approach. The lightly-armed *Hafenschutzflottille* vessels leading the line returned fire with machine guns but before the heavier vessels could join the fray the enemy were gone, *SKA Nr-011* suffering light damage and aborting the troop landing. The inexperience of the patrol commander in unevenly distributing his heavier weapons within the formation led to Kieseritzky issuing strict directives on patrol configuration. The *Artillerieträger* would finally prove their mettle during June and July, with small groups under R-boat escort undertaking coastal bombardments and attacks on enemy shipping.

In June 1943, the 1st UJ-Flotilla was commissioned, comprised of eight converted trawlers stationed initially in Sevastopol before moving to Constanţa. A second UJ-Flotilla was also created in Varna that same month. The men of the Croatian Legion stationed in the Sea of Azov had handed their vessels over to the local German *Hafenschutzflottille* before returning to Croatia on leave. After training with German instructors, they transferred to Varna and were equipped with twelve small *U-Jäger*, averaging 100 tons each, and were designated the 23rd UJ-Flotilla. When Fascist Italy capitulated in September 1943, the existing moratorium on Croatian naval forces operating in their home waters was rescinded and so the Legion was returned to Croatia, the final group leaving the Black Sea on 21 May 1944, bound initially for Trieste. Upon their departure, the 23rd UJ-Flotilla became a registered part of the Kriegsmarine. Some of the repatriated Croatians served aboard various German ships of the Adriatic's *Sicherungsverbände*, while the majority reported for duty with the navy of the Independent State of Croatia.

In June the Black Sea Security Forces were further reinforced by the 30th R-Flotilla, formed of small Dutch boats *RA51*, *RA52*, *RA54*, *RA56* and *R30*. They had traversed the Danube to the Black Sea under the command of KK Eduard von Helleparth. In July the 30th G-Flotilla was set up after a reorganisation of the *Donauflottille*, based in Odessa under the command of Kaptlt Dr Heinrich-Hans Basarke. Croatians formed the basis of the 31st G-Flotilla which was not passed to German control until Spring 1944 when command transferred to KK Helmut Dreschler, *Geleitchef Krim*. The small escort ships were used to escort coastal convoys in Romanian and Bulgarian waters. The last unit formed during 1943 was another Croatian flotilla, the 3rd UJ-Flotilla was created on 16 November 1943 from *Kriegsfischkutter*, later also handed back to German control in April 1944.

The Security Forces were increasingly used in offensive roles in the Black Sea. For instance, in good weather on 7 July three simultaneous operations were carried out against Soviet supply traffic. To bolster the eight operational boats of 1st S-Flotilla, Kieseritzky attached *R33* and *R166* which were ordered to accompany *S40* against the Myskhako landing stages once more. After hours of fighting the three vessels withdrew, *S40* colliding *R33* at high speed and causing considerable damage although they both reached Kerch. The damaged *R33* was taken to Yalta where, on the morning of 19 July, she suffered a direct hit during an air raid and sank. Replacements were soon on hand. '*Räumboote R203* and *R204* were commissioned today for 3rd R-Flotilla in Linz and colours were hoisted.'[75] After sailing down the Danube from Linz the nine boats, *R203–R209*, *R216* and *R248* were soon on strength within the Black Sea.

The Collapse of the Kuban Bridgehead

However, the Eastern Front was crumbling. During July and August 1943 the ambitious German offensive against the Kursk salient had been fought to a standstill and then forced back as Soviet forces launched their own summer counteroffensives. The Wehrmacht's tenuous foothold on the north-eastern coast of the Black Sea came under increasing pressure. By 7 September the battered Seventeenth Army had finally begun evacuating the Taman Peninsula, and three days later the Red Army attacked Novorossiysk with 129 landing craft carrying nearly 9000 troops and forcing the German defenders to evacuate. Anapa was abandoned on 21 September, reducing the German defensive pocket yet further and providing the feared nearby MTB base. On 27 September Temryuk fell to the Soviets and by 9 October the Kuban bridgehead had been destroyed. The final German and Romanian units to be evacuated to the Crimea left the small island of Kosa Tuzla in the Kerch Strait at dawn that day. Although it could not be claimed a victory, the Kriegsmarine had successfully evacuated 97,941 tons of war material, 12,437 wounded, 6329 soldiers, 12,383 civilians, 1195 horses, 2265 head of livestock, 260 motor vehicles, 770 horse-drawn vehicles and 82 guns between 7 September and the end of the withdrawal. Before long, the Axis forces on the Crimean peninsula were isolated as Soviet advances to the north cut off land access.

The intervening months were filled with constant sorties against increasingly daunting Soviet sea and air power. Finally, at 0300hrs on 1 November the natural defensive barrier of the Kuban Strait was crossed by Soviet troops. Despite poor weather and rough seas, 14,000 men of the Soviet 318th Rifle Division and the 386th Naval Infantry Battalion landed in improvised landing craft at Eltigen south of Kerch. With artillery support from the eastern shore and complete aerial superiority, they forced the defending Romanian mountain troops from the coastline and establishing a shaky toehold on Crimean soil, not much wider than the beach itself and under intense fire.

The 3rd R-Flotilla was ordered to set up a patrol line of three boats close inshore in anticipation of further landings and to blockade the beachhead. Kieseritzky despatched MFPs to attempt to patrol the Kuban Strait and lay defensive mines, all of his vessels now being committed to action with no operational reserve. Bad weather and heavy swells frequently disrupted the German patrols while 300 men of the security flotillas that were without assignment were transferred to Army command in a desperate attempt to stop the Soviet advance into the Crimea. The commander of the 3rd L-Flotilla recommended using his landing craft to make an amphibious assault behind the Soviet troops ashore, but the Wehrmacht simply did not have the men available to mount such an operation.

Two days later at Yenikale, north of Kerch, over 4400 men of the 2nd and 55th Guards Rifle Divisions landed in a second amphibious attack that battered its way inland through German and Romanian troops, supported by massed artillery fire from the Taman Peninsula. Reinforcements poured into Yenikale and by 11 November 27,700 men had landed and were holding firm against all counter-attacks.

While the second Soviet beachhead was secure, R-boats supported by S-boats and MFPs kept the Eltigen pocket under heavy siege for almost five weeks, often with close-quarters fighting off the contested coast as R-boats clashed with the enemy vessels attempting to defend the landing ground. The firepower advantage of the Soviet gunboats was nullified by Klassmann taking his boats as close as possible, below the minimum elevation of the Soviet heavy guns. Everything from depth charges to hand-held *Panzerfaust* anti-tank weapons were used by the German crews.

This was achieved by something virtually unique in modern naval warfare – a nautical street fight, waged from nut-shell to nut-shell, during which, as often as not, the opposing ships shaved past each other with only yards to spare . . . It was the days of piracy again. Many of the men must have been reminded of pictures of the great naval battles of the past in which opposing fleets sailed close enough to fire broadsides into each other's hulls. The

Gun crews aboard a *Marinefährprähme* used to bombard Soviet positions in Crimea.

opponents faced each other at pistol range, the hand-to-hand fighting lit up in ghostly fashion by the tracer bullets, searchlights and star-shell. The battle was hot, but the Germans, with their faster and more manoeuvrable boats, kept the upper hand.[76]

Preparing flare pistols for signalling use. R-boats were used to bombard Soviet beachheads as the Wehrmacht's hold on the eastern Black Sea coast came under increasing pressure during 1944.

Finally, a German–Romanian infantry attack on 7 December destroyed the Soviet beachhead, resulting in the capture of 1570 men, 25 anti-tank guns and 38 tanks. However, by then Yenikale was securely held by over 75,000 well-equipped Soviet troops who had reached the outskirts of Kerch. While they proceeded no further during 1943, they had established a firm jumping-off point for a full-scale invasion of the Crimea in 1944, as Partisan activity increased dramatically supported by covert landings of men and equipment from submarines.

On 19 November VA Gustav Kieseritzky was killed by enemy aircraft while leading naval troops against the Eltigen beachhead near Kamysh Burun, FK Karl Mehler of the 5th L-Flotilla being badly wounded. The post of *Admiral Schwarzes Meer* passed to VA Hellmuth Brinkmann, the former commander of the cruiser *Prinz Eugen* and Chief of Staff of MGK Süd. Losses amongst the MFPs in the Kuban area had been heavy, particularly after strong Soviet MTB attacks, and Brinkmann struggled to balance the use of those available between supply of the Army and offensive or defensive naval operations.

Supply convoys were never more important and on 23 November the 4627-ton German freighter SS *Santa-Fe* sailed as convoy Wotan from Constanţa for Sevastopol escorted by the Romanian destroyer *Marasti*, Q-ship *Lola* and *R165*, *R197* and *R209*. The steamer carried twelve StuG III assault guns, two Jagdpanzer tank destroyers and 1278 tons of ammunition

An image claimed to show Kriegsmarine men captured by a Soviet sailor on the Crimean Peninsula.

and fuel desperately needed at the front but was torpedoed early that morning by the Soviet submarine *D4*, breaking in two and sinking in minutes. Twenty-eight crew members were killed and sixteen missing.

The wreck of the *Santa Fe* would claim another victim on 15 December when *UJ101* and *UJ102* were hunting another potential submarine contact in Eupatoria Bay. At 0156hrs *UJ102* dropped a depth charge that resulted in a huge explosion followed by blazing oil on the surface spotted by men aboard the accompanying *U-Jäger*. Of *UJ102* there was no trace found except bodies and wreckage, the depth charge having landed near the wreck of the freighter and detonated the ammunition and fuel aboard.

The dawning of 1944 saw the Wehrmacht hard pressed along the Eastern Front. The Crimea had been cut off to the north as the Soviet Army won the battle on the Dneiper bend forcing German stabilization of the front line further west. Kiev had been liberated by the Red Army on 3 November and Soviet units were at the Eastern edge of the huge Pripet Marshes.

During January *Geleitchef Schwarzes Meer*, KzS Kurt Weyher, was made commander of the newly-established 10th *Sicherungsdivision*. Weyher, former captain of the raider *Orion*, also occupied the post of German Chief of Staff to the Romanian Royal Navy. The 10th *Sicherungsdivision* combined command of all German Black Sea vessels with the exception of S-boats and U-boats, his headquarters established within the Carlton Hotel in Constanţa. Additional units added to Weyher's command during 1944 included the 1st

Kustenschutzflottille Sulina and 2nd *Kustenschutzflottille* Constanţa, formed from small *Kriegsfischkutter* in June to patrol the coastal waters. However, by that stage the battle for the Black Sea had already been decided, despite a desperate rearguard struggle throughout the beginning of 1944.

On 10 February, the Soviet submarine *ShCh216* was sunk by *UJ103* and *UJ106* after attempting to attack an escorted convoy. One torpedo exploded 100m away from *UJ106*, the submarine being detected by hydrophones and subjected to depth-charging after which an oil slick rose to the surface along with splintered wooden panelling, cigarette packs, torn clothes and books. On 18 April it is likely that Lieutenant Boris Gremyako's *L6* was sunk by *UJ104* after an attempted attack on a Romanian convoy. Following depth-charging of the submarine's location, air bubbles and an oil slick marked the presumed end of *L6* and her fifty-six crew.

Meanwhile by 13 March Odessa was under threat from Soviet troops advancing through the Ukraine and the Kriegsmarine began to evacuate, the shipyard at Mykolaiv falling on 29 March. Defending Hungarian troops had withdrawn after contact with the advancing Soviets, while the Germans removed as much material from the yards as possible, transferring it to Galati and Constanţa. The Romanian authorities briefly handed over the Odessa shipyards to the Kriegsmarine, which had previously been employed primarily with the repair of Romanian naval vessels while Varna in Bulgaria had served the requirements of the German security flotillas.

Finally, on 8 April 1944, the Soviet invasion of the Crimea began. Huge numbers of Soviet troops crossed the Kerch Strait, battled through the Crimea and were threatening Sevastopol with capture by the end of the month. The Germans began evacuating the port city and by 8 May, 90,260 able-bodied soldiers and 15,435 wounded had been transported to Constanţa, the city falling the following day as the final German pockets of resistance on the Crimea surrendered. During the struggle for the Crimea, *R204* was sunk by aircraft near Feodosia and *R208* was sunk by a mine in the Danube near Linz, shortly after commissioning into the flotilla.

During June and July the short-lived 10th *Sicherungsdivision* was dissolved and all craft were returned to Brinkmann's control, Weyher being transferred to Crete as *Seekommandant*. The Security Forces continued to protect coastal convoys, now more commonly engaged on evacuating troops north of the Danube to German-held territory as bridges had been demolished. Under Soviet pressure, the Bulgarian Government demanded the withdrawal of German naval forces from the Danube and Black Sea, declaring themselves neutral on 26 August.

Schnellboote and U-boats were ordered to remain in the Black Sea alongside the 3rd R-Flotilla, 3rd AT-Flotilla, 1st UJ-Flotilla, seven minelaying MFPs of the 1st L-Flotilla, two tank-carrying and one workshop

MFP, six transport MFPs and nine converted trawlers of the 2nd *Küsten-schutzflottille*. The remaining craft were to transfer to the Danube beginning on the evening of 22 August. *Räumboote* and *Artillerieträger* operated by night as protection for the eastern flank of the German front lines, patrolling the Sulina estuary alongside Romanian naval units to prevent seaborne landings. Klassmann had command of those operations, his flotilla being provided with six berths 10 miles upstream along the Danube, while the *Artillerieträger* were berthed in Sulina itself where their heavy guns could strengthen the port's anti-aircraft defences and provide protection against Partisans.

Romania Surrenders

Eleven MFPs were already operational on the Danube by 22 August 1944, ten at Izmail and others en route from Constanţa alongside the *Xanten* and *Schiff 19*. Additional craft were being mustered for ferrying duties, the commanders of 1st L–Flotilla, 7th L–Flotilla and 1st *Küstenchutzflottille* being assigned as unit leaders for the transportation of troops across the river. At 1400hrs on 23 August, Brinkmann arrived at Generaloberst Johannes Friessner's head-quarters of Army Group South Ukraine for a situation conference. That day, as the Red Army pierced the Moldavian front, King Michael I of Romania mounted a successful coup, deposing the Antonescu dictatorship and effectively taking Romania out of the Axis. The Romanian authorities offered German forces an unobstructed withdrawal from their country. Hitler, however, was certain that the coup could be reversed and the regional Wehrmacht and Waffen-SS troops were immediately placed on alert to block Soviet advances and counter Romanian 'unrest'. At 0255hrs on 24 August Brinkmann was ordered to take and hold Constanţa.

It was a ridiculous command as he had nothing like the manpower neces-sary to do so. Brinkmann informed Berlin that with his limited resources and Soviet troops only 90km away and advancing unopposed, it was impossible to carry out his orders. Nonetheless, he received further instructions to do the impossible and seize and use Romanian naval craft in the port. On 25 August, after two nights during which Luftwaffe aircraft had bombed Bucharest and other provincial towns in a misguided show of strength, Romania declared war on Germany.

Brinkmann transferred his command post south to Mangalia, planning to board an R-boat bound for Varna from where he could direct operations. However, he did not arrive until the morning of 26 August, prevented from boarding the R-boats by Romanian troops and instead travelling by car. While he was out of contact, Kaptlt Klassmann had been made temporary commander of all Black Sea naval forces and was given identical orders to occupy Constanţa. German naval troops in the port city were now con-gregated around the strongpoint of the Tirpitz Battery as Romanian infantry

The crew of Soviet submarine *S33* photographed with a captured Kriegsmarine ensign.

began to attack. However, Klassmann remained oblivious of his new office, arriving with four R-boats and four MFPs in Varna that evening, the message never having been received as his boats battled against Force 6 winds sweeping the Bulgarian coast.

Ashore, the situation had worsened. German troops had suffered heavy losses in clashes with Romanian forces while the Red Army advanced further into the country. The Black Sea Security Forces had been divided in two, KA (Ing.) Paul Zieb, commander of Black Sea naval shipbuilding, had boarded *UJ110* and taken command of forces retreating along the Lower Danube. He broke through Romanian troops holding the bridge at Cernavodă by using the firepower of the 1st *Kustenschutzflottille* after sailing from Constanţa with nearly sixty mixed Kriegsmarine and Army vessels. Heading towards Silistria, his motley flotilla carried a considerable number of wounded soldiers and women and children as they forced a passage past an imposing Romanian heavy artillery battery south of Bucharest and Romanian river monitors.

From Ruse, Bulgaria, onwards nine MFPs and four *Artillerieträger* sailed in the van, Romanian forces being expected to have occupied Orşova which had been evacuated by its German garrison. Zieb's group was joined by extra steamers, sailing vessels and MFPs carrying more Army wounded, troops going ashore at Ruse and recovering the abandoned equipment of the

Kriegsmarine radio station and installing it aboard an *Artillerieträger*. About 2800 lightly-wounded men, 300 women and children and 800 able-bodied soldiers were disembarked as other vessels of the *Donauflottille* steamed ahead of Zieb's group. Two Romanian monitors were engaged, one being destroyed in flames while *Artillerieträger 913* and *F316* were sunk in the battle at Corabia further upstream. Further ships were hit and set ablaze by Romanian monitors trailing the group, while *Sperrbrecher 192* accompanied by an *Artillerieträger* and minesweepers forced a passage through the Iron Gates and Baziaş, landing troops from the *Sperrbrecher* to briefly occupy the town which was abandoned by retreating Romanian soldiers. *Sperrbrecher 192* captured a number of barges and tugs in an artillery engagement, shooting down a Soviet aircraft between Moldova Nouă and Serbia's Ram Fortress. The *Donauflottille* would continue to function as a fighting unit, strengthened by the additional craft that had fled the Black Sea and providing minelaying and fire support for Army and Waffen-SS troops forced steadily back into Hungary as well as skirmishing with increasingly emboldened Partisan units.

In Varna, Brinkmann assembled the R-boats of the 3rd R-Flotilla that had begun to arrive. Unseaworthy craft had been scuttled in Constanţa, though none of the remaining R-boats were combat-ready. The Constanţa garrison and base personnel were marching to the Bulgarian border to escape the Romanian trap. In Varna Brinkmann also had three *Artillerieträger*, one *Artilleriefahrprähme* and sixteen MFPs in fighting trim, two others having been damaged by bombing. All sixteen vessels of the 2nd *Kustenschutzflottille* were no longer operational owing to either engine damage caused by heavy winter seas or a shortage of weapons. Two *U-Jäger* were also in harbour awaiting shipyard repair.

On 29 August, as Soviet forces occupied Constanţa, Brinkmann received instructions from Führer headquarters that 'under no conditions' were his *Räumboote* to fall into enemy or Bulgarian hands and that the crews should attempt to attach themselves to Wehrmacht infantry units and force their way back to German-controlled territory. Over 4500 Kriegsmarine men had crossed into Bulgaria from Romania; all were advised to attempt to reach Belgrade. On these orders, Varna was evacuated as a functioning German base, all craft to be scuttled. Seven hundred and thirty German troops had been interned at Varna in 'Camp Constantin' by the Bulgarian Armed Forces, Brinkmann negotiating the release of 140 men of the now disbanded 3rd L-Flotilla. With all except the distant *Donauflottille* now disbanded it was the end of the Kriegsmarine's Black Sea Security Forces. After consuming all fuel stores and completing final patrols during which no contact with the enemy was made, the 3rd R-Flotilla scuttled itself in the forenoon off Varna with the exception of one heavily-damaged boat used to return the crews to port before being blown up.

The odyssey of the flotilla was not yet over. Disarmed by Bulgarian troops, the men with Klassmann at their head bluffed their way to a railway yard whereupon they commandeered a locomotive and carriages complete with Bulgarian railwayman to head for Yugoslavia. En route the railwayman deserted and the Germans barely made the Yugoslavian border where more bluff and bluster enabled them to avoid capture by Tito's Partisans before linking up with Wehrmacht troops and joining the general retreat from the Balkans which was by then well underway. At Nish, Klassmann received a radio message from OKM: 'Return to Germany as quickly as possible for reformation of 3rd R-Flotilla.' Their war was not yet over, though they would be returned to combat status only in time to help the desperate exodus of soldiers and refugees before the remorseless advance of the Soviet Army.

Kriegsmarine Security Forces in the South and Italy – April 1944

Oberkommando der Marine Grossadmiral Karl Dönitz

Marinegruppenkommando Süd (Sofia) Admiral Kurt Fricke

Deutsches Marinekommando Italien (Montecatini) KA Meendsen–Bohlken

Kommandant der Seeverteidigung *Westadria* (Venice) KzS Hunaeus
- 2nd Transport Flotilla (Venice)

7th *Sicherungsdivision* (Genoa) KzS Rehm
- 11th R–Flotilla (Rapallo)
- 22nd UJ–Flotilla (Genoa)
- 70th M–Flotilla (Santa Margherita)
- 2nd L–Flotilla (Arencano)
- 4th L–Flotilla (Rapallo)
- 1st Transport Flotilla (Genoa)

Minenschiffgruppe Westitalien

Kommandant der Seeverteidigung *Krim*
- 1st L–Flotilla
- 3rd L–Flotilla

Seetransportchef Schwarzes Meer

Donauflottille (Sementria) KKdR Viktor Mohr

Kommandierender Admiral *Schwarzes Meer* VA Brinkmann 3rd AT–Flotilla
- (Sevastopol)
- *Netzsperrflottille Schwarzes Meer* (Sevastopol)

10th *Sicherungsdivision* (Constanta) KzS Weyher
- 3rd R–Flotilla
- 1st UJ–Flotilla
- 3rd UJ–Flotilla
- 23rd UJ–Flotilla
- 30th G–Flotilla
- 31st G–Flotilla
- 7th L–Flotilla
- *Minenschiff 'Romania'*

Kommandierender Admiral *Ägäis* (Athens) VA Lange
- 12th R–Flotilla (Skaramagas)
- 21st U–Flotilla (Piraeus)
- *Netzsperrflottille Süd* (Piraeus)
- 15th L–Flotilla (Piraeus)

Seetransportcheft Ägäis FK Carl Kolbe
- 4th Transport Flotilla (Thessaloniki)
- 5th Transport Flotilla (Piraeus)

Kommandierender Admiral *Adria* (Abazzia) VA Lietzmann

11th *Sicherungsdivision* (Trieste) FK Walter Berger
- 1st G–Flotilla (Pola)
- 2nd G–Flotilla (Trieste)
- 2nd UJ–Flotilla (Fiume)
- 6th R–Flotilla (Pola)

Seetransportchef Adria FK Lehmann
- 10th L–Flotilla (Trieste)
- 6th Transport Flotilla (Trieste)

8

The 'Inland Seas': The Security Forces in the Mediterranean, Aegean and Tyrrhenian Seas, June 1942 – December 1943

DURING the night of 29/30 April 1942 Hitler and Mussolini had met at Klessheim to discuss the prosecution of the war in the Mediterranean. The decision was made for an operational pause after the planned capture of Tobruk, allowing a joint Italian-German attack on Malta to subdue the island fortress once and for all. With Malta conquered, the supply lines to North Africa would be secured and the Afrika Korps replenished for the advance to the Suez Canal. On 15 June, with Tobruk's capture imminent, Raeder urged Hitler to again support the invasion of Malta (Operation Herkules) but the Führer was dismissive, no diversion of strength being possible during the summer campaign in Russia. Italian reluctance was betrayed by the ease with which they agreed with Hitler's decision and, ultimately, the opportunity was missed to decisively alter the war in the Mediterranean. Herkules was indefinitely postponed and Malta would survive.

'A picture paints a thousand words'. Despite Italy's initial claim on the Mediterranean Sea, Mussolini's forces were increasingly marginalised by the Germans during the course of the war until the country's surrender in September 1943. The few fascist Italian units that remained active at sea contributed little to Germany's stubborn defence of the Southern Front.

216

The Naval Staff particularly regrets the decision concerning . . . [Herkules] as this greatly limits the exploitation of military developments in North Africa, which seem particularly favourable just now. At the same time the future supply to North Africa will continue to depend on continuous action of large air and naval forces in the central Mediterranean.[77]

As the last fighting took place in and around Tobruk the 6th R-Flotilla entered the inner harbour at 1130hrs on 21 June to begin sweeping for mines left behind by the retreating Allies. Strong winds prevented R-boat operations outside of port for 24 hours while Rommel's Panzers continued to race east, crossing the Egyptian border and reaching Sidi Barrani by 24 June. S-boats had already savaged a final troop evacuation from the port and plans to begin shipping supplies to Tobruk were already underway. The harbour and its facilities were captured undamaged, alongside a mountain of supplies including fresh khaki uniforms, cigarettes and even Royal Navy rum. However, the unloading capacity of Tobruk would not exceed an optimistic target of 800 tons per day, meaning that Benghazi remained an essential supply head and coastal convoys under R-boat and MFP protection were required to move supplies east towards the advancing front line.

Allied air forces on Malta had become increasingly effective with the failure to prevent aircraft and fuel reaching the island. Axis convoys from Italy to Tripoli were halted and the the route to Cyrenaica threatened. The vulnerability of these supply lines revived calls for Herkules to be executed, but Mussolini declared that the operation was impossible before September, after massive German-Italian air attacks had battered the island's defences. Only once this had happened, and if the Germans provided sufficient fuel, would the Italian Navy be able to play its part in the invasion.

The crew of a *Marinefährprähme* in North Africa.

Herkules would also require all the local naval forces to support it, though Rommel demanded the continued attachment of R-boats and MFPs to his army to safeguard his vulnerable coastal convoys. He reported that, should the maritime convoys fail to provide an optimum level of supply, his advance on land would only be possible with the compensating factor of complete and undisputed aerial superiority over the RAF.

Therefore, at a time when the war in Russia demanded ever greater Luftwaffe commitment, the Kriegsmarine would have to suffice. Transportation overland was easily disrupted by air attack, there were too few vehicles and it was unable to keep pace with his needs as the Afrika Korps' lines of communication grew ever longer. 'Herkules' would remain on hold.

The R-boats continued to protect small fast convoys of *Marinefährprähme* along the North African coast and at 1800hrs on 29 June *R13* became the first boat to use the newly-captured port of Marsa Matruh in Egypt. By July a makeshift headquarters had been established in the small port for *Räumboote* operations. Allied aerial minelaying around Tobruk had also begun, requiring the *Räumboote* to periodically revert to minesweeping duties to keep the sea lanes clear.

Meanwhile, alongside Italian steamers, MFPs operated in shuttles from Benghazi to Tobruk and onwards to Sidi Barrani. The Italian coaster *Savona* ran aground between Benghazi and Tobruk, requiring unloading by MFPs from the ship's aft holds and causing delays to the movement of cargo east. However, up to 735 tons of material was being unloaded daily in Tobruk, 370 tons of gasoline for use by the Army and Luftwaffe being carried to Sidi Barrani by MFPs on the last day of June.

Nonetheless, the shortage of supplies from Italy began to tell on the Afrika Korps. On 4 July Rommel announced that his entire army had been forced to halt and go over on to the defensive as it awaited supplies, a situation expected to last for two weeks, giving his enemies valuable time in which to muster their own reserves and to reorganise. Consideration was even given to a *Fallschirmjäger* attack on the Suez Canal in order to achieve the final breakthrough that would see the Afrika Korps triumphant, but it was dismissed as quickly as the idea arose. 'Nothing brings the need of extreme speed in expediting supplies into sharper focus than the present predicament which has halted the advance of the Panzer Army to the Nile Delta for lack of forces. It is to be hoped that this pause is only temporary.'[78]

On 18 July five of the 6th R-Flotilla's boats were engaged in convoy duty off the North African coast when they came under attack by enemy torpedo bombers. As the aircraft targeted the escorted steamer SS *Citta di Agrigento*, two R-boats scored hits on the attackers but the Italian ship was still hit four times and sank by the stern in shallow water, though she was later refloated and the cargo successfully unloaded. Mersa Matruh itself also came under

An excellent view of a *Räumboot* taking passengers aboard. Large yet manoeuvrable, R-boats did not have the speed of an S-boat but they packed a formidable punch and could absorb a great deal of punishment in action.

attack by four British destroyers, HMS *Beaufort*, *Dulverton*, *Eridge* and *Hurworth*, which fired twenty salvoes without causing any significant damage but later managed to torpedo the Italian steamer SS *Sturla* as she approached the port under *Räumboote* escort. *Schnellboote* which were sharing the harbour joined the R-boats in the rescue of forty-six crewmembers. The S-boats then foiled a second attempted destroyer attack that night through the use of the Metox radar detector to detect the incoming enemy ships. The port was coming under increasing British air attack, Fleet Air Arm 830 Squadron Albacores sinking the German steamer SS *Brook* in the harbour after her cargo of fuel was ignited by a bomb.

The strain was beginning to tell on the overworked R-boats and MFPs of the Security Forces. Frequent repairs were required and crew fatigue affected performance. Defensive mine barrages to protect the harbours were also being requested by the Italian naval authorities, but there were insufficient vessels or stocks of mines available.

The Commanding Admiral, *Deutsches Marinekommando Italien* [VA Weichold], *Deutsches* makes the following pertinent comment on this discouraging picture.

We have no choice but to use all ships' weapons and to strain German forces to the utmost; great risks and setbacks are unavoidable. However the situation at the front and the weakness of the Panzer Army force us to carry on.

In connection with this comment on the part of its commander from North African headquarters, the *Deutsches Marinekommando Italien* reports from Rome:

a. For the last 3 days the Italian Admiralty has been preparing the minefield for Marsa Matruh. Standard mines type C will be laid by two destroyers in about one week.

b. Two magnetic minesweeping apparatuses will be shipped to Africa on naval barges on 23 July.[79]

Requests for *Marinefährprähme* to be equipped as auxiliary minesweepers were also approved and modifications to craft of the 2nd Landing Flotilla had begun. On 1 August, the 6th R-Flotilla began transferring to Tobruk under nightly British air raids, with the main pier being destroyed early that month. Two R-boats moored in the port of Bardia were also the victims of Allied bombing, the flotilla's first losses since its arrival in the Mediterranean. There were no anti-aircraft guns at Bardia and *R9* was hit and set on fire during the raid alongside MFPs *F347* and *F356*, all of which sank with relatively light casualties. Their flotilla-mate *R11* was also hit and badly damaged, being beached to prevent sinking and enable her potential salvage. Allied air forces were taking advantage of the fact that the majority of Luftwaffe strength had been diverted to the Eastern Front; another MFP loaded with ammunition was sunk in Tobruk harbour during the night of 3 August. Further casualties were inflicted on the 3rd R-Flotilla when *R12* was attacked by six aircraft at 0650hrs two days later, the damaged boat later needing repair in Palermo.

Enemy air raids also increased on Tripoli and Marsa Matruh, though flak defences were reinforced and Italian aircraft began shouldering the burden of convoy escort as Kriegsmarine strength wilted. By 8 August Weichold reported an operational readiness of:

3rd S-Flotilla: two boats ready for action in Marsa Matruh; two in Sula; four in Augusta; four out of commission.

6th R-Flotilla: four boats ready for action in North Africa; two boats out of commission; one boat lost. Attempts being made to salvage *R11* in Bardia.

2nd Landing Flotilla: Of the thirty-five landing craft completed, ten had been lost; three under repair; six returning from complete overhaul; five being equipped. Only eleven MFPs in total were ready for action in North Africa.

Weichold also declared in the same report the urgent necessity of providing armour plating for engines, guns and the bridge and wheelhouse, all vulnerable areas when undre air attack.

The wear and tear and battle damage on the remaining flotilla boats meant that during September *R10, R12, R14* and *R16* were all taken from

North Africa to the yards at Palermo for repairs and overhaul, the journey being made in stages; first to Crete, then Piraeus, the Corinth Canal, Corfu and finally the Sicilian dockyard. During October *R13* was also taken to Palermo, leaving only *R15* on station in North Africa at the beginning of November 1942.

Allied landings to the west and east of Tobruk was carried out at 0045hrs on 14 September, covered by light Royal Navy forces and preceded by a heavy air raid. Italian forces counter-attacked once enemy troops began landing while the Royal Navy shelled Tobruk and the Derna road. By dawn the naval covering force was intercepted and bombed by German aircraft north-east of Tobruk, withdrawing to the east after suffering losses. A second force sighted 60 miles north-east of Marsa Matruh was repulsed with two destroyers and two corvetytes lost to mines and anti-aircraft artillery, and *MTB314* which ran aground.

Four of the available R-boats then began a systematic search of the coast and captured the grounded *MTB314* as well as 130 prisoners, mostly survivors from one of the destroyers. Around noon the situation in Tobruk itself was under control: no significant damage had been caused although fighting still continued at two points against small enemy units which were eventually encircled and annihilated. The Kriegsmarine suffered no casualties and on 20 September their ranks were bolstered when the captured *MTB314* was commissioned into the 6th R-Flotilla as a 'fast *U-Jäger*' designated *RA10*.

Despite the German success at Tobruk, the war in North Africa had reached a decisive turning-point. Rommel's headlong race for the Suez Canal had fatally overstretched Axis supply capabilities. Allied aircraft had taken control of the North African skies as land forces were steadily built up for an impending counter-attack. To the west, Operation Pedestal had reached Malta despite horrendous casualties. Only five of the convoy's merchant ships reached Valletta's Grand Harbour, but those five ships saved the embattled island as a military base. The island would no longer face starvation and the arrival of aviation fuel and machine parts meant that air defence was guaranteed, as well as the ability to strike at Axis convoys from Italy. Once again Rommel's supplies came under attack during August 1942, with 35 per cent of material destined for the Afrika Korps destroyed at sea that month and the figure rising in September. Just as Rommel had appeared poised to strike a decisive blow in Egypt, his supplies were severely depleted once again. Finally, his triumphant advance was halted at El Alamein. Despite the Royal Navy temporarily evacuating Alexandria as German and Italian forces approached, the Afrika Korps would never reach the Suez Canal. While German supply lines were vulnerable and stretched for hundreds of torturous miles, those of the British Eighth Army were short and well protected by air cover. A first battle at El Alamein was fought to a standstill. The second, between 23 October and 4 November, was won by the Allies who enjoyed huge material superiority as well as full access to German communications thanks to the cracking of the Wehrmacht's Enigma code. So began Rommel's slow retreat west.

Operation Torch: the Allies land in North-West Africa

On the day that Rommel conceded defeat in the second battle at El Alamein, the Germans received intelligence reports of another huge convoy in the Gibraltar area, interpreted as most likely being a further relief mission for Malta. However, the enemy shipping swung south as it entered the Mediterranean to approach the shores of Algeria and Morocco: Operation Torch had begun.

The Allied landing served a twofold purpose. Firstly it was a (largely unsuccessful) attempt to meet Stalin's demands for the opening of a second front against the Germans. Secondly – and considerably more realistically – its military aim was to enable the destruction of the Afrika Korps with offensive movement now possible from both east and west while also allowing an opportunity for some kind of Allied rapprochement with Vichy France. Allied planners did not really expect the Vichy forces in Algeria, Morocco and Tunisia to resist the landings, but in fact there were several sharp battles before Allied forces accomplished their initial objectives. While some Vichy units immediately surrendered to the invaders, others remained committed to their stance as an independent nation and fought hard against over-whelming odds. Where the Vichy troops' loyalty lay was frequently a confused issue. It became more polarised after some of the covert Allied political manoeuvring that had been skilfully used with high-ranking Vichy officials became known to Hitler's government and German troops moved to occupy Vichy France itself (Operation Anton) on 10 November. The regime that had been guaranteed nominal sovereignty over its portion of France under the 1940 Armistice was justifiably no longer considered reliable by the German military command. Following Anton's completion, the combined forces of Italy and Germany held all of France as well as the islands of Corsica and Elba and, although the Vichy fleet in Toulon had scuttled itself rather than be captured, the French Mediterranean coast was now available for Kriegs-marine bases, passing into the domain of Ruge's BSW.

In North Africa, *Schnellboote* of the 3rd S-Flotilla based in Trapani were immediately ordered to Vichy-controlled Tunisia, making landfall at La Goulette in Tunis where they blockaded Vichy vessels to prevent their escape and took control of port installations. Tunis boasted a deep-water harbour that would be crucial to any German defence in the west. The minesweeper *Canard* and three other smaller craft were found and disarmed and on 12 November Luftwaffe Oberst Harlinghausen arrived at the head of a makeshift Luftwaffe ground unit to take control of the city, supported by fighters and dive-bombers and paratroopers of *Fallschirmjäger Regiment 5*.

While Tunis was being secured, the other deep-water port of Bizerte to the north-west was also seized, *R12* and *R13* sailing from Palermo to help occupy the harbour in company with two S-boats. In the process, four small Vichy torpedo boats, nine submarines, nine minesweepers and several smaller craft moored in the harbour and the Lac de Bizerte were captured. Two days later *RA10* arrived to reinforce the *Räumboote* and the harbour was effectively under German control. The Allies' failure to risk more with Operation Torch and make landings at both of these Tunisian ports undoubtedly prolonged the Germans' ability to resist. A new local command was established, *Deutsches Marinekommando Tunisien*, KzS Otto Loycke occupying the new post until December when he was replaced by KA Wilhelm Meendsen-Bohlken.

Following the successful occupation of the harbour and its assets, all three R-boats departed: *R12* and *R13* headed to Palermo while *RA10* travelled to the naval basin at nearby Ferryville in preparation for an onward voyage to La Spezia. To the east, Tobruk had been abandoned by Rommel's retreating forces and *R15* left the harbour on 12 November, carrying the city's command staff aboard as they retreated westwards.

Despite this isolated success, the Axis situation in North Africa had undergone a dramatic reversal with little chance of recovering the initiative. Supplies had long been the Afrika Korps' primary problem and the situation deteriorated even further, with the failure to occupy Malta as originally planned returning to haunt the Axis forces. German surface strength was meagre and what units were available were suffering constant battle damage combined with wear and tear of operational use on both the vessels and their crews. Alongside the *Räumboote* and *Marinefähreprahme* in the Mediterranean were the *U-Jäger* of 21st UJ-Flotilla based in Piräus in the Aegean and the boats of *Korvettenkapitan* Grossmann's 22nd UJ-Flotilla that was formed in newly-occupied Marseilles in December 1942; ten requisitioned steamers and French warships of over 1000 tons displacement were armed and ready for service within weeks of the dissolution of Vichy France.

The 22nd UJ-Flotilla went straight into action and on 27 February the flotilla leader *UJ2201* was towing ObltzS Fenker's *UJ2209* to Naples following damage suffered by an air attack. A third boat, *UJ2210*, acted as escort. At 1047hrs, KK Fritz Grossmann's boat *UJ2201* detected a submarine echo at a range of 3000m. Leutnant zur See Otto Pollman's *UJ2210* was ordered to investigate and obtained a firm contact at 1053hrs. Turning sharply to starboard to run the contact down, the trace was lost at a range of 180m as it appeared to be a submarine taking evasive action. An initial pattern of five depth charges was dropped, set between 70m and 120m, further depth charges following until the final pattern of fifteen at 1234hrs. An oil slick was observed on the surface and the contact disappeared. It is believed to have been HMS *Tigris*, lost with all six officers and fifty-six men. Pollmann would go on to become the flotilla's 'Ace' earning the Knight's Cross for a total of fourteen Allied submarines claimed destroyed, although *Tigris* remains his only confirmed victory.

By March 1943 the flotilla had expanded as Ruge reported a provisional organisation of vessels recently requisitioned in Southern France, listing the strength of the 22nd UJ-Flotilla as nineteen vessels and the establishment of *Geleitflottille-Mittelmeer* of nine vessels. Two motor yachts, two motorboats and one customs boat were added to the 6th R-Flotilla. Additionally, one group equipped with cutting kite sweeps and consisting of four vessels, two groups of lobster boats consisting of twelve boats each and one group of minesweeping yawls, also consisting of twelve boats, were now available, while three customs boats, three motorboats and two trawlers were provided for Admiral, Aegean Sea.

The 6th *Sicherungsflottille* which had been established in December 1942 retained the Toulon groups equipped with cutting kite sweeps and with towed coil gear (five boats) alongside the minesweeping tug. This flotilla had evolved from the *Hafenschutzflottille Süd* that had been based on France's south coast and came under the direct command of Ruge as BSW until June 1944 when it was made subordinate to *Kommandierenden Admiral der französischen Südküste*. Plans to enlarge the flotilla to the status of 6th *Sicherungsdivision* were ultimately frustrated by the Allied invasion of France in 1944, but by March 1943, flotilla commander KKdR Hermann Polenz had control over an impressive array of vessels.

That same month, the 7th *Sicherungsdivision* was established at Trapani to control operations along the west coasts of Italy and Sicily. Kapitän zur See Bramesfeld's division initially comprised the 6th and 11th R-Flotillas, 22nd UJ-Flotilla and 3rd and 4th G-Flotilla, but the 2nd and 4th L-Flotillas were soon added, as well as tactical control of the 10th Torpedo Boat Flotilla. During May 1943, Bramesfeld was replaced by FK Karl Bergelt and the division's headquarters moved to Livorno. Bergelt was subsequently replaced by FK Dr Karl Diederichs and the headquarters moved once more to Genoa-Nervi in September 1943.

However, despite the increased strength provided by the captured ships there was little that could be done to turn the tide of battle against ever-increasing Allied naval and air power. Supplies and troops destined for the Tunisian bridgehead, predominantly under Italian escort, were decimated time and again. In Berlin Dönitz intended to support the Italian Navy and with Hitler's agreement flew to Rome to confer first with Mussolini and then the Italian Naval C-in-C Admiral Ricardi on the best way in which Germany could assist the Italians. Ricardi was at first mistrustful of Dönitz's motives, perhaps fuelled by a wounded pride that Germany was interfering in Italian naval affairs. Eventually Dönitz persuaded the Italians to accept a senior German officer with experience in convoy protection for attachment to Supermarina along with whatever requisite ships could be supplied by the Kriegsmarine.

As Director of the German staff attached to Supermarina I appointed VA Ruge. Since the occupation of Northern France in 1940 he had commanded the defences along the Northern and Western coasts of France. Then he had rendered excellent service and had acquired great experience in the protection of coastal waters and of convoys. His work at Supermarina and help given by the Germans in the protection of the convoys themselves were soon to bear fruit, for in April the percentage of ships which reached Tunis safely was higher than in the previous months.[80]

On 6 March 1943 Ruge's detailed report on the escort vessel situation regarding Tunisian supply traffic was submitted to SKL. The report's summation read:

The Tunisian traffic is a decisive factor in the war. Presently available escort facilities are wholly inadequate both at sea and in the air. The convoys cannot be protected to an even approximately satisfactory degree. It is therefore necessary to concentrate on especially valuable convoys in order that at least these may be fairly well protected. In view of the danger of attack by surface forces, which might be particularly disastrous, flanking [mine] barrages must be improved as soon as possible. In addition to other measures which have already been introduced (increase in number of vessels, improvement of minesweeping and communication service and submarine chase etc.) the training and armament of Italian vessels must be improved. The situation will become still more serious, since the British are not yet attacking as heavily as in the Channel. The convoys can be taken through with relatively small losses only if a strong, determined and well-armed naval escort is provided, if the transports also are well-armed and not too slow and if strong air cover is furnished by day. The performance of the Italian escort vessels can be improved to some extent by interchange of officers between German and Italian vessels, by training the Italian officers in German gunnery courses and by armouring the Italian vessels. It is probable that the use of exclusively German-manned vessels would rouse the Italians to better achievements.[81]

Allied Mark XVII mines were found north-west of Bizerte by the 6th R-Flotilla at the beginning of the month, more frequent minelaying following these first attempts to isolate the Tunisian bridgehead. Further aerial mines

Streaming minesweeping gear from one of the smaller auxiliaries used by the Kriegsmarine.

were detected eight miles east of Bizerte near the Axis convoy route which was temporarily closed after a Siebel ferry was lost to a mine off Cape Bon. The first boat of the Bizerte *Hafenschutzflottille* put to sea to take up station on 3 March and at the same time the first *U-Jäger* left Marseilles, *UJ2202* and *UJ2204* putting to sea. The minesweeper *M6024* also departed, en route from Savona to Genoa and from there onward to La Spezia and ultimately Leghorn while *M6022*, accompanied by six auxiliary minesweepers, set out from Leghorn to Naples where she would undergo repairs. *UJ2208* sailed at noon on 3 March from Marseilles, escorting the Italian steamer *Luigi* carrying Luftwaffe supplies to Genoa. At 0330hrs two days later *UJ2208* reported that she had located a submarine 35 miles southwest of Spezia and, at 1235hrs after several attacks, observed large bubbles of air in the water.

Air raids on Cagliari, Naples and Palermo had sunk several German and Italian auxiliary vessels and, with the shipyards coming under intense pressure, by 2 March only a single boat from the 6th R-Flotilla was seaworthy: one was out of action with engine trouble while another had suffered a serious leak caused by a mine explosion. Both *R12* and *R13* had also been damaged during the raid on Palermo as they underwent repairs in the shipyard, later being towed by an Italian steamer to Naples for fresh work to be undertaken.

The few R-boats that managed to put to sea to clear mines east of Bizerta and north of Plane Island were attacked by Allied aircraft that dropped more than seventy bombs, though without causing any damage or casualties. On 7

March, they were also used for rescue duties after the merchant ships *Balzac* and *Estiere* and the torpedo boat *Ciclone* were sunk by mines en route to Tunisia. During this tumult, Weichold was relieved as commander of *Deutsches Marinekommando Italien* by KA Wilhelm Meendsen-Bohlken. The change in command came at a time when the agreement to transfer large R-boats to the Mediterranean via the Seine was rescinded. Instead, immediate plans were begun to move a flotilla of R-boats from MGK West to the Mediterranean. However, there was still the problem of the shortage of transport vehicles for the overland part of the transfer. Hitler had also ordered the despatch of further S-boats to the Mediterranean, but SKL believed that this latest edict should be suspended pending the report of the surveyors studying the new transfer route (Seine–Saône) and then a decision of how many heavy Kuhlemeyer transport trailers could be taken from the existing Elbe–Danube traffic. The R-boats were desperately needed and in view of the small number of Kuhlemeyers available, each S-boat transferred meant that an R-boat was left behind. On 18 March SKL's Quartermaster Division issued preliminary orders that said that the route would be usable within four to six weeks. It was believed, that alongside the R-boats, it would be possible to transfer up to twenty-five *Marinefähreprahme* per month, after further possibilities of using Kuhlemeyer wagons were ascertained with the State Railway. Six were already lying disassembled in Hamburg pending transfer. Meanwhile, the reinforcement of the 6th R-Flotilla was already underway after the decision had been taken to send *R1*, *R3*, *R4*, *R6*, *R7* and *R8*. The small R-boats *R3* and *R4* began their journey from Kiel on 20 March via the Rhine–Rhône canal route, reaching Strasbourg by the end of the month.

The extra strength was desperately needed. Air raids had been heavy but unsuccessful, while *R10* was set on fire and suffered casualties following a PT Boat attack. The damaged boat was later towed to Bizerte. Meanwhile *UJ2203* and *UJ2210* reported successful attacks on a submarine near Cape Milazzo, the target claimed as 'probably destroyed' after four waves of depth-charging.

Small requisitioned French vessels were reshuffled according to individual local requirements; three motor yachts left as *U-Jäger* with the 6th *Sicherungsflottille*; two minesweepers, *M6021* and *M6024*, were turned over to *Deutsches Marinekommando Italien*; six large *U-Jäger UJ2211* to *UJ2216* went to the 22nd UJ-Flotilla; and the steam trawlers *Ctvtnchi* and *Alcyon* joined the Aegean forces. Nine vessels remained with the 6th *Sicherungsflottille* for clearing moored mines.

Bombing of most major Axis ports in Tunisia, Sicily and Italy continued. On 24 March Ferryville was subjected to a heavy raid by B17 aircraft of the North-West African Strategic Air Force that sank an Italian steamer, a captured French destroyer, three *Hafenschutzflottille* vessels, one tank lighter, one Siebel ferry, one landing craft and an 80-ton floating crane and its pier, as well as the Italian submarine *Umbrino*. The latter suffered a direct hit that blew the boat apart, the battered *R10*, in harbour for repair, being caught in the explosion and sunk. However, initial reports that she was a total loss were inaccurate as the boat was operational again in eight weeks with the assistance of the Ferryville arsenal. Fortunately, casualties from the raid were few, though the port was heavily damaged, nearly all the workshops, the power station and the approach roads being virtually destroyed. Ferryville was temporarily suspended as a point of discharge for supply convoys as teams of men worked to repair its facilities. Naples too had suffered severe damage from air raids, limiting its use as a supply head. However, more devastating was an unexplained fire aboard MV *Caterina Costa* that caused the cargo of armoured vehicles, fuel and ammunition to explode, devastating the port and killing 600 people and injuring 3000 others.

At sea the situation had deteriorated. Two of four Italian destroyers – *Lanzerotto Malocello* and *Ascari* – carrying German troops to Tunis were sunk by mines north of Cape Bon, the remaining pair entering La Goulette at 1000hrs while Kriegsmarine rescue operations got underway. The delicate relationship between the Italian and German navies had already become strained. Ruge had made another frank appraisal of deficiencies both within the Italian Navy and the Mediterranean situation:

1.) The enemy mine situation in the Central Mediterranean is less dangerous than it had at first seemed. After systematic channel sweeping and reconnaissance by the Italians, the barrages have been correctly plotted. The situation can be kept in hand in the future. The number of minesweepers and R-boats is gradually increasing. From May 50 Italian motor minesweepers can be counted on.

2.) The Italian escort service is inefficient. It is inexpert in defensive movements and offensive action. It can be improved only by German example and intermixture of crews.

3.) It is not easy to find an organizational solution to this problem. First of all, a post must be found for KzS [Heinrich] Bramsfeld. It would be a good thing if he were appointed German Chief of Staff to the Italian Admiralty at Trapani and also Commander of the German naval forces stationed there. Convoys are directed exclusively by the Italian Admiralty. The Admiral in Trapani has little authority. Chief, Naval Staff commented that very little could be done to change this situation. It was therefore necessary that *Deutsches Marine-kommando Italien* which was directly in touch with the Italian Admiralty, should take a stronger hand. The number of vessels must be increased. At the request of Commander-in-Chief, Navy, the Reichsmarschall, who is now in Italy, is to bring pressure on the Italians to this end. The question of assigning German personnel to the escort services must be examined. German Naval Command must investigate how German personnel can best be distributed among the escort services and whether it would be wise to place German Naval Command under the jurisdiction of the Italian Admiralty. Furthermore, the new staff of the German Naval Command must be manned with suitable fresh personnel.

In regard to the above-mentioned efforts of the Reichsmarschall, Admiral, *Deutsches Marinekommando Italien* reports that, following further verbal and written approaches to the Italian Admiralty made by him and on the basis of a detailed conference with the Reichsmarschall on 6 March, the latter had discussions with Ambrosio and Riccardi on 8 March, during which he requested that all small vessels that can be requisitioned in the Italian area be put into service. The Reichsmarschall pointed out that work has not yet been started on the motor vessels which the Italians seized in the South of France, and demanded that they also be fitted out at once and that the two ex- French despatch boats and three torpedo boats, which are at present in Italian ports, also be employed. The Reichsmarschall offered the assistance of German personnel and will ask the Duce, at today's conference, to issue the necessary orders.

Search for small vessels by German sea transport offices in the ports to which they have access has so far been negative.

However, the loss of the Italian destroyers led Supermarina to refuse the use of further destroyers as troop transports until the appropriated Vichy destroyers reached operational readiness. The Italian Navy maintained that their nine operational destroyers had to be saved for fleet operations in case of an enemy attack on Sardinia or Sicily. Even representations by the supreme Wehrmacht commander in the South, Albert Kesselring, to the Duce failed to have this decision overturned. With bad weather suspending shipping, the remaining alternative was troop transport by air which, however, was not only vulnerable to interception but the available aircraft were already fully committed to supplying fuel and ammunition to the Afrika Korps.

By the beginning of March the Allied troops that had followed Rommel's retreat from El Alamein reached the eastern border of Tunisia, while Torch forces in the West were pressing hard despite temporary setbacks inflicted by Rommel's still dangerous army. Minelaying and minesweeping continued unabated off the Tunisian coast in efforts to protect the fragile supply lines. The 6th R-Flotilla lost *RA10* from its strength when the captured MTB was reassigned to the 7th S-Flotilla, though its service there was brief. Commanded by LzS Brusgatis, *RA10* rescued nine Luftwaffe personnel from a downed Me323 Gigant transport that was part of the evacuation of troops to Sicily, three other surviving soldiers and one body later being retrieved from the same area. However, *RA10* was attacked by British Spitfires at La Goulette and sunk by a direct hit in the engine room, six of the twenty-one crew being killed and eight wounded, with a single Spitfire shot down.

In the afternoon of 1 May, Ruge arrived in Berlin as ordered and reported to SKL for a detailed discussion on the Tunis supply situation that involved representatives of the Italian navy. Ruge voiced the opinion that further supply of Tunis by menas of large surface vessels was futile while the Italians stated their belief that Tunis could no longer be saved and all naval means were better used for the future defence of Sardinia and Sicily.

Chief, Naval Staff emphatically repudiated these objections. It would be a fallacy to believe that the Italian Fleet can prevent an occupation of Sardinia and Sicily. It would not be anywhere near in a position to do so in view of British superiority. The best protection for Italy was the holding of the Tunis bridgehead. As long as this position is held, a landing in Italy or on her islands could hardly be expected. For this reason everything must be done to hold Tunis. Days and weeks might count. To sacrifice the fleet for this task would be of greater benefit than to save it for tasks to come. It is true, all ships would have to be thrown in, in the event of an attack on the islands, but nevertheless, they could not prevent a landing in the face of such enemy superiority.

The decision regarding the holding of the bridgehead in Tunisia rests with the Supreme Command. It will not do for the Navy to suddenly withdraw its support while the other services of the Armed Forces are fighting desperately to hold on. The obligation to the troops battling on land makes it imperative for all naval forces to rally to their support. The alternative in this case is either to hold Tunis, which is tantamount to the Navy committing everything, or to let the armoured corps surrender.

The Supreme Command has issued orders that Tunisia is to be held. The Chief, Naval Staff is convinced that this decision is the only one possible. Therefore, the Navy, too, must throw itself into the task with all means available.[82]

Transport craft embark Afrika Korps light vehicles during the evacuation of Tunisia.

However, nothing could be done to stem the tide of defeat in Tunisia. While reinforcements were en route to the Mediterranean by river and three *Marinefähreprahme* had already crossed France overland, the Afrika Korps were destroying vital installations in Bizerta, the western section of the town being evacuated by the evening of 6 May. Marsala and Trapani came under heavy air attack by B17s that same day, several minesweepers and Siebel ferries being sunk and the ports themselves severely damaged. Reggio and Messina were bombed by B24s towards noon, and in Reggio an ammunition steamer exploding sinking nearby ships, while flak shot down six aircraft and Luftwaffe fighters a seventh.

The office of *Marinekommando Tunisien* was dissolved and a last-ditch evacuation using every possible vessel continued until 10 May when Kesselring suspended seaborne evacuation transport from noon following a discussion with OKW and *Heeresgruppe Afrika*. The Kriegsmarine's small vessels were switched over to the carrying of supplies to the island of Pantelleria midway between Sicily and Tunisia, protected by flanking forces of S-boats. Axis forces in Tunisia finally surrendered on 13 May and 275,000 men went into captivity. The African campaign was over.

Reinforcing the Mediterranean

In April the four captured Vichy torpedo boats from Bizerte that had originally been given to the Italian Navy, were returned to German control. They sailed from La Spezia to Toulon where they were joined by a fifth that had been scuttled but salvaged and repaired by the Italians. The torpedo boats were ready for trials by 2 May: *Bombarde* became *TA9* ('*Torpedoboot Ausland*'), *La Pomone TA10*, *Iphigénie TA11*, *Baliste TA12* and *La Bayonnaise TA13*. However, it soon became clear that the ships were in poor condition, their offensive capabilities also hampered by a lack of ammunition and personnel. Unable to utilise them effectively as torpedo boats, the navy instead relegated them to escort ships and attached then to the 3rd and 4th G-Flotillas that had been established in March 1943. Additionally, the Vichy *Chamois*-class minesweepers *Matelot Leblanc* and *Rageot de la Touche* (both captured in Toulon) were commissioned as *SG14* and *SG15* respectively (*Schnelles Geleitboot*). *SG14* was assigned to the 4th G-Flotilla on 5 June 1943 but would only last in action for two months, being sunk by two Allied aircraft while at anchor in Capri on 24 August 1943. *SG15*, on the other hand, served until the very last weeks of the war. Commissioned into the 3rd G-Flotilla on 3 October 1943, she was later transferred to the 10th Torpedo Boat Flotilla, before being redesignated *UJ2229* on 16 May 1944 and reassigned to the 22nd UJ-Flottilla. On 5 September 1944 she was seriously damaged during an air raid on the port of Genoa but later repaired and rerurned service before eventually being torpedoed and sunk by the submarine HMS *Universal* off

Genoa on 26 April 1945. Additionally, *SG10*, the ex-French fruit carrier *Felix-Henri*, *SG11*, the former French fruit transport ship *Alice Robert* captured in Marseilles, *SG12*, the former fruit transport *Djebel Dira* and *SG13*, the former French passenger ship *Cyrnos* which had been used by the French Navy as a guard ship (*P2*), were also all taken on strength of the 3rd G-Flotilla, all being commissioned on 1 May 1943.

The addition of foreign ships to the Security Flotillas provided a valuable increase in fighting power, despite their sometimes limited effectiveness. Meanwhile the transfer of craft from Germany continued, MFPs and R-boats making the difficult journey by river and road. The vessels left Le Havre after having distinguishing military features removed, being towed along the Seine and Yonne Rivers to the port of Auxerre. There they were lifted from the water and loaded onto the Kuhlemeyer transport trailers pulled by coupled trucks, each ponderous convoy being 90m long. The convoys then joined the N6 to Avallon after crossing Saint-Bris-le-Vineux, Nitry, Joux-la-Ville and Lucy-le-Bois, nearly 5000 labourers having already been conscripted to remove any obstacles that could have hampered the passage of the craft: trees, telegraph poles, road signs and even houses. During April 1943 the mayors of each village along the path were notified by their Prefecture of any planned demolition works, residents being given two days to leave. For example, in the town of Avallon, two petrol pumps were demolished with pickaxes and an unexpected obstacle discovered to be the facade of the hotel L'Escargot,

Limited supply posed difficulties outfitting the large number of vessels of the Security Forces. Captured weapons of all calibres were frequently pressed into German service, such as aboard this small *Hafenschutzflottille* vessel.

which was smashed away by workers under direction of the Organisation Todt while the convoy was delayed for three hours. On 29 June French Resistance members sabotaged a tunnel on the Marne branch canal, the transfer of barges on the Saône and Marne-Saône Canal being briefly interrupted until the transports were re-routed.

By this method the 11th and 12th R-Flotillas were transferred to the Mediterranean in Spring and Summer 1943. *Marinefährprähme* also continued to arrive in Marseilles and during June, 200 Luftwaffe personnel trained in handling Siebel ferries were transferred to the Kriegsmarine in return for an equivalent number of naval flak gunners to be seconded to the Luftwaffe. With the Allies poised to strike north from their newly-conquered African ports, SKL ordered the preparation of ports in the Aegean for use as bases by S-boats and R-boats, KK Maurer's 12th R-Flotilla earmarked for onward transfer to the region. The first four boats of the flotilla to become operational in the Mediterranean carried out minelaying in Sicilian coastal waters on 25 June 1943, putting into Trapani. Meanwhile the remaining craft of the 6th R-Flotilla had rebased in Sicily following the fall of North Africa utilised predominantly for local escort duties, *R13* being unsuccessfully attacked by three aircraft on 25 June while covering transport ships bound for Palermo as the 'Hermann Göring' Panzer Division was transferred from the Italian mainland.

During June, increased enemy activity in the Aegean and fears of attacks on German transport and supply shipping in the area demanded the allocation of an R-boat unit. Hitler and Dönitz both firmly believed that British forces were being held in readiness to counter any Soviet thrust into the Balkans, a region that had long held an irresistible draw for Winston Churchill. Kapitänleutnant Felix Freytag's 11th R-Flotilla was unable to carry out this role as it was still in transit and far from operationally ready, while the 6th R-Flotilla was desperately in need of dockyard overhaul, leaving only the newly-arrived vessels of the 12th R-Flotilla available, the first six boats being scheduled to depart Italy for Greece on 30 June. At that time the overworked 21st UJ-Flotilla was the primary Kriegsmarine escort presence in the region. Konteradmiral Wilhelm Meendsen-Bohlken had moved on from command of *Deutsches Marinekommando Italien* to MGK Nord, being replaced in May by the recently-promoted VA Friedrich Ruge. With the complete agreement of the Italian Navy, Ruge resisted the diversion of the *Räumboot* flotilla as much as possible, emphasising that the boats were urgently needed for defensive minelaying along the vulnerable Sicilian coast and other islands in the Tyrrhenian Sea. While the Italians believed that the Allies would land first on Sardinia rather than Sicily, the common aim of retaining whatever minelaying and minesweeping capabilities in the region resulted in support for Ruge's appeal from the highest echelons of

Friedrich Ruge inspects a minesweeper crew.

Supermarina. Ruge proposed that, in the face of increasing enemy air attacks that required stronger and more numerous convoy escorts, the flotilla's first four operational boats be left in Italy, the next four sent to the Aegean and the remaining four distributed according to whatever the local situation required. However, on 27 June SKL replied that:

> The decision concerning the transfer of the 12th R-Flotilla was made after very careful consideration as, according to the views of Naval Staff, we must at all events avoid sea communication to the Western area of Greece being interrupted by enemy attacks which cannot be detected beforehand, thereby making reinforcement of our defence forces in the Aegean Sea impossible. Therefore a change of decision is not possible, especially as increased enemy activity in the Aegean Sea already makes it urgently necessary now to strengthen defence forces.

Minelaying by the ships *Pommern* and *Brandenburg* established the defensive barrages in Sicilian waters, but Ruge reported sourly that the expansion of the minefields was being 'seriously impaired' by the loss of the 12th R-Flotilla.

The first four *Räumboote* were ready for transfer from to the Aegean by July, moving first to Thessaloniki and then ordered immediately to begin clearing a new submarine-laid minefield detected in the Trikeri Channel, which had been closed after a steamer under *U-Jäger* escort was damaged by what at first was believed to be a mine detonation but later surmised to have been a torpedo attack. The boats of the 12th R-Flotilla would be based initially at Salamis near Athens. In Italy the 7th *Sicherungsflottille* was established under the command of KK Herbert Walter for service in the Tyrrhenian Sea, comprising a large contingent of small converted trawlers that now functioned as minesweepers and *Vorpostenboote*. Initially established in March, the flotilla was soon in service and would later become the 13th *Sicherungsflottille* during 1944, by which stage the Kriegsmarine's back was against the wall in the Mediterranean.

The Battle for Sicily

Within days of Ruge's appeal to OKM to retain control of the few vessels capable of minelaying in his area, his fears were fully realised when agents reported an invasion fleet leaving Algiers for Sicily, the first Allied troops beginning to land in the early hours of 10 July accompanied by heavy naval bombardment as part of Operation Husky.

> *Deutsches Marinekommando Italien* has reported on the distribution and state of readiness of our naval forces as at 1600 . . . The report states that at that time, five boats of 3rd S-Flotilla were ready for action at Palermo and two in limited operational status while three boats at Toulon were non-operational. Five boats of 7th S-Flotilla were ready for action at Cagliari and three boats non-operational at Toulon,
>
> Due to engine trouble, torpedo boat *TA10* put in to Taranto on the evening of 9 July, Torpedo boat *TA9* is ready for action at Toulon and torpedo boat *TA11* is ready for action at Naples. The mine ships *Pommern* and *Brandenburg* are ready for action at Maddalena. The patrol and escort forces and 6th R-Flotilla are on protection duty. One boat of 12th R-Flotilla is en route from Mettunia to Civitavecchia and two boats are en route from Marseille to Leghorn.

Despite the paucity of naval defence around Sicily, the R-boats of the 12th R-Flotilla that were still in Italian waters were ordered to carry out their planned move to the Aegean, German naval intelligence being convinced of probable Allied landings in the Balkans. Meanwhile the two German minelayers began laying minefields in Sardinian waters. In company with the Italian destroyer *Vivaldi* they completed their task off the island's southern coast but were attacked by six torpedo bombers at 1430hrs on 11 July while in the Bonifacio Strait during their return voyage. Three of the planes were shot down but casualties were suffered aboard both minelayers, the captain of the *Brandenburg*, FK Dr Otto Wunder, being killed by machine-gun fire. Both minelayers had been previously been French merchant ships; the 3894-ton minelayer *Brandenburg* was formerly SS *Kita* while *Pommern* had been MV *Belain d'Esnambuc* before they had been seized by the Kriegsmarine and converted.

The main German naval strike force in the Western Mediterranean was made up of the hard-pressed S-boats and U-boats, the latter operating in clear waters that rendered them particularly vulnerable to detection from the air. With the Allies securely ashore in Sicily, Ruge reported to OKM on 12 July that:

> The outcome of the battle of Sicily will probably decide Italy's future attitude. The German Army and Air Force are bringing up more forces into action. Supply requirements are increasing. The enemy Air Force is attacking powerfully. There is a chronic lack of escort vessels. The withdrawal of the first group of motor minesweepers has weakened the defence of Sicily as the Gela barrages could not be laid. Further withdrawals of beats which are specially suited for escort service would, at the present stage, palpably weaken our protection and seriously affect the reputation of the Kriegsmarine.

It was his last appeal for the transfer of the 12th R-Flotilla back to his control and finally SKL relented. They reasoned that it appeared that the Allies were concentrating all their available forces on Operation Husky, rendering a full-scale attack against Greece and its islands extremely unlikely, although submarine attacks and shore bombardment had increased, twelve auxiliary sailing vessel having been sunk by British submarine gunfire on the night of 11 July in the Gulf of Salonika. While the four R-boats that had already reached Salamis would remain in Greece, the seven others which had not yet left Italy temporarily remained with Ruge's forces, though three were still in the process of reconditioning in Marseilles after transit.

The additional boats amounted to only a pin-prick: the Kriegsmarine was hopelessly mismatched against an overwhelming enemy force and was relatively ineffectual in the defence of Sicily. The escort ship *SG13* of Kramer's 3rd G-Flotilla was hit by aerial torpedoes and beached near La Ponta on 12 July with her bows completely blown off. She would later be refloated and repaired as minesweeper *M6063*, only to be sunk in Marseilles in August 1944. *SG10* had been attached to Kramer's flotilla on 1 May 1943 but was sunk after only three months' service on 28 August, torpedoed by HMS *Sickle* near Corsica.

Kapitän zur See Gerhard von Kamptz's 4th G-Flotilla suffered even heavier losses, *SG14* being sunk in an air attack on 24 August and *TA9* destroyed by bombing in Toulon the previous day. The flotilla was disbanded in September and *TA10*, *TA11* and *TA12* were transferred to the 3rd G-Flotilla. On 13 July nine R-boats, *SG10* and five Italian torpedo boats were on escort duty between Sicily, Corsica and Sardinia as supplies and troops were efficiently moved between the islands. By that time a total of twenty-two more MFPs and nine R-boats had left Toulon bound for the Italian front. In

Close-up of the heavy weaponry carried aboard *SF161* of the 10th L-Flotilla.

mid-July SKL Quartermaster Division ordered the formation of the 1st and 2nd Transport Flotillas in the Mediterranean, created from MFPs with military crews in groups of twenty vessels each. They would be placed under the operational and administrative (detached) command of KK Karl Wehrmann's 2nd L-Flotilla that had served so effectively in the North African campaign. The 4th L-Flotilla had also been established in May under the command of KK Erich Zimmermann for operations along the Italian west coast and in the Tyrrhenian Sea, while the 6th L-Flotilla was created in June at Toulon, Kaptlt Werner Breitenstein's unit being formed around a cadre of men from Wehrmann's flotilla and destined to move into the Aegean in August 1943 where it was redesignated the 15th L-Flotilla. To the east, in Trieste, KK Hermann Roth had established the 10th L-Flotilla, under the command of the *Seetransportchef Adria*. To control these various units, FKdR Fhrh Gustav von Liebenstein was appointed commander of a newly-established 2nd *Landungsdivision* in May 1943.

During July Kaptlt Walter Klemm became the new commander of the 6th R-Flotilla as his boats continued to provide convoy escorst. The Wehrmacht's forces in Sicily had been bolstered by the arrival of extra troops and heavy weapons and the defences of the narrow Straits of Messina had been strengthened. Ruge now ordered the Straits to be the focus of extra patrols by Siebel ferries, MFPs and R-boats as German artillery, particularly anti-aircraft guns, were brought into position on both shores. Kapitän zur See Gerhard von Kamptz, of the 4th G-Flotilla, was assigned by Ruge as 'Commander Defences Messina Straits' and placed directly subordinate to his office. Von Kamptz's task was to protect the ferry traffic against enemy light forces and *SG14* and seven R-boats were placed at his disposal. Furthermore, FKdR von Liebenstein (in his capacity as *Seetransportführer*

Messina-Straße) was ordered to provide him with any available naval artillery lighters, combat barges and naval landing craft as required.

On 25 July R-boats *R38*, *R186* and *R188* of the 12th R-Flotilla were despatched from Messina to search for survivors from ten Ju52 transport aircraft that had been shot down, *R186* herself being attacked by fighter-bombers near Spadafora and sunk at 1530hrs with two crewmen killed, the surviving R-boats sustaining light damage while two aircraft were shot down. The search for any survivors from the Ju52s was unsuccessful. That same day events in Rome unfolded that provided a pivotal moment in the battle for Sicily when Mussolini was dismissed by King Victor Emmanuel II as head of the government and replaced by Marshal Pietro Badoglio. Italy had been in steep decline with increased Allied bombing, food shortages and labour strikes for the first time since 1925. The country had had no great appetite for the war even in 1940 and with Italian forces in Sicily on the brink of collapse despite the staunch German defence of the island, the fall of Mussolini was guaranteed. He was subsequently arrested and spirited away to incarceration at Campo Imperatore in the Abruzzo. While Badoglio maintained support for the alliance with Germany in public, he dissolved the Italian fascist party and initiated covert peace talks with the Allies.

In Berlin, the decision to immediately cease the reinforcement of Sicily was taken and contingency plans prepared for evacuating German troops from Sicily, Sardinia and Corsica. Two further operations were hurriedly prepared for potential immediate implementation: Eiche, the rescue of the incarcerated Mussolini by German troops and Student, the planned occupation of Rome by Army Group B under the command of Erwin Rommel and the restoration of Italian fascism. Badoglio's assurances of Italy's commitment to the Axis had been justifiably treated with great suspicion by Hitler's government and in the event of an Italian armistice with the Allies, Operations Achse and Schwarze would also be carried out, the capture of the Italian fleet and the seizure of key Italian military positions on land respectively.

Dönitz was informed at a conference with Hitler in Berlin that in the event of Rome's occupation the Kriegsmarine would be responsible for the seizure of the Italian fleets in La Spezia, Taranto and Genoa as well as Italian merchantmen in all ports. U-boats were also to be used as a cordon to destroy any Italian warships attempting to defect to the Allies, although this proved an abject failure in practice. Dönitz and the majority of senior Wehrmacht officers did not believe that the Fascists would regain control of Italy, Ruge reporting to his superior that Mussolini's resignation had been 'accepted without protest anywhere'. However, Hitler retained his belief that a liberated Mussolini would rally the country behind him once again as an Axis ally. Regardless, Germany's defensive lines would be shortened in the event that Italy collapsed entirely.

The heavy *Artillerieträger SF161*, which was bombed in the Messina Strait on 16 August 1943 and later scuttled.

Before long the decision had been taken to begin bringing any unnecessary troops out of Sicily, the full-scale evacuation only getting underway on 11 August. By skilful withdrawal of defensive lines and extremely effective Kriegsmarine transport services under the protection of a heavy concentration of artillery and flak units, the Wehrmacht managed to successfully extricate its troops from the lost battle for Sicily in daylight with minimal interference from Allied air or naval forces and redeploy them in Calabria. The evacuation, masterminded by von Liebenstein, was completed by 17 August with the successful transporting of 52,000 German troops (including 4444 wounded), 14,105 vehicles, 47 tanks, 94 guns, 1100 tons of ammunition, and about 20,700 tons of equipment and stores. The Italians had recovered 62,182 men, 41 guns and 227 vehicles with the loss of only one of their own motor rafts and the train ferry *Carridi*, which was scuttled when Allied troops entered Messina. Sicily fell to the Allies the following day. The evacuation has been described by some as a 'miniature Dunkirk' but in fact it was far more successful than that, as the troops that returned to Calabria did so in excellent fighting order after a highly skilful defensive battle against overwhelming odds.

Boats of the 11th R-Flotilla had finally begun to achievet operational readiness and the delayed transfer of the 12th R-Flotilla to the Aegean was resumed during August. The 6th R-Flotilla had meanwhile relocated to Anzio and Nettuno. On 13 August RAF Beaufighters sank *R6* near Civitavecchia as she escorted the Italian freighter *Carbonello* sailing from Olbia. Three crewmen were killed in the attack that left the R-boat on fire and sinking.

Elsewhere, both *SG10* and *SG14* were sunk during the latter days of August. *SG14*, which had successfully defended the Messina crossings from air attack while carrying troops, was sunk by a direct hit from a fighter bomber during an air raid on Sapri, 80 miles south-east of Naples at 1646hrs on 24 August. Two of the attacking planes were shot down while eight German crewmen were killed and twenty wounded. Four days later the former French fruit carrier *SG10* was escorting two Italian lighters and a water tanker from La Maddalena to La Spezia in company with *UJ2208* and *UJ2209* when HMS *Sickle* fired four torpedoes at 0657hrs, two of them hitting *SG10* which sank in less than a minute. Eighty-five crewmen were lost and 122 rescued by the other ships of the convoy while the *U-Jäger* dropped thirty-five depth charges, at least five of them close to the submerged boat before she escaped the area.

The Allies attack Italy – Italy Surrenders

There was little doubt that the Allies would press their advantage in and assault Italy itself once Sicily had fallen and the expected attack began on the morning of 3 September when British troops crossed the Straits of Messina onto the 'toe' of Italy in Operation Baytown. Kesselring had decided to fight his battle further north and they faced no serious resistance. Nonetheless, the British advanced with painful caution over obstacles and inhospitable terrain, and five days after the landing Eisenhower announced the negotiated surrender of Italy. Those naval forces that remained loyal to the deposed Mussolini became known as the *Marina Nazionale Repubblicana* while Mussolini himself was later freed from incarceration by German paratroopers on 12 September as part of the successful Operation Eich, flown to Germany and browbeaten into forming a new fascist regime, the 'Italian Social Republic', proclaimed on 23 September 1943. Dönitz was thereafter proved correct as the majority of Italian troops failed to rally to the new banner.

Meanwhile, German units executed Operation Achse just as further Allied forces landed at Taranto on 9 September, the Allied attack carried out at short notice following an Italian offer to surrender the port and its military units intact. Kesselring correctly surmised that neither Baytown nor the new attack, Slapstick, were the primary Allied invasion, which landed that same day at Salerno, code-named Operation Avalanche. American Lieutenant General Mark Clark's Fifth Army landed at Salerno and despite some local successes was soon fighting a desperate battle against aggressive attacks by Kesselring's troops and Luftwaffe aircraft. Clark initially was thrown into a panic and proposed evacuating his troops from the four small beachheads that they had become penned into, but he was overruled by Allied Supreme Command.

While chaos broke out on land, the 6th R-Flotilla suffered its own casualties during the attack on Salerno, both ObStrm Hartwig's *R7* and

ObltzS Reichelt's *R13* being caught in the harbour when the guns of the Allied invasion fleet bombarded the port, suffering damage and then scuttled by their crews with depth charges. Two R-boats, one towing the other, were also unsuccessfully attacked by HMS *Seraph* with gunfire between Corsica and the Italian mainland, the submarine crash-diving after only firing six rounds to avoid Luftwaffe aircraft. However, Lt N. L. A. Jewell was more fortunate with his next two attempts:

> 1028 hours – Sighted two tank landing craft [barges *Eva* and *Margot*], again one towing the other. Surfaced in position 42°48'N, 10°43'E to engage with gunfire. After three rounds had been fired the enemy also opened fire and soon found the range. Fortunately the second landing craft caught fire shortly afterwards. The crew was seen to jump overboard. Fire could now be concentrated on the first landing craft which soon also caught fire. Both burnt furiously for about one hour. Eight further tank landing craft escorted by two R-boats then appeared forcing *Seraph* to dive. Several more of these 'convoys' were seen during the day.
>
> 1645 hours – Sighted two armed barges. Surfaced in approximate position 42°48'N, 10°42'E and engaged with gunfire. Both were hit before *Seraph* was forced to dive when aircraft approached. When these had passed *Seraph* surfaced again and continued the action. After several more hits the crew of the leading barge abandoned ship. The second barge was then engaged and after two hits ran herself ashore. The crew rapidly abandoned ship. *Seraph* closed to 1000 yards and obtained two more hits after which she started to burn. She blew up violently a few minutes later. *Seraph* then set course for the first barge and the last three rounds of 3' (star shell) were fired into her with apparently no success. *Seraph* then closed with the intention to board and place a demolition charge. When she came alongside smoke was seen coming from the hold and with the second barge's fate in mind *Seraph* cast off and set off at high speed. This barge was seen to explode at 1855 hours.[83]

After days of heavy fighting, the Salerno beachhead was finally secured with the aid of overwhelming aerial and naval bombardment and Kesselring's forces were driven back. Meanwhile Operation Achse met with mixed results, the majority of Italian capital ships escaping capture by the Wehrmacht, either sailing intact to Malta or North Africa and surrendering to the Allies or being scuttled in harbour. The battleship *Roma*, sailing in company with the fleet from La Spezia, was caught by Luftwaffe bombers and sunk using Fritz X guided bombs and a number of destroyers, torpedo boats and smaller craft were also sunk by the Luftwaffe and Kriegsmarine. Some were captured intact, particularly in Crete and Greece where the German garrisons outnumbered their erstwhile allies. In the Aegean four Italian torpedo boats, two destroyers, one minelayer, five MAS boats, six auxiliary minesweepers, fourteen small auxiliary naval vessels, two tankers, two troop transports and two freighters were taken over.

Also in La Spezia was Contrammiraglio Federico Martinengo, commander-in-chief of the Italian Navy's anti-submarine forces. The announcement of the Armistice found him in Rome and he did not reach his headquarters in La Spezia until the morning of 9 September where he ordered every operational submarine chaser to move south and surrender to the nearest Allied forces. After issuing his instructions he too left the port aboard the submarine chaser *VAS234*, in company with her sister-ship *VAS235*. During early afternoon the two Italian vessels encountered a *rotte* of R-boats off Gorgona Island who commanded them to stop and surrender. Martinegro attempted to flee towards the coast of nearby Cala Scirocco where Italian coastal artillery could support him but a heavy exchange of gunfire followed during which Martinengo, who had taken the helm of *VAS234*, was hit and killed instantly. The boat burst into flames, though the remaining crew managed to beach her and escape before the shattered craft exploded.

Elsewhere, Italian warships and units of the security flotillas also clashed as the Germans attempted to carry out their instructions as part of Operation Achse. In Corsica's Bastia harbour the resulting battle destroyed seven German vessels; MFPs *F366*, *F387*, *F459*, *F612* and *F623* as well as *U-Jäger UJ2203* and *UJ2219*.

Bastia hosted both Italian and German warships and upon the declaration of the Italian Armistice the assembled commanders of each side reached a 'gentlemen's agreement' that the German forces would be permitted to depart for the Italian mainland unhindered. The Italian *Ciclone*-class torpedo boats *Ardito* and *Aliseo* and the merchant ships *Sassari* and *Humanitas* were in the harbour, while the *Gabbiano*-class corvette *Cormorano* remained on picket duty outside it. However, tension mounted in the port, Italian anti-aircraft gunners opening fire on passing German aircraft while civil unrest broke out, French civilians supported by Italian troops seizing control of the citadel, the railway station and the main roads. Obeying their instructions under Operation Achse, the Germans launched a surprise attack in an attempt to capture the Italian ships, starting at 2345hrs. Two groups of German soldiers stormed the *Ardito*, killing 70 of the 180 crew and damaged her severely. Both merchant ships were also taken with heavy Italian losses.

The torpedo boat *Aliseo* had just sailed from the harbour when the German attack began and shortly after dawn a counter-attack by Italian infantry of the *10° Raggruppamento Celere Bersaglieri* recaptured the port and all three vessels. The *Aliseo* was captained by Carlo Fecia di Cossato, a submarine 'Ace' who had served with distinction in the Atlantic aboard the BETASOM boat *Tazzoli* and been awarded, amongst other decorations, the Knight's Cross by the Kriegsmarine. Following the successful recapture of Bastia, all German vessels were ordered to leave, whereupon they were fired upon by 76mm Italian coastal batteries, being damaged *UJ2203* and several of the MFPs. *Aliseo* then attacked the German convoy and battle commenced. *UJ2203* opened fire on *Aliseo*, one 88mm shell hitting the engine room, temporarily disabling her. Repairs were swiftly completed, however, and the torpedo boat engaged the convoy, sinking each ship in succession, *UJ2203* exploding at 0820hrs after suffering several direct hits. *UJ2219* was also destroyed ten minutes later when her magazine exploded. In the next five minutes *Aliseo* also sank *F366*, *F459* and *F623* as *Cormorano* arrived to help force *F387* and *F612* to run aground where they were abandoned and destroyed. A 43-ton Luftwaffe service motorboat, *FLB412*, was also sunk by the corvette. Twenty-five German survivors were picked up by *Aliseo*, which proceeded in company with the damaged *Ardito* towards Portoferraio, the damaged ship later being abandoned there and captured by the Germans.

Operation Achse had resulted in a significant number of smaller warships and merchantmen being seized. Italian and French ports that had been held by Italian troops were occupied by the Wehrmacht, and Corsica, Elba and strategically-valuable Aegean islands were also taken, though some only after pitched battles with Italian troops who at first refused to capitulate. Sardinia was immediately evacuated by German forces which transferred to Corsica where French resistance fighters rose up against the occupying troops. The Partisans were soon engaged in heavy fighting with troops of *Sturmbrigade 'Reichsführer SS'* and the 90th Panzergrenadier Division, supported by Italian paratroopers loyal to the fascist cause. The remaining Italian garrison defected to the Allies and on 15 September an SOE-trained French battalion landed on the island to support the uprising.

The Maquis rebellion on Corsica was largely held in check and the German decision to evacuate the island was confirmed on 17 September once the harbours of Bastia, Porto Vecchia and Bonifacio and their connecting roads were once more firmly in German hands. An occupation force was landed at Porto Farraio by a hastily-assembled flotilla comprising the torpedo boat *TA9*, the fast escort vessel *SG11* and four R-boats escorting four troop-carrying MFPs. Troops were still being moved from Sardinia to Corsica and from there to the Italian mainland using both maritime and air transport in another successful operation planned and executed once again by von Liebenstein, this time having been appointed *Seetransportführer Korsika*.

25,800 men, 4650 vehicles, 4765 tons of supplies, 66 medium anti-tank guns, 78 heavy anti-tank guns, 12 light and 12 heavy infantry guns, 62 tanks, 37 assault guns, 23 armoured cars, 23 light and eight heavy field howitzers, four 10cm guns, 119 88mm guns, 147 20mm guns and 30 20mm 'Vierling' guns were evacuated from Sardinia in all. The steamers *Champagne* and *Anjou*, the war transports *KT8* and *KT31*, ten Marinefährprähme, five tugs, and five pinnaces are available for the traffic between Corsica and the mainland. To this tonnage nine steamers totalling about 10,000 GRT, the war transport *K16*, the fast escort vessel *SG11*, the [night-fighter control ship] *Kreta* and some more pinnaces will be added by 22 Sept . . . and 23 naval landing craft, seven Siebel ferries, three LCIs, eight torpedo boats, the war transport *KT2* and two Italian war transports will be seized at Maddalena, as soon as the Sardinia traffic ceases.[84]

However, the strain on the Kriegsmarine was beginning to tell. *Schnellboote* and U-boats were waging desperate rearguard actions while struggling to remain operational in any numbers. By 21 September the 11th R-Flotilla had eight operational vessels and the 12th R-Flotilla only three, with five boats from both flotillas undergoing a short period in dock The 6th R-Flotilla could only field two operational vessels, the remaining seven out of action. All the R-boats were based at Rapallo. The torpedo boat *TA9* of the 3rd G-Flotilla was due for dockyard repairs but remained operational, as did *SG11*. The 22nd UJ-Flotilla was down to only two operational craft with eight in dock undergoing overhaul or repair.[85] The minelayer *Pommern* remained operational in Toulon harbour.

That same day both the minelayer *Brandenburg* and the night-fighter control ship *Kreta* were sunk by HMS *Unseen* about seven nautical miles north-east of Isola di Capraia, Italy. The two ships were being escorted by *R189* and *R201* accompanied by two Arado seaplanes when Lt. M. L. C. Crawford hit each ship with a single torpedo each after firing four torpedoes. *Kreta*, the ex-French postal and passenger ship SS *Ile de Beauté*, had been built in 1930 at the Deschimag Werft, Bremen, captured after the fall of France and subsequently converted into a night fighter control ship. Her main armament was two 105mm and two 75mm guns augmented with smaller flak weapons and she carried Freya AN (FuMo303) and Würzburg D (FuMo213) radars. Twenty-five German crewmen were reported missing and thirty wounded (seven seriously) from *Brandenburg*, with five killed or missing and eleven wounded (four seriously) from *Kreta*. A total of 486 survivors were picked up and later landed at Leghorn by the R-boats after brief attempts at depth-charging the British submarine which escaped by going deep after firing.

In Corsica escalating Maquis attacks and Allied aerial bombardment hampered the embarkation of forces due for evacuation to the mainland. Transport convoys were reduced to sailing by night due to air attacks but that only increased the danger from aggressive Allied submarine patrols. On 22 September the Polish submarine *Dzik* attacked a convoy comprising *F420*, *F360*, *F587*, *F616*, *F450* and *MZ749* that had left Bastia for Piombino. At 1802hrs the boat's periscope was sighted to port and disappeared following a short bombardment. Only 23 minutes later four torpedoes arced toward the convoy, one hitting *F420* in the stern and the rest narrowly missing *F360* and *F450*. The MFP sank within ten minutes with ten crew members missing, the remaining nine and the embarked infantry being rescued.

At 0349hrs on 24 September HMS *Ultor* attempted to torpedo the 9946-ton former French tanker *Champagne* engaged upon evacuation duties, but missed with two torpedoes fired while surfaced in bad visibility. The tanker was under R-boat escort and the track of the first torpedo was spotted, *Champagne* turning away as the R-boats engaged. *R178* opened fire and hit *Ultor* as she dived, though inflicting little real damage. No depth charges were dropped and the British submarine crept away.

Later, at 1945hrs that same night, *Ultor* again found *Champagne* emerging from Bastia harbour under R-boat and *Geleitboote* escort, firing four torpedoes of which two struck home. The escorts began depth-charging, but only eight were dropped as they hunted the submarine for two hours. The tanker was beached south of Bastia as Siebel ferries began unloading her deck cargo before she was finished off with a third torpedo, this time from HMS *Uproar* on 27 September.

The British submarine HMS *Sybil* attempted an attack on six other MFPs travelling in convoy on 29 September. A single shallow-set torpedo was fired towards *F611*, *F553*, *F554*, *F619*, *F610* and *F622* that passed 15m astern of *F610*. *Sybil* had already sunk the 2910-ton German merchant ship *Saint-Nazaire* eight nautical miles west of Sestri Levante as the steamer travelled from Genoa to La Spezia under escort by *R38* and *R187*. The R-boats had rescued twenty-one survivors, thirty-eight others being killed in the attack.

The ferry traffic between Corsica and the mainland was subjected to heavy enemy air attacks and hampered by bad weather. The 2969-ton SS *Tiberiade* was damaged by aircraft and capsized in Bastia while damage to dockyard installations dramatically slowed the embarkation of heavy vehicles and weapons. The smaller pinnaces and R-boats suffered damage due to the heavy seas, while the dockyard struggled to repair them every day and night. The transfer of troops by aircraft was also disrupted by weather and heavy air attacks, though three MFPs shot down two of seven attacking aircraft on 29 September. However, that same day, Allied aircraft from Sardinia destroyed four Ju52 transport aircraft laden with troops. By 2 October only about 6000 men, 1500 soft-skinned vehicles and numerous artillery pieces remained on the island, all armoured vehicles having been shipped off, *R212* narrowly being missed by submarine torpedoes while escorting a convoy near Bastia the following day which was the last shipment of materiel to the mainland: 2282 men, 222 prisoners, 328 vehicles, 51 artillery pieces and 77 tons of supplies. Bastia was under heavy artillery fire as the final retreating Germans demolished the harbour facilities and sank the teamer *Sassari* as a blockship. Only after they had embarked did the commander of Corsica's German troops, General von Senger und Etterlin, leave with his staff. Two R–boats stood by off the coast at Bastia until 0300hrs the next morning to pick up any stragglers. Meanwhile, at 2300hrs, von Liebenstein announced the evacuation complete, Hitler later sending a congratulatory message to Kesselring:

> The withdrawal of troops, including their heavy arms and equipment, from Sardinia and Corsica to the mainland was an exceptional feat. It was hardly to be hoped that this evacuation from one island to the other and thence by sea to the mainland would be completed so successfully.
>
> The German forces, pushing though the treacherous Badoglio troops, shelled from the sea and attacked from the air by strong enemy formations, made their way to Bastia, recaptured it and there held out against the attack of regular de Gaulle troops until evacuation to the mainland was completed in spite of numerous enemy submarines.
>
> I express my fullest appreciation. to the Commander on Corsica, General Von Senger und Etterlin, to the troops under his command as well as to the Naval and Air Force escort and transport units and to their Commanders.

The withdrawal had cost the Germans one infantry landing boat, seven MFPs, two *U-Jäger*, one tug, three Siebel ferries, one barge and three steamers sunk and 31 dead and 101 wounded. From at least forty air attacks, fifteen attacking aircraft had been shot down and from eight submarine attacks one enemy submarine was, erroneously, claimed as sunk.

War in the Aegean Sea

By the time that the evacuation of Corsica had been completed the feared British incursion into the Aegean had also begun with nearly 4000 British troops spread across the Dodecanese Islands by early October 1943. On the day that Italy had surrendered, the 30,000 Italian troops on Rhodes had been exhorted by British leaflets, and later two British majors parachuted onto the island, to subdue the island's 7000-strong German garrison. However, after just two days of sharp fighting the Italians surrendered at 1220hrs.[86] Partisans had risen on the island of Euboea and taken control of the ports, while Zante, Cefalonia, Corfu and Volos also seemed under imminent threat of surrender to Greek guerrillas as Italian troops began handing them their heavy weapons, refusing to surrender to the Germans.

In the Athens area, the 1st Company of the Brandenburger Regiment's *Küstenjäger Abteilung* had been placed under the command of KK Dr Brand's 21st UJ-Flotilla. Upon receipt of the Achse codeword they promptly seized an Italian torpedo boat and a destroyer – *San Martino* and *Calatafimi* – in Piraeus harbour which were later recommissioned into the Kriegsmarine as *TA17* and *TA19*.[87] Allied pressure mounted as uncertainty over the intention of Italian troops and Greek Partisan activity increased. During the afternoon of 12 September HMS *Rorqual* shelled Stratoni harbour east of Thessaloniki, another enemy submarine being sighted 30 miles south of Piraeus. Wehrmacht reinforcements for the naval port commanders of Volos and Khalkis were being rushed to the area, while two R-boats ferried an assault detachment from Piraeus for the defence of the radar station at Ariopoli on the southern Peloponnesus.

To the north, on 14 September the Greek submarine *Katsonis* was detected while surfaced by *UJ2101* and attacked. The submarine was on her seventh war patrol and had landed Commandos on Euboa on 11 September. Ordered to patrol off Nicaria, the commander Lt V. Laskos intercepted two sailing boats and discovered after interrogating the crews that a captured French ship *Simfra* was due to pass nearby carrying German soldiers on leave. The following day Laskos was surfaced and questioning another boat's crew when he spotted a ship in the distance. At first believing it to be the expected troop transport, Laskos was late in crash-diving his boat after discovering it to be *UJ2101* escorting a small local convoy. *Katsonis* was still shallow when depth charges forced her to the surface, the hydroplanes jammed, seawater entering the fractured hull and chlorine gas beginning to spread throughout the boat. As soon as *Katsonis* broke the surface the German gunners opened fire and after a lengthy exchange of shots disabled the Greek boat. Laskos ordered his crew to return fire with the submarine's deck gun but the gunners were soon killed by machine-gun fire. The skipper himself attempted to man the gun but was also hit and killed as *UJ2101* finally rammed *Katsonis* sending her to the bottom with thirty-two crewmen killed, including a British W/T operator Leonard Joseph Smith. One officer, one British Chief Petty Officer 2nd Class and thirteen Greek crewmen were captured, while the boat's IWO and two petty officers swam for nine hours to reach Skiathos and Pilio. Aboard the *U-Jäger* one man had been killed in the engagement and another twelve wounded.

The occupation of Corfu was postponed on 16 September because the decision was taken to first tackle Italian resistance on Cephalonia. The garrison of the island of Skarpantos surrendered unconditionally while Syra required extended negotiation. The 525 officers and 11,500 men of the Acqui Division had been on Cephalonia since May 1943, the division's 18th Regiment having detached for garrison duties on Corfu. The division's commander, General Antonio Gandin, was a veteran of the Eastern Front where he had been awarded the Iron Cross. He also had naval coastal batteries, torpedo boats and two aircraft at his disposal. Following the Italian armistice, Gandin began negotiating the fate of his command with Oberst Johannes Barge, commander of the Wehrmacht's 2000-strong 966th Fortress Grenadier Regiment also present on the island and with whom Gandin had a good relationship. Corfu's Italian commander flatly refused to surrender, while on Cephalonia Gandin eventually agreed to give up his division's weapons by 16 September while withdrawing from strategic positions on the coast. However, at 0700hrs on 13 September, Italian artillery batteries opened fire on their own initiative on a convoy of five MFPs carrying three 150mm artillery batteries to the port of Argostoli. Machine-gun fire hit Btsmt Gottschalk's *F495* when only 50m from the pier, three artillery rounds then hammering the starboard quarter, the boat later capsizing. *F494* was also hit, suffering four dead and three severely wounded, who were later flown to hospital in Athens. The damaged *F494* was towed into the harbour at Lixuri by a Greek ship.

Negotiations completely broke down and Gandin, with the backing of most of his officers and men, finally decided that his unit would fight. German troops of the 1st *Gebirgs* Division and 104th *Jäger* Division were embarked as '*Kampfgruppe Hirschfeld*' under the command of Major Harald von Hirschfeld aboard the *R210, UJ2015* and MFP *F131. R194* acted as escort and the hospital ship *Gradisca*, manned by a German prize crew, was stationed in Prevesa ready to remove Italian prisoners. Preparations for the attack were handicapped by a lack of available vessels, but Ju87 Stukas began to bomb the Italian positions on 17 September in preparation for the amphibious landing.

Meanwhile the newly-commissioned *UJ2111* was dispatched to Kythnos and Andros with the order to disarm the Italian garrisons there. Army Group South expected enemy landings to begin soon, particularly on the Ionian Islands which would effectively cut German coastal traffic along the west coast of Greece, and indeedon 17 September British troops occupied Leros and Samos. Royal Air Force aircraft were now operating from the airfield on Kos and a convoy consisting of the steamers *Pluto* and *Paul* escorted by *UJ2104* was attacked by seven low-flying Beaufighters at 1430hrs south of Naxos, whilst on passage from Piraeus to Rhodes. The escort's commander and both officers of the watch were severely wounded and one of two escorting Arado 196s of *Seeaufklärungsgruppe* 126 was shot down. The pilot, Fritz Schaar, ditched his badly-damaged aircraft after which he and his radio operator Herbert Schneider were rescued by *UJ2014*, the battered aircraft being taken in tow but it gradually sank as its holed floats filled with water. Expecting a second air strike, *UJ2104* radioed for urgent fighter cover as a Dornier floatplane unsuccessfully tried to find the convoy and rescue the wounded. The convoy proceeded on its way until 2330hrs when they were attacked by the destroyers HMS *Faulknor*, HMS *Eclipse* and HHMS *Queen Olga* near Astypalaia. While both merchant ships were sunk, the escort *UJ2104* was severely hit and began flooding in two parts of the damaged hull, with multiple casualties from shell fragments scattered throughout the boat. Many crewmen and at least one of the Arado crew jumped overboard to escape what

Fritz Schaar's Arado 196 damaged by enemy aircraft near Naxos and being taken in tow by
UJ2104.

they believed to be a sinking ship, the two merchant ships burning fiercely in
the background. After seven hours in the water they washed ashore on the
north coast of Astypalaia. Meanwhile, the remaining men aboard the *U-Jäger*
had coaxed their shattered boat into Maltezana Bay on the island's south-
east side, carrying survivors from the two other ships, where they dropped
anchor and, after realising that the Italians were no longer allies, prepared
their boat for scuttling. 'Last report: "Crew of *UJ2104* taken prisoner by
Italians – boat ready to be blown up."'[88] The tiny Italian garrison of the island
treated the German survivors well, although the Italian commander believed
them to be the spearhead of a German occupation force and asked for
reinforcements, two MAS boats – *MS12* and *MS23* – being despatched from
Leros with troops aboard to hold the island.

In Piraeus, VA Werner Lange (*Kommandierender Admiral Ägäis*) had
requested dive bomber support and Junkers Ju88 aircraft were despatched
to assist that afternoon. The MAS boats, in company with two small motor
sailing boats, had recovered the shipwrecked survivors on the island's north
coast and werer returning them to Maltezana Bay when the Ju88s attacked;
both MAS boats were sunk and only frantic waving and Morse signals from
the German survivors prevented an attack on the other boats. The Ju88s
departed and eventually the Germans reached their destination, the survivors

being billeted in a hospital under Italian guard while the dead were buried. A small British landing party later took the prisoners aboard HMS *Faulknor* which transported them to a prisoner of war camp in Egypt.

The capture of the German survivors reinforced the British belief that Germany was preparing to attack the Dodecanese after reinforcing Rhodes and Crete. This train of thought ultimately led to any gathering of forces that their intelligence detected – such as the 1st *Gebirgs* Division before its deployment to the Ionian Sea – being seen as a move to the East, rendering other German operations free from Allied interference. However, while this was of some small benefit to the Kriegsmarine units within the Western Aegean and Tyrrhenian Seas, they still lacked naval power in the region.

> The development of the situation in the Aegean Sea demands that naval landing craft and Siebel ferries be immediately dispatched there in order to maintain the supply traffic along the coasts and between the islands, and also for the defence of the ports and straits against the insurgents. As disclosures made in our propaganda broadcast have made a transfer from the Black Sea to the Aegean Sea impossible, the only way left is to transfer these craft by overland routes to Thessaloniki or Kavalla, where facilities for immediate assembly are available. It is therefore requested that the sections of as many naval landing craft as possible be shipped at once to Thessaloniki and those for Siebel ferries to Kavalla. Please state how any naval landing craft and Siebel ferries are to be expected and when the sections will arrive, so that the necessary preparations for their assembly may be made.[89]

On 17 September *Kampfgruppe Hirschfeld* landed on Cephalonia and fighting raged until the last Italians surrendered at 1100hrs on 22 September. The Italian conscripts of the Acqui Division were no match for the veteran *Gebirgsjäger* and while 300 German troops were killed, the Italians lost 1315 men. A single R-boat was despatched to the harbour of Argostoli to take control of the two Italian torpedo boats still there. On 24 September, SKL recorded a single pair of sentences that inadequately describe what happened next: 'The island of Cephalonia is in our hands. The bulk of the Italian division there has been annihilated.' Beginning on 21 September, even before the end of hostilities, Hitler had ordered that due to the 'perfidious and treacherous' behaviour of the Italians on Cephalonia, no prisoners were to be taken. Over the week that followed over 5000 men of the Acqui Division were shot, including Gandin. It was a pattern repeated to a lesser degree on other islands. 'Mopping up operations on Cephalonia have been completed. The Italian General and all the officers have been shot.'[90]

On the island of Paros, the Italian defenders fled upon the arrival of German patrol vessels, abandoning their weapons. German troops attempted a second landing on Corfu, beginning in the early morning of 24 September. An earlier attempt by a task force of thirteen MFPs and commandeered trawlers carrying two companies of men from the 1st *Gebirgs* Division had been repulsed on 13 September after having lost one ship to defensive fire, with three damaged and six others suffering engine trouble. The second assault, code-named Operation Verrat, was mounted with *UJ2105*, *R194*, *R195*, *R211*, the light S-boat *LS6* and four MFPs carrying the veteran *Gebirgsjäger*. This time the assault force was landed successfully and began fighting to recapture the island. *UJ2105* suffered a direct hit from Italian coastal artillery, killing one man and wounding six others including the skipper ObltzS Keller. Artillery fire also damaged *R195*, wounding six men and *R211* was hit be heavy machine-gun fire. As the German vessels returned to Ignumenitza they were attacked by Italian aircraft, which sank *LS6* and damaged *R194* and *F131*. However, by 26 September Corfu was firmly in German hands.

> On Corfu in all about 600 Italians were shot or taken prisoner. About 10,000 unarmed Italians surrendered, most of them in closed formations. The officers will be dealt with in accordance with the Führer directive. The following material was captured: eight batteries, the arms and equipment of eight infantry battalions, one trench mortar battalion, and one anti-aircraft defence company; moreover stores and munitions. Our casualties were: seven killed, including two naval ratings, and 45 injured. Investigations as to the whereabouts of the former German island garrison have not yet been completed. (The naval and air force personnel are said to have been taken to Brindisi by the Italians).[91]

The Italian garrison on Syra was taken prisoner while fighting continued briefly on Andros and Euboa. In Northern Euboea, fifty Italian officers and artillerymen deserted to join the Greek partisans, removing the breech blocks of the guns. A company of men from the 4th SS *Polizei* Division was transferred to the island, but was soon surrounded and required further SS reinforcements landed by MFPs.

Throughout the region Italian prisoners of war that had survived the shocking purges carried out by the Wehrmacht were being transported aboard captured Italian merchant ships to incarceration on the mainland or deportation to Germany. However, in many cases their ordeal was only just beginning. On Rhodes the 3428-ton Italian SS *Gaetano Donizetti* which had been seized on the Italian armistice arrived on 19 September to bring weapons and ammunition to German troops on Rhodes. Once there she loaded 1576 prisoners into the cargo hold and sailed on 22 September, heading south-west. The ship was escorted by *TA10* commanded by *Oberleutnant zur See* Jobst Hahndorff. At 0110hrs the following morning they were sighted ten miles from Rhodes by the destroyer HMS *Eclipse* which immediately opened fire. The overcrowded *Gaetano Donizetti* was hit and went down in seconds with all her German crew and Italian passengers. Hahndorff's ship was badly damaged, with both engines destroyed and the engine room gutted by fire with five men killed and another four injured. Able to keep his disabled ship afloat, Hahndorff was soon assisted by other vessels that towed him to Prasso Bay where the ship was scuttled at anchor after any weapons that could be removed from *TA10* had been taken ashore.

This disaster was not the only one to befall Italian prisoners of war. The men were crammed into every available space aboard a few ships and following the sinking of *Gaetano Donizetti*, Allied aircraft also unwittingly sank the steamer *Sinfra* north of Souda – carrying 204 German soldiers, 2389 Italian prisoners and 71 Greek convicts aboard – with only 539 of the prisoners being rescued. The steamer *Marguerita* was sunk by a mine west of Patras on 13 October with five German guard and 550 Italian prisoners lost. On 8 February 1944 the British submarine HMS *Sportsman* torpedoed the steamer *Petrella* north of Souda with 3173 Italian prisoners on board, of which 2670 perished and on 12 February the 2127-ton steamer *Oria*, escorted by *TA16, TA17* and *TA19*, ran into heavy weather while passing through the straits between the islands of Serifos and Kythnos, the escort commanders' advice to turn west to avoid the coast being repeatedly ignored until the steamer ran aground near Cape Sounion, the ship breaking apart and only six guards, seven crew members, including the captain, and forty-nine Italian prisoners were saved. More than 4100 men were killed in the disaster.

To the east the Dodecanese islands of Kos, Leros and Samos were in enemy hands, their Italian garrisons finding common cause with whatever British and Greek forces had been rushed to help hold the islands. By 18 September Symi, Astypalaia and Ikaria were also in British hands. This fulfilled a long-held ambition of Winston Churchill's who was obsessed with possession of the Balkans. As well as wishing to regain a British strategic initiative in a period where American military power had begun to dominate, the British Prime Minister fervently believed that Allied occupation of the Dodecanese would bring Turkey into the war on the Allied side. He was, of course, sorely mistaken.

Operation Accolade called for a direct attack on Rhodes and Karpathos and had been formulated by the British High Command at the beginning of 1943. It envisioned a total of three infantry divisions, an armoured brigade and supporting troops to be used to capture the islands and dominate the entire Eastern Aegean, supported by heavy air cover. However, the American refusal to take part resulted in the required invasion shipping being redirected to the Italian campaign. Upon the Italian armistice, smaller British and Greek units were rushed to take control of as many Dodecanese islands as possible before the Germans could counter the move. They, however, failed to take control of the greatest prize – Rhodes – which was swiftly seized by the Germans.

A Beaufighter attacks German troop-transporting *Marinefährprähme* traffic during Operation Accolade.

In Berlin a Führer meeting that included Feldmarschall Baron von Weichs and Dönitz was held on 25 September. Both Von Weichs and Dönitz urged the evacuation of the Greek islands as they were 'of no value in a defensive situation such as this', being able to be cut off from supply and starved into submission while German troops were occupied with maintaining control over Partisan activity on the Greek mainland. Hitler, however, demurred, as he believed that Germany's allies in the south-east and Turkey would lose confidence lest a show of force be made. He was even willing to accept the eventual loss of men and material in the area as long as German prestige was upheld. Admiral Kurt Fricke (*Oberbefehlshaber der Marinegruppenkommando Süd*) passed on Hitler's directive to VA Lange: the Aegean was to be held.

The German commander on Crete, Generalleutnant Friedrich-Wilhelm Müller, was ordered to retake Kos and began to swiftly formulate plans. Kos now hosted two Spitfire squadrons, an RAF regiment with 20mm AA guns, 1st Battalion, Durham Light Infantry, a company from 11th Parachute Battalion, 1st Airborne Division and a company of men from the Special Boat Service. There also remained 3500 men of the original Italian garrison. Initial heavy bombardment by Luftwaffe aircraft of *Fliegerkorps* X – now freed from service in the Ionian Sea after the subjugation of the Italian garrisons – rendered the airfield unusable, both Spitfire squadrons being withdrawn to Cyprus and such severe casualties were caused amongst the British para-troopers that they too were withdrawn. The air raids widened to include Leros and on the morning of 26 September HMS *Intrepid* was badly damaged and HHMS *Queen Olga* sunk in Port Laki.

The Luftwaffe now had local air supremacy and following days of aerial bombardment, Operation Eisbär began. On 3 October 2000 German troops that included Panzergrenadiers, Brandenburgers and even some tanks, boarded five steamers, six MFPs and two converted trawlers, escorted by eight *U-Jäger* and four minesweepers of KK Mallmann's 12th M-Flotilla that had bwwn transferred to the Aegean, the armada setting sail from Piraeus, Suda and Candia in three groups, and rendezvousing west of Naxos to become Convoy 'Olympus'. Operational control rested with VA Lange and tactical control at sea with the commander of the 21st UJ-Flotilla, KK Günther Brandt. The landing was scheduled for 0400hrs on 3 October and between 0400 and 0430hrs the first wave of troops went ashore. Two landings were made on the south coast at Camare Bay and Capo Foco by 0700hrs, attacked by enemy aircraft of which two were shot down. The northern landings at Marmari, Tingachi and Forbici came under sporadic mortar fire and shelling as well as air attack; three of the attackers were brought down by flak. At 0630hrs a Brandenburger *Fallschirmjäger* company was also dropped directly on the cratered airfield.

Kriegsmarine losses were recorded as 'insignificant' (fifteen dead and seventy wounded), the unloading of troops being assisted by two armed fishing vessels, several motor boats and cutters. By 1500hrs four *U-Jäger* and two of the steamers were ordered to leave Kos, and were shelled while passing the island of Callno. Intelligence reports were received that indicated fresh Royal Navy forces were sailing to the island and Brandt decided to withdraw his vessels and begin their return journeys, avoiding direct courses and leaving behind the last four MFPs which were still loaded. Although the steamer *Citta Di Savona* and *UJ2102* were strafed by Beaufighters, only minor casualties were suffered and all of the invasion fleet returned to port. By 0600hrs on 4 October all organised resistance had ceased and Kos was in German hands.

A battalion of German infantry was then rushed to the island in a small convoy comprising the 852-ton Greek MV *Olympos*, skippered by Master Dimitris Mazarakis, and MFPs *F308*, *F327*, *F336*, *F494*, *F496* and *F532* escorted by *UJ2111*. The convoy was given the highest priority, an operation to take Naxos, Paros and Antiparos by Wehrmacht troops transported from Syra by MFPs of KK Dr Ado Brune's *Küstenschutzflottille Attika* being postponed in in favour of the Kos convoy due to limited shipping space being available. Although a risky proposition with British attention squarely focussed on Kos, two MFPs, a captured Italian MAS boat and the 12th R-Flotilla had all successfully transferred to the island. The battalion of troops was intwnsws to garrison Kos while the assault troops currently in possession would immediately mount an attack on Leros, the MFPs of the convoy to be used later in both the Leros assault and the occupation of

Kalymnos that lay unprotected halfway between the two islands. The convoy sailed with *UJ2111* leading *Olympos*, flanked by *F496*, *F532* and *F336* to port and *F494*, *F327* and *F308* to starboard.

However, reports of approaching British warships were correct; the cruisers HMS *Penelope* and *Sirius* in company with destroyers HMS *Faulknor* and *Fury* were nearby, part of a larger deployment specifically ordered to intercept German invasion traffic. At 0401hrs on 7 October the submarine HMS *Unruly* sighted 'a number of darkened ships' east of the island of Amorgos. After tracking on a parallel course, Lt. J. P. Fyfe turned to attack with a spread of four torpedoes, all of which missed but were not spotted by the Germans. He radioed a sighting report to summon surface forces and, after giving chase, closed for surface action at 0600hrs.

> Gun action stations. Position was now 36°49'N, 26°16'E. Opened fire on the rear Siebel ferry [*sic*]. The second round hit and after two more hits, shifted target to the next Siebel ferry [*sic, F532*] which was hit twice. The first target was now on fire. The gun then malfunctioned. After it was cleared one round was fired at the larger merchant vessel. It hit. Fire was then shifted to a Siebel ferry [*sic*] coming out of the smoke. Hit it at least twice. The merchant then also came out of the smoke and fire was re-opened on this ship. It was hit eight times. It was then seen to be stopped and being abandoned. Altered course to the East to set off in chase of the remainder of the convoy. During the chase they opened fire on *Unruly* and therefore the chase was abandoned at 0635 hours.[92]

The aftermost MFP to port, *F496*, was badly damaged by the attack, stored ammunition catching fire and the commander and two men being killed instantly, the boat's Number 1 seriously wounded in both eyes and his right arm. Amongst the remainder of the crew only two men escaped unscathed. Sinking by the stern, the shattered vessel limped to a bay in Astypalaia where she was beached and the remaining crew captured by Italian troops.[93] A surviving officer reported the event for the 12th *Küstenschutzflottille Attika* War Diary:

> After the gun battle I checked the number of ships and found that steamer *Olympos* and a barge were missing, this later turned out to be *F496*. I reported my observation to *UJ2111* by signal, but received no reply. Shortly thereafter, I repeated a proposal for me to retrace our course and search for the two missing ships. *UJ2111* replied: 'Four hostile destroyers to port'. Thus, a hunt for the missing ships became impossible. Especially since it seemed to me as if the submarine had probably returned to the site of the action.

As the Greek motor vessel dropped out of the convoy, the remainder of the German ships were found by the Royal Navy cruisers and destroyers who opened fire on the massively outgunned convoy. Within minutes the German ships were burning.

> After the cruiser had had shot up all of the MFPs, they sailed again past the floating wreckage and survivors and fired with small calibre artillery and flak machine-guns among the soldiers. The Commander of *UJ2111* and some of our soldiers observed the commander of *F336* and several other survivors killed by this. All of the MFPs were in flames and they then exploded in succession and sank quickly; except for *F327* which stood vertically with the stern above the water for a few hours.

The British warships continued to fire on men in the water and in rubber dinghies with tracer ammunition before withdrawing, later coming under sporadic unsuccessful Luftwaffe attack, while three R-boats, an MAS boat and aircraft converged on the scene and began rescuing survivors. In the confusion that followed, the three R-boats were also attacked by Luftwaffe aircraft, but without serious casualties. Other convoys en route to Kos were diverted as two extra MFPs were despatched to assist in the rescue. In total 1027 men were recovered with 150 missing.

Bitter recriminations immediately followed the destruction of the convoy. In Berlin OKM had been oblivious to the convoy's existence, later assuming it to be an intended attack on Leros of which they had not been informed. Fricke responded to strongly-worded messages from Berlin with a full breakdown of events, including a copy of an order issued by Army Group E that demanded troops sent directly to Kos to act as relief for the forces already there, freeing them for an attack on Leros:

> 1. In the unanimous opinion of Army Group E, Naval Group South and Air Force Command, Southeast, the immediate occupation of the island of Leros is decisive for maintaining the Aegean stronghold.
> 2. I therefore order that:
> a. The island of Leros is to be attacked and occupied at latest on 9 October, if possible on 8 October, by forces under the command of Lt. General Müller in accordance with basic operational plan discussed and agreed on 5 October. It is necessary to act with extreme daring and to accept all risk before the British transfer further reinforcements to the island.
> b. It is the task of Admiral, Aegean to carry out the naval part of this operation at once, setting aside all objections and avoiding all runs not essential for the success of the operation. Plans for carrying it out are to be reported to me at once. The date for attack – 9 October – is definite unless developments in the situation make a change necessary, in which case I will personally make the decision.
> 5. Fliegerkorps X will continue support of the operation with combined forces.
> 4. Lt. General Müller has been advised by radiogram accordingly.[94]

Fricke also expressed his opposition to orders for the convoy to sail before enemy dispositions were fully known. However, the Kriegsmarine was absolved of a certain amount of responsibility for the disaster as orders had been received from General Löhr at Army Group E to carry out the risky troop transfer 'despite any reservations', before Luftwaffe forces were worn down by constant attrition. The attack on Leros, code-named Leopard, would still take place, but the timetable that had been set for 8 October would suffer an inevitable delay of 24 hours.

With the urgency of Leopard now agreed throughout the Kriegsmarine hierarchy, troops of the 10th Battalion, 999th Light 'Afrika' Division – a penal unit that had first seen service in Tunisia – were embarked in Piraeus aboard the minelayers *Drache* and *Bulgaria*. Elsewhere four other convoys were also bound for Kos: three R-boats from Milos; *UJ2101*, MFP *F131* and the armed fishing vessel '*2*' from Syra; coastal auxiliary patrol boats *GA41*, *GA44* and *GA45* from Castron; and, as a substitute for the *Olympos* convoy, the steamer *Ingeborg*, two MFPs and an armed fishing vessel escorted by *UJ2102* from Piraeus, departing at 1100hrs.

Unfortunately, *Drache* and *Bulgaria* were found by HMS *Unruly* which had received aerial reconnaissance reports of the German ships and attacked at 1523hrs five miles south of Amorgos. Four torpedoes were fired, one of which hit and sank *Bulgaria* carrying 285 soldiers and a crew of 81; thirty-nine men were killed in the sinking.

Drache later reported British warships scouring the area near Kalymnos with star shells and searchlights during the early morning on 10 October, and the convoy centred on *Ingeborg* was ordered to take refuge in Mykonos rather than risk yet more losses to the Royal Navy after the steamer's captain and four crewmen were wounded by an air attack. While frantic efforts were made to keep the Leopard timetable going, the good weather also broke in the Aegean and this, combined with the arrival of USAAF P38 Lightning fighters that had begun to cause the Luftwaffe problems, finally forced a postponement of the assault on Leros in increments that ultimately delayed it until November. By then it was reasoned that German crews would be operational aboard captured Italian destroyers and torpedo boats and the build-up of troops in the Dodecanese completed. *Drache*, for her part, also laid a mine barrage off Kalymnos for the protection of planned Leopard shipping, which would later sink the destroyers HMS *Hurworth* and *Eclipse* and blow the bows off HHMS *Adrias*, though the latter would reach Alexandria for repair. All three had been running supplies to Leros, which was becoming increasingly isolated. Finally, with the Luftwaffe still operating effectively, the British were forced to rely on the submarines HMS *Rorqual* and *Severn* to shuttle supplies to the island.

Skirmishes also continued between the Allied naval and air forces and German Security Forces. On 14 October a convoy made up of the steamers

Kari and *Trapani* carrying Wehrmacht troops bound from Piraeus for Kos departed under escort by *UJ2109* and *UJ2110* along with *R211* at 1550hrs on 14 October. A second convoy consisting of the steamer *Ingeborg* and other vessels was scheduled to depart an hour later. An Allied reconnaissance aircraft was sighted while the convoy was east of Naxos, the ships turning to pass north-east of Amorgos, enemy naval forces briefly sighted that evening but evaded.

At 1100hrs the following day HMS *Torbay* found the small convoy and hit *Kari* with two torpedoes. The 1925-ton steamer carried 500 troops aboard and was sunk by the attack, the escorts dropping seventeen depth charges near *Torbay* but failing to damage her. While *R211* hove-to around the wreck with *UJ2110* in order to attempt to rescue survivors, *UJ2109* and *Trapani* continued on course. The R-boat was initially unable to recover any of the shipwrecked men due to increasingly heavy seas, two crash boats despatched from Milos being forced to return because of bad weather and a Dornier Do24 floatplane attempting to assist crashing on take-off and sinking. However, *R211* would eventually pull 130 men from the sea and take them to Kos while *UJ2110* was able to rescue 180 survivors, some of whom were severely wounded. The coastal patrol boat *G42* later scoured the area without success, although fifty other survivors were known to have reached the tiny island of Levitha but were unable to be recovered straight away on account of what SKL noted as 'the unsettled situation and weakness of our naval and air forces.' In due course they were able to overpower the small British garrison aided by some Brandenburger paratroopers. A second Do24 managed to later find twenty other survivors and recover them from the sea, flying them onward to Kos and in total 320 of the 500 men carried were eventually rescued.

The two remaining ships of the convoy, *Trapani* and *UJ2109*, also ran out of luck on 17 October when they were sighted and attacked by HMS *Hursley* and HHMS *Miaoules* off the east coast of Kalymnos. The Germans put in to Atti Bay, where *UJ2109* was shot up at close range and sank, *Trapani* and MFP *F338* also being set ablaze. The MFP's stern, crew cabin and engine were completely destroyed by the fire, but the ammunition lockers were flooded to prevent an explosion and the shattered hulk was towed back to Kos and beached by Bootsmaat Piersen and his crew. The *UJ2109* had started life as British minesweeper HMS *Widnes*, sunk in Crete during the German invasion of 1941 and subsequently raised, repaired and recommissioned as an *U-Jäger*. Five of her crew killed during her sinking at Kalymnos. The damaged *Trapani* was shelled again by British destroyers the following day, her bow being set ablaze but she remained afloat.

The steamer *Ingeborg* had disembarked her passengers on 20 October, lying at 24-hours readiness to sail for Kalymnos. On 28 October *Ingeborg* and an armed fishing boat transferred from Syra to Naxos, joined by a customs launch for the onward voyage to Kalymnos via Candie and south of Astypalaia in order to disembark troops. At 0227hrs on 29 October HMS *Unsparing* commanded by Lt. A. D. Piper sighted the darkened steamer and a little over two hours later fired four torpedoes, one of which hit *Ingeborg* as *Unsparing* went deep anticipating a counter-attack. When no depth charges were dropped, Piper rose to periscope depth.

1011 hours: Fired one torpedo at an R-boat which was laying stopped to pick up survivors from the ship sunk earlier that day. It hit and the target was seen to disintegrate. A second vessel, a landing barge, that had also been picking up survivors, was now seen to get underway.

1014 hours – Four depth charges exploded. These may have come from the ship that was just sunk.

1015 hours – Two depth charges exploded quite close. These were most likely dropped by the landing vessel that came down the torpedo track before *Unsparing* took avoiding action.

1034 hours – Four more depth charges were dropped but these were much further off.

Piper had torpedoed the commandeered customs cutter designated *GA49* as she picked up survivors, *KFK3* later arriving to rescue 111 men from the sea. Of the 408 men aboard *Ingeborg*, 306 were eventually saved.

Despite this materiel erosion and the superiority of the enemy naval forces, Germany was ascendant within the Aegean, albeit temporarily. Astypalaia was occupied by German troops on 22 October who liberated the forty-eight German prisoners on the island. The Italian garrison of 670 men and 100 British soldiers were captured; the wreck of *UJ2104* was found listing in harbour and the burnt-out *F496* still had some of its original cargo.

Battle for the Dodecanese: the German capture of Leros

Operation Leopard and the capture of Leros and the elimination of the British presence in the Dodecanese remained the Germans' top priority in the Aegean. By the beginning of November 1943 the British garrison had swelled to about 2500 troops and Leopard was scheduled for 9 November. The plan involved thirteen Infantry Landing Boats (IO), two MFPs, thirteen escort vessels (*U-Jäger*, escort boats and coastal patrol boats) as well as two ex-Italian destroyers and two torpedo boats to be used as a covering group. Early in the morning of 6 November the landing flotilla entered Nausa Bay (Paros Worth), vessels brought from Naxos and Milos bringing the total strength up to twenty-five landing craft and thirteen escort vessels, divided into four groups including the ex-Italian destroyers and torpedo boats of 9th

Torpedobootflottille. However, that same morning they were detected by aerial reconnaissance and attacked at 1335hrs by eight Beaufighters, *R184* and *R43* suffering casualties and being put out of commission.

On 7 November, amid security concerns, the operation was renamed Taifun and as the shipping required for the assault assembled, they suffered further Allied air harassment, *R195* taking engine damage and *R34*, *R194* and *R211* all in Piraeus for repair. Finally, after several false starts, Taifun began on 12 November. As planned, the voyage to Leros started with two groups east and west of Kalymnos the previous night. *R195* had been damaged by an air attack at 0124hrs and was forced to withdraw, while at 0210hrs a small enemy craft was destroyed near Telendo by *R210*, and a British patrol vessel captured by *UJ2101* near Telendo and brought into Kalymnos.

Under heavy defensive fire, troops began landing on the eastern coast of Leros at 0521hrs, those destined for the west coast turning away at 0543hrs five miles south-west of the island under heavy fire from land. Stukas were called in to neutralise the British artillery and the western landing being rescheduled for 1245hrs. However, heavy fire still defeated them, Bootsmaat Gebert's *IO93* being hit by mortar fire that detonated stored ammunition and fuel, the boat sinking east of Alinda Bay but with only two men wounded. The attack was broken off under cover of darkness, and those vessels that survived redirected to land on the eastern coast The supporting torpedo boat *TA18* was hit in the boiler and her speed reduced while *TA17* had her guns silenced by shell hits, all the torpedo boats later breaking off and returning

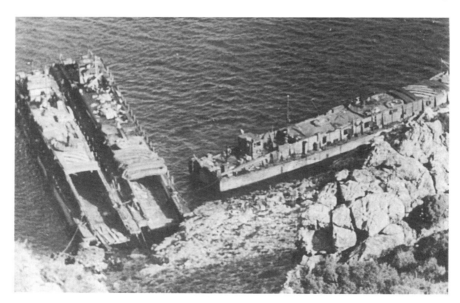

Marinefährprähme unloading Brandenburger troops on Leros during Operation Taifun.

to Syra for refuelling, towing naval landing craft *F370* whose engines were out of action. Brandenburger *Fallschirmjäger* landed at 1330hrs, suffering 40 per cent casualties in strong winds after dropping from lower than planned as the battle continued into the night.

The rescheduled landing of the troops of the western group on the eastern side of Leros was carried out at about 0600hrs the following morning under heavy fire in an all-out attack by *U-Jäger* and R-boats, the weather having deteriorated considerably overnight, rendering a repaired *R195* unable to land her twenty-eight passengers. *F129* was hit by artillery fire and sunk near Alinda Bay while *F331* was hit by HMS *Echo* and sunk. At 1030hrs when entering Kos, *R102* picked up a British radio operator and sailor from the destroyer HMS *Dulverton* that had been scuttled after Luftwaffe attack. For days the battle raged until, on 16 November, the Allies surrendered and Leros was taken. Samos was soon bombed into submission and smaller islands evacuated by whatever Allied troops were present. The Dodecanese was firmly in German hands, though attrition would continue to whittle away whatever strength the Kriegsmarine possessed with Allied naval and air attacks continuing undiminished. Hitler expressed his appreciation on the execution of the operation by a message to *Wehrmachtsbefehlshaber Südost* (Commanding General, Armed Forces, Southeast) Generaloberst Alexander Löhr: 'The capture of Leros, embarked on with limited means but with great courage, carried through tenaciously in spite of various setbacks and bravely brought to a victorious conclusion, is a military accomplishment which will find an honourable place in the history of this war.'

Korvettenkapitän Brandt moved all available vessels of his 21st UJ-Flotilla to the Samos area, with their focal point of operations the waters north of Vathi and south of Tigani Bay until the Army was ready to undertake Operation Damokles, the seizure of Samos using Luftwaffe ground troops, which was the last Allied stronghold in the Dodecanese. On the eve of the operation two S-boats transporting a Wehrmacht officer with surrender terms was received after one previous failed attempt, this time the senior Italian officer agreeing to lay down his arms, Samos capitulating at 1000hrs on 22 November. The majority of British soldiers had already evacuated the island but 4000 Italian troops passed into captivity and there were no summary executions.

For the British the loss of the Dodecanese was a disaster. Only a tiny force left on Kastellorizo remained which, despite some isolated commando raids, the Germans were content to ignore. Nonetheless, Churchill continued to clutch at the straws of Accolade and an Allied assault on Rhodes. On 24 November, at the Cairo Conference, Churchill renewed his demand for the attack. Face to face with General Marshall, Churchill said: 'His Majesty's Government can't have its troops standing idle. Muskets must flame.'

Marshall replied, 'Not one American soldier is going to die on [that] goddamn beach.' The subject was not raised publically again.

HMS *Torbay* returned to wreak havoc on 27 November when Lt. Robert Clutterbuck sighted the 2609-ton German troop transport *Palma* travelling empty off Karlovassi, Samos, under escort by the convoy leader *UJ2110* with *R210* astern. The faint trace of the submerged submarine had just been detected to starboard by *UJ2110*'s S-*Gerät* when two shallow-running torpedoes hit *Palma* amidships and sent the steamer down quickly although the entire crew and the ship's anti-aircraft weapons were saved. *UJ2110* subjected *Torbay* to severe depth-charging, flooding the boat's aft periscope and causing some leaks in the hull. As Clutterbuck crept away, the boat touched the bottom at 240 feet but was able to escape, rising to periscope depth and observing the hunter and three Arado aircraft still searching for him, three other *U-Jäger* soon arriving to join in the fruitless search.

The fall of Italy caught German forces in the Adriatic unprepared. Venice was captured by two S-boats that bluffed the Italian garrison, while on land Operation Istrien was launched by Rommel's Army Group B; the 2nd SS Panzer Corps occupying Trieste and the Yugoslavian coastal region. The office of *Kommandierender Admiral Adria* was established in Sofia, soon moving to Belgrade and later Trieste. Vizeadmiral Joachim Lietzmann was in command until July 1944 and to him would fall the task of building up whatever forces he could assemble from a woefully undeveloped area. His initial area of responsibility ranged from Fiume to Valona, the Italian coast remaining under control of *Deutsches Marinekommando Italien*. The demarcation line that separated the two naval commands matched that which divided Army Group E (Italy) and Army Group F (Balkans); the border between Mussolini's Italian Social Republic (RSI) and the Independent State of Croatia (NDH). Upon Lietzmann's request his area was later extended to include the whole of Istria to the mouth of the Tagliamento.

Lietzmann's Security Forces would comprise whatever captured vessels could be accumulated as well as MFPs and Siebel ferries, some moved overland from Genoa to the Italian Adriatic coast, while local dockyards were ordered to immediately begin construction of new MFPs. The surviving boats of Klemm's 6th R-Flotilla were transferred to Venice via the River Po as soon as the evacuation of Corsica was completed, these R-boats being the oldest and smallest still in service.

War in the Adriatic

With little offensive capacity available, the Germans relied on minelaying in the Adriatic. At first, due to a scarcity of minelaying craft, the minefields were laid along the Dalmatian coast rather than the envisioned barrage stretching between Cape Gargano to the island of Korčula that would effectively close the approaches to the central Adriatic. Though 1372 moored mines, 1600 explosive floats and 50 ground mines had been allocated to Lietzmann, most were still in transit from depots in Germany by the end of the month due to increasing transport difficulties resulting from Allied bombing. Italian mine stocks were to be used, as well as captured Italian minelayers and the C2M-type MFP *F483*. This minelayer had been constructed at Cantieri Navali Riuniti in Palermo, Italy, and commissioned on 29 November 1942 into the 2nd L-Flotilla. Commanded by Bootsmann Ferstel, *F483* had transferred briefly to the 10th L-Flotilla based at Trieste and had already been minelaying south of Ancona in October when she was attacked by low-flying aircraft, suffering two minor casualties and being peppered with 190 bullet holes. Upon the boat's arrival in Venice, Ferstel and his crew were assigned to *Hafenschutzflottille* Venice, though remaining committed to minelaying. On 19 November, while sowing a field north of Benedetto. *F483* was intercepted by the destroyers HMS *Quilliam* and *Loyal* patrolling and providing gunfire support off Italy's Adriatic coast. *F483* was disabled during the skirmish in which *Loyal* herself was hit by German coastal batteries before withdrawing. The MFP was beached broadside-on and the heavy cargo of mines broke free of their rails and shifted, many falling in to the shallow water. Too dangerous to recover, the MFP was scuttled with shellfire from an 88mm flak battery.

Further MFPs and Siebel ferries were trickling through to the Adriatic to bolster the meagre Kriegsmarine forces, two R-boats also earmarked for the move – *R190* and *R191* – being temporarily held up by a demolished bridge at Genoa and difficulties on the River Po. A new escort flotilla was formed on 8 October from Italian ships captured in Trieste, Venice and Pola, initially designated the 11th *Kustenschutzflottille*. Commanded by KKdR Jürgen von Kleist, this new unit was originally planned to comprise six converted steamers and three torpedo boats, but would eventually be made up of the torpedo boat/destroyers *TA20* (ex-*Audace*), *TA21* (ex-*Insidioso*), *TA22* (ex-*Giuseppe Missori*), *TA36* (*Stella Polare*), *TA37* (ex-*Gladio*), *TA38* (ex-*Spada*) and the cruiser *Niobe*, the latter crewed by a mixed German-Croatian complement. A rash of Italian torpedo boat and MAS boat defections to the Allies while engaged in escort duties in the Adriatic after pledging allegiance to Mussolini's new Republic resulted in Kriegsmarine unwillingness to use any Italian crews aboard the new units; even the amalgamation with Croatian naval perosnnel only being an absolute last resort, the difficulties in multi-national crews felt to outweigh the exigencies of manpower shortage.

The ex-Italian *TA22* was in action in October supporting German and Croatian Ustaše ground troops engaged in pushing Yugoslavian Partisans back from Rijeka as part of a co-ordinated offensive to take control of the Dalmatian coast that had been left abandoned by the surrender and defection of the

Pre-war portrait of a crewman from the 2nd *Geleitflottille*. Though the F-boats had been a complete design failure, the concept of Escort Flotillas remained and they saw service in the Mediterranean.

Italian occupation troops. However, *TA22* was fired on several times by Partisan artillery and the inexperienced crew proved wholly inefficient, suffering slight casualties and being forced back to Trieste for further training.

> Fitting-up and commissioning of the . . . 11th *Kustenschutzflottille* is to be speeded up by all available means. Besides this, all vessels in the area of Admiral, Adriatic which are suitable for escort duty are to be requisitioned, fitted-up and commissioned as soon as possible. Admiral, Adriatic is to regard it as his most important task to ensure supplies to the 2nd *Panzerarmee* by sea and especially to provide the necessary escort forces for this.
>
> 2. German Naval Command, Italy will carry out minelaying operations on the East coast of Italy, for which torpedo boat *Audace* (*TA20*) is required, if possible in such a way that *TA20* can be placed at the disposal of Admiral, Adriatic at the beginning of November.
>
> . . . The 11th *Kustenschutzflottille* is being formed under Admiral, Adriatic. Three Italian torpedo boats (one already in service) and six steamers converted into escort vessels have so far been requisitioned for this Flotilla and are being fitted-up. All these vessels are expected that further vessels suitable for escort duty will be taken over. Instructions for speedy requisitioning, fitting-up and commissioning of such vessels have been given.
>
> Besides the above, steps have been taken to transfer motor minesweepers and PT boats from the Western Mediterranean overland (Genoa–Piacenza–River Po). These vessels are, however, not expected to be in operational readiness in the Adriatic until December.[95]

All available forces were mustered to help secure the maritime communications links that ran along the Dalmatian coast and through the Partisan-held islands. Those off Šibenik were captured by the end of October, Generaloberst Lothar Rendulic Sibenik, the commander of the 2nd *Panzer-armee*, acknowledging the 'good co-operation and support afforded by the Kriegsmarine'. Fishing boats were pressed into service for minesweeping operations in the Faresina Channel, fitted with German sweeping gear and defended by an SS armoured regiment stationed on the nearby coastline. The rugged terrain and Partisan activity rendered overland transport difficult at best, the Kriegsmarine being responsible for keeping maritime supplies for the land operations available and efficient. Coupled with the military necessity was the transport of bauxite and iron ore which was no longer possible by sea while the Dalmatian islands were held by Partisans and patrolled by British coastal forces. The alternative was vulnerable rail transport, eventually paralysed in September 1944 by the bombing of the rail bridge over the Sava River.

On 11 November *TA21*, *Niobe* and the steamer *Ramb III* took part in offensive landing operations as part of Operation Herbstgewitter, putting troops ashore on Krk, Cres and Lošinj. Men of the 7th SS *Gebirgs* Division 'Prinz Eugen' were embarked aboard *Ramb III*, three Siebel ferries and numerous smaller vessels. The escorting *TA21* and *Niobe* were augmented by the coastal defence boat *Najade* and German seaplanes, capturing several auxiliary sailing vessels which were attempting to escape and taking prisoners that included eight British troops.

A second combined operation was planned – Herbstgewitter II – for early December with the purpose of clearing the island of Korčula but suffered continual postponement due to materiel deficiencies, damage and losses caused by Allied air supremacy, and bad weather. Of the planned troop transport deployment only Siebel ferry *SF264* was available by 16 December although the urgent delivery of *SF193* and *SF267* had been ordered in good time. However, *SF193* was out of commission in Trieste with bad leaks in the engine's cooling system and *SF267* lay in Zadar harbour disabled by damage to the drive gear. *SF268* was out of action in Trieste while *SF192* was ready for service but trapped in Dubrovnic until the coastal waterways could be secured. Furthermore, *TA20* was briefly out of commission due to a serious leak in the forward part of the ship.

An auxiliary sailing vessel carrying 800 life jackets for Herbstgewitter II and 80 cans of gasoline for the Siebel ferries was sunk by Allied fighter aircraft on 16 December and two days later *SF193* was rushed into service following repair but was surprised by the British *MTB637* while carrying 29 infantrymen, 800 lifejackets and 22,000 litres of petrol destined for armoured vehicles at Ploča. The Siebel ferry caught fire and was driven ashore near

Brač where the burning hulk was hit by Partisan machine-gun fire: six men were killed, eleven missing and twenty-nine later rescued, the crewmen being used to man captured the Italian minelayer *Pasman*. Meanwhile, *SF267* was pushed into action, despite her damaged gear, to carry 400 life jackets to the troop convoy loading area at Ploce east of Dubrovnik. With bad weather preventing Luftwaffe air cover, the commander of V *SS Gebirgs Korps*, Obergruppenführer Artur Gustav Martin Phleps refused to carry out Operation Herbstgewitter II until both Kriegsmarine and Luftwaffe support could be assured.

In December the 11th *Kustenschutzflottille* was dissolved and the 11th *Sicherungsflottille* created in its place; the command structure and unit organisation remaining the same although auxiliary vessels were frequently attached to KKdR Jürgen von Kleist's command as the situation warranted. *Niobe* ran aground on 21 December off Silba Island causing minor leaking but still remaining serviceable, while the semi-repaired *TA20* prepared to begin operations north of Brač with only one functioning propeller as part of the delayed Herbstgewitter II that began on 22 December. Earlier that morning, the stranded *Niobe* was hit by two torpedoes from *MTB226* and *MTB298* which launched a surprise attack while the tug *Parenco* was attempting to refloat her. One torpedo struck forward in the empty magazine and the second aft, the tug being hit by a third torpedo and exploding as the Germans returned fire. Both MTBs avoided retaliation and sped away, *Niobe* breaking in two and losing nineteen crewmen killed including the medical officer and chief engineer and fifteen seriously wounded. The ship's commander and twenty men remained aboard the wreck to dismantle whatever guns could be salvaged while the remainder were taken by tugboat to Pola.

Despite this, Herbstgewitter II was a resounding success for the Germans; over 1150 Partisans were killed, captured or missing and mountains of weapons and ammunition captured as well as twenty-one coastal vessels, some of British origin, four motor boats and 160 smaller boats taken by the Kriegsmarine. After such a disaster the Yugoslavian Partisans began to withdraw from all of the Dalmatian islands apart from Vis with its valuable airstrip. German operations continued into 1944 to capture Hvar, Brac and Solta against opposition from Partisan rearguards, Mljet being occupied on the last day of December without opposition.

9

The Mediterranean, Adriatic and Aegean, January 1944–May 1945

ON 3 January 1944, MGK West reported that the situation regarding Security Forces on the southern French coast could only be described as 'catastrophic'. Proper minesweeping, escorting of convoys or anti-submarine patrols could not be carried out due to a complete lack of vessels and crews for the 6th *Sicherungsflottille*. Alongside the six MFPs that had already been approved for conversion to minelayers, requests were urgently made for reinforcements, including fourteen more to be fitted as minelayers, doubling as gunboats for convoy escort purposes. Twenty of the larger Type D MFPs were to be used as *U-Jäger*, capable of carrying adequate anti-submarine gear and also being used as gunboats. A monthly output of at least five MFPs was considered essential from yards in southern France, though delays in reaching the output led MGK West to propose that at least some

A minesweeper's mascot playing on the after deck.

267

MFPs currently in Italy should be fitted out as *U-Jäger* and transferred to them immediately. Furthermore they asked that smaller French yards build *Kriegsfischkutter*, the necessary materials to outfit them as minesweepers, *U-Jäger* and harbour defence vessels being shipped directly from Germany. Merchant shipping needs would have to be a secondary consideration for all regional shipyards.

British submarines had begun operating from a forward base at Maddalena in Sardinia during December. HMS *Uproar* patrolled between Cannes and Monaco and HMS *Untiring* and *Ultor* sailed off the French Riviera and Toulon respectively. HMS *Unseen* also departed to relieve HMS *Uproar* while HMS *Universal* took up position between Rapallo and La Spezia.

During their December missions HMS *Unseen* was anything but, as she broke surface on 21 December, being sighted by patrolling German vessels 140 miles south of Toulon and depth-charged with a pattern of five that caused minor damage. HMS *Universal* torpedoed and sank the 2497-ton freighter *La Foce* at 1120hrs east of Genoa, Lieutenant C. Gordon RN estimating the target as a '5000-ton tanker' and hitting her with two of four torpedoes fired. The ship's escort hunted the submarine for two and a half hours, dropping forty-five depth charges but failing to cause any damage, though she was claimed sunk by *UJ2208*. HMS *Uproar* also patrolled the Gulf of Genoa, sighting a 'merchant travelling in ballast' on 19 December (actually a *Marinefährprähme*) under escort by a destroyer and *UJ6076* '*Volontaire*' and closing for a submerged attack. Firing four torpedoes, Lieutenant L. E. Herrick DSC RN missed with every one of them as he had wrongly estimated the depth and they passed under the shallow-draught vessel, Herrick being unable to make a second attack. Free French submarines were also active in the area and on the afternoon 22 December *Casabianca* found the same westbound convoy and attacked with a spread of four torpedoes. The 916-ton ex-French trawler *UJ6076* was hit and sunk with only fifteen survivors rescued. Other unsuccessful torpedo attacks were reported by MFPs, particularly those detailed to cover the minelayer *Niedersachsen* as she laid defensive minefields south of Genoa.[96] One week after the loss of *UJ6076*, some German retribution was had when the Free French submarine *Protee*, on patrol off Toulon, was sunk by *UJ2208*.

On Christmas Day MGK West reported to OKM that the loss of *UJ6076* had further aggravated the catastrophic situation of the 6th *Sicherungsflottille* with only one *U-Jäger* remaining in the area and she having been out of service for weeks. At least two fully-operational craft from the Italian area were urgently requested, to be temporarily under the command of KK Hermann Polenz's 6th *Sicherungsflottille* and returned when the conversion of other vessels was complete or by 1 March 1944 at the latest. On 15 January 1944 SKL recorded that they considered that:

Auxiliary warships were in short supply in the Mediterranean and Adriatic at the beginning of 1944 and the regional Security Forces struggled to combat increased Allied submarine patrols, lacking both surface firepower and ASW vessels.

. . . the south-eastern area, particularly the Adriatic and Aegean, is a distinctly weak spot in our defensive system. Matters are extremely difficult because transport facilities are poor and often interrupted, and the only way to improve them is to resume the sea traffic along the Dalmatian coast and from the Adriatic to the Aegean. Bearing these facts in mind, after the Italian collapse in October 1943 Naval Staff decided to concentrate our strength in the Eastern Mediterranean and issued appropriate orders.[97]

Unfortunately for the Kriegsmarine there just were not the ships available to alter this situation. Despite crash building of MFPs and the continued conversion of captured Italian torpedo boats and destroyers, the numbers could not lie. Allied materiel superiority had been guaranteed by the declaration of war against both the Soviet Union and the United States, while Germany and its satellite states were bled dry. Nonetheless, work continued on conversion of as many captured, seized or requisitioned vessels as possible.

In the Adriatic the prospective minelayer *Pasman* had run aground in fog while on passage from Zara to Pola for outfitting. The small 130-ton ex-Yugoslavian minelayer had first been captured by the Italians in April 1941, then seized by the Germans following the Italian armistice in September 1943. She was intended to be handed over to the Croatian Ustaše Navy but grounded in Kozja Draga Bay on Ist Island, the crew of twenty-four German sailors and four Croats being captured by a boarding party from Partisan ship *NB3*. After the prisoners were removed *Pasman* was demolished with explosive charges. Immediate plans to rescue her crew were made for the night of 6 January, the mission to be spearheaded by torpedo boat *TA22* with

NB3 of the Yugoslav Partisan Navy. The crew of this gunboat boarded the stranded minelayer *Pasman*, capturing twenty-four Germans and four Croats.

two *Hafenschutzflottille* vessels. The addition of the obsolete torpedo boat, the first of six, had considerably strengthened the force available to the 11th *Sicherungsflottille* although her baptismal mission was foiled by bad weather and engine trouble that compelled her to break off and put into Pola for repairs to her Tosi steam turbines. The operation was repeated without *TA22* on the night of 8 January, although there was no trace of the missing German crewmen.

Partisan gunboats continued to skirmish with Security Forces in the Adriatic while British aircraft attacked German-held ports. The German imperative to occupy the Dalmatian coast and those islands still under Partisan control was restated during January 1944 by MGK Süd. Those islands considered to be in the 'first priority group' were already under German control with the exception of Brijuni near Pola while Brač and Šolta were to be captured in Operations Morgenwind I and Morgenwind II respectively. Hvar would be occupied as part of Operation Walzertraum. But, unbeknownst to the Germans, following their heavy losses in Herbstgewitter II, Tito's forces had already made the decision to abandon the remaining Dalmatian islands and concentrate their forces on Vis.

Wehrmacht infantry transported by *Marinefährprähme* took Šolta on 12 January in Morgenwind II and Brač the following day with only minor resistance from Partisan rearguards being encountered, though the shallows and roadsteads for both islands had been mined. Landings were then made

Artilleriefährprähme towing transport barges carrying Wehrmacht vehicles.

in two waves against Hvar as Walzentraum on 19 January. Although one landing craft struck an anti-tank mine that the Partisans had buried at the water's edge, killing twenty-one men, the invasion was virtually unchallenged. *TA22* had previously reported detonations on the island during a reconnaissance patrol, indicating that it was possibly being prepared for evacuation. After a shore bombardment, the Germans stormed ashore and headed swiftly inland opposed by only thirty-seven Partisans left as a rearguard while the remainder evacuated to Vis.

While the three Dalmatian islands were being occupied, the German garrisons on the islands of Ugljan and Pašman were being hard pressed by Partisan attacks. The repaired *TA22* and coastal patrol boat *G107* were sent to reconnoitre the coastal waters and both were fired upon by artillery and machine guns near Pašman. Returning fire, the ships took damage, *G107* later being declared a total constructive loss. *Hafenkommandant Zara*, FK Herbert Winkelmann, later reported that it had been shellfire from the German garrisons on Pašman and the Yugoslavian mainland, the gunners and observers having failed to see the recognition signals given by both vessels.

German forces were unable to occupy the remaining Dalmatian islands due to the shortage of troops but they were to be kept 'under observation by the available forces'. Their inability to take the stronghold of Vis and the island of Lastovo left perfect starting-points for continuous enemy naval and air activity against German supply convoys. Both islands provided secure harbours for light forces and the unloading of supplies. Though Vis had a primarily hilly

Maintenance of a 20mm flak cannon in harbour.

interior, part of the central plain was cleared to provide an airstrip capable of hosting RAF fighters, beginning with four Spitfires of the 'Balkan Air Force', and allowing emergency landings by disabled Allied bombers.

Vis became a major Partisan stronghold, Churchill having backed a decision to help fortify the island in January 1944. Tito moved his headquarters to the island and over 1000 British troops arrived alongside Royal Navy MTBs. The Dalmatian coast was never to be secured by the Kriegsmarine and reinforcements were constantly transferred from the Italian front to the Adriatic, the 11th *Sicherungsflottille* being redesignated 11th *Sicherungsdivision* in March 1944. By that stage, the division's strength in the Adriatic amounted to 1st, 2nd and 3rd G-Flotillas, stationed in Pola, Venice and Trieste respectively; 2nd UJ-Flotilla (Fiume); and 6th R-Flotilla (Pola) with the minelayer *Ramb III* attached.

A rather curious attachment to the 11th *Sicherungsdivision* occurred during September 1944 when the 22nd S-Flotilla, comprised entirely of LS and captured Italian MAS boats, was added briefly to their numbers. Originally formed in Surendorf, Germany, in December 1943 and equipped with small coastal S-boats (KS-boats), the flotilla had been largely manned by Croatian crews training under the command of Kptlt Friedrich Hüsig. The five boats were handed over to the Croatian Navy on 9 September,

German minesweeper captain at sea.

transferred from Lignano to Rijeka where they formed the Croatian KKS-Flotilla (*Kroatische Küsten-Schnellbootsflottille*) and made subordinate to 11th *Sicherungsdivision*. However, none of the boats saw action after they attempted to desert to the Partisans during December 1944, all the crews being arrested and court-martialled.

The desperation of MGK West to reinforce the Security Forces on the southern French coast had been rendered unnecesary on 15 August 1944 when General Alexander Patch's US Seventh Army landed on the French Riviera in Operation Dragoon. During the invasion the 6th *Sicherungsflottille* was briefly renamed the 'Rhone Flotilla' as it retreated upriver before being disbanded in August 1944. In Italy, Allied troops had landed at Anzio during January 1944 and, despite a startling reluctance to advance, finally broke out of their beachhead and captured Rome. The battle for Monte Cassino was over by May after five months of agony for both sides and Allied troops were slowly advancing on the Gothic Line in Northern Italy.

The surviving boats of the 11th R-Flotilla in the Ligurian Sea were engaged in desperate minelaying alongside MFPs, their ranks depleted by constant air attacks. The flotilla was officially disbanded on 23 September 1944, the remaining serviceable boats – *R162, R189, R198, R199, R212* and *R215* – being transferred to the 22nd UJ-Flotilla and unseaworthy vessels

273

sunk in Genoa harbour. The flotilla continued to fight until 1945, the last seven boats being blown up in Genoa harbour on 25 April 1945.

The Security Forces that had battled so valiantly in the Aegean during 1943 were suffering a gnawing casualty rate from which they could never recover. An air raid on Piraeus on 11 January helped to reduce operational numbers with the destruction of eight German and one former Italian minesweepers, two *Vorpostenboote*, two former Italian patrol vessels, one decoy ship and various smaller vessels including several motor boats, two oil lighters, a tug and some small Greek auxiliary sailing vessels. Kriegsmarine casualties in the raid were remarkably light at twelve killed, five missing and fourteen wounded although 500 Greeks were killed. As the operational forces continued to escort supply and troop convoys between the mainland and the Greek islands despite increasingly effective submarine and air interdiction, developments on the Eastern Front would finally settle the issue of the occupation of the Balkans.

General Wagner arrives in Symi to sign the surrender of German forces on Rhodes. Wagner (third from left) was taken to the British destroyer aboard *KJ25*, the captured British *HDML1381* which had been operated by the Special Boat Squadron.

By the middle of 1944 the advance of Soviet forces into south-eastern Europe and Bulgaria's withdrawal from the Axis had threatened to cut off the troops in Greece and Hitler granted Löhr's Army Group F permission to withdraw from mainland Greece and the islands in the Ionian and Aegean Seas. On 27 August the evacuation of the Aegean islands was ordered, air transport missions beginning within three days using 106 Ju52 transports. The ships of the Security Forces helped protect the maritime convoys that followed and between 30 August and the end of October 1944, the Kriegsmarine had evacuated 37,138 soldiers, 380 being lost from 29 ships that were sunk by the Allies – over half of the number used. The Luftwaffe evacuated 30,740 soldiers in 2050 separate flights.

On 31 October the last four boats of the 12th R-Flotilla – *R185*, *R195*, *R210* and *R211* – had withdrawn to Thessaloniki and they were scuttled in the harbour, the flotilla being officially disbanded as its men joined the trains of German troops streaming back to the shrinking borders of the Reich.

However, several 'fortresses' remained. Crete, Rhodes and the Dodecanese islands remained unchallenged throughout the remainder of the war apart from small-scale Allied raids. On 8 May 1945, Generalmajor Dr Otto Wagner surrendered Rhodes, Generalmajor Hans-Georg Benthack surrendering Crete the following day. Somewhat ironically, as the garrison on Crete awaited occupation troops after submitting to the smaller British 28th Infantry Brigade, they received an emergency message from the Brigadier General P.

Detonating or sinking a mine with gunfire.

G. C. Preston that the Brigade was under attack by Communist ELAS guerrillas, a German *kampfgruppe* with assault guns rescuing the encircled British and driving the Greeks away.

In the Adriatic, British – and later French – naval forces continually challenged Kriegsmarine Security Forces during 1944 while Partisans mounted seaborne landings on several islands supported by the Royal Navy and Commando units. These raids achieved varying degrees of success, but always served to keep German occupation forces off balance. During the second half of the year the Royal Navy despatched the 22nd Destroyer Flotilla and additional MTB units into the Adriatic, the destroyers' most significant action being an attack by HMS *Avon Vale* and *Wheatland* on *TA20*, *UJ202* and *UJ208* as they sailed out of Zara on 1 November. The two destroyers opened fire at a range of 4000 yards and both *U-Jäger* were soon in flames. The supporting torpedo boat *TA20* of the 2nd G–Flotilla attempted to intervene and was herself also sunk. The battle was also remarkable because it resulted in the awarding of four Knight's Crosses, three of them posthumously. The commander of 2nd G–Flotilla, KK Friedrich-Wilhelm Thorwest, had been aboard *Führerboot TA20* and was killed in the action; the skipper of *TA20*, ObltzSdR Heinz Guhrke was also killed, as was the skipper of *UJ202*, ObltzSdR Heinz Trautwein. Only ObltzSdR Klaus Wenke, the commander of *UJ208*, survived. All four were awarded the honour on 5 November 1944, MGK Süd recording a suitable swansong for the all such units and men: 'In

Vorpostenboot lookouts.

the award with four Knight's Crosses we recognise the so-often hidden heroism of the Security Forces and this well-deserved honour.'

The Kriegsmarine presence in the Adriatic, Tyrrhenian and Aegean seas was whittled down throughout 1944 and into 1945. The original Mediterranean *Räumboote* – 6th R-Flotilla – had transferred to the Adriatic in January 1944. They had lost two boats, *R1* and *R3*, to bombing in Toulon but by the middle of the month *R4*, *R8*, *R12*, *R14*, *R15* and *R16* had successfully relocated to Venice, stationed in the ex-Italian Arsenal where they were overhauled for the next two months. Once complete they were to be based at Opatija on the Istrian Peninsula before moving to Pola. Throughout the six months between April and September 1944 they primarily conducted minelaying missions by night, LzS Wimmer-Lamquet's *R12* being sunk by a mine in the Adriatic near Pirano on 5 September with ten crewmen killed. One reinforcement was taken on strength with the addition of *R187* at the end of the month, the boat having belonged to the 12th R-Flotilla but having been sunk twice by enemy bombing in harbour and subsequently repaired each time. By November 1944, *R10* had been repaired after battle damage and the flotilla's strength remained constant into the first months of 1945 as they continued minelaying, pushed further back towards the waters around Pola and Venice by Allied and Partisan advances. Eight R-boats (*RD115–RD122*) were nearing completion in the shipyards at Monfalcone, and another eight (*RD123–RD130*) in Venice while smaller yards had sixteen in various states of completion. However, few would see active service and those that did were too late to turn the tide. Obersteuermann Klein's *R4* was disabled while at sea by rocket fire from Allied aircraft on 2 February and *R14* was bombed and put out of action in Monfalcone harbour on 16 March.

The final weeks of the war saw Security Forces assisting the evacuation of personnel from Istria as the Partisans advanced. With five operational boats left, flotilla commander Klemm also continued minelaying, LzS Frieß' *R15* being sunk in a skirmish with British MTBs on 16 April 1945. Test runs were made with newly-commissioned boats *RD116* and *RD127*; however, the latter was destroyed by American troops as they attacked Verona on 28 April, all boats under construction in Venice also being destroyed apart from *RD128*, which was towed without an engine to Trieste. On the last day of April the incomplete boats in Monfalcone were blown up as New Zealand troops were poised to take the city and by 2 May when the 9th Brigade, New Zealand Division, entered Trieste, the last three operational boats of the flotilla – *R8*, *R10* and *R16* – were set ablaze by their crews who surrendered to the New Zealanders.

Kriegsmarine Security Forces in Western Europe and North Sea – April 1944

Oberkommando Der Marine Grossadmiral Karl Dönitz

Marinegruppenkommando West (Paris) Admiral Krancke

Marineoberkommando Nordsee (Wilhelmshaven) Admiral Förste

Befehlshaber der Sicherung West (**BSW**) (Paris) KA Breuning

Befehlshaber der Sicherung der Nordsee (**BSN**) (Wilhelmshaven) KA Lucht

2nd *Sicherungsdivision* (Souverin-Moulin)	3rd *Sicherungsdivision* (Nostang)	4th *Sicherungsdivision* (La Rochelle)	6th *Sicherungs-Flotilla* (Marseilles)	1st *Sicherungsdivision* (Utrecht)	5th *Sicherungsdivision* (Cuxhaven)
FK von Blanc	KzS Bergelt	KzSdR Lautenschlager		KzS Knuth	KzS Bentlage
2nd R-Flotilla (Dunkirk)	2nd M-Flotilla (Benodet)	8th M-Flotilla (Royan)		1st AT-Flotilla (Rotterdam)	7th M-Flotilla (Cuxhaven)
4th R-Flotilla (Boulogne)	6th M-Flotilla (Concarneau)	10th M-Flotilla (Plaimboeuf)		1st M-Flotilla (Rotterdam)	21st M-Flotilla (Wesermünde)
8th R-Flotilla (Bruges)	24th M-Flotilla (Brest)	26th M-Flotilla (Coueron)		11th M-Flotilla (Wesermünde)	27th M-Flotilla (Cuxhaven)
10th R-Flotilla (Ouistreham)	40th M-Flotilla (Brest)	28th M-Flotilla (Pauillac)		32nd M-Flotilla (Terneuzen)	13th R-Flotilla (Wesermünde)
14th R-Flotilla (Dieppe)	46th M-Flotilla (St Malo)	42nd M-Flotilla (Les Sables d'Olonne)		34th M-Flotilla (Ijmuiden)	1st Sp-Flotilla (Cuxhaven)
36th M-Flotilla	2nd Vp-Flotilla (St Malo)	44th M-Flotilla (La Pallice)		9th R-Flotilla (Vlaardingen)	8th Vp-Flotilla (Wesermünde)
38th M-Flotilla (Le Havre)	7th Vp-Flotilla (Brest)	4th Vp-Flotilla (Bordeaux)		8th Sp-Flotilla (Vlaardingen)	11th Vp-Flotilla (Wesermünde)
15th Vp-Flotilla (Le Havre)	6th Sp-Flotilla (Concarneau)	6th Vp-Flotilla (St Nazaire)		13th Vp-Flotilla (Rotterdam)	12th Vp-Flotilla (Wesermünde)
18th Vp-Flotilla (Bruges)	14th UJ-Flotilla (Lorient)	2nd Sp-Flotilla (Royan)		14th Vp-Flotilla (Rotterdam)	
2nd AT-Flotilla (Boulogne)				20th Vp-Flotilla (Rotterdam)	
6th AT-Flotilla (Channel Islands)					

10

Elimination: Allied Forces mount Operations against the Security Forces, 1944–1945

I N the Channel and North Sea, January 1944 began with patrol vessels and minesweepers periodically unable to operate due to rough seas and high winds by day combined with bright moonlit nights. Of the few vessels that put out, both *V1411* and *FJ23* ran aground and came very close to capsizing before salvage vessels refloated them both. As a result of the stormy weather, on 11 January a large number of drifting mines were found and sunk by gunfire, *Hafenschutzflottille* Wilhelmshaven alone accounting for thirty-two of them.

With the U-boats driven out of the Atlantic, Allied troops doggedly fighting their way through Italy against a tenacious and skilful German defence, retreat in the East and the rise of Tito's Partisans with Allied support in the Balkans, fears of an invasion of mainland Europe were high for the New Year. On 19 January Hitler ordered the following 'heavily fortified coastal defence areas' in the West to be 'Fortresses': Ijmuiden, Hook of Holland, Dunkirk, Boulogne, Le Havre, Cherbourg, St. Malo, Brest, Lorient, Saint-Nazaire and the Gironde Estuary north and south. Should invasion come, they were to be held at all costs and with all available means, regardless of the military situation elsewhere.

By the New Year, the three *Sicherungsdivisionen* under the command of KA Erich-Alfred Breuning, who had replaced Ruge as BSW after the latter's departure to Supermarina, had expanded considerably from their initial deployments nearly four years previously. The 2nd *Sicherungsdivision*, commanded by KzS Max Freymadl since February 1943, had received five extra flotillas:

8th R-Flotilla: formed in Cuxhaven in October 1941 and transferred to Brugge, officially active from January 1942.
2nd AT-Flotilla: formed in Brugge during January 1943 and moved first to Dunkirk and then onward to Boulogne in June.
10th R-Flotilla: constituted on 1 Marrch 1942 at Cuxhaven and then moved to Ouistreham.
14th R-Flotilla: formed January 1944 at Dieppe.

6th AT-Flotilla: formed during February 1944 in Rotterdam, transferred to Isigny during May, basing between Jersey, Guernsey and Aurigny.

The 3rd *Sicherungsdivision*, commanded by KzS Karl Bergelt since July 1943, had been bolstered by the addition of two new flotillas:

24th M-Flotilla: constituted on 1 November 1942 from crews of the 12th M-Flotilla; stationed originally at Pri1oldy near Brest, then St Malo and from August 1944 in the Channel Islands.
6th M-Flotilla: reconstituted after having been disbanded on 27 January 1942 and the crews transferred to form the 21st M-Flotilla. The flotilla reformed on 15 May 1942 using Type 39 (mob) minesweepers and was stationed first in Royan before moving to the Breton port of Concarneau.

By 1944 KzS Anselm Lautenschlager's 4th *Sicherungsdivision* had also expanded. From his headquarters in La Rochelle, he now controlled these new units:

6th Vp-Flotilla: created on 1 January 1943 from ex-trawlers of the 7th Vp-Flotilla and 14th and 44th M-Flotillas, stationed at Saint-Nazaire.
10th M-Flotilla: created on 15 April 1943 in Cuxhaven and transferred to Plaimboeuf near St Nazaire and 26th 26th M-Flotilla; formed on 1 January 1943 from *M40*-class ships and based at Couëron.
28th M-Flotilla: formed with nine *M40*-class minesweepers at the beginning of December 1942 using crews of the disbanded 18th M-Flotilla, and the 4th Vp-Flotilla which had been transferred from the North Sea to Bordeaux.

Among Lautenschlager's command was the 4th Vp-Flotilla, commanded by KK Wilhelm Cyrus, formerly commander of *V1304* and the 6th Sp-Flotilla.[98] During January 1944 moves were made to hand the flotilla over to Italian personnel that had remained in the Gironde following the Italian armistice, professing loyalty to Mussolini's Italian Social Republic. Konteradmiral Breuning, however, had considerable doubts about the wisdom of such a decision, uncertain of their steadfastness in the face of the difficult tasks required of a Vp-Flotilla.

No clear verdict can be given on this point at present, particularly on their political reliability. Nevertheless every effort is being made to realise the ordered objective of handing over the 4th Vp-Flotilla to the Italians. The final verdict depends on the results attained by the re-training programme and the measures ordered by Group West. These provide that, effective immediately, Italians of all ranks who have undergone re-training will relieve 50 per cent of the German crew on boats engaged on active operations under German command.

Vorpostenboote at sea in the Bay of Biscay.

The purpose of this measure is to weed out unsuitable elements, improve the reliability of the others and enable us to reach a definite verdict. If the policy proves a success, the percentage of Italians will be increased. *Befehls-haber der Sicherung West* [Breuning] states in conclusion: 'Even with optimum results from the re-training and educational programme, the operational value of the 4th Vp-Flotilla will decrease as the number of Italian personnel increases. The shortage of forces also entails heavy demands on trawler flotillas. Whether Italian crews will be able to stand up to the average of up to 25 days a month at sea still remains to be seen.'[99]

Combined with the expansion of the Security Forces in Biscay, the Kriegsmarine established battle schools for minesweeper crews, training them in land warfare in the event of Allied invasion or encountering Resistance activity. Aboard *M275* of the new 10th M-Flotilla, Maschinenhauptgefreiter Otto Schütze remembered a distinguished visitor to his new unit:

From 1940 to 1943 I was with the 38th M-Flotilla in Le Havre. I had a really good relationship with a French family that lived near our barracks; I knew them because they did our laundry. At the beginning of September 1943 I was transferred to *M275*, part of the 10th M-Flotilla at Paimboeuf. Our flotilla was given missions around Biarritz. In April 1944 we were part of a large group of soldiers that formed in a combat school hidden amongst some pines. Our flotilla chief, KK Josephi, visited the school with *Feldmarschall* Rommel on 13 April.

Operation Tunnel: the Royal Navy anti-shipping campaign

The Royal Navy had meanwhile embarked upon concerted efforts to eliminate the threat of Germany's naval forces to an invasion fleet embarked upon the planned opening of the 'Second Front' during 1944. Relatively ad-hoc formations of ships with no specific unit structure were gathered together as task forces to begin systematic sweeps of the English Channel under specific operational guidelines. Operation Tunnel began in October 1943 and would eventually cover months of individually-numbered operational patrols along the westernmost Channel region. Unfortunately, the first such mission intended to intercept the blockade breaker *Münsterland* that had been carrying a valuable cargo of raw materials from Japan, ended in disaster when on 22 October the cruiser HMS *Charybdis* was sunk by *Münsterland*'s torpedo boat escort, the destroyer HMS *Limbourne* also being so badly damaged that she was later scuttled.

Although the first Tunnel mission had ended in a bitter blow to Britain's coastal forces, lessons were learned that resulted in greater cohesion within assembled task forces, trained to operate as a single unit, and drilled in both mutual fire support and communications. The 6408-ton *Münsterland* had been shepherded into Cherbourg following the attack, immediately coming under prolonged air attack that same day. Thirty-six RAF Typhoons armed with 1000lb delayed-action bombs were sent to sink the ship, escorted by Spitfires of 601 and 132 Squadrons. The British aircraft flew through thick mist at sea level that blanketed the English Channel before attacking the ship and *Vorpostenboote* stationed nearby to provide flak cover between 1513hrs and 1531hrs. With nearly 200 flak guns in the area and defending Fw190 fighters, four Spitfire pilots were lost and seven Typhoons shot down, two pilots later being rescued by RAF launches. *Münsterland* was hit and set on fire and a *Vorpostenboot* sunk. *Münsterland* was ordered onward, though this proved more difficult than expected. Heinrich Ziemsen of the 4th R-Flotilla recalled the difficulties involved in *Münsterland*'s planned voyage to Germany.

From August 1941, I was stationed as Maat with the 4th *Räumboote* Flotilla. I assisted in bringing through many vessels, but we were unlucky with the *Münsterland*, It might well be said that the *Münsterland* was followed by a 'jinx'. The first time we convoyed the *Münsterland* the area off Boulogne was seething with fast vessels so that our commanding officer was compelled to abandon the enterprise. After a few days, we should have tried again, but unfortunately it went very foggy and we had to go back to harbour. The sailors on the *Münsterland* were thoroughly 'fed-up'. In the long run everybody's nerves were on edge with continually coming out and going back again. Then the command came again to leave port and this I believe was on 31 December 1943. Visibility on that particular night was rather poor. On top of that, the *Münsterland* met with a net-barrier, which had been put up outside the harbour entrance. Her propeller fouled the nets and thus it was impossible to manoeuvre her, and the ship drifted towards Cap Gris Nez.

Then the *Münsterland* was towed back to Boulogne. At the pier where the railway station used to be, the *Münsterland* was made fast. In order to free the propeller from the nets, the forward tanks were filled so as to facilitate work on the propeller. This work naturally took some considerable time. I believe that it was on the 31 December, but cannot be sure. After the *Münsterland* was put in order, we prepared to leave again. The convoy ships were mine-sweepers, mine-destructor vessels, reconnaissance ships and converted ferry-boats. Our vessel which was a minesweeper was in position astern of the *Münsterland*. We had the task of laying silver-foil [i.e. chaff] when we were within range of your Battery. We used to call your Battery 'Suitcase Alley'. Here in Germany, we used to call the big shells 'suitcases'. When we saw your fire, we used to count up to 72. At 73, we heard the explosion. In order to put you off the scent, we sometimes sailed quickly, and sometimes slowly. At the same time we laid silver-foil in order that your radar might be confused. Your shooting was sometimes accurate and sometimes too far ahead, until you recorded the first hit. The *Münsterland* was hit several times. Your fire was so well directed that our vessel was unable to reach the *Münsterland*. Those shells which fell into the sea exploded on the bottom. Had they burst on the surface our boats would have looked like sieves. Your shells had no splinter effect.

When a shell burst a considerable amount of mud rained down on the decks. Then the *Münsterland* began to sink, but still remained with the upperstructure above water. Some of the crew of the *Münsterland* were killed in the icy waters through heart-failure on account of plunging too quickly into the sea. After having taken off all the people, we made for Calais at full speed.[100]

Aboard *Münsterland* five merchant seamen were killed and twenty-five wounded, two of them severely, while naval gunners aboard lost six dead, six severely wounded and thirty-nine lightly wounded during the sinking.

While Tunnel operations yielded some results with the sinking of Torpedo Boat *T29* during April 1944, new operations were mounted to counter the threat posed by U-boats and surface vessels in the Western theatre. Minelaying operations utilised both shallow and deep-water mines with mixtures of trigger types to strengthen existing minefields and clog the entrances to Channel harbours.

Meanwhile British coastal forces continued to attack German convoys with gunfire and torpedoes. While these fierce battles frequently resulted in damage and loss to both sides, results were just as frequently overestimated. For example, during March 1944 six converted trawlers of the 18th Vp-Flotilla were heavily engaged by British MTBs off Blanc Nez. Estimating the attackers' strength at ten boats (in fact a total force of four, two of which became separated and failed to attack) the battle was short and furious and resulted in the destruction of *MTB417*, which was hit by shellfire from *V1810* and *V1811* and exploded with the loss of all nineteen men aboard. The

Sperrbrecher 10 'Vigo' going down on 7 March 1944 after hitting a mine; sunk with one man missing.

accompanying *MTB418* attempted to approach the burning boat to search for survivors but was forced away by the heavy barrage. Dönitz himself sent a congratulatory message for the estimated four enemy MTBs destroyed while on the British side the commander of *MTB418* was decorated for a spirited single-handed attack that had resulted in the claimed sinking of an R-boat. Of course this in no way belittles the genuine accomplishments of either side. Fast-paced naval actions, particularly those in darkness, were confusing with frequent misidentification of vessels and misinterpretation of results.

The Baltic, 1944

In the East the Baltic States were coming under direct Soviet pressure. With troops now pushing against the Estonian border the 1st and 3rd M–Flotillas in Kotka were ordered to maintain one-hour readiness and two *Artillerie-fährprähme* in Aseri kept at 30-minutes' readiness in the event of Soviet landings on the Estonian coast. Destroyers and S-boats were also kept on alert, but their strength was too limited without the support of the Security Forces. The ice had cleared from the Gulf of Finland during April and May 1944, allowing Soviet vessels to operate again. The original Porkkala net barrier had been found to be in poor condition by the Germans. In many places it was no longer effective against submarines on the surface, and attempts at buoying up the sagging nets failed as most net tenders were still in dock for repairs and the decision was made to lay new nets. Patrolling was stepped up to force any sighted submarine underwater where the existing nets still had at least some effectiveness and fully-operational minefields lay in wait. Six minesweepers of the 25th M-Flotilla and twelve *Vorpostenboote* were established as a dedicated patrol force when weather permitted. However, with generally poor conditions their effectiveness rapidly declined, the *Vorpostenboote* returning to port if the sea state passed 5, minesweepers once it passed 7. The forces available for the defence of the Eastern Baltic were negligible owing to enforced dockyard overhauls during winter that had been further delayed by Allied bombing. The solution was the transfer of vessels guarding the Skagerrak to the East to prevent Soviet submarines penetrating into the Baltic. Nine converted whalers of the 17th Vp-Flotilla – each equipped with revolving directional hydrophones and sonar – would then become available for the Gulf of Finland. Following their withdrawal, BSO was compelled to order the curtailment of measures for intercepting blockade runners attempting to pass through the Skagerrak from Sweden, patrols off the Swedish coast or stationing of vessels at the intercepting position on the eastern edge of the Skagerrak declared area being no longer possible due to a lack of ships.

Beginning in March four destroyers, the minelayers *Linz*, *Roland* and *Brummer* and the craft of the 24th L-Flotilla supported by minesweepers and

R-boats laid minefields that by the end of May would cover 17 nautical miles from a mere 600m offshore at Hungerburg, Narva Bay, to the island of Suur Tütarsaar. The barrage was extended to Suursaari but not without cost, *Roland* being sunk by a mine on 21 April with 235 men killed.

While Soviet submarines may not have become the threat that was anticipated during 1944, aircraft had increased their anti-shipping missions exponentially. Using anywhere between ten to seventy aircraft per mission, the Soviet air force began mounting up to four attacks daily on the Kriegsmarine ships, resulting in severe damage, sinkings and an average loss of fifty men daily from the German forces. While during 1944 eight ships both military and merchant were lost to mines and four to submarines, fifty-eight were sunk by Soviet aircraft and a further 112 damaged.

Operation Neptune: 6 June 1944

In occupied France, Allied air attacks against Channel defences and ports had increased in intensity during May and early June. However, as bad weather buffeted the Channel it was considered unlikely that the expected invasion would come yet. The majority of Kriegsmarine vessels were in port waiting for the bad weather to break before resuming patrol and escort duties. During the early morning of 6 June MGK West was informed of enemy parachute landings near Caen and on the Cherbourg Peninsula, but even at that point Krancke recorded that – like the Army and Luftwaffe commands – it was

Part of a newsreel film showing Erwin Rommel aboard a *Vorpostenboot* during a tour of inspection of the Atlantic Wall. Rommel knew the Allies wouldn't come ashore at a major port, but his last-minute building drive of Normandy's coastal defences did not stop Allied troops successfully landing.

unlikely to be a full-scale invasion and no increased defensive patrolling was ordered within the Seine Bay on account of the 'unfavourable tide conditions and the weather'. He was, of course, mistaken.

> The invasion has begun. Following an almost uninterrupted attack against our defence positions along the Channel coast between Cherbourg and Ostend carried out during the last days and nights by strongest air forces, the time has come – from the military point of view – for a large-scale landing attempt as soon as the weather conditions are favourable. Although during the night of 5 June the weather could not be regarded as favourable – north-west wind with a velocity from 4 to 6 and even more, a strongly clouded sky and low cloud cover – the enemy decided to venture upon the undertaking, apparently hoping for an improvement of the weather conditions which have been forecasted for the next days. Thus all considerations and abstract speculations have been silenced. The strain that prevailed in all quarters was solved. The war entered into its decisive stage as far as Germany is concerned. Once again there is an opportunity to bring about a quick decision of the war by a short but energetic fight.[101]

The Allies had begun Operation Neptune, the assault phase of Operation Overlord, the invasion of North-West Europe. Leading the Allied invasion fleet were the minesweepers, clearing paths through the defensive barrages that the Germans had desperately attempted to create. Opposing the Allied armada in the Normandy area, Breuning's Western Security Force mustered a total of 163 minesweepers of all types, 57 *Vorpostenboote* and 42 *Artillerieträger*. Four *Artillerieträger* of the 6th AT-Flotilla were sunk during the day. *AF62*, *AF67* and *AF72* were all trapped in Port en Bassin, but their weapons were capable of fire support and so they were subordinated to the local Army commander. Their guns helped to ensure that the American landings at Omaha Beach were bitterly contested, but return naval artillery fire severely wounded Kaptlt Friedrich Schad, his place temporarily being taken by the commander of the 46th M-Flotilla, Kaptlt Armin Zimmermann. To the west, ObltzS Joswig's *AF64* was disabled by enemy action in Isigny and scuttled.

At Bénouville the bridges over the Orne and Caen Canal had been captured by British airborne troops, landed during the early morning to prevent German reinforcements from reaching the nearby British and Canadian beaches. The glider-borne attack led by Major John Howard succeeded in taking the bridges and prepare to hold them against the inevitable German onslaught.

> Further attacks were launched on the battalion position during the afternoon. At one period, as a novelty, two gunboats came up the canal. Fire was held

until they reached the bridge when one of them was put out of action by a PIAT fired by Howard's force from the bridge area. The second one turned round and made off quickly while the first one opened fire with its gun (which was remote controlled) and shot up my HQ area. There were several lucky escapes and only one slight casualty. The crew of the boat were taken prisoner.

The same boats, or similar ones, had been shooting up the battle outpost at the battery position 105765 (Lieutenant Parrish) [nearly two kilometres downstream from the Bénouville bridge]. This outpost found that the position was, as thought, abandoned and so they occupied it themselves and remained there all day without incident other than the trouble with the gunboat. This trouble cost the outpost one killed and one wounded.[102]

Confusion still exists over exactly which German vessels mounted the attack on what is now known as Pegasus Bridge, not to mention which boats accidentally shelled German troops of the 21st Panzer Division as they engaged the British around the bridges. It has been attributed previously to both *V206 'Otto Bröhan'* and *V212 'Friedrich Busse'* which had both been in the area, as well as *R221* of the 10th R-Flotilla. These boats were generally stationed in Ouistreham, moored behind the canal lock gates near the sea. On the eve of the Allied invasion Kapitänleutnant Herbert Nau's flotilla numbered ten R-boats – *R180, R182, R213, R214, R217, R218, R219, R221, R224* and *R234* – plus their tender *M546 'Von der Lippe'*. All except *R221* had proceeded to Le Havre during the previous day for planned minelaying, *R221* being it the small yard within the Hérouville basin at Blainville–sur–Orne undergoing repair when the invasion broke. However, it is most likely to have been vessels of Ouistreham's *Hafenschutzflottille Kanalküste*. Major Howard later recalled that the German captain was 'an eighteen- or nineteen-year-old Nazi, very tall, spoke good English. He was ranting on in English about what a stupid thing it was for us to think of invading the Continent, and when his Führer got to hear about it that we would be driven back into the sea, and making the most insulting remarks, and I had the greatest difficulty stopping my chaps from getting hold and lynching that bastard on the spot.'

The three named vessels were indeed upon the Caen Canal that day and were all disabled. However, they were downstream of the bridge and every account of the attack on Howard's men records the boats coming from seaward. *R221* was attacked by aircraft in the Hérouville basin and disabled, scuttled by her crew. *V206 'Otto Bröhan'* was also scuttled in the canal in front of the coaling dock near Bassin Saint Pierre in Caen itself. *V212 'Friedrich Busse'* was also scuttled at the Blainville–sur–Orne shipyard. The *Hafenschutzflottille Kanalküste* lost six vessels that day.

As the seaborne assault was developing, the Cherbourg-based mine-sweepers of the 5th M-Flotilla were also sent east around Cape Barfleur and

V206 'Otto Bröhan' scuttled in the Caen Canal in front of the coaling dock near Bassin Saint Pierre.

those of the 9th M–Flotilla were sent west. The minesweepers found nothing and returned to harbour. Three torpedo boats of the 5th T–Flotilla and six serviceable boats of the 15th Vp–Flotilla departed Le Havre at 0415hrs to attempt to make contact with the enemy.

Weather: wind West 6–7, sea 3–4, heavy clouds, low clouds, good visibility . . .

0510 at buoy A2 course 217 degrees. Use small calibre guns (KKG) and hand grenades. Continuously overflown by aircraft.

0503 opened fire. Towards the sea artificial fog banks.

0522 in between these silhouettes, enemy units.

0525 fire opened by *PA2* with 10.5cm, then recognised as larger units. Enemy opens fire with medium calibre on our formation. Our T-Boats turn on return course for harbour, I turn 180 degrees, since way is blocked by heavy units. Continuous air defence . . .

0545 heavy explosion *V1509*, high water column, probably hit by a mine. At the same time under fire by heavy ships artillery.

0548 . . . Boat slowly sinking by the stern.

0550 *V1511* rescues survivors. T-Boats attacking again distract fire away from *V1059/11*.

From 0600 to 0610 *V1511* under fire by bracketing salvoes. Opposing formation has come closer, heavy splinter effects. Wounded and dead on *V1511*. Rescue measures broken off. One rescue float with eight men left behind. Following return to harbour sea rescue boat sent.

0600 order to move up the Seine. Since bar of the Seine can only be passed from 0930, formation held before bar of the Seine.

0615 *V1509* sunk. Bow visible for a while. Enemy air surveillance continuously engaged. Enemy units fire on coast and our boats. Since bar is only passable from 0930, decide to take on pilot, hand over severely wounded and replenish ammunition, and enter harbour for a period at 0715. During this time receipt

FT 0625/72 order to enter harbour for BSW forces. Patrol boats fastened as last formation in Le Havre between 0735 and 0745. During entering harbour observed drops in sea area, probably mines. *V1511* enters harbour with 35 survivors and two dead from *V1509*. 26 missing. *V1505* eight severely wounded. *V1511* four wounded. *V1506* three times bottom scraping with propeller. *V1505* and *07* light grounding before bar of the Seine. *V1506* ready with some issues.

Ammunition consumption: 10.5cm 68 rounds, 8.8 cm 55 rounds, 3.7cm 1,410 rounds, 2cm 15,900 rounds, 15mm 1,910 rounds, 13.2mm 812 rounds.[103]

Though the torpedo boats sank the Norwegian destroyer HNoMS *Svenner* there was little that the Security Forces could achieve in the face of such overwhelming odds. Massively outnumbered and outgunned, they were used for the continued laying of so-called 'Blitz' minefields in a belated attempt to obstruct the invasion while Luftwaffe aircraft also dropped mines in hazardous low-level missions. The security flotillas suffered a steady stream of damage and casualties over the days that followed the invasion, Allied air and naval supremacy being virtually unassailable.

Naval forces at Brest were placed on alert as soon as the invasion had begun, *M4031 'Pesce Spada'* being sunk that day while minesweeping outside of the harbour entrance. The last remaining destroyers stationed in the West – *Z24*, *Z32* and *ZH1* – alongside the torpedo boat *T24* departed for an ill-fated attempt to attack the Allied invasion fleet, encountering the enemy at around 0130hrs

Minesweeper in dock with extensive damage following Allied air attack. The Security Forces were completely overwhelmed by Allied sea and air power around the time of the Normandy landings.

on 9 June and suffering the loss of *ZH1* sunk and *Z32* driven ashore and abandoned, the surviving crew being rescued by boats of the 2nd Vp-Flotilla. The remaining two damaged ships escaped to the Gironde where they would later be sunk by RAF Coastal Command Beaufighters during August. U-boats had also been sent from Brest in a last-ditch attempt to thwart Operation Neptune. As Hitler still believed that the Normandy landings were in large part designed to draw forces away from a second invasion site, he ordered most of the formidable 36-boat 'Landwirt' group to remain in reserve, only the fifteen stationed in Brest being ordered to attack immediately. Of these only seven were equipped with the *schnorchel* allowing them to proceed to the battle submerged, the remainder being ordered to 'proceed on surface at top speed to English Coast'. In the words of Herbert Werner, commander of *U415*:

> The message was even more insane than our present standing order from Headquarters. It required me and seven of my friends . . . to remain on surface and race unprotected toward the Southern English coast at a time when the sky was black with thousands of aircraft and the sea swarmed with hundreds of destroyers and corvettes.

The results were predictable as they encountered a storm of Allied surface forces and aircraft. Of the fifteen U-boats that put to sea from Brest, only five got anywhere near the Allied fleet and a meagre four actually came to grips with the enemy. German successes amounted to *U621* sinking *LST280* near Le Havre and *U764* blowing the bows off the escort destroyer HMS *Blackwood* on 15 June, herself being damaged in counter-attacks and forced to return to base. It was a predictable disaster and as Allied forces built up their strength ashore over the days that followed, there was nothing that the Kriegsmarine could do to stop them.

On D-Day itself, the Allies lost only three destroyers, one minesweeper, one MTB and one PT boat either sunk or damaged beyond repair. While Allied naval losses for June 1944 included twenty-four warships and thirty-five merchantmen or auxiliaries sunk – over a quarter of them by mines – and a further 120 vessels damaged, the overall force deployed for Operation Neptune included 6939 vessels: 1213 warships, 4126 landing ships and landing craft, 736 ancillary craft and 864 merchant vessels.

Schnellboote that still gamely attempted to attack and last-ditch *Klein-kampfverbände* human torpedo and explosive motorboat missions also failed to have any appreciable effect. The Security Forces were forced away from Normandy to both west and east while suffering steady losses.

With the neutralising of the threat posed by destroyers and U-boats the Allies had virtually secured the western flank of their Normandy invasion front. The S-boat service was dealt a severe blow by a heavy RAF bombing raid on Le Havre, while the Royal Navy turned its attention to the remaining German vessels stationed on the French Atlantic coast. A new initiative code-named Operation Dredger targeted the escort vessels that rendezvoused with U-boats off Brest, Lorient and Saint-Nazaire and safeguarded their passage to and from harbour. Dredger began on 5 July 1944 and an Anglo-Canadian task force of cruisers and destroyers patrolling near Ouessant sighted two U-boats under escort by *V715 'Alfred I'*, *V728 'Vierge de Massabielle'*, *V713 'Leipzig'*, *V729 'Marie Simone'*, *M4013 'Othello'* and *M4045 'Uwe'*.

The first salvo hit *V715*, badly wounding her captain LzS Thiess and disabling her rudder as fires broke out aboard. Over the 30 minutes that followed the two U-boats dived to safety while the Germans returned a steady fire that actually deterred their attackers, who withdrew after suffering casualties and damage. However, *V729* and *V728* were both seriously damaged while *V715* drifted powerless and burning. The decision was made to abandon her at the south-east corner of Fromveur Channel and at approximately 0600hrs she finally sank after *Schnellboote S145* and *S112* from St Malo rescued her survivors.

The Dredger missions were repeated; during the night of 7 July destroyers HMS *Tartar* and HMCS *Huron* attacked Kaptlt Armin Zimmermann's 46th M-Flotilla near the Channel Islands and sank both *M4601* and *M4605* while a week later *Tartar*, HMCS *Haida* and ORP *Blyskawica* sank *UJ1420* and *UJ1421* near Ile de Groix, Lorient.

RAF Coastal Command had been freed of its commitment to support of the landings in Normandy by this stage and was also able to continue attacks against enemy shipping, including in the Bay of Biscay. On the last day of June they attacked *M12* and *M21* of Benodet's 2nd M-Flotilla as they travelled in company with *UJ1408*. Twenty-seven Mosquitoes and Beaufighters of Coastal Command's 235, 404 and 248 Squadrons hit the *U-Jäger* repeatedly and she capsized and sank at 1456hrs with two dead, four missing and twenty-nine wounded. A single attacking aircraft was shot down by nearby land-based flak and crashed into the sea south of Pointe de Penmarc'h.

Operation Kinetic: the British assault on Security Forces in the West

Although the Security Forces were suffering the death by a thousand cuts, the Allies were determined to deliver the final blow to the Kriegsmarine in the West. The British Admiralty devised a plan for August 1944 that would be code-named Operation Kinetic to force a decision along the Atlantic Coast. With strong support from Winston Churchill, Vice-Admiral F. H. G. Dalrymple-Hamilton was in overall command aboard HMS *Diadem*. The operation had two goals: the elimination of the Kriegsmarine in the West and assistance for American ground forces' approach to France's Atlantic coast. Despite fierce combat amidst the hedgerows of Normandy and skilful German defence, Allied forces had pierced the German lines, American troops breaking through at Avranches and racing both into Brittany to the west and towards the Seine south of Paris. By 25 August Paris had been liberated while in Finisterre, Brittany, the prize was to be the deep-water harbour at Brest, home to two U-boat flotillas and many vessels of the 3rd *Sicherungsdivision*.

With the Atlantic U-boat ports threatened, the Allies knew through Enigma decrypts that Dönitz intended to evacuate his boats to occupied Norway, allowing them to remain active in the Atlantic and also in greater strength in Arctic waters. The Royal Navy formed escort groups and task forces to intercept not only U-boats in transit but also the remaining surface strength in the West, while Coastal Command moved 19 Group's patrol areas to focus upon the Bay of Biscay, reinforced by two squadrons of 16 Group Beaufighters.

On 1 August, as Operation Kinetic began, urgent appeals were heard in Hitler's headquarters from Generalfeldmarschall Günther von Kluge, Chief of Army Group D, that all available men to the 'last man and the last gun' be placed at his disposal as American troops poured into Brittany. Correspondingly Hitler ordered the 'combing out' of units to provide infantrymen for the trenches around the ports that he had declared 'fortresses'. Even Breuning's Security Forces were expected to contribute men, though they were fully engaged against the enemy at sea. Breuning further encouraged the construction of ad-hoc anti-tank detachments and weapons. Accordingly *Sp1* '*Saar*' landed fifty-five men and several of its 20mm anti-aircraft guns at Brest's *Port de Commerce* after which they were swallowed up by the forthcoming ground battle. On 2 August France's Resistance members received their call to rise up against the Germans with a coded message over the BBC, while the US 6th Armoured Division smashed through the outskirts of Dinan.

Over the weeks that followed, Kinetic obliterated what had remained of the Security Forces in western France. As the Americans advanced on land many German Army units abandoned defensible positions leaving naval radar stations, lighthouses, searchlight batteries and minor ports vulnerable, they, in turn, frequently being abandoned. However, as the American spearheads approached Brest they encountered German *Fallschirmjäger* who were not prepared to give way, a battle amongst the trees at Huelgoat leaving thirty Sherman tanks destroyed. Order was gradually imposed upon the Wehrmacht's land defence, while at sea the Kriegsmarine was destroyed.

The array of ships sunk by combined naval and air attacks during Kinetic is dizzying. During the three-week offensive the Germans lost twelve U-boats (four to surface ships, three to air attack, three to combined surface ship and air attack and two to mines), seventeen large ships, two destroyers, one torpedo boat and sixty-two vessels of the Security Forces. Operation

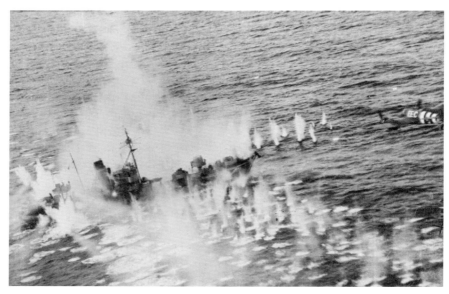

Operation Kinetic: Beaufighters attack the Security Forces in the Bay of Biscay.

Kinetic reached its climax on the night of 23 August after the Americans had begun their direct assault on Brest.

As the city came under siege the seven surviving operational vessels of the 7th Vp-Flotilla commanded by KK Ludolf Jacobi were ordered by Breuning to break out of Brest and head for Lorient. The experienced men of the flotilla were considered too useful simply to become ground troops in what was widely considered a hopeless battle. For safety the seven ships were split into two groups leaving with an interval of an hour between them. They assembled on the River Aulne, near the medieval abbey of Landévennec, seeking some cover from the constant Allied air raids over Brest itself. At approximately 1115hrs the first convoy of the three slower and older ships, *V702 'Memel'*, *V729 'Marie-Simone'* and *V730 'Michel-François'* slipped away, hugging the shoreline as they headed South. Within minutes they had been detected by Force 27, centred on the cruiser HMS *Mauritius*, which set course to intercept. The Germans in turn detected the oncoming threat with their Seetakt radar and the three ships scattered to attempt to reach any friendly port. Star shells arced overhead at 0209hrs and in their haste both *V702* and *V730* ran aground on the Gamelle Plateau before Audierne. After attempting to return fire but suffering serious damage and heavy casualties, the ships were abandoned and finished off by shellfire from HMCS *Iroquois*. *V729* did not survive for much longer, her commander ObltzS Luddecke beingwounded and LzS Ernst Meyer taking command and running the ship toward the beach at Audierne to give the wounded aboard a chance to escape ashore. By

0245hrs the Allied guns fell silent and *V729* was little more than wreckage.

Following the rapid destruction of the first German convoy, the Anglo-Canadian force soon detected a radar trace of the next four, *V719* '*Neubau 240*', *V714* '*Neubau 168*', *V717* '*Alfred III*' and *V721* '*Neubau 308*'. The converted trawler '*Alfred III*' was the only ex-merchant of the group, the remainder all purpose-built *Vorpostenboote* displacing around 500 tons, with raked bows and relatively heavy armament. From the mast of *V714* flew the Iron Cross pennant of the *Flotillenboot*, signifying that KK Jacobi and his reduced staff were aboard. At 0408hrs the battle began and as the Germans laid smoke while firing all weapons, they immediately began to take casualties. *V719* ran aground on the Penhors rocks in front of Pouldrezic, IIWO ObltzS Walbrun being killed along with six crewmen as the remainder abandoned ship. Likewise *V721* ran aground, the German crew firing machine-guns and cannon until a British flak round killed commander ObltzS Bremer and his men abandoned ship under the direction of IWO LzS Jacobs. *V714* was sunk in sight of Audierne, smashed to pieces by heavy salvoes while grounded on the Gamelle reef while *V717* also grounded on the reef. While the German crew abandoned their ship they displayed a white cloth to ward off any further gunfire and HMS *Ursa* drew alongside and landed a prize crew to search the ship and assist wounded men. Finally HMCS *Iroquois* sent a single torpedo into the stranded boat and she was ripped in two. Eight Kriegsmarine men near the ship were killed in the explosion, including the ship's IWO ObltzS Scholz. The 7th Vp-Flotilla was no more. In 1974 one of the veterans who had

The end of *V717* '*Alfred III*'; finished off with a torpedo from HMCS *Iroquois*.

been aboard HMCS *Iroquois*, Midshipman Charles Croucher, was quoted as saying of the uneven match 'it wasn't combat, but an execution'.

The total cost to the flotilla that day was fifty-four dead, twenty-four missing, and forty-four wounded. Over 250 sailors who escaped swam to shore, many becoming involved in the desperate land battle being waged between German troops and American soldiers supported by French Partisans of the FFI (*Français Forces de l'Interieur*). In Brest, on 20 September 1944, the 7th Vp-Flotilla was formally disbanded. Further along the Biscay coast, all of the German-held ports had taken very heavy damage with the security flotillas no longer recognisable as coherent fighting units. Heinz Hunke was part of the crew of *M486*:

> I was stationed at Saint-Nazaire from January 1941 to September 1944, firstly as part of the 6th M-Flotilla then in the 26th. The emblem of that flotilla was the coat of arms for Saint-Nazaire. The flotilla commander was KK Marguth who lived in a villa near the beach called 'Vieil Armour'. In 1943 when the 16th M-Flotilla was disbanded the crews were transferred to the new minesweepers of the 26th M-Flotilla. I was based on *M486*. Our last sortie began on 5 August 1944 and at 0030hrs on 6 August near l'ile d'Yeu our ship was attacked by surprise. It was destroyed and sunk. I was one of only three survivors from a crew of 98. We waited for about 15 hours in the water before being picked up by a *Sperrbrecher*. Despite the fighter bombers, we arrived at

Sperrbrecher 26 'Mostrand'. This 3549-ton ex-Norwegian freighter was sunk by Coastal Command bombs and torpedoes on 30 August 1944.

Saint-Nazaire and from there we were given eight days leave at La Baule. At the end of the month of August, just as Saint-Nazaire was about to be encircled and turned into a fortress, we received our orders to return to Germany. Only three minesweepers still existed in the port. We left by foot and then bicycle to Dijon and from there we were taken by Kriegsmarine truck to Cuxhaven in the North of Germany. I actually still had good luck with me as I was the only man to stay in the port, the rest of the crews were sent to the Eastern Front.[104]

The *Sperrbrecher Tellus* had been loaded with *Schnorchel* parts in Brest and sailed South to deliver them to other ports, Dönitz having ordered the equipping of all available U-boats with the device in an attempt to evacuate them through the Allied noose to Norway. *Tellus* managed to break out of Brest, despite losing her *Vorpostenboote* escort, and had narrowly escaped destruction before heading to La Rochelle where she was later found by enemy aircraft. MaschHptGef Otto Schütze was aboard the escorting minesweeper *M275* when they encountered Kinetic forces.

On 14 August Saint-Nazaire was attacked by rocket-firing fighter bombers. The ships that were at anchor there received orders at 2000hrs as the flotilla chief arrived: 'ObltzS Fischer's *M275* and Kaptlt Schurig's *M385* leave harbour to escort the blockade breaker *Tellus* near La Rochelle. I wish the best of luck to the ships and crews.'

Near L'ile d'Yeu at about 0045hrs we were first attacked by a four-engine bomber that tried to bomb us, the first salvo landing 70 metres from our ship. Some hours later we were engaged by two destroyers, one of them hit by our 105mm gun. Our commander had been gunnery officer aboard a cruiser and his experience came in handy. But, *M385* and *Tellus* were sunk and our *M275* was stranded on a sandbank.

A French fishing boat flying the tricolour rescued the best part of our crew and the wounded. The sailors then took refuge in the dunes. I stayed aboard with some of my comrades and we saw two torpedoes heading towards our minesweepers, but they missed! We left the ship with our rifles aboard a dinghy in which we had mounted a machine-gun. On land, the sailors were being attacked by British aircraft. Once the danger had passed and high tide came in we actually reboarded our ship and freed her from the sand returning to Sables-d'Olonne!

Once in port we began repairing the damage. This time we were attacked by many more aircraft. The only men that stayed on the ship were those manning flak weapons; the rest took shelter in the bunkers. For the first time they opened fire on us with rockets. Fortunately the minesweeper was barely touched. The following day, the port commander ordered us to sail. We were attacked again by machine-gun fire from a four-engine bomber. On 17 August we finally left the port of Sables-d'Olonne and we returned to La Pallice. There we had some security. After mounting two more actions to recover encircled infantrymen, our minesweeper was hidden in the U-boat base. Our flak cannon were taken off and given to an infantry battalion near Marans.[105]

Ultimately thirty-one U-boats would successfully escape the Biscay ports which were soon all under direct attack. Saint-Malo had fallen on 17 August, minesweepers of the 24th M-Flotilla stationed within the port leaving on 6 August for the Channel Island. As they departed a minesweeper shelled the cathedral spire, which collapsed causing severe damage to the building's structure, maintaining that the spire was being used as an observation post by 'terrorists'. Oberst Andres von Aulock, commander of the German garrison, was furious and informed Breithaupt that they had 'hardly covered the Kriegsmarine with glory'.

On 18 August German forces were ordered to evacuate southern and south-western France apart from those troops within the surviving fortresses of western France. The costly battle that destroyed Brest ended on 18 September with the German surrender, by which time the port was useless to the Allies and also unnecessary. The advance through eastern France had gathered a remarkable pace since the collapse of the German defence of Normandy and with Cherbourg secured at the end of June, they were already in possession of a deep-water port which was brought into limited use by the middle of August. Unwilling to lose so many troops taking the remaining 'fortress' ports which were no longer necessary and barely functioned as naval bases, the Allies invested each one and put them under siege until the end of the war. Only Bordeaux fell on the last day of August but with German troops holding both shores of the Gironde River estuary to the north-west it was unusable.

I was a Corporal in the navy and near the end of the war was assigned to the 4th Vp-Flotilla on *V404* based at Bordeaux, France. After the invasion of Normandy by American and English troops, all German military bases in Southern France gave up. We were assembled into company strength and marched or driven north, although the order was to retreat to Germany. During the night of September 7, 1944, we stayed in a big meadow. At morning roll-call we were told that we were to be prisoners of the Americans. We were to put up no fight. After receiving instructions, the officers were to hand over 20,000 soldiers and all weapons.

During our march, we were escorted by only a few jeeps. In the area around the city of Rennes, we were disarmed and driven to a big meadow, which was surrounded by a chain-link fence. We were surrounded by white and black soldiers as well as a few officers. There wasn't a single building in the whole area. When no [American] officers could see, the black soldiers would sell us apples from a nearby orchard. We also got a knife from them so that we could trim branches into tent pegs. For eight days we stayed in this meadow. There was very, very little to eat and it rained every day. Then we were taken by landing craft to England.[106]

In the besieged ports there was little naval warfare to be conducted. With Allied mastery of the skies the few ships that remained operational were trapped within range of the ports where flak defences could protect them. However, some *U-Jäger*, *Vorpostenboote* and smaller vessels of the *Hafen-schutzflottillen* continued to make routine patrols off the harbours in order to prevent any possible landings or infiltrations. Limited raids were also mounted on outlying islands either to disrupt French communications or to capture whatever supplies and provisions could be found. The remainder of Breuning's Security Forces were fed into the front lines. Oberfähnrich Halmut Zülsdorff of the 6th Vp-Flotilla recalled the destruction of his unit and subsequent relegation to fighting as infantry in the Saint-Nazaire pocket.

In August 1944 most of the ships of 6th Vp-Flotilla were disarmed and the crews were sent to join the naval artillery units. I was part of the group sent to the 'Batterie Hai' at Saint-Brevin. We were lodged mainly in a villa and I believe it was not hit once by the enemy during my stay there. After a few weeks I was transferred to the edge of the Fortress to a battery that was part of 'Kampfgruppe Josephi'. The command post was situated in a chateau above Pornic, about 500-metres from our battery. Inside the command post a group of generators provided electricity. The battery, named 'Ursula', was commanded by Oberleutnant Salm and was equipped with four captured French 75mm flak guns. We had a Renault truck for relocating if needed, but not a lot of fuel. Our sector was actually very very calm and we spent a lot of time using a bicycle to visit local farmers to obtain provisions.[107]

While the Atlantic coast was lost to German control, flotillas from the Normandy region retreated steadily eastwards. Only the 2nd Vp-Flotilla, 24th M-Flotilla and 46th M-Flotilla moved to the Channel Islands which were now even more isolated by the Normandy invasion. While air attacks took a steady toll on the remaining security vessels, accidents also damaged valuable infrastructure. On 3 August an explosion inside Dunkirk's R-boat bunker, caused by a short-circuit during welding operations that allowed current to flow into the ignition cable of an explosive charge, caused its partial collapse and destroyed the workshop. A harbour tugboat, water-tank vessel and mine barge sank in the harbour though fortunately the mines did not explode. Twenty-two men were killed in the explosion and twenty-five more wounded.

By the time that Brest had fallen to the Americans, British and Canadian troops had pushed into Belgium and Luxembourg in the west. Dieppe was abandoned and occupied by the Allies at the beginning of September without opposition, while Le Havre began evacuating during the night of 23 September, which was completed within a week and falling to the Allies after a 48-hour assault. Boulogne and Dunkirk were placed under siege, Boulogne finally surrendering on 27 September after five days of fighting while Dunkirk would hold out until the final German surrender.

By the end of Kinetic, MGK West had ceased to exist in real terms and a restructuring of the Western Kriegsmarine command was instigated during September and October. *Marinegruppenkommando West* itself was dissolved on 20 October and replaced by the limited office of *Marineoberkommando West*, commanding all of the Atlantic fortifications and all troops within the fortresse ports still held by the Wehrmacht.

Konteradmiral Breuning's BSW was disbanded on 30 September 1944, KA Bütow's *Befehlshaber der Sicherung der Ostsee* following in November, the flotillas still under its control forming the basis of the new 10th *Sicherungsdivision*. Konteradmiral Lucht's *Befehlshaber der Sicherung Nordsee* was also dissolved, but not until January 1945 when its constituent units passed over to the 1st *Sicherungsdivision*. In place of these commands came the new office of *Befehlshaber der Sicherungsstreitkräfte* (B.d.Sich.) under the command of KzS Bergelt on 10 November 1944, who was replaced by KA Lucht in the New Year, Bergelt serving as his Chief of Staff until the war's end. This new office was originally based in Albeck near Swinemünde before relocating to the headquarters ship *Helgoland* in Kiel in March 1945.

At a lower level FK von Blanc's 2nd *Sicherungsdivision*, KzS Karl Bergelt's 3rd *Sicherungsdivision* and KzS Hans John's 4th *Sicherungsdivision* were all dissolved in September 1944. All that remained of the original divisions were KzS Knuth's 1st *Sicherungsdivision*, responsible for Security Forces in the North Sea and German Bight, and KzS Kurt Thoma's 5th *Sicherungsdivision* headquartered aboard the ship *Helgoland* in Cuxhaven.

New formations had also been created during the first half of 1944. Kapitän zur See Max Klein's 8th *Sicherungsdivision* had been established in April 1944 for service in the Skagerrak and Kattegat, Klein moving his headquarters from Copenhagen to Aarhus during June. *Konteradmiral* Böhmer had formed 9th *Sicherungsdivision* on 17 June 1944, responsible for the Eastern Baltic to the Pomeranian coast from the headquarters ship *Rugard* in Windau, replaced by FK von Blanc in October. Within the Adriatic, KzS Walter Berger's 11th *Sicherungsdivision* still functioned while those units active in waters around the Italian coast were under the control of KzS Rehm's 7th *Sicherungsdivision*.

The Eastern Front

The Eastern Front had been steadily driven back during 1944. While the front line near Kirkenes had remained more or less static, by the end of January the siege of Leningrad had been lifted and within two months Soviet troops had reached the Estonian border and were approaching Latvia in the north, while they battered their way into Poland and had reconquered nearly all of the Ukraine. However, the offensive of January 1944 that ended Leningrad's agony did not immediately improve the situation of the Soviet Baltic Fleet. Despite overwhelming Soviet aerial superiority, German and Finnish minesweepers continued to monitor the nets and minefields of Seeigel that had barred access to the Baltic while the Soviets attempted some shambolic landings on the Finnish coast which were badly co-ordinated and easily destroyed. It was, of course, only a temporary lull. *Artillerieträger*, *Vorpostenboote* and some small coastal minesweepers moved into Lake Peipus to help support German Army units facing the Soviets while minelaying continued in the Eastern Baltic. On 20 June, heavy Soviet air raids on the naval mine depot at Kirkkomansaari sank the transport ship *Otter* with 146 EMC mines aboard and the Finnish minelayer *Pragas 17* that had embarked 124 KMA (snag) mines. The bombing also destroyed 200 EMC, 54 FMC and 66 KMA mines ashore as well as 107 cutter buoys and 49 explosive buoys, the MFP *F140* being damaged and grounded, and was not salvaged until July 1945.

While the fighting in Normandy raged, Soviet forces finally attacked the Finnish lines in an effort to force Finland out of the war. The defenders began retreating in disarray under fire from supporting ships of the Soviet Baltic Fleet and attempting to ward off amphibious landings that were more skilfully executed than previously. The Germans rushed whatever surface forces and vessels of the security flotillas to the area – including the cruiser *Prinz Eugen* under escort by destroyers, torpedo boats, the minesweepers *M403*, *M423*, *M460* and MFP *F10* as gunnery support (Operation

Funeral of two men from a *U-Jäger* crew in Norway.

F224 of the 21st L-Flotilla carrying troops in northern Norway.

Rotbuche). Six *Artilleriefährprähme* were transferred to Kotka and placed at the disposition of the Finns in the eastern region of the Gulf of Finland, 1st R-Flotilla was transferred from to Kotka for the defence of Narva Bay and as minesweeper escort for Operation Drosselfang an attack on Soviet forces in the Koivusaari-Piisaari area spearheaded by the new torpedo boats *T30* and *T31* that had sailed from Helsinki to Kotka. Six MFPs of the 24th L-Flotilla were moved to Kirkomansaari and placed at the disposition of the Finns while minesweepers of 1st, 3rd and 25th M-Flotillas were to operate from Kotka. All of the forces allocated for the support of the Finns were directly controlled by KA Böhmer, commander of the 9th *Sicherungsdivision* in close liaison with the Finnish Navy.

The Security Forces on Lake Peipus were caught in a tug of war between BSO and the commander of the Wehrmacht's XVIII Corps. While the Army wanted those units present to carry out aggressive attacks against Soviet naval forces on the lake and fishing boats supplying the enemy with food, the Kriegsmarine maintained that the meagre forces available were intended as a line of defence, lacking the necessary offensive strength to take the battle to the enemy. Rather, they would treat the eastern banks of the lake as the Soviet front line and react to incursions from that direction. At 2100hrs on 18 June the Peipus boats reported capturing a rowing boat with spies aboard, seizing a 'large number of maps'.

On 19 June Operation Drosselfang began and the torpedo boats *T30* and *T31* alongside *Nettelbeck*, and *M29*, as well as *Artillerieträger* and R-boats were ordered to attack Soviet vessels reported south of Piisaari at 1740hrs. En route they were repeatedly attacked by four small gunboats, ten *MO-4* class submarine chasers and fourteen MTBs as well as supporting aircraft, shooting down two fighter-bombers and setting a patrol boat ablaze with gunfire. However, *T31* was torpedoed and sank with seventy-six men killed and six captured by the Soviets. The surviving torpedo boat, *T30*, was forced to retreat with damage and one man killed while *Nettelbeck* was hit by a bomb and had to be towed back to Helsinki; *M29* was also damaged and required docking for repair. They had blundered into cover for Soviet landing forces which were later attacked by the 1st R-Flotilla. Four R-boats and four *Artillerieträger* on temporary attachment to the flotilla attacked the Russian troops that same afternoon, shelling their landing point on the eastern coast of Piisaari. Bunkers and sheds on the beachhead were set on fire while frequent air attacks were beaten off. The Soviets' landing boats were destroyed but both *R119* and *R120* were damaged and both guns aboard *AF49* knocked out.

A joint operation code-named Steinhäger was devised for an assault on the Soviet positions on the tiny island og Narvi in the Gulf of Finland. Strong German supporting forces were to suppress Soviet positions by artillery bombardment while Finnish troops landed and destroyed all enemy positions before withdrawing. The torpedo boats *T8*, *T10* and *T30* were supported by the minesweepers *M15*, *M18*, *M19*, *M22* and *M30* of KK Dr Emil Kieffer's 3rd M-Flotilla and the R-boats *R67*, *R68*, *R76* and *R249* of Kptlt Walter Erich Schneider's 1st R-Flotilla. Finnish patrol boats would land the 108-man Finnish assault unit with direct MTB and torpedo boat support.

At 2240hrs on 27 June the German ships were in position with torpedo boats to the north, *M15*, *M19* and *M22* to the west and *M18* and *M30* to the north-east. Awaiting the order to commence firing, they were surprised by Soviet artillery on the island opening their own barrage, beginning a seven-minute exchange before the Soviets suddenly stopped. Five small Soviet craft appeared to the east of the island and while the Germans carried on their own bombardment until 2315hrs, a sudden flurry of shells from the island hit *M19* four times, causing slight damage. With no communication between the Finns and Germans, confusion ensued as Finnish craft approaching the island believed that the Kriegsmarine fire support had retreated and so the landing was called off.

The whole operation was under Finnish command under which Commander, 3rd M-Flotilla was in charge of the German forces. The combat group did only fire upon the isle of Narvi and silenced the batteries on the island with the exception of one gun at a distance of seven kilometres. The landing attempt was not carried out upon order of the Finnish commander. No reasons for his decision are known so far . . . The results seem rather poor in comparison with, the relatively strong forces on our side.[108]

It had been the second German setback in the Gulf of Finland during June, though the Kriegsmarine had successfully transported the 122nd Infantry Division and the 303rd *Sturmgeschützbrigade* to Finland to face the Red Army offensive. The Soviets had launched their land attack across the Karelian Isthmus and were making good headway while south of the Baltic the attack against the Estonian front line was expected to commence at any time.

Security Forces manning the 'Seeigel' mine barrage came under increasing pressure in July while German merchant traffic west of the minefields suffered the attention of the Soviet Air Force which, during the course of twenty-six attacks in July, sank a single freighter and damaged two others. The Kriegsmarine lost the minesweepers *M20* and *M413*, the MFPs *F237* and *F498* and the *Vorpostenboot V1710* along with the flak ship *Niobe*, all sunk by the attacks, while *M3, M14, M15, M19, M29, M30, M453, M460, M3114, V1703, V1705* and *F259* were damaged.

In August the *Artillerieträger* on Lake Peipus came under severe strain as Soviet forces carried out landings in the straits between Lake Peipus and Lake Pleskau, creating a beachhead 7km deep. The *Artillerieträger* went into immediate action, two of them leaving Praaga with five *Vorpostenboote* to

Troops disembark during the evacuation from the East in 1945. The vessels of the Security Forces helped thousands of military personnel and civilians escape the remorseless advance of the Red Army.

harass the Soviet landings. Under KK Paul Kahle, the commander of the 4th *Artillerieträger* Flotilla, the vessels were heavily shelled and returned fire, silencing the Soviet guns. German troops were able to temporarily push back the Soviet advance while the *Artillerieträger*s 88s continued to bombard the landing stage. Casualties were caused by frequent air attacks, but the flotilla successfully disengaged, earning the written gratitude of the Commander-in-Chief of Army Group North.

On 18 August the flotilla was heavily bombed with some casualties and damage, the withdrawal of the land front due to close the mouth of the Emajõgi River to the *Artillerieträger*. With troops needing to be lifted off the island of Piirisaar and the defence of the Western and Northern shores of Lake Peipus the main operational priority, plans were made to employ the *Artillerieträger* within the secondary waterways of the Emajõg as floating batteries or, in the worst case, strip them of their weapons for use ashore. Two days later Army Group North placed Kahle and his boats under the command of *Kampfgruppe* Narva to cover the evacuation of Piirisaar and four *Artillerieträger* and two *Vorpostenboote* provided fire support on the night of 21 August, men from the other flotilla vessels being employed as infantry in the ground fighting that followed. Thirteen patrol boats were protecting Lake Wirz, while it was planned to use two of Kahle's *Artillerieträger* to protect the bridgehead at Praaga, another to defend the bridge and flank at Kavastu, another to protect the flank at Kastre and supporting the army and two in Haslava to protect the flank of the endangered town of Tartu.

However, strong Soviet forces broke through Estonian troops and captured Tartu after forcing a crossing of the Emajõg. The units of the III SS Panzer Corps were nearly cut off between Lake Peipus and Narva Bay as Kahle and six officers, his staff and support company as well as crews of decommissioned vessels joined the infantry to defend the outskirts of Tartu. By that stage most of the unit's *Artillerieträger* had been destroyed, only *MAL14* and *23* engaging Soviet gunboats on Lake Peipus at 0645hrs on 26 August in the mouth of the Emajõg River.

On 30 August, KK Paul Kahle was killed in action near Tartu, his last boats passing directly under the command of II Army Corps though the few that were left were soon lost to Soviet air attacks. The 4th AT-Flotilla was officially dissolved in September by which time a cease-fire had been agreed between Finland and the Soviet Union, a full Armistice being signed on 10 September. Although Finland would not declare war on Germany until March 1945, they were now effectively in conflict with the Wehrmacht as the removal of German forces from Finnish territory had been an Armistice stipulation. The Germans withdrew from Finnish harbours as further Soviet advances shattered the German lines in Russia during Operation Bagration and the

Tartu Offensive into Estonia, resulting in the fall of Tallinn on 20 September.

The Wehrmacht were aware of the possibility of a Finnish withdrawal from the war and had devised a planned withdrawal from Finland code-named Operation Birke. To cover Birke two further operations were required, code-named Tanne West and Tanne Ost. The former entailed the capture of Finnish coastal artillery on the Ahvenanmaa and Åland islands in order to safeguard the planned withdrawal by sea, while the latter was an assault on Suursaari Island in the event that the Soviets landed there. Situated in the heart of the Gulf of Finland, the island was strategically valuable as it not only provided the perfect platform from which to guard the extensive mine barrages that had been laid over the previous years, but two radar installations had also been built there; 'Thor', for aerial surveillance, and 'Marder' for both surface ships and aircraft. Both were operated by twenty-six German personnel, who received orders to destroy their equipment, which they did, followed by successive orders countermanding this action.

With faulty intelligence about the strength and likely reaction of the island's Finnish garrison, the German landing force was a mixed bag of troops that included Kriegsmarine infantry and artillerymen, Luftwaffe flak troops and some Army infantry and engineers (equipped with twenty *Sturmboote*), all under the command of KzS Karl-Conrad Mecke, com-mander of Swinemünde's flak and naval artillery school. The Security Forces that transported the troops into action comprised three minesweepers and two *Flakjäger* of the 3rd M-Flotilla, four R-boats of the 1st R-Flotilla, MFPs of the 21st and 24th L-Flotillas, supported by gunfire from 7th AT-Flotilla, a requisitioned Estonian tugboat *Pernau* and the *Schnellboote S67*. The small fleet was commanded by the minesweeping flotilla's senior officer, KKdR Dr Emil Keiffer. Nearby torpedo boats, stationed to the west of Suursaari, were to provide supporting fire if required,

The German force used the evacuation of the twenty-six radar men as a reason to justify approaching the island, though the arrival of such a large number of ships immediately gave the lie to this stated intention. As *R249* entered the island's harbour a little after midnight on 15 September, she sailed to the pier and began to tie up even as Finnish troops shouted that they had not been granted permission. Kieffer disembarked and met with the Finnish commander Lieutenant-Colonel Martti J. Miettinen to request that the Finns hand the island over to German control. Miettinen refused and despite threats of overwhelming German force, Kieffer's mission was frustrated. Granted permission to make radio contact with his superiors, Kieffer radioed Mecke who ordered the invasion to begin. Hidden troops aboard *R249* began setting up machine guns in the harbour and captured the few Finnish sentries present as the remaining German ships entered the bay and began unloading the invasion force. At 0030hrs Finnish troops opened fire.

Marinefährprähme heading west in the Baltic with refugees and soldiers aboard.

By daybreak both sides had been battered by artillery and small-arms fire. Although the Germans had established a beachhead, they were pinned down by highly-motivated Finnish troops who occupied the island's high ground. Plans to land half of the German force elsewhere on the island had been foiled and Kieffer had ordered them all disembarked in the harbour which was now crowded with men and boats. The punishment that the Security Forces ships took was severe: *M15* had taken several shell hits to her waterline and fuel tanks, *M19* and *M30* were both severely damaged, *R29* was leaking following a collision with a minesweeper; *R72* and *R119* were damaged but afloat, and *R76* had been hit twice with her skipper and four crewmen killed. Leaking heavily, the boat was ordered to break off the action and head for Estonia. The MFPs had taken severe damage. *F866* and *F867* had been the first to attempt to land their troops, *F866* finally transferring Army engineers to small *Sturmboote* rather than reach the harbour pier while *F867* was hit repeatedly in harbour. A third, *F173*, was hit by Finnish artillery and drifted into a minefield where it detonated a mine and sank, *F866* being damaged by the blast. *F822*, carrying ammunition and a radio vehicle, was shelled and caught fire. The German forces ashore were, in fact, out of radio contact until the third wave of troops landed, by which time their entire mission was a disaster. The lack of radio meant that the potential support of the distant destroyers was never called for.

The commander of the 7th AT-Flotilla, KK Dr Theo Sonnemann, had already landed on the island to oversee his part of the operation, charged with command of both the artillery and landing craft. However, he was then unable to get back to any of his remaining vessels, twice attempting to reach them by

Sturmboote and twice being sunk by Finnish gunfire and swimming back ashore.

Unable to make contact with the various units ashore and aware that the mission had gone badly wrong, Kieffer called off the attack at 0450hrs, the surviving ships being ordered to the northern side of the island to regroup, while *Artillerieträger* then turned back to continue to provide fire support for the men ashore. To compound the problems faced by the Tanne Ost forces, Finnish MTBs arrived with the daylight and torpedoed *R29* and *Pernau* as the main fleet began its return to Tallinn, claims that they destroyed three large minesweepers were grossly exaggerated. Soviet aircraft harried the departing ships all the way back to Estonian coastal waters, then returning to add their weight to the counter-attack against the German troops on Suursaari.

Within 24 hours Tanne Ost was over. At least 155 Germans were killed, 175 wounded and 1056 able-bodied men surrendered to the Finns who lost 36 confirmed dead. Among the prisoners was KzS Karl-Conrad Mecke, who at one point had been wounded and treated in a Finnish field hospital, walking back to his own lines when he realised that he was unguarded. About sixty-four men managed to escape by undamaged *Sturmboote* to the small island of Pein Tytarsaari and on 17 September S-boats rescued some Kriegsmarine personnel from there, including the commander of 7th AT-Flotilla, Dr Sonnemann, who had finally managed to get off shore. The battle marked the opening of hostilities between Finland and Germany, Tanne West subsequently being cancelled.

To the north, the Soviet demand for the expulsion of all German troops from Finland, kick-started what is now known as the 'Lapland War'. As the Wehrmacht prepared to evacuate troops from their positions in Finnmark that had remained virtually unchanged since 1941, there were frequent though at first relatively minor skirmishes. Gradually, however, pressure intensified on the retreating Germans until full-scale fighting erupted and the Wehrmacht instigated a scorched-earth policy that devastated the entire region. The Kriegsmarine Security Forces in the north retreated to Norwegian harbours further south and Kirkenes was completely demolished and abandoned by the Germans on 25 October. A new Wehrmacht defensive line was established at Lyngenfjord with hurriedly-constructed bunker complexes into which the troops who had mounted an organised and orderly retreat moved. Finnish troops were unwilling to advance beyond their border and thus the lines became static again. Hammerfest, the most northerly Norwegian port at that time, was abandoned in October and the town burnt to the ground as its Norwegian inhabitants were forcibly moved south.

In the Gulf of Finland the Kriegsmarine evacuated 4049 soldiers, 3336 wounded, 332 evacuees, 746 vehicles and 42,114 tons of supplies from Finnish harbours, the final ships sailing from Kotka on 21 September after German troops destroyed the harbour installations.

The Security Forces continued to operate in the Baltic Sea. The loss of Finland as an ally meant that Soviet naval forces were simply able to side-step the dense mine barriers in the eastern Baltic and sail through clear channels in Finnish coastal waters. Nonetheless, their dogged and deter-mined missions to lay mines, patrol minefields, hunt for enemy submarines and provide escort for the large ships – such as the cruiser/destroyer *Kampfgruppe 2* that sailed into the Eastern Baltic centred on the *Prinz Eugen* and *Lützow* – continued despite the Third Reich clearly being defeated on all fronts. The day-to-day routine reports record casualties, losses and successes with an undiminished regularity that would require many pages to relate here. A single Soviet air attack could sink a *Vorpostenboot*, a converted trawler that had already weathered years of war in harsh natural environments that would put its crew to the test during arduous weeks of combat at sea. Their place within Kriegsmarine history is largely forgotten or, unforgivably, ignored. But, without them, the larger vessels whose stories are told more frequently would never have been able to put to sea with any security; minefields, submarines and aircraft would have stopped their missions before they had begun. However, there is no space to list all the vessels and all the men who served and lived or died aboard those vessels during the Second World War, let alone its final few months.

By September 1944 mainland Estonia was being evacuated by the Germans in Operation Aster, with both land and naval evacuation skilfully handled as Generalfeldmarschall Ferdinand Schörner's Army Group North moved south and west around the Gulf of Riga to Courland where it was subsequently cut off as Soviet troops advanced into East Prussia during October 1944. There it would stay until the German surrender, successfully supplied by hard-pressed merchant convoys under R-boat escort.

The Eastern Front stood on the Vistula River at the end of the year, but a January offensive carried it west, ultimately to the gates of Berlin. The *Donauflottille* fought artillery engagements against advancing Soviet armour as the Security Flotillas in the Baltic began aiding the desperate flight of refugees while also fighting a rearguard action against crushing Soviet material superiority. Over two million people were shuttled back to Germany between January and April 1945. In the West Hitler had squandered his final reserves in the Ardennes, and the Kriegsmarine was being pushed back along the shrinking coastline of Hitler's Thousand Year Reich.

The Western Front

However, even when the odds were hopeless, the Kriegsmarine's little ships could still show their teeth. The garrisons of the Channel Islands had been left to wither on the vine by the Allies. Shortages of both food and coal became critical during the winter of 1944/45, the latter providing inspiration for a raid on mainland France. Four *Fallschirmjäger* prisoners of war and FzS Leker, captured at Brest, had escaped from an American prisoner-of-war camp at Granville. Hiding amongst a working party in the harbour area and passing themselves off as interpreters, they managed to slip away and stole an American landing craft, Leker apparently having masterminded the plan. Using a pocket compass and sketch-map they reached Maitress Ile in the Minquiers group where German sentries at first fired on them but later directed them to Jersey once their identity was established. The escapees reported that Granville harbour was generally full of ships discharging coal bound for Paris, while the United States Army maintained a signal station on the South Pier and a radar station nearby. The newly appointed garrison commander of the Channel Islands, VA Friedrich Hüffmeier, authorised the planning of a raid both to restore some morale and pride to the flagging spirits of the forgotten garrison and also to obtain badly-needed coal. The method of attack was devised by senior officer of the 24th M-Flotilla, Kaptlt Carl-Friedrich Mohr, who had assumed command of the flotilla following the death of FK Fritz Breithaupt on Christmas Day. Breithaupt, winner of the Oak Leaves to his Knight's Cross in February 1944 and having served in the minesweeper service for the duration of the war, was killed in a Heinkel He111 plane crash as he accompanied Leker and possibly the escaped *Fallschirmjäger* to Berlin on what was, at best, a perilous flight. Intercepted over Bastogne, where the Battle of the Bulge was raging, by an American fighter, the plane went down with no survivors.[109]

Mohr would lead the attack aboard *Schnellboot S112*, a strong contingent of nearly 600 Luftwaffe, Kriegsmarine and Army troops being carried aboard *M412*, *M432*, *M442* and *M452* of the 24th M-Flotilla, *AF65*, *AF68* and *AF71* previously of the 2nd Vp-Flotilla and transferred to the 46th M-Flotilla, *M4613* of the 46th M-Flotilla, *V228* and *V229* of the 2nd Vp-Flotilla, *FK01*, *FK04*, *FK56* and *FK60* of the *Hafenschutzflottille Kanalinseln* (the latter the captured landing craft used by the escapees) and a seagoing tugboat. Their plan was to land in the harbour and destroy the installations and the nearby radar station while troops created a diversion by attacking the Hotel des Bains where senior American officers were present. The withdrawing force would commandeer vessels loaded with coal for the return to the islands.

The initial attempt was thwarted by bad weather and the presence of an American patrol boat, the raid being postponed until the night of 8 March 1945. The assault force departed St Helier after nightfall and reached Granville at approximately 0100hrs, guided by harbour lights burning as if it were peacetime. The three *Artillerieträger*, led by flotilla commander ObltzSdR Otto Karl, were positioned between the Ile Chausey and St Malo to intercept potential Allied patrols while two minesweepers stationed themselves between

Jersey and the Cotentin Peninsula. The remainder headed into harbour, spearheaded by two minesweepers. Upon being challenged by semaphore they replied with the same challenge, creating enough confusion to allow their entry to the harbour unmolested. The two ships landed at the pier while the *Vorpostenboote* made to land troops at the beach by the Hotel des Bains. Firing broke out straight away, but the German assault force established firm positions and were able to fend off counter-attacks. However, they had miscalculated the tide, three of the four colliers in harbour running firmly aground in an ebbing tide. They were the prize and so towing them to the Channel Islands by use of the tugboat was obviously impossible for all but the 1200-ton SS *Eskwood*. While demolition teams sabotaged the engines on the three remaining ships – shooting the captain of the *Kyle Castle* after he failed to co–operate – and demolished cranes, locomotives, wagons, lock gates and fuel dumps, *Eskwood* was seized and set sail.

An American submarine chaser, *USPC 564*, was intercepted by the three *Artillerieträger* and sunk with fourteen men killed and eleven rescued as prisoners while the rest of the assault force disengaged. The planned attack on the radar station had failed due to the low tide preventing a close–enough approach to land troops, *M412* running aground and blown up during the retreat. The German force had liberated sixty-seven German prisoners and taken a number of American soldiers and officers as their own priosners. Friedrich Ruge, who had moved to a position in OKM after departing Army Group B in August 1944, recorded that it was through 'a sound plan, thorough preparation, and complete secrecy had enabled the Channel Isles to strike a shrewd blow. Compared with the battle in Germany, it was no more than a pinprick, yet it was the best they could do for their suffering country.' Mohr was awarded the Knight's Cross on 11 March 1945 with Otto Karl also receiving his ten days later.

By that stage of the war the exodus of refugees fleeing East Prussia before the Soviet advance had become a tidal wave of humanity. The Kriegsmarine threw ships into defending the remaining military enclaves and embarkation points for civilians desperate to reach the West. *Artillerieträger* of the 8th AT-Flotilla, which had been fighting constantly against the Allies in the West since D-Day, transferred to the Baltic during April 1945 and tasked with assisting in the defence of Wolgast and the evacuation of Peenemünde. An SS demolition commando destroyed the Karnin Lift-Bridge connecting the island of Usedom to the mainland in a vain attempt to hold the Soviet advance while AF77 removed the last Luftwaffe personnel from Peenemünde itself. On 2 May, *AF75* and *AF77* engaged T34 tanks with direct fire near Freesendorfer See, but nothing could halt the enemy. Amidst relentless attack from land, sea and air, the Kriegsmarine Security Forces were pushed back to Germany, taking as many people as they could with them. On 5 May 1945,

24-year-old Knight's Cross holder ObltzS Gerd-Dietrich Schneider, commander of the 8th AT-Flotilla was in Eckernförde.

> There, later, I met up again with my other boats *AF104*, *AF107* and *AF109*. On 6 May at 1600hrs we weighed anchor and set course for the Danish island of Svenborg. During the voyage on 7 May . . . I received radioed instructions that at 1600hrs we were to lower our battle flag [*Kriegsflagge*]. So, I had all boats made fast and the crews lined up at the specified time. The battle flag was struck and then we continued our journey. Towards midday on 8 May we returned to Eckernförde where the harbourmaster forbade our entering the port and mooring. So I headed to Kappeln and at 2100hrs we made fast. One day later we ran on to Sieseby, reaching there on 10 May. In Kappeln there had been too many ships and boats, but here on the estern bank of the Schlei we had some peace. By 3 June 1945 we had held our final muster and I finished my diary.

Postscript

THE end of hostilities in Europe did not mark the end of Germany's minesweeping service. The German Minesweeping Administration (GMSA) was formed on 21 June 1945, under the authority of the Royal Navy Commander-in-Chief for Germany, Vice Admiral Sir Harold Martin Burrough. Commodore H. T. England was made commander of the GMSA while KA Fritz Kraus was Chief Administrator.

The German sailors that formed the GMSA were not volunteers; they were disarmed military personnel subject to the same disciplinary code as in the Kriegsmarine. Initially they served in their wartime uniforms (with

The *Kriegsabzeichen für Minensuch, Ubootsjagd and Sicherungsverbände:* service badge for minesweepers, submarine chasers and security vessels. Awarded after either three operational sorties, one successful sortie, six months active service, being wounded in action or being aboard a vessel sunk by enemy action. Designed by Otto Placzek.

national symbols removed) but were issued dark blue British battledress and specific GMSA insignia on 25 May 1946. The sailors were paid a moderate wage and had equivalent rights to those they had during wartime military service.

The GMSA was divided into six divisions (*Räumbootdivisionen*), their headquarters at Glückstadt and later Hamburg.

> 1st Division: Schleswig-Holstein.
> 2nd Division: West Germany (Cuxhaven).
> 3rd Division: Denmark.
> 4th Division: Norway.
> 5th Division: Netherlands.
> 6th Division: Bremen (American division).

Approximately 840 vessels were used at the outset of minesweeping operations, but over the years many were retired from service and by the beginning of 1947 the service comprised the following active vessels:

> 84 M-class Minesweepers.
> 63 R-boats.
> 62 *Kriegfischerkutter*.
> 6 *Sperrbrecher*.
> 5 converted trawler minesweepers.
> 110 auxiliary vessels.

The GMSA was disbanded as a result of Soviet pressure in 1948 by which time they had cleared 2721 naval mines, and had lost ten vessels and 348 men killed.

Appendices

Appendix 1: Kriegsmarine Security Forces, December 1940

December 1940 (West)

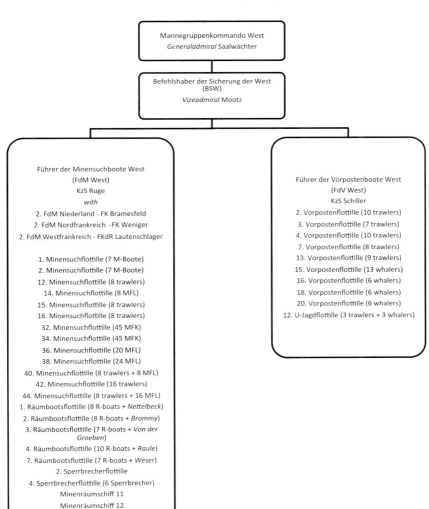

Marinegruppenkommando West
Generaladmiral Saalwächter

Befehlshaber der Sicherung der West
(BSW)
Vizeadmiral Mootz

Führer der Minensuchboote West
(FdM West)
KzS Ruge
with
2. FdM Niederland - FK Bramesfeld
2. FdM Nordfrankreich -FK Weniger
2. FdM Westfrankreich - FKdR Lautenschlager

1. Minensuchflottille (7 M-Boote)
2. Minensuchflottille (7 M-Boote)
12. Minensuchflottille (8 trawlers)
14. Minensuchflottille (8 MFL)
15. Minensuchflottille (8 trawlers)
16. Minensuchflottille (8 trawlers)
32. Minensuchflottille (45 MFK)
34. Minensuchflottille (45 MFK)
36. Minensuchflottille (20 MFL)
38. Minensuchflottille (24 MFL)
40. Minensuchflottille (8 trawlers + 8 MFL)
42. Minensuchflottille (16 trawlers)
44. Minensuchflottille (8 trawlers + 16 MFL)
1. Räumbootsflottille (8 R-boats + *Nettelbeck*)
2. Räumbootsflottille (8 R-boats + *Brommy*)
3. Räumbootsflottille (7 R-boats + *Von der Groeben*)
4. Räumbootsflottille (10 R-boats + *Raule*)
7. Räumbootsflottille (7 R-boats + *Weser*)
2. Sperrbrecherflottille
4. Sperrbrecherflottille (6 Sperrbrecher)
Minenräumschiff 11
Minenräumschiff 12

Führer der Vorpostenboote West
(FdV West)
KzS Schiller
2. Vorpostenflottille (10 trawlers)
3. Vorpostenflottille (7 trawlers)
4. Vorpostenflottille (10 trawlers)
7. Vorpostenflottille (8 trawlers)
13. Vorpostenflottille (9 trawlers)
15. Vorpostenflottille (13 whalers)
16. Vorpostenflottille (6 whalers)
18. Vorpostenflottille (6 whalers)
20. Vorpostenflottille (6 whalers)
12. U-Jagdflottille (3 trawlers + 3 whalers)

December 1940 (North)

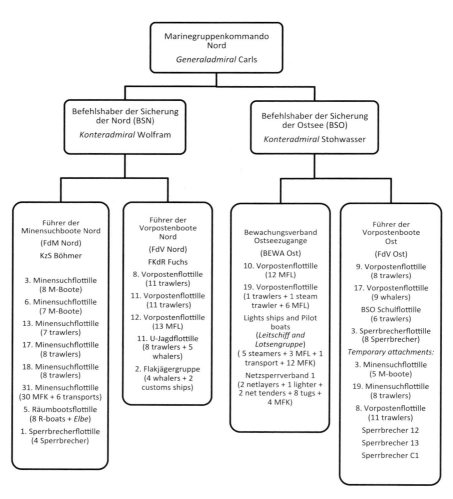

Marinegruppenkommando Nord
Generaladmiral Carls

Befehlshaber der Sicherung der Nord (BSN)
Konteradmiral Wolfram

Befehlshaber der Sicherung der Ostsee (BSO)
Konteradmiral Stohwasser

Führer der Minensuchboote Nord
(FdM Nord)
KzS Böhmer
3. Minensuchflottille (8 M-Boote)
6. Minensuchflottille (7 M-Boote)
13. Minensuchflottille (7 trawlers)
17. Minensuchflottille (8 trawlers)
18. Minensuchflottille (8 trawlers)
31. Minensuchflottille (30 MFK + 6 transports)
5. Räumbootsflottille (8 R-boats + *Elbe*)
1. Sperrbrecherflottille (4 Sperrbrecher)

Führer der Vorpostenboote Nord
(FdV Nord)
FKdR Fuchs
8. Vorpostenflottille (11 trawlers)
11. Vorpostenflottille (11 trawlers)
12. Vorpostenflottille (13 MFL)
11. U-Jagdflottille (8 trawlers + 5 whalers)
2. Flakjägergruppe (4 whalers + 2 customs ships)

Bewachungsverband Ostseezugange
(BEWA Ost)
10. Vorpostenflottille (12 MFL)
19. Vorpostenflottille (1 trawlers + 1 steam trawler + 6 MFL)
Lights ships and Pilot boats
(*Leitschiff and Lotsengruppe*)
(5 steamers + 3 MFL + 1 transport + 12 MFK)
Netzsperrverband 1 (2 netlayers + 1 lighter + 2 net tenders + 8 tugs + 4 MFK)

Führer der Vorpostenboote Ost
(FdV Ost)
9. Vorpostenflottille (8 trawlers)
17. Vorpostenflottille (9 whalers)
BSO Schulflottille (6 trawlers)
3. Sperrbrecherflottille (8 Sperrbrecher)
Temporary attachments:
3. Minensuchflottille (5 M-boote)
19. Minensuchflottille (8 trawlers)
8. Vorpostenflottille (11 trawlers)
Sperrbrecher 12
Sperrbrecher 13
Sperrbrecher C1

December 1940 (Norway)

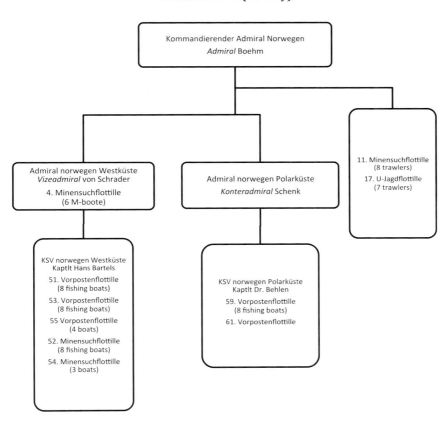

Kommandierender Admiral Norwegen
Admiral Boehm

Admiral norwegen Westküste
Vizeadmiral von Schrader
4. Minensuchflottille
(6 M-boote)

Admiral norwegen Polarküste
Konteradmiral Schenk

11. Minensuchflottille
(8 trawlers)
17. U-Jagdflottille
(7 trawlers)

KSV norwegen Westküste
Kaptlt Hans Bartels
51. Vorpostenflottille
(8 fishing boats)
53. Vorpostenflottille
(8 fishing boats)
55 Vorpostenflottille
(4 boats)
52. Minensuchflottille
(8 fishing boats)
54. Minensuchflottille
(3 boats)

KSV norwegen Polarküste
Kaptlt Dr. Behlen
59. Vorpostenflottille
(8 fishing boats)
61. Vorpostenflottille

Appendix 2

Knight's Cross Winners of the *Sicherungsstreitkräfte*

OAK LEAVES

Minesweepers

Breithaupt, Fritz, KK	10 Feb 44, commander 24th M-Flotilla
Kamptz, Gerhard von, FK	14 Apr 43, commander 8th M-Flotilla
Palmgren, Karl, KK	11 Jul 44, commander 38th M-Flotilla

U-Jäger

Pollmann, Otto, ObltzS	25 Apr 44, commander *UJ2210*

Räumboote

Kamptz von, Gerhard, FK	14 Apr 1943, commander 8th R-Flotille

Minenschiff

Brill, Dr Karl-Friedrich, FKdR	18 Nov 1943, commander '*Juminda*'

Sicherungsdivision

Blanc, Adalbert von, FK	06 May 45, commander of 9th Sicherungsdivision (unconfirmed)

KNIGHT'S CROSS

Minesweepers

Bartels, Hans, Kptlt.	16 May 40, commander *M1*
Bergelt, Karl, K.z.S.	03 Aug 42, commander 1st M-Flotilla
Blasberg, Kurt, ObltzS	07 Sep 44, commander *M3619* and Gruppenführer
Bögel, Hermann, LzS	15 Oct 42, commander *M4040*
Breithaupt, Fritz, KK	03 Aug 41, commander 12th M-Flotilla
Feller, Wolfgang, ObltzSdR	17 Jun 45, Gruppenführer, 36th M-Flotilla (unofficial)
Heynsen, Rudolf, KKdR	20 Apr 45, commander 27th M-Flotilla
Hölzerkopf, Arnulf, KK	14 May 44, commander 8th M-Flotilla
Jesse, Rudolf, ObltzSdR	26 Aug 44, commander 8th M-Flotilla
Kieffer, Dr Emil, KK	03 Dec 44, commander 3rd M-Flotilla
Klünder, Erich, KK	12 Aug 44, commander 5th M-Flotilla
Lehmann, Paul, KK	24 Sep 44, commander 42nd M-Flotilla
Mohr, Karl-Friedrich, Kptlt.	11 Mar 45, commander 24th M-Flotilla
Rehm, Hans. KK	31 Dec 41, commander 2nd M-Flotilla
Ruge, Prof. Friedrich, Kommodore	21 Oct 41, F.d.M.West
Schneider, Walter-Erich, Kptlt.	05 Nov 44, commander 25th M-Flotilla
Thoma, Kurt, KK	06 Oct 40, commander 2nd M-Flotilla

Räumboote

Anhalt, Wilhelm, Kptlt.	03 Jul 44, commander 4th R-Flotilla
Brökelmann, Jost, KK	14 Jun 42, commander 2nd R-Flotilla
Dobberstein, Werner, Kptlt.	04 Sep 41, commander 5th R-Flotilla
Forstmann, Gustav, KK	28 Jul 41, commander 1st R-Flotilla
Godenau, Arthur, StbsObStrm	31 May 40, commander *R17* (1st R-Halbflottille)
Goetzke, Axel. LtzSdR.	27 Dec 41, commander R61 (5th R-Flotilla)
Grundmann, Erich, Kptl.(Ing.)	31 May 40, flotilla engineer 1st R-Flotilla
Hoff, Carl, Kaptlt	09 May 45, commander 1st R-Flotilla (unconfirmed)
Holst, Waldemar, KK	03 Dec 42, commander 4th R-Flotilla
Kamptz, Gerhard von, KzS	06 Oct 40, commander 2nd R-Flotilla
Klassmann, Helmut, Kaptlt	22 Dec 43, commander 3rd R-Flotilla
Maurer, Otto, KK	03 Jul 43, commander 12th R-Flotilla
Merks, Hans Joachim, Kptlt.	28 May 45, commander 2nd R-Flotilla (unconfirmed).
Muser, Alfred, Kaptlt	12 Aug 44, commander 8th R-Flotilla
Nau, Herbert, Kptlt	11 Jul 44, commander 10th R-Flotilla
Nordt, Otto, Kaptlt	06 Sep 44, commander 14th R-Flotilla
Pinkepank, Georg, KK	12 Aug 44, commander 2nd R-Flotilla
Rixecker, Karl, StObstrm.	31 May 40, commander *R23* (1st R-Flotilla)

Vorpostenboote

Fischer, K.-H., Steuermannsmaat	03 May 43, Steuermann *V722*
Fischer, Dr Walther, KK	08 May 43, commander 13th Vp-Flotilla
Flügel, Otto, Steuermannsmaat	03 May 43, Steuermann *V1525*
Loewer, Kurt, KK	24 Jun 44, commander 11th Vp-Flotilla
Martienssen, Ekkehard, ObltzS	29 Jun 44, commander *V203*
Porath, Rudolf, LzS	08 Oct 41, commander *V1806*
Rall, Dr Viktor, KKdR.	10 Jun 44, commander 15th Vp-Flotilla
Schulz, Karl, ObltzSdR.	26 Aug 44, commander *V1509* and Gruppenführer
Stamer, Heinz, KK	20 Apr 45, commander 8th Vp-Flotilla
Tellgmann, Eugen, ObltzS	05 Oct 44, commander *V1313*
Wulff, Erich, ObltzS	24 Apr 44, commander 18th Vp-Flotilla

U-Jäger

Brandt, Dr Günther, KK	23 Dec 43, commander 21st UJ-Flotilla
Kaden, Wolfgang, Kptlt	18 Dec 40, commander *UJ116*
Jungnickel, Edgar, ObltzS	10 Sep 44, commander *UJ1430*
Pollmann, Otto, LzS	19 May 43, commander *UJ2210*
Trautwein, Heinz, ObltzSdR	05 Nov 44, commander *UJ202*
Wenke, Klaus, ObltzSdR	05 Nov 44, commander *UJ208*
Werther, Helmuth, OBltzSdR	08 Nov 44, Grpfhr. i.d. *Minenschiffe, Küstenschutzflotille Attika*, 21st UJ-Flotilla
Wünning, Joachim, KKdR	22 Oct 44, commander *Drache* and temp comm. 21st UJ-Flotilla

Wunderlich, Friedrich, KKzV   03 Dec 42, commander 14th UJ-Flotilla

Sperrbrecher
Palmgren, Karl, KKzV   03 Aug 41 commander *Sperrbrecher IX* and *I*

Geleitbooten
Guhrke, Heinz, ObltzSdR   05 Nov 1944, commander *TA20* (2nd G-Flotilla)

Thorwest, Friedrich Wilhelm, FKdR   05 Nov 44 (posthum) commander 2nd G-Flotilla

Landungsflottillen
Brauneis, Erich FK   28 Dec 44, commander 24th L-Flotilla
Liebenstein, Gustav Frhr. Von, FK   03 Sep 43, commander 2nd L-Division and *Seetransportführer Messina-Straße.*

Artillerietrager
Haxthausen, Elmershaus von, Kptlt.   03 Jul 44, commander 2nd AT-Flotilla.
Karl, Otto, ObltzSdR   21 Mar 45, commander *AF65*
Schneider, Gerd-Dietrich, ObltzS   03 Oct 1944, commander 8th AT-Flotilla
Minenschiff
Brill, Dr Karl-Friedrich, KKdR   27 Dec 1941, commander *Cobra* and '*Minenschiffgruppe Cobra*'

Sicherungsdivision
Blanc, Adalbert von, FK   27 Nov 44, commander 9th *Sicherungsdivision*

Böhmer, Kurt, KA   06 Oct 40, Chief of Staff, BSN
Bramesfeld, Heinrich, K.z.S.   21 Jan 43, commander 2nd *Sicherungsdivision*

Knuth, Hermann, K.z.S.   24 Sep 44, commander 1st *Sicherungsdivision*
Lucht, Ernst, KA   17 Jan 45, *Befehlshaber der Sicherung der Nordsee*

Philipp, Hans-Otto, KK   30 Dec 44, commander 1st *Küstensicherungsverbande*s

Stohwasser, Hans, KA   30 Nov 40, *Befehlshaber der Sicherung der Ostsee*

Weniger, Karl, K.z.S.(posthumous)   15 Nov 41, commander 2nd *Sicherungsdivision* (killed 1 Oct 41).

Wolfram, Eberhard, KA   25 May 41, *Befelshaber der Sicherung der Nordsee*

Appendix 3: Security Units

NOTE: I have taken a liberty with the nomenclature of these German units. Whilst retaining their German titles I have numbered them in the English manner. Strictly speaking, what I list as the '1st *Vorpostenflottille*' should be written in German as '1. *Vorpostenflottille*'. I hope that this Anglo-German linguistic collision doesn't interfere with these lists.

PATROL BOATS

1st *Vorpostenflottille* (Small steamers)
Commissioned on 1 October 1939. Redesignated **3rd** *Sperrbrecherflottille* on 1 October 1940.
Saw brief service in the western Baltic before transfer to *Sperrbrecher* duties.

2nd *Vorpostenflottille* (Trawlers, KFK)
Commissioned during September 1939 with eight trawlers and disbanded in December 1944.
Served in the North Sea, later based in St Malo for Channel service. After the Overlord landings, the flotilla moved to the Channel Islands, headquartered at St Helier.

3rd *Vorpostenflottille* (Trawlers)
Commissioned on 3 October 1939 with eight trawlers, serving in the Baltic and then as convoy protection between the Elbe River and The Netherlands. After Operation Barbarossa, the flotilla moved to Libau, patrolling the Gulf of Finland.

4th *Vorpostenflottille* (Trawlers, French escort ships)
Commissioned in September 1939 with eight trawlers and disbanded in September 1944.
Served in the North Sea before moving to the French Atlantic coast and operating between Bordeaux and Bayonne.

5th *Vorpostengruppe*
Commissioned in September 1939 and disbanded on 22 May 1940 after service in western Baltic.

6th *Vorpostengruppe*
Commissioned in September 1939, transferred to the North Sea and *Führer der Sonderverbände West* command in January 1940. Disbanded on 22 May 1940. Reformed on 1 January 1943. Disbanded in September 1944 (Trawlers, KFK). Served the western French coast, based at Saint-Nazaire.

7th *Vorpostenflottille* (Trawlers)
Commissioned on 22 September 1939 and disbanded in September 1944.
Based in Kiel before transfer to Brest.

8th *Vorpostenflottille* (Trawlers)
Commissioned in September 1939 and disbanded in 1945.
Saw service in the North Sea, ending the war as convoy protection between the Elbe and Rotterdam. Headquartered at Bremerhaven and Cuxhaven. Upon the disbandment of **13th Vp-Flotilla** in March 1945, that unit's last three ships joined the 8th.

9th *Vorpostenflottille* (Small trawlers)
Commissioned with nine trawlers on 27 September 1939, disbanded on 23 April

1945. Served in the western Baltic, Kattegatt and Skagerakk before moving East, headquartered at Aalborg.

10th *Vorpostenflottille* (Coastal motor boats, Herring boats)
Commissioned in Wesermünde in September 1939 using small coastal vessels before those craft were discharged and replaced with larger herring boats. It was renamed **10th** *Sicherungsflottille* on 1 October 1943. Served in the North Sea, the Baltic and the Danish Kattegat, Belt and Sound.

11th *Vorpostenflottille* (Trawlers, flakships)
Commissioned in September 1939 from eight trawlers. Additional newly-built ships were added before the remains of 2nd *Flakjäger-Flottille* were also added.

12th *Vorpostenflottille* (Fishing boats, MFPs)
Commissioned on 26 September 1939 in Wesermünde from eight fishing boats. It was disbanded in December 1947.The flotilla served in the North Sea, operating from Cuxhaven, Esbjerg, Wesermünde, Borkum, Norderney, Hörnum, Tönning and Terschelling. At the end of the war the remaining ships of the flotilla were assigned to the *Deutschen Minenräumdienst* (GMSA) and attached to the 6th *Minenräumdivision* in Wesermünde operating under American control.

13th *Vorpostenflottille* (Trawlers)
Commissioned in September 1939 and disbanded in January 1945.
Served in the North Sea and then the Netherlands and Belgium. Upon disbandment the surviving ships transferred to **8th**, **14th** and **20th Vp-Flotillas**.

14th *Vorpostenflottille* (Trawlers)
Commissioned on 1 February 1943 in Rotterdam initially with captured trawlers, later replaced by German ones, and disbanded in 1945 at the capitulation.
Served as convoy escort along the Dutch coast.

15th *Vorpostenflottille* (Trawlers)
Commissioned on 26 September 1939 and disbanded at the capitulation in 1945.
Serving initially in the North Sea before transfer to Le Havre. After the D-Day landings most ships were lost, the remainder moving to Norway, based at Kristiansand Süd.

16th *Vorpostengruppe*
Commissioned in July 1940, redesignated **16th** *Vorpostenflottille* on 20 September 1940.

16th *Vorpostenflottille* (German and French Trawlers)
Commissioned on 20 September 1940 from French and German trawlers and finally disbanded in July 1945.

17th *Vorpostenflottille* (German whalers, fishing boats)
Commissioned in June 1940 from German whaling boats and disbanded in 1945. Based in the Baltic, between 1942 and 1944 tasked with monitoring the minefields in the Gulf of Finland.

18th *Vorpostengruppe*
Commissioned in July 1940 and redesignated **18th** *Vorpostenflottille* on 3 October 1940.

18th *Vorpostenflottille* (French trawlers, KFK)
Commissioned on 3 October 1940 and disbanded in 1945.

Served in the English Channel until D–Day whereupon the trawlers were sent to southern Norway as convoy protection. The remaining ships were redistributed amongst 32nd M-Flotilla, 12th Vp-Flotilla and 6th *Sicherungs-Flotilla*.

19th *Vorpostenflottille* (Fishing boats)
Commissioned in July 1940, redesignated **5th** *Sicherungsflotille* on 1 October 1943. Served in Danish waters, based at Aarhus.

20th *Vorpostenflottille* (Dutch, Belgian, German trawlers)
Commissioned in July 1940 and renamed **20th** *Minensuchflotille* after the end of the war.

51st *Vorpostenflottille* (Norwegian fishing boats, R–boats and older S–boats)
Commissioned in Bergen on 23 December 1940 and disbanded in June 1945.

53rd *Vorpostenflottille* (Norwegian whalers)
Commissioned on 23 December 1940 from Norwegian whaling boats. Disbanded in June 1945.

55th *Vorpostenflottille* (Norwegian vessels, KFK)
Commissioned in December 1940 from Norwegian vessels and disbanded in June 1945.
Based in Floorvag, the KFKs were transferred to Kiel after the end of the war to undertake minesweeping.

57th *Vorpostenflottille* (Norwegian Whalers, German trawlers, MFP)
Commissioned in June 1940 as **6th** *Küstensicherungsflotille*, redesignated 57th *Vorpostenflottille* in November 1940. Disbanded in June 1945.

59th *Vorpostenflottille* (Norwegian Whalers, German trawlers, MFP)
Established in February 1941. Disbanded in June 1945. Stationed in Sandnessjöen and engaged in coastal escort and patrol on the Norwegian coast.

61st *Vorpostenflottille* (Norwegian trawlers, Customs boat, British trawler)
Established in November 1940. Disbanded in June 1945. Based in Bodo and engaged in coastal convoy protection in northern Norway.

63rd *Vorpostenflottille* (Norwegian vessels, KFK)
Established in May 1944 from the *Narvik Hafenschutzflottille*. Disbanded in 1945. Security and escort duty in northern Norway

64th *Vorpostenflottille* (Norwegian fishing boats, MFP, KFK)
Established in June 1944 from *Trondheim Hafenschutzflottille*. Disbanded in 1945. Divided into five groups, based in Hysnes and patrolling northern Norwegian coast.

65th *Vorpostenflottille* (*U-Jagdboote*, Norwegian fishing boats, floating torpedo battery, KFK)
Established in May 1944 from *Hammerfest Hafenschutzflottille*. Disbanded in summer 1945 after serving on the Northern and Polar Norwegian coasts.

66th *Vorpostenflottille* (Norwegian vessels, floating torpedo battery, MFP, KFK)
Established in May 1944 from *Sandnessjöen Hafenschutzflottille*. Disbanded in summer 1945. Stationed in Rörvik.

67th *Vorpostenflottille* (Norwegian vessels, KFK)
Established on 1 July 1944 in Kirkenes. Disbanded in summer 1945 after serving on the Polar and north Norwegian coasts.

68th *Vorpostenflottille* (Norwegian vessels, KFK, MFP, floating torpedo battery) Established in May 1944 from *Molde Hafenschutzflottille*. Disbanded in summer 1945.

SPERRBRECHER

1st *Sperrbrechergruppe*
Established in September 1939; redesignated in July 1940 **1st** *Sperrbrecherflottille*.

2nd *Sperrbrechergruppe*
Established in September 1939; redesignated in July 1940 **2nd** *Sperrbrecherflottille*.

4th *Sperrbrechergruppe*
Established October 1939; redesignated in July 1940 **4th** *Sperrbrecherflottille*.

6th *Sperrbrechergruppe*
Established October 1939; redesignated in July 1940 **6th** *Sperrbrecherflottille*.

1st *Sperrbrecherflottille*
Established in July 1940. Disbanded 1946. Operated in the Baltic and German Bight.

2nd *Sperrbrecherflottille*
Established on 1 July 1940 from the **2nd**, **4th** and **6th** *Sperrbrechergruppe*. Divided into 2nd and 6th *Sperrbrecherflottille* on 1 July. Disbanded in September 1944. Operational in Dutch waters (1940), the Bay of Biscay (1940–4). *Sperrbrecher 7* was temporarily assigned to the Baltic and Great Belt.

3rd *Sperrbrecherflottille*
Established on 1 October 1940 from the *1st Vorpostenflottille*. Disbanded in 1946. Operational within the western Baltic clearing departure channels for U-boats through the Great and Small Belts and the Sound.

4th *Sperrbrecherflottille*
Established in June 1940 as *Sperrbrechergruppe Niederlande*. On 29 September 1940 redesignated **4th** *Sperrbrecherflottille*. In autumn 1941 components formed cadre for the **5th** *Sperrbrecherflottille*.
The flotilla was dissolved in July 1943.

5th *Sperrbrecherflottille*
Established in November 1941 from parts of the **4th** *Sperrbrecherflottille*. During December 1941 renamed **8th** *Sperrbrecherflottille*.

6th *Sperrbrecherflottille*
Established on 1 July 1941 from a cadre of the **2nd** *Sperrbrecherflottille*. Flotilla dissolved in September 1944. Operational from Nantes and later Concarneau for escort of U-boats.

8th *Sperrbrecherflottille*
Established on 9 December 1941 after the renaming of **5th** *Sperrbrecherflottille*. Dissolved at the capitulation in 1945. Operational in the North Sea, off Dutch coast and at the end of the war in Danish waters.

MINESWEEPERS

1st *Minensuchflottille* (Type 16 and *M35* minesweepers)
Established in 1924. Disbanded in summer 1946.
Operational Areas: September 1939, Bay of Danzig; April 1940, Operation Weserübung; 1940–2, North Sea, the Netherlands, France and Bay of Biscay; 1942, Irben Strait and the Baltic Islands; 1942–4, Dutch waters and the North Sea.; 1944–5, the Baltic.
The flotilla received constant reinforcement from the dissolution of other flotillas (**4th, 6th** and **8th**)

2nd *Minensuchflottille* (*M35* minesweepers)
Established in 1936. Disbanded in August 1944.
Operational Areas: September 1939, Bay of Danzig; 1939–40 North Sea; April 1940, Weserübung; 1940–4, the Netherlands, the English Channel and Western France.
Reformed on 1 February 1945 and served until the capitulation. Disbanded in November 1947 after service in the GMSA (*M43* minesweepers).
Operational Area: 1945, the Baltic

3rd *Minensuchflottille* (*M35* minesweepers and *Flakjäger*)
Established in April 1940. Disbanded in summer 1945.
Operational Areas: 1940, Northern Norway; 1942, Finnish waters.

4th *Minensuchflottille* (Type 16 and *M35* minesweepers)
Established in September 1939. Disbanded in March 1945.
Operational Areas: 1939–40, North Sea; April 1940 Operation Weserübung; 1940–1, North Sea and Dutch waters; June 1941 battle of Ösel and Dagö; 1941–2, Biscay; 1942–5, Norwegian west coast.

5th *Minensuchflottille* (*M35* minesweepers)
Established in November 1940. Disbanded in October 1947.
Operational Areas: 1940–1, North Sea and southern Norway; 1941–2, minelaying between Memel and Sweden, Eastern Baltic; February 1942, Operation Cerberus; 1942–5, Norway and North Cape.

6th *Minensuchflottille* (*M35* minesweepers)
Established in September 1939 from Type 16 minesweepers. Disbanded on 27 January 1942.
Operational Area: 1939–42, North Sea.
Reformed on 15 May 1942 in Royan. Disbanded in Concarneau in August 1944 (*M35* and *M40* minesweepers)
Operational Area: 1942–4, Bay of Biscay.

7th *Minensuchflottille* (Type 16 minesweepers)
Established in September 1939. Disbanded in March 1940.
Operational Areas: September 1939, the Baltic; October 1939, Polish waters; 1939–40, North Sea.
Reformed on 21 January 1942. Disbanded in November 1947 (*M35* minesweepers and F-boats).
Operational Areas: 1942, German Bight; 1942–5, waters between the Elbe and Rotterdam, North Sea.

8th *Minensuchflottille* (*M35* and *M40* minesweepers)
Established on 14 March 1941. Disbanded at the capitulation in 1945.
Operational Areas: 1941–4, Bay of Biscay; 1944–5, Saint-Nazaire.
After capitulation served in French minesweeping service with German crews and French officers.

9th *Minensuchflottille* (*M40* minesweepers)
Established on 15 March 1943. Disbanded in June 1947.
Operational Area: 1943–5, northern Norway. Served with GMSA after the capitulation.

10th *Minensuchflottille* (*M40* minesweepers)
Established in Cuxhaven on 15 April 1943. Disbanded in September 1944.
Operational Area: 1942–5, Bay of Biscay.
Crews transferred to Saint-Nazaire infantry as *Marinegrenadierabteilung Josephi*.

11th *Minensuchflottille* (Large German trawlers)
Established on 22 September 1939. Dissolved on 1 August 1942, crews moved to **23rd M-Flotilla**.
Operational Areas: 1939–40, the Baltic; April 1940, Norway; 1940–2, Norwegian west coast.
Reformed in August 1943. Disbanded in February 1945 (*M40* minesweepers).
Operational Area: 1943–5, North Sea.

12th *Minensuchflottille* (Large German trawlers)
Established in September 1939. Disbanded in October 1942 and boats transferred to **46th M-Flotilla**, crews to **24th M-Flotilla**.
Operational Areas: 1939–42, North Sea, Dutch waters and the English Channel.
Reformed in November 1944. Disbanded November 1947 (*M43* minesweepers).
Operational Areas: 1944–5, the Baltic, North Sea.

13th *Minensuchflottille* (Large German trawlers)
Established on 28 September 1939. Disbanded on 31 December 1942 and crews transferred to **27th M-Flotilla**.
Operational Areas: 1939–40, the Baltic; April 1940, Operation Weserübung; 1940–2, North Sea between the Elbe and the Netherlands.

14th *Minensuchflottille* (German Loggers)
Established in September 1939. Disbanded on 31 August 1941.
Operational Areas: 1939–41, North Sea, Dutch coast and Northern France.

15th *Minensuchflottille* (Large German trawlers)
Established on 24 September 1939. Disbanded in March 1943.
Operational Areas: 1939–40, the Baltic; April 1940, Operation Weserübung; 1940–3, Norway.

16th *Minensuchflottille* (Large German trawlers)
Established on 5 October 1939. Disbanded in January 1943 and crews transferred to **26th M-Flotilla**.
Operational Areas: 1939–40, North Sea; 1940–3, the Netherlands, North and West France.

17th *Minensuchflottille* (Large German trawlers)
Established on 22 September 1939. Disbanded on 30 November 1942 and the crew transferred to **25th M-Flotilla**.

Operational Areas: 1939–40, the Baltic; April 1940, Operation Weserübung; 1940–2, North Sea and Norway.

18th *Minensuchflottille* (Large German trawlers)
Established on 26 September 1939. Disbanded on 30 November 1942 and crews transferred to **28th M-Flotilla**.
Operational Areas: 1939, North Sea; 1940, the Netherlands, Belgium, Northern France, the English Channel and Norway.

19th *Minensuchflottille* (Large German trawlers)
Established in September 1939. Disbanded on 8 October 1943 and crews transferred to **29th M-Flotilla**.
Operational Areas: 1939–40, the Baltic and Skagerrak; April 1940, Norway, Kattegat and Skagerrak; 1940–3, Kattegat and Skagerrak.

20th *Minensuchflottille*
Established in Kiel after the capitulation from trawlers of the **20th Vp-Flotilla**, **1st Sich-Flotilla** and **2nd Sich-Flotilla** for minesweeping with the GMSA.

21st *Minensuchflottille* (Type 16 and *M40* minesweepers)
Established on 27 January 1942 from crews of the former **6th M-Flotilla**. Disbanded in April 1945.
Operational Areas: 1942–5, North Sea, Norway, the Baltic.

22nd *Minensuchflottille* (*M40* minesweepers)
Established on 1 September 1941. Disbanded at the end of 1947.
Operational Areas: 1941–5, North Sea, Norway, the Baltic; after the war in Danish waters with the GMSA.

23rd *Minensuchflottille* (*M40* minesweepers)
Established on 1 August 1942 from crews of **11th M-Flotilla**. Disbanded in 1947.
Operational Areas: 1942–5, Norway; 1945, the Baltic; after the war service with the GMSA in Norwegian and Danish waters and Skaggerak.

24th *Minensuchflottille* (*M40* minesweepers)
Established on 1 November 1942 from crews of **12th M-Flotilla**. Disbanded at the capitulation in 1945.
Operational Areas: 1942, the English Channel; 1944, Channel Islands.

25th *Minensuchflottille* (*M40* minesweepers)
Established on 1 December 1942 from crews of **17th M-Flotilla**. Disbanded in November 1947.
Operational Areas: 1942–3, North Sea, Norway; 1944, Gulf of Finland; 1945, the Baltic.

26th *Minensuchflottille* (*M40* minesweepers)
Established on 1 January 1943 from crews of the **17th M-Flotilla**. Disbanded in August 1944.
Operational Area: 1943–4, Bay of Biscay.

27th *Minensuchflottille* (*M40* minesweepers)
Established on 1 January 1943 with crews from **13th M-Flotilla**. Disbanded in 1946.
Operational Areas: 1943–4, the Netherlands and waters between the Elbe and Rotterdam; 1945 North Sea.

28th *Minensuchflottille* (*M40* minesweepers)
Established on 1 December 1942 from crews of **18th M-Flotilla**. Disbanded in August 1944.
Operational Areas: 1942–4, the English Channel, Bay of Biscay.

29th *Minensuchflottille* (*M40* minesweepers)
Established in October 1943 from crews of **19th M-Flotilla**. Disbanded in June 1945.
Operational Areas: 1943–5, Kattegat and Skagerrak.

30th *Minensuchflottille* (*M40* minesweepers)
Established on 15 March 1943. Disbanded at the capitulation in 1945.
Operational Area: 1943–5, Norway.

31st *Minensuchflottille* (Dutch cutters and loggers)
Established in September 1940. Disbanded at the end of 1947.
Operational Areas: 1940–1, the Netherlands; 1941–5, Gulf of Finland.

32nd *Minensuchflottille* (KFKs and R-boats)
Established on 16 June 1940. Disbanded at the capitulation in 1945.
Operational Area: 1940–5, the Netherlands.

34th *Minensuchflottille* (Dutch fishing boats, KFKs)
Established on 13 June 1940 as *Küstenminensuchflottille Holland*. Renamed **34th M-Flotilla** in July 1940. Disbanded at the capitulation in 1945.
Operational Area: 1940–5, the Netherlands.

36th *Minensuchflottille* (Dutch fishing boats, KFKs)
Established in July 1940. Disbanded at the capitulation in 1945.
Operational Areas: 1940–4, the Netherlands; 1945, the Baltic.

38th *Minensuchflottille* (Dutch fishing boats, KFKs)
Established on 4 July 1940. Disbanded at the capitulation in 1945.
Operational Areas: 1940–4, the English Channel, the Netherlands and Belgium; 1944–5, Kattegat.

40th *Minensuchflottille* (French trawlers, loggers and cutters)
Established on 1 July 1940. Disbanded in September 1944.
Operational Area: 1940–4, Bay of Biscay (Brest).

42nd *Minensuchflottille* (French fishing boats)
Established in July 1940. Disbanded on 15 September 1944.
Operational Area: 1940–4, Bay of Biscay (Les Sables d´Olonne)

44th *Minensuchflottille* (French trawlers and loggers)
Established in November 1940. Disbanded in September 1944
Operational Area: 1940–44, Bay of Biscay (Blaye)

46th *Minensuchflottille* (French trawlers and fishing boats)
Established on 8 December 1941. Disbanded in May 1945
Operational Area: 1942–5, Bay of Biscay (3rd *Sicherungsdivision*)

52nd *Minensuchflottille* (Small Norwegian fishing boats)
Established in December 1940. Disbanded on 30 September 1944.
Operational Area: 1941–5, Norwegian (Bergen).

54th *Minensuchflottille* (Small Norwegian fishing boats)
Established in December 1940. Disbanded in 1944.
Operational Area: 1940–4, Norway (Bergen).

56th *Minensuchflottille* (Norwegian fishing boats and whalers)
Established in June 1940. Disbanded at the capitulation in 1945.
Operational Area: 1940–5, Norway (Trondheim).
70th *Minensuchflottille* (Italian vessels)
Established in July 1943. Redesignated **13th** *Sicherungsflottille* in October 1944.
Operational Areas: 1943–4, West Italian coast and the Riviera.

MOTOR MINESWEEPERS

1st *Räumbootsflottille*
Established in the Baltic 1937. Disbanded at the end of 1947.
Operational Areas: September 1939, Bay of Danzig; 1939–40, the Baltic and North Sea; April 1940, Operation Weserübung; 1940–1, the Netherlands, the English Channel; 1942–4, Gulf of Finland; 1945, the Baltic.
2nd *Räumbootsflottille*
Established in the North Sea, autumn 1938. Disbanded in August 1944
Operational Areas: 1939–40, North Sea; April 1940, Operation Weserübung; 1940–4, The Netherlands, the English Channel (Dunkirk).
3rd *Räumbootsflottille*
Established in spring 1939 in North Sea. Disbanded in August 1944.
Operational Areas: 1939, Bay of Danzig; 1939–40, North Sea; 1940–1, the Netherlands, Northern France; 1941, transport to Black Sea; 1942–4, Black Sea.
4th *Räumbootsflottille*
Established in 1 April 1940. Disbanded in summer 1945.
Operational Areas: 1940, North Sea; 1940-4, the Netherlands, Belgium, the English Channel; 1944–5, Skagerrak, Southern Norway.
5th *Räumbootsflottille*
Established in August 1939. Disbanded at the end of 1945.
Operational Areas: 1939–40, the Baltic; 1940–1, Northern Norway; 1941, Gulf of Finland; 1941–5, Northern Norway.
6th *Räumbootsflottille*
Established on 28 July 1941 from small R-boats of **5th R-Flotilla**. Disbanded in April 1945.
Operational Areas: 1941–5, Mediterranean, Tyrrhenian Sea, Ligurian Sea, Adriatic Sea.
7th *Räumbootsflottille*
Established 15 October 1940 in the Netherlands from crews of **11th R-Flotilla**. Disbanded on 28 November 1946.
Operational Areas: 1940, The Netherlands, Belgium; 1941–5, Northern Norway.
11th *Räumbootsflottille*
Established on 4 September 1939. Disbanded in October 1940
Equipped with Finkenwerder Fishing boats as 'Auxilliary R-boats'
(*Hilfsräumboote*). Boats passed to *Hafenschutzflottillen*. Crews to **7th R-Flotilla**.
Operational Areas: 1939–40, the Baltic, Denmark, the Netherlands, Belgium.
Reformed in September 1942. Disbanded on 23 September 1944 with boats transferred to **13th** *Sicherungsflottille* and **22nd** *U-Jagdflottille*.
Operational Areas: Southern France, Western Italy, Corsica, Sardinia.

329

12th *Räumbootsflottille*
Established on 1 May 1942 in Brugge. Disbanded in February 1945.
Operational Areas: 1942–3, sea area between Boulogne and Wimereux; spring 1943, transferred via French canals and rivers to Marseille; 1943–5, Adriatic Sea, Ionian Sea, Aegean Sea.

13th *Räumbootsflottille*
Established on 15 November 1943. Served in GMSA after the capitulation, transferred to Bundesmarine in 1957.
Operational Areas: 1943–5, North Sea, German Bight.

14th *Räumbootsflottille*
Established in December 1943. Disbanded in summer 1946.
Operational Areas: 1943–4, the English Channel; 1944–5, German Bight; 1945, the Baltic, Denmark.

15th *Räumbootsflottille*
Established on 1 July 1944. Disbanded at the capitulation in 1945.
Operational Areas: 1944–5, the Baltic, Gulf of Finland.

16th *Räumbootsflottille*
Established in October 1944. Disbanded on 25 November 1947.
Operational Area: 1944–5, Norway.

17th *Räumbootsflottille*
Established in July 1944. Used as training boats. Disbanded in 1947.
Operational Areas: 1944–5, Eastern and Central Baltic.

21st *Räumbootsflottille*
Established in July 1943. Disbanded in 1946.
Operational Area: 1943–5, Norway (Bergen)

25th *Räumbootsflottille*
Established in summer 1945. Disbanded in 1946. Not operational during the war.

30th *Räumbootsflottille*.
Established in June 1943. Disbanded in August 1944.
Operational Area: 1943–4, Black Sea.

SUBMARINE HUNTERS

1st *U-Bootsjagdflottille*
Established in June 1943. Disbanded in August 1944.
Operational Area: 1943–4, Black Sea.
Reformed in Swinemünde on 30 October 1944. Boats transferred to **6th** *Sicherungsflottille* and Stettin Police on 16 December 1944.
Operational Area: 1944, the Baltic (Swinemünde)

2nd *U-Bootsjagdflottille*
Established in March 1944. Disbanded on 7 December 1944. Surviving boats passed to **2nd** *Geleitflottille*.
Operational Area: 1944, Adriatic Sea.

3rd *U-Bootsjagdflottille*
Established in spring 1944. Disbanded in August 1944.

Operational Area: 1944, Black Sea.

Reformed in Swinemünde on 30 October 1944. Disbanded in summer 1945.

Operational Areas: October 1944–January 1945, the Baltic (Pillau); 1945, the Baltic (Gotenhafen, Hela).

11th *U-Bootsjagdflottille*

Established in September 1939 in Flensburg. Disbanded in June 1945.

Operational Areas: 1939–41, the Baltic; 1941–5, Kattegatt, Skaggerak, North Sea, Norway

12th *U-Bootsjagdflottille*

Established in September 1939 in Wilhelmshaven. Disbanded in May 1945.

Operational Areas: 1939–41, North Sea, Kattegat; 1942–3, Norway, Northern Norway; 1944–5, Gulf of Finland, Baltic Sea.

13th *U-Bootsjagdgruppe*

Established in September 1939 with ten trawlers. Transferred to **14th** *U-Bootsjagdflottille* in 1940. Operational Area: 1939–40, Baltic Sea.

14th *U-Bootsjagdflottille*

Formed in May 1940 from **13th** *U-Bootsjagdgruppe*. Disbanded at the capitulation in 1945.

Operational Areas: 1940–1, Norway (Stavanger); 1942–4, Bay of Biscay; 1944–5, Lorient.

17th *U-Bootsjagdflottille*

Established on 28 July 1939 in Kiel. Disbanded at the capitulation in 1945.

Operational Areas: 1939–40, the Baltic; 1941–5, Norway (Stavanger).

21st *U-Bootsjagdflottille*

Established in December 1941 in Piräus. After loss of all boats disbanded in October 1944.

Operational Areas: 1941–4, Aegean Sea, Mediterranean Sea.

22nd *U-Bootsjagdflottille*

Established in December 1942 in Marseilles. Disbanded on 27 April 1945.

Operational Areas: 1942–5, Western Mediterranean, Ligurian Sea.

23rd *U-Bootsjagdflottille*

Established in May 1944 in Constanţa. Disbanded in June 1944.

Operational Area: 1944, Western Black Sea.

ESCORTS

Geleitfottille

Estabished 1938 by the amalgamation of original **1st** and **2nd** *Geleitflottille* comprised of the unsatisfactory *Geleitboote*. Disbanded March 1940

Operational Area: North Sea.

1st *Geleitflottille*

Established in Trieste in March 1944 from captured Italian torpedo boats. Disbanded on 28 February 1945 and vessels transferred to 9th *Torpedobootsflottille*.

Operational Area: Adriatic Sea.

2nd *Geleitflottille*

Established March 1944 in Fiume from captured Italian torpedo boats, coastal steamers, motor ships and auxiliaries. Disbanded at the capitulation in 1945.
Operational Area: Adriatic Sea.
3rd *Geleitflottille*
Established in March 1943 from captured Vichy torpedo boats. Disbanded July 1944.
Operational Areas: North Africa, Italy, Sicily.
Reformed from *Hafenschutzflottille Venice* in December 1944. Disbanded at the capitulation in 1945.
Operational Area: Adriatic Sea
4th *Geleitflottille*
Established in March 1943 at La Spezia. Disbanded in August 1943.
Operational Areas: Italy, Sicily.
Reformed in April 1945. Disbanded in May 1945.
Operational Area: the Baltic.
5th *Geleitflottille*
Established in April 1945. Disbanded at the capitulation in 1945.
Operational Area: the Baltic.
30th *Geleitflottille*
Established in July 1943 from elements of the **Donauflottille**. Disbanded in June 1944.
Operational Area: Black Sea
31st *Geleitflottille*
Established in September 1942 from various artillery carriers. Disbanded in May 1944.
Operational Area: Black Sea

SECURITY FLOTILLAS

Subordinate to *Sicherungsdivision*, primary responsibilities local convoy escort, mine clearance and guarding harbours and net barrages. Not to be confused with *Hafenschutzflottillen* which were controlled by regional *Seekommandant* (Coastal Sector Command).
1st *Sicherungsflottille*
Foremd on 1 October 1943 from *Küstenschutzflottille westliche Ostsee*. Served until the capitulation and formed a flotilla of the **1st** *Minenräumdivision* of the GMSA after the war.
Operational Area: Western Baltic (Warnemünde).
2nd *Sicherungsflottille*
Established on 1 October 1943 from *Küstenschutzflottille mittlere Ostsee*. Disbanded in May 1945.
Operational Areas: Pomeranian coast, Rügen Island (Stettin).
3rd *Sicherungsflottille*
Established on 1 October 1943 from *Küstenschutzflottille Preußenküste*. Disbanded in May 1945.
Operational Area: Bay of Danzig (Gotenhafen).

4th *Sicherungsflottille*
Established on 1 October 1943 from *Küstenschutzflottille Kleiner Belt*.
Disbanded in July 1945.
Operational Area: Little Belt (Fredericia).
5th *Sicherungsflottille*
Established on 1 October 1943 in Denmark from **19th** *Vorpostenflottille*.
Disbanded in June 1945.
Operational Area: Great Belt (Korsör).
6th *Sicherungsflottille*
Established on 16 December 1942 from *Hafenschutzflottille Süd*. Redesignated
Rhone-Flotilla after invasion of Southern France, August 1944.
Operational Areas: French Mediterranean, Rhône River.
Reformed on 16 December 1944 from flotilla staff of **1st** *U-Jagdflottille*.
Disbanded in summer 1945.
Operational Area: 1944–5, central Baltic (Swinemünde).
7th *Sicherungsflottille*
Planned for Mediterranean. Expanded to **7th** *Sicherungsdivision*.
8th *Sicherungsflottille*
Established on 1 October 1943 from *Hafenschutzflottille Kopenhagen*.
Disbanded in May 1945.
Operational Area: The Sound (Copenhagen).
9th *Sicherungsflottille*
Established on 1 October 1943 from **9th** *Vorpostenflottille*. In August 1945
became **39th** *Minensuchflottille* with GMSA.
Operational Area: Kattegat (Aalborg).
10th *Sicherungsflottille*
Established on 1 October 1943 from **10th** *Vorpostenflottille*. Disbanded in June
1945.
Operational Areas: Kattegatt, Great Belt, The Sound.
11th *Sicherungsflottille*
Established in May 1943 in Trieste from **11th** *Kustenschhutzflottille*. Evolved
into **11th** *Sicherungsdivision* on 1 May 1944.
Operational Area: Adriatic Sea.
12th *Sicherungsflottille*
Established on 1 October 1943 from Danish *Hafenschutzflottillen*. Disbanded in
June 1945.
Operational Area: The Great Belt.
13th *Sicherungsflottille*
Established in February 1944. Disbanded in May 1945.
Operational Areas: Mediterranean, Ligurian Sea.
14th *Sicherungsflottille*
Established on 10 July 1944 from *Küstenschutzflottille Reval*. Disbanded in
1945.
Operational Area: Eastern Baltic Sea (Tallinn).
15th *Sicherungsflottille*
Established in August 1944. Disbanded in June 1945.

Operational Areas: Western Baltic Sea, Skagerrak (Thyborön, Esbjerg).
16th *Sicherungsflottille*
Established in September 1944 from *Hafenschutzflottille Esbjerg*. Disbanded in
May 1945.
Operational Areas: Western Baltic Sea, Skagerrak (Esbjerg).

ARTILLERY CARRIERS

1st *Artillerieträgerflottille*
Established on 25 April 1943 in Wesermünde.
Operational Area: North Sea
2nd *Artillerieträgerflottille*
Established in September 1942. Disbanded at the capitulation in 1945.
Operational Areas: 1942–4, the English Channel; 1944 *5th Artillerieträger-flottille*, German Bight.
3rd *Artillerieträgerflottille*
Established in February 1943 from **3rd** *Marineartillerieleichterflottille*.
Originally designated *Artillerieträgerflottille Asowsches Meer*. Disbanded in
September 1943.
Operational Area: Sea of Azov.
Reformed in February 1944. Disbanded in September 1944.
Operational Area: Black Sea.
Reformed on 1 January 1945 from **21st** *Landungsflottille*. Disbanded at the
capitulation in 1945.
Operational Area: Baltic Sea.
4th *Artillerieträgerflottille*.
Established in January 1944. Disbanded in September 1944 after vessels scuttled.
Operational Area: Lake Peipsi.
5th *Artillerieträgerflottille*.
Established in February 1944. Disbanded in February 1945.
Operational Areas: North Sea, Skagerrak, the Baltic.
6th *Artillerieträgerflottille*
Established in February 1944 in Rotterdam. Disbanded on 30 August 1944.
Operational Areas: the English Channel, the Netherlands.
7th *Artillerieträgerflottille*.
Established in August 1944. Disbanded at the capitulation in 1945.
Operational Area: Eastern Baltic.
8th *Artillerieträgerflottille*
Established in April 1944 in Rotterdam. Disbanded at the capitulation in 1945.
Operational Areas: 1944, the English Channel; 1945, the Baltic.

ANTI-AIRCRAFT

2nd *Flakjägerflottille*
Established in July 1940. Disbanded on 25 April 1943 and vessels transferred to
3rd Vp-Flotilla, 11th Vp-Flotilla, 1st Sp-Flotilla, 3rd M-Flotilla.
Operational Area: North Sea.

LANDING CRAFT

1st *Landungsflottille*
Established in Varna on 26 February 1942. Disbanded in August 1944.
Operational Areas: Black Sea, Sea of Azov.

2nd *Landungsflottille*
Established in October 1941. Disbanded in February 1944 and vessels passed to
4th L-Flotilla.
Operational Areas: North Africa, south-west Italy.

3rd *Landungsflottille*
Establish in October 1942 in Berdyans'k. Disbanded in August 1944.
Operational Areas: Sea of Azov, Black Sea.

4th *Landungsflottille*
Established in May 1943 in Toulon. Disbanded at the capitulation in 1945.
Operational Area: Tyrrheanian Sea.

5th *Landungsflottille*
Established in April 1943 in Kerch. Disbanded in November 1943 and vessels
transferred to **3rd** and **7th L-Flotillas**.
Operational Areas: Sea of Azov, Black Sea.
Reformed in Kirkenes in July 1944. Disbanded in April 1945.
Operayional Area: Norwegian Polar Coast.

6th *Landungsflottille*
Established in June 1943 in Toulon. Transferred to the Aegean and renamed **15th**
L-Flotilla in July 1943.
Operational Areas: French South Coast, Ligurian Sea, Tyrrhenian Sea.
Reformed in June 1944 in Hammerfest. Disbanded at the capitulation in 1945.
Operational Area: Northern Norway.

7th *Landungsflottille*
Established in July 1943 in Varna. Disbanded in September 1944.
Operational Area: Black Sea.

8th *Landungsflottille*
Established in January 1942. Disbanded in November 1942.
Reformed in September 1944 in Tromsø. Disbanded at the capitulation in 1945.
Operational Areas: Northern Norway, Polar coast.

9th *Landungsflottille*
Established in Narvik in June 1944. Disbanded in March 1946.
Operational Area: Norwegian Polar coast.

10th *Landungsflottille*
Established in May 1943 in Trieste. Disbanded at the capitulation in 1945.
Operational Areas: 1943, retreat from Sicily, Sardinia, Corsica; 1943–5, Adriatic
Sea.

11th *Landungsflottille*
Established in Rotterdam in January 1943. Disbanded at the capitulation in 1945.
Operational Areas: North Sea, the Baltic.

12th *Landungsflottille*
Established on 1 December 1942. Disbanded in February 1945, craft transferred
to **3rd** *Sicherungs-Schullflotilla* (Security School Flotilla).

Operational Area: the Baltic

13th *Landungsflottille*

Established in December 1941 from *Erprobungsverband Ostsee* (Baltic Testing Unit) Disbanded at the capitulation in 1945.

Operational Area: the Baltic

15th *Landungsflottille*

Established from 6th **L-Flotilla** in July 1943. Disbanded in November 1944.

Operational Area: Aegean Sea.

17th *Landungsflottille*

Established in December 1941 from *Erprobungsverband Ostsee* (Riga). Disbanded in March 1942 and vessels transferred to **21st** and **27th L-Flotillas**.

Operational Area: the Baltic.

18th *Landungsflottille*

Established on 15 January 1942. Disbanded in April 1943.

Operational Area: the English Channel.

21st *Landungsflottille*

Established in 1 April 1942 from **17th L-Flotilla**. Redesignated **3rd AT-Flotilla** on 1 January 1945.

Operational Area: Eastern Baltic Sea.

22nd *Landungsflottille*

Established on 20 September 1942 in Swinemünde. Disbanded in February 1943.

Operational Area: Norway.

23rd *Landungsflottille*

Established on 1 October 1942 in Swinemünde. Disbanded in April 1943.

Operational Area: Norway.

24th *Landungsflottille*

Established on 15 February 1943 from **27th L-Flotilla**. Disbanded at the capitulation in 1945.

Operational Area: the Baltic.

27th Landungsflottille

Established from 17th L-Flotilla in April 1942 in Gulf of Finland. Disbanded on 15 February 1943 and vessels transferred to **24th L-Flotilla**.

Operational Area: Gulf of Finland.

RIVER PROTECTION

Donauflottille

Established in Linz in 1938. Divided in half in July 1943, one half for service in the Black Sea region (becoming the **30th** *Geleitflottille*), the remainder within the Danube. On 1 January, 1945, the *Donauflottille* was divided once again into the 1st and 2nd *Donauflottille*. Disbanded at the end of the war.

Operational Area: The Danube, Black Sea.

Space prevents all Security Flotillas and all of their craft to be listed here. For further flotilla structures and ship attachments go to:

www.lawrencepaterson.com

Notes

1 Annual Report of Minesweeping, 1 November 1936 — 31 October 1937 ADM1/9566.
2 'The Lohmann Affair', Central Intelligence Agency. https://www.cia.gov/library/center-for-the-study-of-intelligence/kent-csi/vol4no2/html/v04i2a08p_0001.htm
3 Gerhard Both, *Without Hindsight*, pp85–7.
4 Alongside his German military awards – which culminated in a posthumous Knight's Cross – Weniger was the recipient of two foreign medals during his Kriegsmarine service; the Bulgarian Military Merit Cross awarded in 1936 and the Danish Order of Danebrog, Knight, dated 26 July 1939. Weniger would later die aboard an R-boat near Dieppe on 1 October 1941 as Chief of the 2nd *Sicherungsdivision*.
5 Erich Raeder, *Grand Admiral*, p203.
6 Deschimag comprised: Aktiengesellschaft 'Weser' (A.G.Weser), Bremen; Vulkan-Werke Hamburg A.G. (sold to Howaldtswerke Kiel in 1930); Joh. C. Tecklenborg A.G., Wesermünde (closed in 1928); AG Vulcan Stettin (closed in 1928); G. Seebeck A.G., Geestemünde; Actien-Gesellschaft 'Neptun', Rostock (rendered bankrupt in 1935); Nüscke & Co. A.G., Stettin (bankrupted in 1928); and Fredrichswerft A.G., Einswarden (stopped shipbuilding in 1935 and moved into aircraft production).
7 The International Treaty for the Limitation and Reduction of Naval Armament, commonly known as the London Naval Treaty, was made between the United Kingdom, the Empire of Japan, France, Italy and the United States and signed on 22 April 1930. Within its terms it sought to regulate submarine warfare and limit naval shipbuilding.
Article 8 of the treaty stipulated that:
'Subject to any special agreements which may submit them to limitation, the following vessels are exempt from limitation:
  (a) Naval surface combatant vessels of 600 tons (610 metric tons) standard displacement and under . . .'
8 2nd M-Flotilla and 2nd R-Flotilla were based in Cuxhaven; *Geleitflottille* and 1st R-Flotilla in Kiel; 1st M-Flotilla and 3rd R-Flotilla in Pillau.
9 This declaration of non-belligerance violated the terms of the pact, although so had Hitler by his unilateral decision to go to war. However, Italian reluctance provoked some ire in Germany and would lay a foundation of suspicion and resentment that would forever hamper military co-operation between the two nations.
10 SKL KTB 1 October 1939.
11 *Oxhöft* was later used by the Kriegsmarine as a hydrographical survey ship.
12 *Heisternest* underwent conversion to Kriegsmarine specifications before being used as a minesweeping research ship based in Kiel. Later, under the command of LzS Friedrich Fischer, the ship sailed to Nantes for Atlantic tests, where she was hit by USAAF B17

bombing on 16 September 1943 and declared a constructive total loss. All the remaining ships survived the war, although when *Rixhöft* was renamed *TF48*, the former Polish auxiliary *Smok* which had also entered German service was renamed *Rixhöft* and was sunk on 2 March 1945 near Warnemünde.

13 http://www.cassiodor.com/Artikel/4873.aspx

14 *New York Times*, 6 November 1939.

15 HMS *Sturgeon* War Diary, ADM 199/1837.

16 SKL KTB 22 November 1939.

17 The wreck was later salvaged and repaired during 1940.

18 *Leipzig* had been so badly damaged by HMS *Salmon* that after repairs she only ever served as a training ship. Philips was awarded the DSO and promoted for his claimed sinking of the cruiser and skilful attack and evasion.

19 Röhrig was transferred to the *Scharnhorst* as Second Gunnery Officer after repatriation. He was relieved of this post and promoted to KKdRes shortly before the ship's sinking, transferred to *Schiffsartillerieschule* III (S.A.S.III) in Saßnitz-Dwarsieden which he later commanded between 11 February 1944 and May 1945.

20 Extract from LtComm Jackson's report on the sinking of his submarine, filed with the Admiralty on 25 June 1945 after his release from a prisoner of war camp.

21 Grau transferred the U-boat service in January 1941. Petzel transferred first to command the 6th M-Flotilla before the Donau Flotilla in July 1941. He was killed in action on 9 November 1941.

22 SKL War Diary 7 January 1940.

23 In July 1940, the diving vessel *Oldenburg*, assisted by vessels of the 17th UJ-Flotilla, attempted to locate the wreck to recover secret documents but with little success. Timm was awarded the Iron Cross 2nd Class. He later transferred to the U-boat service.

24 SKL KTB 9 January 1940.

25 That same night an He111 was shot down at about 0032hrs when approaching the island of Borkum from the west having been mistaken as British by Kriegsmarine flak gunners.

26 Report to MGK West by Bartels: 'Secret report on the sinking of four Danish fishing cutters'; http://www.wlb-stuttgart.de/seekrieg/miszellen/40-02-24.htm

27 Winston Churchill *The Second World War*, Vol. 1, p449.

28 The ship was originally named *Posidonia* until rechristened by the Kriegsmarine in February when she was taken into the military. The wreck still bears the original name on the stern. It is not clear whether the tanker was sailing as part of the *Weserübung See* transport waves or whether it was an additional sailing.

29 SKL KTB 8 April 1940.

30 The *Olav Tryggvason* was taken into the Kriegsmarine and renamed *Albatros II* on 11 April, to commemorate the torpedo boat she had damaged. Five days later, on 16 April, she was renamed again, as the *Brummer*, after an artillery training ship torpedoed in the Kattegat 14 April 1940. *Rauma* was repaired and recommissioned as *Kamerun* on 18 April 1940. *Kamerun* first served as a *Vorpostenboot* in the *Hafenschutzflotille* Oslo, later being converted into a minelayer. *Kamerun* spent her entire war in Norway and was part of the German Minesweeping Administration (GMSA) after the German surrender in 1945. *Albatros* had suffered under fire from the 5.9in guns of the Bolaerne battery; while escaping ten rounds from 8750 yards the torpedo boat ran hard aground in fog at 1318hrs southeast of Bolaerne Island and was a total loss.

31 SKL KTB 23 April 1940.

32 SKL KTB 15 April 1940.

33 On 27 April the 8500-ton German merchant ship *Liege* was sunk by one of the mines;

the 4601-ton steamer *Johann Wessels* was damaged by another on 5 May 1940. Three days later, on 8 May 1940, the 1151-ton steamer *Gerda* also hit a mine and sank bringing the total claimed by *Tyr*'s minefield to three supply ships, two *Vorpostenboote* and a launch.

34 Feldt would later transfer to the S-boat service. *Schiff 221* was later taken into the Bergen Hafenschutzflottille as *NB01 'Ratte'* before being redesignated *V5501 'Ratte'* and joining the 55th Vp-Flotilla. *Tyr* was pressed into German service laying defensive minefields in April.

35 Italy had declared herself a 'non-belligerent' upon the outbreak of war in 1939, Mussollini recognising that his country was unprepared for full-scale war. Despite German disappointment, he remained uncommitted until immediately before the collapse of France, forced to declare war in order to attain territorial demands already planned.

36 HMS *Express* and *Esk* were sunk by German mines while on a minelaying mission north of Texel on 31 August 1940.

37 *NSI* became *Sperrbrecher 141*, *NSII Sperrbrecher 142*, etc. in numerical order until *NSIX* as *Sperrbrecher 149*.

38 HMS *Narwhal* laid another successful minefield — FD19 — on 12 June west of the Norwegian coast which would sink a Norwegian steamer and fishing boat as well as the 173-ton *NB15* (ex *Oyulf*) on 16 August and on 13 October three 50-ton ex-Norwegian fishing vessels that had been commissioned into the Kriegsmarine as minesweepers for the 52nd M-Flotilla: *M5207 'Gnom'*, *Kobold 1* and *Kobold 3*.

39 Ulrich Mohr, *Atlantis – The Story of a German Surface Raider*, Werner Laurie, London, 1955, p93.

40 SKL KTB 8 May 1940.

41 BETASOM was the Italian acronym for Bordeaux Submarines: 'B' (Beta) for Bordeaux and 'SOM' an abbreviation of *Sommergibile* (submarine).

42 Bartels' apparent ability to think outside of the norm was not to be wasted and would later lead to him being assigned command of the fledgling *Kleinkampverbände* and its myriad midget weapons.

43 On 7 April 2000, this Victoria Cross was presented in perpetuity to Campbell's elder brother, the stipulation being made that it was to be regarded as an award for the entire crew.

44 *Coastal Command; The Air Ministry Account of the Part Played by Coastal Command in the Battle of the Sea, 1939-1942*, HMSO, London, 1943, p138.

45 Mallmann Showell, *Führer Conferences on Naval Affairs*, 29 June 1943, p337.

46 SKL KTB 10 February 1942.

47 Mallmann Showell, *Führer Conferences on Naval Affairs*, 22 May 1941, p199.

48 SKL KTB 10 June 1942.

49 Admiral Black Sea KTB 8 June 1942. KK Fritz Petzel, a veteran of the Spanish Civil War, had been killed in action on 9 November 1941.

50 615 Sqn Operations Record Book.

51 Mallmann Showell, *Führer Conferences on Naval Affairs*, 13 November 1941, pp2401.

52 Rossow and Reischauer swapped command as Rossow relieved him as senior officer of the 3rd R-Flotilla. He was killed in action on 1 October 1941 in the air attack off Dieppe that killed Weniger.

53 *F154* would later be used for landing operations in the attack against Tobruk, stranded in a storm east of Ras el Aali while fully loaded and wrecked, though the cargo was salvaged.

54 SKL KTB 20 June 1942.

55 *The Conduct Of The War At Sea; An Essay by Karl Dönitz*, Division of Naval Intelligence, 15 January 1946, p22.

56 https://www.the-saleroom.com/en-gb/auction-catalogues/dixnoonanwebb/catalogue-id-dix-no10020/lot-11b6c4a3-7f50-43bd-a5a6-a5fb00b57f43

57 3rd, 5th, 7th, 13th, 17th, 18th and 21st M-Flotilla, 5th R-Flotilla, 1st Sp-Flotilla, 8th, 11th, 12th and 17th Vp-Flotillas, 2nd *Flakjäger* Flotilla and 12th UJ-Flotilla.

58 Somewhat ironically, on 12 December 1943 *U593* sank HMS *Tynedale* with a torpedo in the Mediterranean, the U-boat then being sunk by a retaliatory 'Swamp' operation that lasted until the following day.

59 Braeuer, *Fortresse Saint Nazaire*, p170.

60 SKL KTB 28 March 1942.

61 Admiralty Interrogation Report.

62 Brereton Greenhous, 'Operation Flodden: The Sea Fight off Berneval and the Suppression of the Goebbels Battery, 19 August 1942', *Canadian Military Journal*, Autumn 2003.

63 SKL KTB 19 August 1942.

64 *Komet* herself would not survive the English Channel. She was attacked by a strong force of destroyers and MTBs while under torpedo boat escort on 13 October. In a confusing action that saw her open fire on her own escorts, the raider was sunk by torpedo with the loss of her entire crew.

65 The *Küstenschutzflottille Ostland* would later become 14th *Sicherungsflottille* on 15 July 1944.

66 Ruge, *The Soviets As Naval Opponents 1941-1945*, pp30–1.

67 USS Blackfish Patrol Report. NARA Catalog ID:4697018. World War II War Diaries, Other Operational Records and Histories, compiled ca. 01/01/1942 - ca. 06/01/1946, documenting the period ca. 09/01/1939 - ca. 05/30/1946. Record Group:38.

68 *V722* rejoined her flotilla later in the year after repairs. At 0115hrs on the morning of 6 May 1944 she detonated an aerial mine laid by RAF bombers near the mouth of Anse de Berthaume and went down with 27 of her 36-man crew.

69 SKL KTB 29 August 1943

70 There is debate about how much the increase in armament output was down to Speer and how much was already underway that he eventually took credit for. But that is beyond the scope of this book.

71 Admiral Black Sea KTB 14 October 1942.

72 Admiral Black Sea KTB 31 October 1942.

73 Admiral Black Sea KTB 27 April 1943.

74 Admiral Black Sea KTB 23 May 1943.

75 Admiral Black Sea KTB, 28 June 1943.

76 Becker, *Swastika at Sea*, pp117–18.

77 SKL KTB 21 June 1942.

78 SKL KTB 4 July 1942.

79 SKL KTB 22 July 1942.

80 Dönitz, *Ten Years and Twenty Days*, p360.

81 SKL KTB 6 March 1943.

82 SKL KTB 1 May 1943.

83 ADM 199/1841.

84 SKL KTB 19 September 1943.

85 The flotilla had also lost its commander Fritz Grossmann, severely wounded during

April and hospitalised until June. His place had been taken by KK Friedrich Wunderlich.

86 On 19 September, between 1584 and 1835 Italian naval and air force prisoners – considered to be more belligerent than their army counterparts – were herded onto the captured Italian MV *Donizetti* bound for mainland Greece. During the voyage the ship was intercepted and sunk by HMS *Eclipse* with no survivors.

87 The destroyers *Turbine*, *Castelfidardo* and *Solferino* were also seized that day in Piraeus, later recommissioned as *TA14*, *TA16* and *T18* respectively.

88 SKL KTB 18 September 1943.

89 Report from MGK Süd.

90 SKL KTB 25 September 1943.

91 SKL KTB 30 September 1943.

92 ADM 199/1824

93 After the recapture of Astypalaia, weapons aboard the burnt-out MFP were salvaged for further use.

94 SKL KTB 7 October 1943.

95 SKL KTB 21 October 1943.

96 Between September and the end of 1943, a total of 3804 mines had been laid in the area, covering an area of 315 miles.

97 SKL KTB 15 January 1944.

98 Cyrus was killed in action on 10 September 1944.

99 SKL KTB January 1944.

100 Letter from Heinrich Ziemsen to Mr Mallinson, former officer of the British 540 Coast Regiment, dated 10 September 1954;
http://sussexhistoryforum.co.uk/index.php?topic=590.0

101 SKL KTB 6 June 1944.

102 Field Report written by Lieut.Col. Commanding 7 (L.I.) Bn The Paratp Regt, R.G. Pine-Coffin, 29 June 44: *Appendix I Action Fought at Ranville and Benouville brs on night 5/6 June and day 6 June 1944*. National Archives catalogue number WO 171/1239.

103 *Radio Call Gkdos 18897 from Chief of Staff 15th Patrol Boat Flotilla. Short AAR concerning sea and air combat during enemy landing 6 June 1944*. KTB 2nd *Sicherungsdivision*, 6 June 1944.

104 Braeuer, *Fortresse Saint Nazaire*, p150.

105 Ibid., pp151–2

106 Karl-Hans Friedrich, in Hoza, *PW: First Person Accounts of German Prisoners of War in Arizona*, p35.

107 Braeuer, *Fortresse Saint Nazaire*, p143.

108 SKL KTB 28 June 1944.

109 Huffmeier informed the Kriegsmarine personnel under his command of the death of Breithaupt 'who the enemy never managed to touch in all his time at sea' and flags were flown at half mast on 5 January.

Bibliography

Barnett, Correlli, *Engage The Enemy More Closely*, Hodder & Stoughton, London, 1992.

Bekker, C. D., *Swastika At Sea*, William Kimber, London 1953.

Bohn, Roland and Le Berre, Alain, *Chronique D'Hier, Tome II*, Self-published, 1994.

Both, Gerhard, *Without Hindsight*, Janus Publishing Company, London, 1999.

Bräckow, Werner, *Die Geschichte des deutschen Marine-Ingenieur-offizierkorps*, Stalling Verlag, Hamburg, 1974.

Brandt, Karl and Schiller, Otto, *Management of Agriculture and Food in the German-occupied and Other Areas of Fortress Europe*, Stanford University Press, 1953.

Braeuer, Luc, *Fortresse Saint-Nazaire*, SPEI-Pulnoy, 2002.

Churchill, Winston, *The Second World War*, six volumes, Cassell & Co, London, 1954.

Cruickshank, Charles, *The German Occupation of the Channel Islands*, Guernsey Press Company, 1975.

Dönitz, Karl, '*Ten Years and Twenty Days*', George Weidenfeld and Nicolson Ltd, London, 1959.

Escuadra, Alfonso, *Bajo las banderas de la Kriegsmarine. Marinos de españoles en la Armada Alemana (1942-43)*, Editorial Fundación Don Rodrigo, Spain, 1998.

Leroux, Roger, *Le Morbihan en Guerre*, Joseph Floc, Mayenne, 1978.

Grier, David, *Hitler, Donitz, and the Baltic Sea: The Third Reich's Last Hope, 1944-1945*, Naval Institute Press, Annapolis, 2013.

Guard, J.S., *Improvise and Dare*, The Book Guild, Lewes, 1997.

Haarr, Geirr, *The Battle for Norway: April–June 1940*, Seaforth Publishing, Barnsley, 2010.

_____, *The Gathering Storm: The Naval War in Northern Europe*, Seaforth Publishing, Barnsley, 2012.

Hoza, Steve, *PW: First Person Accounts of German Prisoners of War in Arizona*, E6B Publications, Phoenix, Arizona, 1995.

Isby, David, *The Luftwaffe And The War At Sea 1939-1945*, Chatham Publishing, London, 2005.

Johnson, Brian, *The Secret War*, British Broadcasting Corporation, London, 1978.

Kent, Captain Barrie, *Signal: A History of Signalling in the Royal Navy*, Permanent Publications, 2004.

Lohmann, W. and Hildebrand H. H., *Die Deutsche Kriegsmarine 1939 – 1945* (three volumes), Podzun Verlag, Bad Nauheim, 1956.

Kurowski, Franz, *Kampffeld Mittelmeer*, Ullstein, Berlin, 1984.

Mallmann Showell, Jak P., *Führer Conferences on Naval Affairs*, Chatham Publishing, London, 2005.

Mann, Christopher and Jörgensen, Christer, *Hitler's Arctic War*, Brown Partworks, London, 2002.

Meister, Jürg, *Der Seekrieg in den osteuropäischen Gewässern, 1941-45*, J.F. Lehmanns Verlag, München, 1958.

Müller, Wolfgang and Kramer, Reinhard, *Gesunken und Verschollen*, Koehlers Verlag, Herford, 1994.

Nesbit, Roy Conyers, *The Strike Wings*, William Kimber, London 1984.

Polmar, Norman and Noot, Jurrien, *Submarines of the Russian and Soviet Navies, 1718-1990*, Naval Institute Press, Annapolis, 1991.

Raeder, Erich, *Grand Admiral*, De Capo, Boston, 2001. First published USNI 1960 as '*My Life*'.

Rohwer, J, and Hümmelchen, G., *Chronik des Seekrieges 1939-1945*, Gerhar Stalling Verlag, Oldenburg, 1968.

Ruge, Friedrich, *The Soviets As Naval Opponents*, Naval Institute Press, Annapolis, 1979.

Stellmann, Georg, *Tagebuch und Briefe eines Minensuchers 1939-1946*, Books on Demand, Norderstedt, 2006.

Studt, Johannes, *Als Matrose auf einem Minensuche*, Books on Demand, Norderstedt, 2004.

Tarrant, V. E., *The Last Year Of The Kriegsmarine*, Arms and Armour Press, London, 1994.

Weichold, Eberhard, *Axis Naval Policy and Operations in the Mediterranean, 1939 to May 1943*, Washington Navy Dept., 1951.

Weinberg, Gerhard, *Germany and the Soviet Union*, E.J. Brill, Leiden. 1954.

Wilson, Kevin, *Men Of Air*, Phoenix Publishing, London, 2008.

Winton, John (ed.), *The War At Sea*, Book Club Associates, London, 1974

Articles

Dunn, John, and Stoker, Donald, 'Blood On The Baltic', *Naval History Magazine*, Vol. 13, No 2 (April 1999).

Index

344